The Theater
of Lee Blessing

ALSO BY PHILIP ZWERLING

After-School Theatre Programs for At-Risk Teenagers
(McFarland, 2008)

EDITED BY PHILIP ZWERLING

*The CIA on Campus: Essays on Academic Freedom
and the National Security State* (McFarland, 2011)

The Theater of Lee Blessing

A Critical Study of 44 Plays

PHILIP ZWERLING

McFarland & Company, Inc., Publishers
Jefferson, North Carolina

LIBRARY OF CONGRESS CATALOGUING-IN-PUBLICATION DATA

Names: Zwerling, Philip author.
Title: The theater of Lee Blessing : a critical study of 44 plays / Philip Zwerling.
Description: Jefferson, North Carolina : McFarland & Company, Inc., Publishers, 2016. | Includes bibliographical references and index.
Identifiers: LCCN 2016015016 | ISBN 9780786471102 (softcover : acid free paper) ∞
Subjects: LCSH: Blessing, Lee—Criticism and interpretation.
Classification: LCC PS3552.L43 Z84 2016 | DDC 812/.54—dc23
LC record available at https://lccn.loc.gov/2016015016

BRITISH LIBRARY CATALOGUING DATA ARE AVAILABLE

ISBN (print) 978-0-7864-7110-2
ISBN (ebook) 978-1-4766-2437-2

© 2016 Philip Zwerling. All rights reserved

No part of this book may be reproduced or transmitted in any form or by any means, electronic or mechanical, including photocopying or recording, or by any information storage and retrieval system, without permission in writing from the publisher.

Front cover photograph of Lee Blessing by Michal Daniel

Printed in the United States of America

McFarland & Company, Inc., Publishers
 Box 611, Jefferson, North Carolina 28640
  www.mcfarlandpub.com

For Clare

Table of Contents

Preface   1

Introduction   5

1. The Beginning   7
   The Authentic Life of Billy the Kid 12

2. The Estrogen Plays   19
   Nice People Dancing to Good Country Music 20; *Independence* 27; *Riches* 33; *Eleemosynary* 39

3. On Fields of Dreams   45
   Oldtimers Game 46; *Cooperstown* 49; *Cobb* 50; *Fantasy League* 56; *The Winning Streak* 57; *For the Loyal* 61

4. A Walk and a View   67
   A Walk in the Woods 67; *A View of the Mountains* 78

5. The Headline Plays   84
   Two Rooms 85; *Down the Road* 93; *Lake Street Extension* 100; *Patient A* 104; *The Rights* 111; *Going to St. Ives* 112; *Chesapeake* 116; *34th and Dyer* 119; *Whores* 120; *Wood for the Fire* 127; *Seven Joys* 130

6. The Race Plays   134
   Black Sheep 134; *Flag Day* 139; *Perilous Night* 144

7. Love Is All There Is   149
   Thief River 150; *The Roads That Lead Here* 156; *A Body of Water* 159; *The Scottish Play* 165; *Lonesome Hollow* 169; *Great Falls* 174; *Into You* 179; *Uncle* 181

8. The Rushmore Plays   188
   Fortinbras 188; *Tyler Poked Taylor* 193; *Reagan in Hell* 195; *When We Go Upon the Sea* 196

9. The Plays of Life, Death and Immortality — 202
Cold Water 202; Heaven's My Destination 204; A User's Guide to Hell Featuring Bernard Madoff 208; Unknown 213; Courting Harry 214; The Hourglass Project 219

10. Writing for Movies and Television — 223

11. Curtain — 226

Appendix 1. The Awards — 235

Appendix 2. The Napkin Play — 238

Appendix 3. The Plays — 240

Chapter Notes — 246

Bibliography — 263

Index — 265

Preface

The Theater of Lee Blessing: A Critical Study of 44 Plays, unlike some other books, lives up to its title. Here you will find information on and a discussion of almost every play written by this contemporary American playwright. This afternoon I sit at my desk covered with various editions of Blessing's plays in anthologies, acting editions, and collections devoted solely to his work. In fact, I now find that over the last five years I've read more plays by Lee Blessing than I have plays by William Shakespeare—in part because Blessing wrote more plays than Shakespeare. Usually such a statement would require some allusion to the fact that quantity does not equal quality. I want to resist that rather trite formulation. Quantity does matter. Lee Blessing's 48 plays, full-length and ten-minute, or somewhere in between, all but the very latest produced on U.S. stages and at least 31 of them published or filmed, constitute an unrivaled body of work that has helped enliven American theater in both the second half of the 20th century and first half of the 21st century. Somewhere, right now, one of his plays is likely unfolding onstage. It would be simply impossible to imagine contemporary American theater without Lee Blessing.

Though he writes on a myriad of subjects, from nuclear arms negotiations, in his most famous play *A Walk in the Woods*, to family dysfunction, feminism, pedophilia, racism, and homophobia, it is fair to say that Blessing always writes about *something* and his themes reach theatergoers and readers consistently on both an emotional and intellectual level. I have grouped my discussion of his plays by general theme and chronologically within the thematic groupings I've identified. But I warn a reader that Blessing's subjects often resist categorization. As a playwright, he rarely repeats himself by subject or style. Also, a warning about dates in this chronology: since Blessing writes, rewrites, revises, workshops, and then revises again, many of these plays have evolved over many years. The dates I use are the dates of productions or publications rather than the dates they were first written.

In an interview conducted with Blessing at Denison University in Granville, Ohio, Professor Kevin Wetmore asked, "Is Lee Blessing the Best Kept Secret in American Theater?"[1] The answer may be yes. This book aims to change that.

I've taught playwriting at the University of New Orleans (as a graduate student), Ursinus College, outside Philadelphia (with the rather grand title Playwright in Residence), and the University of Texas Pan American, now the University of Texas Rio Grande Valley, in deep south Texas (as director of the MFA program in creative writing) over the past 20 years. I've had plays produced on campus and, once, just once, commercially. The term "minor playwright" overstates my case but helps explain my appreciation for the nearly 50-year career Lee Blessing has carved for himself in American theater.

As I warn my students, few professions yield less recognition and less financial success than playwriting. In theater it is still true that one can make a killing but one cannot make a living. And yet for 45 years Lee Blessing, almost alone among his peers, has largely supported himself through his craft. Even Tony Kushner (his *Angels in America* succeeded as a smash critical success on Broadway and a film for HBO) had to admit, in a comment more about our culture than his own skills, "Its almost impossible for a playwright in the U.S. to make a living. You can have a play like I did with *Angels*, and it still generates income for me, but it's not enough for me to live on and have health insurance."[2]

I began this project over four years ago after meeting Blessing at a playwriting workshop he conducted for the Playwrights' Foundation in San Francisco. I had previously enjoyed productions of his plays *A Walk in the Woods* and *Eleemosynary* and especially enjoyed meeting their author, who seemed both down to earth and immensely talented. Following the workshop he cooperated with me in producing an interview which was published in the literary journal *34 Parallel* in October 2011. When I discovered, to my surprise, that no one had yet produced a book-length study of his work I pitched the idea to McFarland, and this is the result. I interviewed Blessing four times face to face, traveling to California, and countless times by email. I traveled to Austin on two occasions to visit the Harry Ransom Center which archives his scripts, photos, diaries, etc. I tracked down the two masters theses and two doctoral dissertations written about his plays. I read his plays. I also got divorced, earned tenure, traveled around the world, and remarried. But, the sheer quantity of his work slowed me down. At one point I told him jokingly that my job would be a lot easier if he had died like Karl Georg Büchner, author of just two plays, both masterpieces, *Danton's Death* and *Woyzek*, at the tender age of 23. Blessing responded: "Sorry to keep writing plays (for so many reasons!), but I'm sure you'll catch up eventually."[3] I think now I have caught up, though Blessing is probably sitting at a computer right now, writing a new play as you read this.

Many people have helped me with this project. First and foremost I must thank Lee Blessing himself who sat for multiple face-to-face and countless email interviews, provided electronic copies of scripts, posed for photos, and overall made the research for this book an engaging, educational, and delightful experience for me.

Let me acknowledge the aid of the Harry Ransom Center at the University of Texas, Austin, repository of Blessing's personal memorabilia, play scripts, theater posters, theater reviews, etc., and to librarians Bridget Gayle Ground, Richard B. Watson, and Patrice S. Fox. I appreciated librarian Michael L. Gilmore especially, for injecting a sense of humor into the often grim archive reading room.

I'd like to thank the University of Texas Pan American for a Faculty Development Grant in 2010 that allowed me to attend a Playwrights' Foundation Workshop in San Francisco taught by Lee Blessing, and the UTPA Library and its humanities librarian Virginia Gause for ordering and making available all Blessing plays in print.

Theaters and photographers generously provided the pictures and releases for this book. I want to thank the Guthrie Theatre and Michal Daniel, Illusion Theatre, History Theatre, Actors' Theatre of Louisville, the Contemporary American Theatre Festival, and photographers A. Vincent Scarano and Susan Johann.

Introduction

Theater has grown, evolved, developed from the first caveman, or woman, who, sitting around the fire at night describing how they had taken down a bison and feeling words alone insufficient, picked up their spear and reenacted the hunt for their fellow Neanderthals, first crouching low and then running at the animal and driving their weapon deep into its heart. Aristotle called theater "an imitation of an action" and the more gripping, unnerving, dangerous the action, the more dramatic the imitation by firelight or, later, onstage. The Classical Greeks staged theater festivals twice a year as religious rites, with the High Priest of Dionysius seated front and center as the majority of the Athenian population, men, women, and slaves, attended in amphitheaters carved out of hills to hold 15,000 people. Tragedies outnumbered the comedies and the Satyr Plays, evoking fear and pity for the protagonist undone by his or her own finest qualities. Shakespeare held "a mirror up to nature" for us to see the human failings, ambition, greed, and jealousy of kings and queens. Henrik Ibsen, Anton Chekov, August Strindberg, and Arthur Schnitzler outraged early 20th century audiences with their critiques of bourgeoisie society and, later, American playwrights like Eugene O'Neill, Tennessee Williams, and Arthur Miller gave us tragedies of the common man and woman in plays of lust, despair, and inner torment. Somewhere, however, we lost our way. Theater changed from transformational experience to disposable entertainment. Society lost interest and turned to cinema, television, and the computer screen.

Lee Blessing once told me: "The purpose of theater is to shake you up, not give you a warm glow. That's the job of the circus." He added:

> Theater audiences have become so unambitious. We had such a rich theater from the mid–20th century to the end of the 20th century. Theater has now become so expensive that audiences only want to spend the money to see something they know in advance they will like.[1]

Introduction

In February 2014, the *Denver Post* engaged in a fool's errand, asking 177 theater professionals—directors, actors, professors, producers, etc.—to rank the most important American plays ever written. We could predict the results: *Death of a Salesman, Angels in America, A Streetcar Named Desire, Long Day's Journey into Night,* and *Who's Afraid of Virginia Woolf?* made the top five.[2] Notice, they asked folks to name the most *important* plays, not the *best* plays. They offered no parameters for what makes a play important. With such an ill-defined mission, these responders actually ranked 263 American plays! You can understand that *Raisin in the Sun* makes the list at number 7, not only as a great play but as the first play by an African American woman to premiere on Broadway, formerly the "Great *White* Way," where only white playwrights had been produced. But what accounts for the absence of the 1931 play *Green Grow the Lilacs*, by Lynn Riggs, the first Native American playwright produced on Broadway, which later served as source material for Richard Rodgers and Oscar Hammerstein's *Oklahoma!*, or *Roger Bloomer*, from 1923, the first American expressionistic play by John Howard Lawson? What makes a *good* play? What makes an *important* play? To my shock, not one play by Lee Blessing appeared on the list. I didn't write this book to correct that oversight. Blessing needs no defense from me.

But I have set out here to do something no one else has yet done: to examine Lee Blessing's body of work over a 45-year period and his significant contribution to American theater. The *New York Times* called Blessing "America's most imaginative playwright on public issues,"[3] and I think they got that right. His plays may amuse and entertain, but, just as importantly, they make us think, reexamine our beliefs and prejudices and enter into a dialogue, sometimes even an argument, with the playwright. In his *Poetics*, Aristotle listed the qualities of great tragedy as plot, music, spectacle, idea, diction, and character, listing plot as most important with character second. I quibble with Aristotle here because I think idea, which he ranked third, really leads the way. The play that makes us think lets us grow, learn, and develop as human beings. As you will see here, Lee Blessing's plays do exactly that.

CHAPTER 1

The Beginning

The Authentic Life of Billy the Kid

Like most playwrights, Lee Blessing was born. Unlike most of them he was born in the U.S. Midwest and that has made all the difference. Born Lee Knowlton Blessing on October 4, 1949, in Minneapolis, to Frank and Harriet Blessing, he grew up in the small city of Minnetonka with his two brothers, Guy and Dean. Minnetonka, with a population of less than 20,000 in 1950, lies eight miles west of Minneapolis. His father founded Lintex Corporation, supplying linens to hotels,[1] and his mother, as was the case with so many other women at the time, stayed home to raise her children.[2] In one interview, Blessing called his upbringing "bland,"[3] but in a speech at his former high school while accepting a distinguished alumni award in 2011, he said: "I had a wonderful time growing up in Minnetonka."[4]

In a 2008 interview, Blessing described his parents as "extremely average, pleasant, normal people. Nobody in my parents' generation ever went to college. They didn't go to theater."[5]

One theater critic, after meeting Blessing, noted, "Normality hangs on him like an anchor" and called him a "relatively happy, relatively sane, relatively whole human being who has tried to add complexity to his life."[6] This accords with my own view based on multiple interviews and meetings with the playwright over the last four years. Blessing is generous with his time and money, whimsical, soft spoken, and though he has a healthy ego, he is not egotistical. In speaking of him one might invoke the stereotype of "Minnesota Nice" to describe his public demeanor. Minnesota Nice usually incorporates the characteristics of courtesy, reserve, and mild manners. When I tried to accuse Blessing of "niceness," he deflected the charge with his usual dry humor: "Well, it's easy to be nice in Minnesota since we're far enough away from the center of all evil, Chicago."⁷ Though he moved away from his hometown decades ago, he returns annually to Minnesota, telling an interviewer:

> We always come for Christmas. My wife, [playwright] Melanie [Marnich], has family in Duluth. And I grew up in Minnetonka.... I lived in New York for 12 years and now I'm in L.A., but Minnesota is in my heart.⁸

Lee Blessing, at a rehearsal for *Thief River*, Guthrie Theater, Minneapolis, Minnesota; 2002, photograph by and courtesy of Michal Daniel.

Blessing's middle-school report cards show him scoring off the charts in vocabulary, reading, and language. His math skills always ranked lowest of all, however.⁹ At Minnetonka High School, one English teacher, William Chisholm English, recalled his "impish smile, quirky humor, and restless nature."¹⁰ He began writing as early as eighth grade.¹¹ Soon, his interest turned to theater:

> I was 13 or 14 when the Guthrie [Theater] came to town. That was a powerful event for me. I fell in love with theater and, from that point on, wanted to be an actor. I wrote poetry. I even went to Iowa for grad school as a poet. But five years later, I emerged as a playwright.¹²

Blessing says that the first time he wrote a play was in high school.

> I did it to get out of writing a term paper. I said to one teacher: "You don't want to read another 30-page paper. I can write you a one-act play." And he let me.¹³

He told another interviewer a slightly different story:

> I was writing poetry and stories a lot. Then I got an assignment to write a short play. So I wrote one about me and an imaginary friend. My next play was also about me and an imaginary friend. After that I decided to make most of my characters real people.¹⁴

Deeply involved in theater in high school, Blessing did sound for a production of *The Diary of Anne Frank* and acted in a number of plays that can hardly be called standard high school fare: *Beggar on Horseback*, the 1924 play by George S. Kaufman and Marc Connelly; as the title character in *Biedermann and the Firebugs*, written in 1953 by the Swiss playwright Max Frisch, and as Bert in Harold Pinter's *The Room* (1957), with which he traveled to the State High School League District 18 One-Act Play Festival competition. He graduated Minnetonka Senior High School on June 8, 1967, and went off to the University of Minnesota for two years, but not before experiencing a family tragedy: his brother Dean was killed in a single-car accident just four days after turning 20. Blessing told me:

1. The Beginning

> It was an inexplicable accident. No one saw him drinking. He was alone in the car and hit a tree in 1967 before seat belts were required in cars. If he'd been belted in he would have walked away from the accident. I was 17½ at the time.[15]

Deeply affected by his brother's death, Blessing tried to write about it:

> The first time I wrote a play it was to get out of writing a paper in high school. I ended up writing a play that no longer exists. The second play, when I was at the University of Minnesota as a freshman, was about my brother's death in a car accident.[16]

The oldest of the three brothers, Guy, still lives in Minnesota and teaches high school shop classes.

While a sophomore at the University of Minnesota, Lee Blessing moved from merely writing plays to staging one over three nights during his summer vacation. He recruited local friends and advertised in Minnetonka with hand-drawn posters: "I got an A-plus on a play [I] wrote and decided to see what it looked like on stage."[17] Titled *They Don't Name the Parts Though* (not currently in his professional résumé and no script seems to have survived) he described it as "a one-act *avant-garde* tragicomedy dealing with the ceremonies of death."[18] It premiered in 1968, staged in a carriage house at an estate on the shores of Lake Minnetonka. Tickets sold for $1.25. Years later, Peter Vaughn wrote:

> Blessing remembers it as being about "a death in the family filled with all sorts of creative writing. I wrote, directed, produced and starred in it, as I remember. Luckily, no one asked me to explain it."[19]

Lee Blessing, Eugene O'Neill Theatre Center, Waterford, Connecticut; c. 2001, photograph by and courtesy of A. Vincent Scarano.

Then he did something fairly unusual for a Minnesotan: he transferred across the country to tiny Reed College, in Portland, Oregon, with an enrollment of around 1,200 students. As he told me:

> Growing up in Minnesota [and then] going to the University of Minnesota was almost automatic, but after two years I wanted to find a small school and, having only been to the Pacific Northwest as a kid, I chose Reed.[20]

His Reed profile, written in 1969, displays a certain sophomoric sense of humor. Asked for his Church preference, he replied: "Coptic." For special interests or hobbies, he listed: "Making love and constant introspection—usually done simultaneously." When asked for his preference in sports, he wrote: "Baseball, football, basketball, tennis, golf, peace." As to which vocations he favored, he stated, perhaps facetiously, that he had yet to choose between becoming a "fisherman [or the] preeminent writer of the twentieth century." And, finally, as to his prospects upon leaving college, he wrote: "Grisly."[21]

At Reed, he acted in *The Great American Desert*, written by Joel Oppenheimer in 1961. Foreshadowing one of Blessing's own plays, it featured Billy the Kid in its chorus of western heroes. He directed *Out to Sea*, a one-act absurdist drama by Slawomir Mrozek, the Polish playwright, and acted in the same production with his friend Eric Overmyer as two men adrift at sea on a raft. I would have loved to have seen this production featuring two future famous writers. Overmyer went on to success as a playwright (*On the Verge* may be his most famous play) and as featured writer for such TV shows as *Homicide: Life on the Streets*, *Law and Order*, and *The Wire*. The two teamed again in a Reed production of Burt Shevelove and Larry Gelbart's musical farce *A Funny Thing Happened on the Way to the Forum*, with Overmyer as Seneca and Blessing as Proteus, and yet again in the men's chorus in Aristophanes's *Lysistrata* at Lewis and Clark College, and in Samuel Beckett's *Endgame*, with Blessing as Nagg and Overmyer as Hamm. Blessing recalled the latter play in his 2001 commencement speech at Reed:

> I have only one memory left of my days here: hunching half nude and freezing in an oil drum while my erstwhile roommate Eric Overmyer got all the good lines.[22]

He graduated Reed with a B.A. in English in May 1971 and returned to Minneapolis. There, he appeared on stage at the Cricket Theatre in *The Police*, another absurdist play, this one by Slawomir Mrozek. A reviewer mentioned the young actor by name: "Lee Blessing as the [sergeant] who dreams of arresting somebody has some fine moments."[23] But Peter Altman, in the *Star*, disagreed: "The unskillfulness of [director] Lawless' actors may not have allowed him much interpretive freedom as director. Leading players ... and Lee Blessing ... all appear to lack control and a necessary knack for understatement."[24] Blessing eventually segued out of acting because he had trouble memorizing lines; better, he told me, "to write the lines" than learn them.[25]

Upon graduation from Reed in 1971, his parents offered him a choice of graduation gifts: a used car or a six-week trip to the Soviet Union. Blessing chose the trip and that, as they say, was that. On the trip, Blessing, who had studied the Russian language and literature in college, met regular Soviet citizens and even made a friend of one of them. Years later, that trip helped inspire him to write *A Walk in the Woods*.

1. The Beginning

Returning to the States, Blessing had choices to make: what would he do with his life? And, if he really wanted to be a writer, how could he support himself?

> I've dedicated myself to being a writer since undergraduate school. And I've carefully kept myself from learning to do anything else in order to stay a playwright.... I originally wrote about things any suburban boy might write about—baseball, the old West.... What I'm trying to do is expand from themes that were easy and available—to deepen as an artist.[26]

Supporting himself meant working as a mail carrier and store clerk.[27] He paid his expenses and sought jobs that left his mind free for writing:

> "[I chose jobs that] required the least [amount of] intellectual effort. I worked as a clerk in a stationery store and had a number of retail jobs. And I maintained a very modest lifestyle in order to keep expenses low. I just wanted to write plays, to write them as well as possible, and to get them out there and see what happened. Basically, in 1980, I took a vow of poverty." ... Blessing estimated the last time he got a paycheck every two weeks from a full time job was in 1973 when he was a mail carrier.[28]

His lifestyle distressed his parents at first:

> [His father] Frank talked about Lee after graduating from Reed: "I tried to persuade him to go into law. I told him the difficulties of trying to make a living in the art world. I was concerned about the troubled lifestyles of successful people in the theatre and art world. I had read that Hemingway, Truman Capote and Tennessee Williams led terrible personal lives. That's why I wasn't happy when Lee said he wanted to be a playwright. [Frank argued his case until sunrise, and throughout those long hours] Lee was very patient with me. He's a good listener. [Finally, as the sun rose, Lee answered,] "I don't want to be a lawyer. I want to be a playwright." He beat the odds. He finally made a believer out of me."[29]

Now committed to writing, Blessing applied to the University of Iowa Writing Workshop, where he earned a masters of fine arts degree in poetry in 1976. We get a taste for his poetry in the first and last poems on his MFA thesis chapbook. The first poem in full:

> I haven't written a poem yet Over 20 years old
> Over a week cognizant
> I have been seeing and imploring you All morning
> You haven't looked up once.
> What's a flag pole sitter to do?[30]

The last entry in the chapbook, "Sistena with Dirty Words," closes with this stanza:

> Cunt, cock, piss, shit, fuck, fart.
> At night, feel the warmth and pressure of
> Your hands. So much we have no name for.[31]

Unlike most other writers earning an MFA, Blessing re-enrolled at Iowa to earn a second MFA, this time in playwriting, in 1979:

> I slowly segued from poetry to playwriting while at the University of Iowa Writers Workshop. I took MFAs in both forms, and while I was just as successful getting my poetry published in little magazines, etc. as my classmates, there was always something arduous for me in the process of writing poetry. I never felt fully articulate in the form. I didn't think naturally in images and seemed to be more intrigued by what people said to each other. Not surprisingly, I found myself using a good bit of dialogue in my poems. Playwriting was somehow different. The more plays I wrote—the more plays I read—the more I felt that every corner of meaning was now somehow exposed to me, and I was free to explore what and wherever I wished. I no longer felt "tongue-tied," I suppose. And of course, relative to the money-free world of poetry, playwriting looked downright lucrative. The first plays I wrote were in high school and as an underclassman in college. I'm happy to report they are gone forever. I do recall that my friends and I produced the first of them on an estate which once saw a performance by Dame Sybil Thorndike. Only friends and family were invited, and the piece was wildly well received.[32]

Lee Blessing, at a rehearsal for *Thief River*, Guthrie Theater, Minneapolis, Minnesota; 2002, photograph by and courtesy of Michal Daniel.

Or, as Blessing told me: "I chose playwriting over poetry because poets can't make a living. Of course playwrights only do marginally better"[33] While at Iowa, Blessing directed *Bad Dreams in the White House* by Fred Hoffman. Judith Rew, reviewing the play for the *Daily Iowan*, wrote: "[The play] represents humor at its finest, combined with word play, satire, fantasy, slapstick, and song and dance numbers."[34]

The Authentic Life of Billy the Kid

Blessing's own plays, produced at Iowa, included the full-length *Animals*, in which the central character, a normal 16-year-old named Dan, suddenly starts acting like an animal. His friends and family first shun him but later admire and emulate him. One day he stops acting like an animal as suddenly as he had begun and the experience seems but a phase he went through. Other Blessing plays produced during his student years at Iowa included a one-act play, *Lunatics, At the Post Office*, in 1974, and, most importantly for his future career, *The Authentic Life of Billy the Kid*, in 1975. But, at the time, even with two MFAs in hand, prospects didn't look good.

> My dad was glad that I had found some way of making a living. I enrolled in grad school at the age of 25 after knocking around. My parents provided some financial aid, like keeping my car running. But then I exited grad school at age 30 without a job résumé.[35]

First, a student deferment and then a high number in the draft lottery kept him out of the Vietnam War, but he insists: "I wouldn't have served had I been drafted."[36] Then all that hard work of researching and writing and rewriting and workshopping *The Authentic Life of Billy the Kid* paid off. Photos taken in 1979 show a bearded Lee Blessing preparing, whether he knew it or not, for a very big year. Six years earlier he happened to be listening to a Ry Cooder song, "Billy the Kid" about the notorious gunslinger and outlaw.[37] Inspired by the song, Blessing began researching the subject and writing ever-changing drafts of a play on the subject, a play which combined what would become his lifelong interest in the interweaving of fact and myth, society's fixation with celebrity, and an evolving bent for mixing characters, both dead and alive, onstage.

The song led him, first, to a book by man claiming to be the living Billy the Kid, and then to a book by Billy's killer, Marshall Pat Garrett, entitled *The Authentic Life of Billy the Kid*. The result: Blessing's script entitled "The Real Life of Billy the Kid," retitled some years later as *The Authentic Life of Billy the Kid*, won the American College Theatre Festival award for best script over 400 entries submitted from across the nation, which in turn led to its publication by Samuel French Publishers. As a result, Blessing received the first of many invitations to workshop his writing at the Eugene O'Neill Theater Center in Waterford, Connecticut. Adapted for video, the NBC affiliate WRC-TV broadcast the play in Washington, D.C. Blessing's professional playwriting career had commenced.

Few Old West mythic figures rival outlaw Billy the Kid and Sheriff Pat Garret for romantic staying power in the national imagination. Legend credits Billy with 21 six-gun killings, one for every year of his young life (1859–1881). This homicidal murderer began life as Henry McCarty, son of Irish immigrants in New York City, and serially adopted the aliases William H. Bonney and William Antrim. Shot dead at midnight in a darkened room by sometime friend, sometime lawman, sometime bartender and sometime customs agent Pat

Garret, Billy entered the American psyche as the quintessential "good boy gone bad," the ageless anti-hero. The subject of some 20 movies from 1930 to 1991, a myriad of books and television shows as well as four other plays, Billy and Pat, like our dream of the Old West, never really went away. And never really existed, either.

Billy's death at Garrett's hands, either in self-defense or as a shot in the back, depending upon historical conjecture and argument, might have passed into forgotten history if not for two events. In 1882, in desperate financial straits, Garrett, reliant upon the florid ghost writing of Marshall Ashmun "Ash" Upson, released his own tale of the famous outlaw in *The Authentic Life of Billy the Kid*. Though a financial failure in Garrett's lifetime, the book has survived through ten reprintings, through 1976. In 1950, "Brushy" Bill Roberts, discovered by a researcher in Texas, stepped forward to claim he was the real Billy the Kid and that Garrett had killed another young gunslinger, Billy Barlow, by mistake. The year 2015 saw plans for an exhumation of Billy's grave in Lincoln, New Mexico, for DNA testing and a court petition for a death certificate, which had never been issued in the case.[38]

Could Billy the Kid have, in fact, survived into the 20th century? On one level: who cares? But on another level, and more importantly: why do we obviously care so much? Blessing set out to explore the latter question in his first successful play. Though years later Blessing called it "a terrible play,"[39] he explained what he had learned in the process, saying:

> You can put way too much research into a play. A play isn't a treatise. No one's depending on our report to decide how to move their troops around. We're writing plays … about human emotions and how to use them.[40]

You can see how he applied that lesson to such a later play as *A Walk in the Woods*, where he scrupulously excised all discussions of technical arms control issues like throw weight, MIRVS (Multiple independently targetable reentry vehicles), ABMs (anti-ballistic missile systems), and the like, which real arms negotiators would undoubtedly haggle over but which would put theatergoers to sleep.

Blessing researched (over-researched?) the lives of William Bonney and Pat Garrett to write a two-act play set on Garrett's New Mexico ranch the night before Garrett's own death, as he is visited by an odd threesome: ghostwriter Upson, hired killer Jim Miller, and a man who may or may not be Billy the Kid himself. The whole era calls for investigating connections and coincidences. The New Mexico governor who offered Billy a pardon was Civil War General Lew Wallace, who wrote the best-selling *Ben-Hur: A Tale of the Christ* the year before Billy's 1881 death, and Garrett's own killers were successfully defended in court by one Albert B. Fall, a thoroughly corrupt lawyer who went on to become a judge, a governor, a senator, and the secretary of the interior under President Harding when, as the perpetrator of the "Tea Pot Dome" scandal, selling public leases for personal enrichment, he became the first cabinet member to go to jail.

(You can see how easily I got off track here. History has many uses and, though often inherently dramatic, it becomes difficult to tease apart the events and personalities to, as Blessing said, expose the human emotions within.)

The play opens at Garrett's rundown cabin where he lives alone, fifteen years after writing his memoir, the kind of exposition Blessing would later excise. Ash Upson, for example, has a long and unnecessary early speech about Garrett's ruined relationship with President Theodore Roosevelt, who recruited his "Rough Riders" in New Mexico for service in the Spanish-American War.[41] The stage setting alone tells us all we need to know about how far Garrett has fallen financially; the story about Roosevelt would likely confuse an audience with little knowledge of Garrett's later life.

Soon, Ash has ushered into Garrett's cabin his "driver," a young man named Billy Barlow. They are visiting Garrett with a proposition and we learn that Upson no longer writes for small-town newspapers, but has evolved into a novelist:

> I now write novels, under a variety of names, about the true West: its heroes, its devils, the men I know and knew and those I never met.[42]

You mean, says Garrett: "Goddamn yellow-back dime novels without a line of truth in them."[43] This leads them both to trading quotes from the book Ash wrote about Billy under Garrett's name. Little of this advances the play's action. Finally, on page 16 of the published script, Ash gets to the point of his visit: his driver is none other than the *real* Billy the Kid. Garrett doesn't recognize him because, as Ash says: "You haven't seen him in 26 years, six months, and 15 days."[44] Garrett's not buying it:

> Don't tell me he's the Kid, 'cause even if he is, he ain't! I killed him! I am the man who killed Billy the Kid.[45]

But Billy Barlow has the Kid's story down pat, even as to how he escaped the night Garrett shot not the Kid but Billy Barlow, the name then assumed for all the succeeding years by none other than the real Billy the Kid.

Ash advertises Billy's story as an entree into show business careers for all three of them, allowing them to turn a long-ago and largely forgotten killing into a long-running and lucrative road show. "Think of it!," says Ash in purple prose:

> A dramatic reenactment of the monumental moment when you two, each the paragon of your chosen field, met in the dead zone between law and lawlessness—Pete Maxwell's darkened bedroom.[46]

Signaling the theme of the commodification of history, Ash adds: "It's not realism people want—it's the real item."[47]

The play takes an eerie turn at the end of Act 1 when Billy badgers Garrett into a shocking and largely unexplained admission:

> BILLY: I'm Billy the Kid. Now you tell me if that's a lie. Admit it. Admit it's me.
> PAT: (Quietly) I know it's you.[48]

Garrett agrees to the money-making tour, though he worries it will make him "the man who didn't kill Billy the Kid."[49] A knock at the door interrupts their reenactment of the shooting as a Mr. Miller arrives to purportedly discuss buying Garrett's ranch. Act 1 closes with the knock. If you know your Pat Garrett history, you know Miller's arrival bodes ill.

Act 2 commences as the cabin door opens and Jim Miller enters. Reality and myth collide as Pat confirms Billy's identity, "the resurrection of Billy the Kid"[50] but they set to arguing over the number of the Kid's victims: 21, as Billy claims, or no more than six, as Pat maintains? Can reality exist next to legend? Which would the public prefer ... and pay for?

> ASH: Pat, what are you talking about? What do you want to do?
> PAT: I want to tell the truth.
> ASH: The truth?[51]

A mere six homicides won't draw crowds for their tour. They need to inflate the kill list, not unlike the bloated weekly tallies of enemy deaths reported by U.S. troops in Vietnam served to rally, for a limited time, public opinion at home. Miller shares his news: a bunch of men in town plan to ambush Garrett the next morning. Garrett doesn't think they have the guts for it. Billy gets drunk and taunts Garrett about their shared past rustling cattle though Garrett, a former lawman himself, will not admit to having broken the law. Pat goes for his gun but Billy beats him to it. Each threatens to shoot the other. Billy prophesizes: "Someone's gin' to kill someone."[52]

Oddly enough, Ash ignores Billy's warning and asks the two to reenact the evening of the Kid's death at Garrett's hands on July 14, 1881, for the edification of Mr. Miller, though he does disarm them both first. As Ash says: "This is what we call show business. This is the West."[53] We can only suspect things will not end well.

After the brief show Billy asks the $64,000 question of his audience: "Was I—you know—real?"[54] With Garrett and the Kid still fussin' and feudin', Ash reaches a startling conclusion:

ASH: I'll just have to get a new Pat Garrett.
PAT: What?
ASH: I'll get an actor and just tell everybody he's you. It'll work just as well.[55]

The *appearance* of the real (an actor) trumps the real (Pat Garret himself). The mythic American West of cowboys and indians, gunslingers, lawmen, and killers, looms larger than truth, made up of lies we tell ourselves for our enjoyment and wish fulfillment.

Mr. Miller, however, wants to give us a foretaste of the next day's planned assassination and now he enlists Ash and Garret in acting it out as well. They mime the action and Miller punctuates the climax with a shot at Garrett, adding: "That's how it could happen. That's all I'm saying."[56] The action wraps up quickly. When Billy suddenly dashes into all this high-stakes play-acting, Pat Garett shoots him dead. Ash and Miller go on their way. Garret remains with the Kid's corpse at the curtain. History has been righted. Pat Garrett killed Billy the Kid (again) and tomorrow Jim Miller, Deacon Miller of the Methodist Church, hired assassin, will kill Pat Garrett just as the history books record.

It's easy to see what doesn't work in *The Authentic Life of Billy the Kid*. Long speeches and a quest for accurate historical detail suck the life out of the characters and render them museum exhibits. We can predict the action and never really begin to care about any of the people onstage. But the script wrestles with big ideas that leave us thinking after the final curtain: Is history truth or just a collection of well-known lies we agree to repeat? Is celebrity based on fact or self-aggrandizing stories? If we can't know the past, how do we comprehend the present?

Blessing returned to these themes in numerous later plays, from *Fortinbras* to *Cobb*, and, as he refined his craft, stripped away the unnecessary exposition, the long speeches, the extraneous characters, to get to the heart of the theme.

Producers continue to stage *The Authentic Life of Billy the Kid* as late as this year (2015) and it continues to garner positive reviews. In January 2015, Julie Petrucci wrote of one production at the ADC's Corpus Playroom Theatre at the University of Cambridge:

> At times funny and at times chilling…. Personally I felt the play was rather wordy and a tad too long but everything was handled with great expertise.[57]

And a production at The Spot in Arroyo Grande, California, earned this review from Ann Weltner in *New Times*:

> Blessing, better known as the playwright of *Fortinbras* and *A Walk in the Woods*, knows how to create nuanced situations and complicated, perhaps even tortured relationships, and *The Authentic Life* is a perfect study of this.[58]

Also reviewing the production at The Spot, Joan Crowder wrote: "*The Authentic Life of Billy the Kid* is a gripping play, based on history and sprinkled with dry humor."[59] Like the legend of Billy the Kid, Blessing's play, having launched his professional career, lives on.

While I am not writing a biography of the playwright, I know readers want some inkling of how his personal life and professional life intertwined. Blessing moved in with Jeanne Blake, who had collaborated with him as actor, dramaturge, and director, in 1982, and they married in 1986. She brought to the union two children from a previous marriage. Blessing called her influence "pervasive and profound"[60] and their collaboration "an artistic partnership."[61] In fact, Blessing based his play *Riches*, originally *War of the Roses*, in part on stories Blake told him about her own first marriage. Blessing and Blake divorced in 2000.[62] Blessing began dating fellow playwright Melanie Marnich in 2004; they married in 2008. Blessing described her as "not only a playwright but another Minnesota playwright.... I was glad there was no language barrier."[63] Marnich, who has won prizes for her plays, showcased in regional theaters, has succeeded in Hollywood, writing for three years for the HBO series *Big Love*, the Showtime series, *The Big C*, the AMC drama, *Low Winter Sun*, and, most recently, she served as a co-executive producer and writer for *The Affair*, also on Showtime. Blessing taught as head of the Graduate Playwriting Program at Mason Gross School of the Arts, Rutgers University, 2001 through 2013, his first and last full-time teaching position, although he has lectured and taught part-time at over 40 U.S. universities and colleges. He was named Professor Emeritus at Rutgers University in 2014 and moved from New York City to Los Angeles in 2012, packing his belongings and driving west in a Penske truck to be with his wife. They live now in the Hancock Park section of Los Angeles.

Chapter 2

The Estrogen Plays

Nice People Dancing to Good Country Music
Independence
Riches
Eleemosynary

After writing *The Authentic Life of Billy the Kid* and *Old Timers' Game* with all male characters, Blessing set himself a task, an "assignment,"[1] in his words, from 1982 to 1985 to write a series of plays "which revolved around women."[2] He wrote four: *Nice People Dancing to Good Country Music* in 1982, *Independence* in 1983, *Riches* in 1984, and *Eleemosynary* in 1985, one after the other, to growing critical and popular acclaim.

They were the first of his plays to include female characters and served several purposes. Politically, Blessing saw that "a society which so often suppresses real women will suppress fictional ones as well"[3] and that liberating fictional women on stage supported their struggle in the real world. Personally, he saw that

> once you attempt to look at the world through the eyes of the other sex—no matter how imperfectly—you see a very different world. The moment my writing left the realm of the exclusively male, many simple and rigid "certainties" began to disappear for me, and were replaced by something far more uncertain and rewarding—opening into the future, I thought, instead of the past.[4]

Years later he offered a more flip answer to why he began creating female characters:

> At one point I realized I had written 13 male roles in a row and didn't know anything about women. I wanted to learn—and besides, I couldn't get a date.[5]

These are family plays, nuclear and extended, but plays in which male characters are absent, in *Independence* and *Eleemosynary*, or less powerful than the women, in *Nice People* and *Riches*. These women are not necessarily smart or happy or powerful, but they are, untethered from male control, deeply involved in their own quests for wholeness and fulfillment. They often do not, strangely enough, spend their time thinking about men, trying to attract men, or needing men.

The chronological progression of his writing is interesting because, I believe, each play is better than the last. We can see him sharpening his message and dialogue (though *Riches* remains my personal favorite of all Blessing's plays) as his skills culminate in the final script, *Eleemosynary*, a richly complementary meshing of theme, character, and minimalist staging that has made it one of his most appreciated and produced works.

Nice People Dancing to Good Country Music

Nice People Dancing to Good Country Music, the title inspired by a sign Blessing sighted outside a Dew Drop Inn in Louisville as he walked from his apartment to the theater each day,[6] is as loose and rambling as its title. Originally a one-act (the second act written first as a stand-alone play, an *entr'acte* for the Humana Festival, and the new first act, "Toys for Men," written later, at the suggestion of Humana director Jon Jory, to form one full-length play, or in Blessing's words: "two plays that live together. They're not quite married but they're real close."[7] *Nice People* unfolds in Houston among five slightly "zany" but "cute" characters who would find a welcome on a slightly off-kilter TV sitcom, where the thinness of their characterizations would be covered by the endearing oddities of their quickly recognizable stereotypical behaviors. Blessing says it began as a "fond tribute to some 'good ol' boy' comedies. However it quickly shifted into a 'good ol' girl' comedy."[8]

Act 1 introduces the three male characters, Jim Stools, a 41-year-old bar owner and former biker; Roy Manual, his 30-year-old friend and bar patron; and Jason Wilfong, the 15-year-old son of Jim's live in girlfriend, Eva Wilfong. It opens in the street-level bar parking lot, while the second act, dominated by the female characters Eva and her niece Catherine Empanger, takes place above the bar, at a symbolically higher level.

Blessing sometimes struggles with character names that fail as symbols but too often survive as jarring oddities. Jim Stools's bar has stools, no doubt; Roy Manual is a manual laborer, digging ditches for a living; and Eva, or Eve, is the first and paradigmatic woman beguiling every man since the beginning of time. In an interview with the author in December 2012, Blessing expressed surprise when I pointed out these name correlations, telling me he hadn't seen

Nice People Dancing to Good Country Music: Church novice Catherine (Kerstin Kilo, right) asks her aunt Eva (Kirtin Coan) for advice on dealing with men. Actors Theatre of Louisville (Kentucky); 1982, photograph by David S. Talbot; courtesy of Actors Theatre of Louisville.

the connection between Jim's last name and the seats in his bar or Eva's relation to Eden. While allowing the name Wilfong came from a former utility infielder for his beloved Minnesota Twins baseball team, he told me that he usually just found his characters' names in a big book of baby names, without aiming for symbolism.[9] Perhaps naming characters is more prosaic than we thought and critics with overheated imaginations read meaning into places where it does not reside.

At the opening curtain we find Jim hammering away on his battered pickup. He is attempting to get it to start so he can escape before giving in to his urges to "murder" Jason, who is visiting for the summer and who has been breaking beer bottles, eating all the chips in the bar, and even burning the money in the cash register. Jason is scheduled to go home to Minnesota (the state of Blessing's own nativity and childhood) the next day, but Jim, as he explains to an incredulous Roy, cannot stifle his murderous feelings for even one more day. Roy has hunted Jim down to find out the identity of a comely young woman he saw Eva lead through the bar an hour earlier. Told she is Eva's niece, Roy says he hopes to "get to know her better"[10] because "I think I may love that girl."[11] He adds: "Fate's gonna keep slapping us together until we can't come apart no more."[12]

Jason, nicknamed "Jay Bob" by Jim, in an initial and ham-handed attempt to make the teenager feel at home in Texas, enters and, not seeing Jim under the truck, takes a tire iron to the old heap, adding several new dents. Jim tackles the kid and is on the point of violence when Jason threatens to tell his mother what Jim has done so she will leave him. Jim surrenders before this threat and Jason beats a retreat into the bar.

This leaves the space clear for Roy and Jim to comically discuss the place of women in men's lives. Roy has had little luck with women, saying: "They hit me all the time, 'cause I say stupid things. I can't help it.... It's time I got serious about a woman."[13]

Jim responds: "No man in his right mind wants to get serious about a woman." He recounts the series of changes Eva has wrought in his life, from paving the parking lot, to upscaling the bar from a biker bar to The Nice People Bar, to even making Jim give up his beloved Harley-Davidson motorcycle.[14] Jim is convinced of one unassailable fact: "Whenever a woman comes to stay, you're gonna lose something."[15] Rather than sell his bike, Jim dropped his Harley off a cliff in Utah, and tells Roy: "Eva June calls motorcycles toys for men. Like that's a bad thing. Like men don't need toys."[16]

Jim's supposed attachment to his Harley and an outlaw biker lifestyle do not convince this motorcyclist (current bike a 2005 Kawasaki ZZR 1200) and I wonder if Blessing ever rode himself. A real Hog rider would likely rhapsodize about his late bike: of all the models and years of Harleys out there, did Jim bond with a knucklehead or a shovelhead? Did he have a big old Road King or a Fat Boy? What personal modifications did Jim make to the bike to make it his own: added chrome, special pipes, seat, ape bars? (I added Muzzy pipes, a Corbin seat and Givi trunk to my bike.) And just where *is* his tattoo? Jim is more a generic biker than a specific person.

Jim's story of loss and change explain his cynical attitude to the whole idea of love:

> Roy, you don't know what you're messing with here. Love. You may as well say you're ready for a hurricane or an epidemic, or a flood. Love don't repair your life, it wrecks it.[17]

While Jim bemoans his loss of freedom it is hard to take his remarks too seriously as he made his choice freely and doesn't seem ready to toss Eva off a cliff and resume his motorcycle riding. Roy, on the other hand, is ready to give up just about anything for a love of his own, even for a woman he has never met and has only seen from afar for a few seconds. The scene ends as Jason returns just long enough to tell Jim, and the audience, but not Roy, who is conveniently offstage, that Catherine, the object of Roy's new love is a nun, further complicating Roy's infatuation. The first act closes, appropriately enough, with the song "(I Can't Help) Falling in Love with You" playing on Jim's truck radio.

Act 1 might be called a slice-of-life drama rather than a play in that it has no rising action, no climax, and no resolution. No character changes, goes on a journey, or learns anything. It is mostly talk, with little action. As the first act in a two-act play (actually written a year after the second half) it now does little more than lead us into Act 2.

Nice People unfolds over several hours in a single day and Act 2 takes us upstairs to an outdoor deck on the third floor, two stories above the bar, for a second half dominated by two female characters, the symmetrical flip side of Act 1, the yin to Jim and Roy's yang. Here we find Eva and her niece Catherine, women who, once they work out their own fears and issues, will descend the stairs to enter the (lower) world of men at the end of the play.

On the rooftop deck we quickly learn that Catherine is not a nun, but a novice on the brink of being washed out of her convent and that Eva left her husband, Robert, for being "a deadly human being. Deadly dull."[18] Robert, "a professor of Latvian"[19] not only bored Eva but oppressed her by requiring her to study Latvian history as well. So when Eva ran into Jim while changing planes at an airport all he had to say was "I got a bar in Houston. Interested?" And she was.[20]

As Eva tells Catherine the change in men has meant a change in her from a "dead hum coming out of someone else's machine ... to an honest-to-God human being."[21] But she has no plans to marry Jim because: "Living together is having somebody around. Marriage is having somebody around your neck."[22] Eva is just as sour on the idea of love as Jim in Act 1:

> Love is an evil pain in the butt. For years I was in love with a man who had more passion for Latvian self-rule than he had for my body. You can stick love.[23]

Though Eva has found her fulfillment in fixing up the bar, pounding nails into railings, rehanging shingles, paving the parking lot, and converting the bar into a restaurant, Catherine is facing her own moment of decision between celibate religious life and a reentry into a secular world of love and lust and fools like Roy Manual. Her order sent her on a retreat to think things through when, just a month earlier, Catherine started using dirty words at the convent, calling a nun, first, "Sister Shit,"[24] and then "Fart Face."[25]

She also began reciting the backs of Wheaties boxes and barking like a dog during devotions and while working in the garden. Catherine, a psychologist tells her, has developed this irrepressible behavior as an unconscious means of escaping her order. Blessing never uses the diagnosis Tourettes Syndrome, the real-life condition a reader would immediately assume Catherine has, perhaps because in real life Tourettes has a genetic and not psychological cause, appears first, most frequently, in childhood rather than adulthood and because only 10 percent of those afflicted shout profanities, though this is the most widely popularized hallmark of the syndrome.

Sadly, Catherine is more cartoon than character: a pretty 22-year-old virgin capable of cursing like a sailor whose first thought after leaving the cloisters seems to be finding a man. All of which fits conveniently with the theme of the play. (If I am being hard on Blessing it is because this is his third professionally produced play and the last time his characters exist solely to serve a playwright's needs. After *Nice People* there are no more cartoons and no more characters concocted for the benefit of the plot.)

Eva opposes Catherine's newfound interest in Roy, an interest based on nothing more than his interest in her which, in itself, is based on a three-second glimpse of the young woman, telling her: "… it takes time to learn men. They're tricky. It's not a natural relationship."[26]

Above the bar, Jason, running from Jim who has threatened to kill him again, tries to prove Eva's warning by dancing with Catherine who rebuffs his advances.

> CATHERINE: I am your cousin…
> JASON: You're not that much older than me.
> CATHERINE: Jay Bob. Listen to me. I—am—your—cousin.
> JASON: So, there won't be all that getting-to-know-you crap.[27]

She finally slaps him and he bursts into tears.

Roy then enters this feminine retreat and handles matters only slightly more decorously:

> CATHERINE: I'm going back to the convent, that's all there is to it.... I'm not ready for the world again.
> ROY: Yeah, it's a bitch, ain't it?[28]

And later:

> ROY: I think God works in mysterious ways.
> CATHERINE: (*Violently*) Of course He does, as far as you can see! You're stupid! I know exactly how God works. He's created this incomparably lovely, incomparably stupid world for us to live in, and now He sits back and watches us break our hearts over it. I can't imagine how anyone can make love at night and then read the papers the next morning.
> ROY: I do that all the time.
> CATHERINE: How? How can you reconcile the two?
> ROY: Making love and reading the papers? (She nods. He pauses, shrugs.) I only do the crossword puzzle.
> CATHERINE: The murders! Wars! Starvation! What about those?
> ROY: They're in another section...[29]

When Roy pushes Catherine for a date, her odd reaction of blurting out nasty words returns:

> CATHERINE: I'm saying odd things. Aren't I?
> ROY: You sure are.
> CATHERINE: Well don't take offense. I mean it's not you or your tiny penis.[30]

Jason bursts in again, pursued by Jim who, swearing vengeance for the slur of having been told "You're not a real cowboy,"[31] lifts Jason above his head and tosses him over the railing to the bar below. Jason falls out of sight and is met by hooting offstage derision as the bar patrons catch him in a blanket. This is a nice bit of theatricality and the first real action of a play that has been mostly talk, occurring just moments before the final curtain.

The men all return to the bar, their lower sphere, leaving Eva and Catherine alone. Catherine, harkening back to her conversation with Roy about rationalizing making love and then reading the newspapers' daily tally of human tragedies, offers an unsatisfying answer to an insoluble reality:

> CATHERINE: I know what my problem with the world is. I know what it is.... I'm trying to understand the world. That's my problem.... I mean, why should the world explain itself to me?[32]

Eva offers an existentialist take, with no fear or trembling:

> EVA: Hell, the world never explains itself. You just gotta make something up. That's what I did. I made up a whole new way of life.[33]

Catherine and Eva exit to get something to eat and the last words we hear are from Hank Williams's classic "I'm So Lonesome I Could Cry."[34]

Nice People breaks no new ground in the long history of comic explorations of male/female relationships. Some of the tropes are cultural throwbacks, like Eva's plan to "improve" Jim, Jim's disempowerment at Eva's hands, Catherine's foul-mouthed subconscious, Roy's desperate willingness to love any proximal female, and Jason's nastily rebellious teenager.

Two things are interesting, however: Blessing's willingness to create unsympathetic characters and his continuing theme of change. We don't necessarily like any of the five characters, and that is by the writer's design. Eva is insufferably self-satisfied, Jim whines, Jason simpers, Catherine is clueless, and Roy is needy. We might not like that in any of them but we do, at the same time, glimpse a bit of our own flaws in each of them. We'll see in his succeeding plays how Blessing feels freer and freer to create ambiguous, ambivalent, and flawed characters just like the real people we all know.

In an interview several years ago, Blessing told me:

> I suppose, for me, the most common thematic thread connecting my plays is loneliness. Most of my plays show people breaking apart, or staying apart, in one way or another. Happy families, even happy relationships, are a rarity in my work, generally achieved at high cost and often short-lived.[35]

Eva, Jim, Jason, Catherine, and Roy are in flux, leaving behind old ways that seemed fixed (Jim wedded to his bar and his Harley; Eva wedded to a dull husband; Catherine wedded to the convent; Roy, alone and lonely; and Jason, dedicated to being an obnoxiously rebellious adolescent) and trying out new identities (Jim as a dutiful partner, Eva as the partner in charge, Catherine as a woman in and of the world, Roy as a potential marriage partner, and Jason as an evolving adult).

Blessing makes copious use of classic country music in the play as befits the play's setting in a Houston bar. The songs are obviously chosen to underline, contradict, or comment upon the action of the play. But this is a "talky" play, and the music helps mask the lack of action onstage; a talkiness that is broken only once, when Jim heaves Jason over the railing, a dramatic stage picture that stays with us, even though we don't actually see all of it.

Nancy Scott, in the *San Francisco Examiner*, wrote:

> All five of these people are larger than life, twice as preposterous, and entirely engaging.... although much of the dialogue is so glib you could use it for mayonnaise.[36]

While Carla Waldemar, in the *Twin Cities Reader*, opined:

> It's love at first sight for this piebald lot—theirs for each other and ours for them. With wacko humor rooted in warm compassion Blessing has created four failures born again.[37]

And David Hawley, in the *St. Paul Pioneer Press*, summed it up well:

> Blessing isn't out to write a great play or deliver a passionate message, but he knows his business.... with a talent for writing gags he conserves his best lines so that they emerge from the characters' mouths and not from the playwright's pen.... [The five characters] ... are somewhat familiar stage creations.... But they are better than cartoons and ultimately they make you feel good about the business of living.[38]

Nice People is an entirely personal, nonpolitical, play. Well written, in a mechanical, everything-fits-together kind of way, with no sharp surprises or unsettling pokes at an audience's preconceptions, it has nothing profound to say about marriage, the church, or feminism, its seeming subjects, beyond the lives, skewed attitudes, and *faux pas* of five quirky people, although the dominant role of the female characters as created by a male writer was a rarity for its time and, in that sense, a political statement. The play remains popular on university stages, with productions mounted as recently as 2012.

Independence

Things changed with Blessing's next play, *Independence*, with all female characters and his first gay character, whose interpersonal struggles play out on a larger generational, social, and political stage. Blessing decided to set a play in Iowa, a state he knew well from his work at the Writers Workshop at the University of Iowa in Iowa City, for 70 years the premier writers' training program in the country. There he earned, first, an MFA in poetry, and then a second MFA in playwriting because, he said, "As poorly as playwrights get paid, poets earn even less."[39] Originally a 1981 one-act, he titled the play *Summer in Clinton*, after the town of that name. This shorter play featured the three sisters without Mom, and was set in Jo's apartment. At the play's climax, Kess and Sherry witness Don, who does not appear in *Independence*, arrive with a gun.[40] All that changed in rewrites.

In his travels across Iowa, Blessing encountered the town of Independence, population 6,000 or so, in the northeast quadrant of the state and home to the Independence State Hospital, formerly the Iowa State Hospital for the Insane. After visiting the town and the hospital, where staff gave him a tour, he decided it would serve well as the play's setting with the matriarch of the family volunteering at the state hospital where her daughter had once committed her.[41]

Unlike *Nice People* this play met with opposition for its less than nice people: their dirty language, sexual orientation, and mores. In Buncombe County, North Carolina, a high school drama teacher who had taught at the same school for 11 years, was abruptly transferred. She had chosen *Independence* for her advanced acting class to perform in a statewide competition, in which they placed second. Students' parents had given express permission for their children to work on the play. However, when they returned from the competition and performed scenes from the play by invitation from another class, whose parents had not been consulted in advance, a public uproar resulted, as reported in the *San Francisco Chronicle*:

> The play contained profanity, took God's name in vain, blasphemed the name of Jesus, presented sexual promiscuity, premarital sex, adultery, and homosexuality conservative Christians complained in an ad in the Asheville [NC] Citizen-Times.[42]

Dramatic ironies abound. The play is titled *Independence* but takes place in multiple symbolic prisons: the prison of a small town (Independence, Iowa, with a population of 6,000, we are told), the prison of a house, the Briggs family home, and the prison of a family presided over by a manipulative and authoritarian matriarch. And some people, like that stage matriarch and those parents in North Carolina, were not at all sure *Independence*, with all its messiness, was such a good thing for their children.

The characters in *Independence* include: the family matriarch, Evelyn Briggs, age 53; the eldest daughter, Kess, 33; the middle daughter, Jo, 25; and the youngest daughter, Sherry, 19. Teresa Durbin, who wrote her doctoral dissertation at Bowling Green State University on the conflicts in "Twentieth-Century American Plays with Three Sisters" and studied *Independence* as well as *Crimes of the Heart* by Beth Henley and *The Sisters Rosensweig* by Wendy Wasserstein, concluded:

> The fact that there are three sisters in each of these plays is not a coincidence. The frequent occurrence of the number three in geometry, astrology, theology, literature, and even sports demonstrates its significance to all aspects of both ancient and modern cultures: three wishes, three bears, three little pigs, three bases, three strikes, three outs.[43]

Of course, a premise involving three sisters raises the dramatic possibilities for the author. Two sisters allow for a single conflict between them, but three sisters allows for six potential conflicts: sister 1 versus sister 2, sister 1 versus sister 3, sister 2 versus sister 3, sisters 1 and 2 versus sister 3, sisters 1 and 3 versus sister 2, and sisters 2 and 3 versus sister 1. Adding but one extra character increases the potential for conflict by 600 percent.

The three sisters in *Independence* can even be seen as surrogates for their shared mother. In her book, *The Secret Between Us: Competition Among Women*, Laura Tracy writes:

> In a way, sisters plot up their mother's life. Each sister develops into an alternative version of Mother. One sister may become like Mother, doing what she does, sharing her pleasures, her tastes, her dislikes.... The other sister may actualize, in her life, choices her

mother didn't make—not marrying, experiencing her mother's distastes as her own desires.[44]

For example, Sherry and Jo have stayed at home with their mother and both have gotten pregnant prior to marriage, as did their mother, but Kess moved out of her mother's home and, as a lesbian, is not likely to marry a man.

(It is interesting to note that, in this situation of life imitating art, Blessing himself grew up with two brothers—and no sisters—but has yet to write a play about three brothers.)

The Inciting Incident(s) which occurs prior to the play's action are an injury to Jo's neck caused by her mother hitting/pushing her off a six-foot drop, and Jo's out-of-wedlock pregnancy. The Point of Attack, the event that starts all of the action of the play, is Kess's unannounced return home after a four-year absence in response to Jo's plea for help following her injury. These twin terms help in any play analysis. In *Hamlet*, for example, the Inciting Incident is the murder of King Hamlet, and Shakespeare's Point of Attack is the appearance of Hamlet's ghost demanding that his son, also named Hamlet, avenge his murder. The Inciting Incident occurs prior to the action of the play, prior to curtain, and causes a rupture in the "world" of the play, creating a challenge or problem for the characters to work out. The author's Point of Attack comes soon after the curtain's rise and gives meaning to everything that follows. In the case of *Hamlet*, Shakespeare saves the Point of Attack until Scene 5 of Act 1, when the ghost demands of Hamlet: "Avenge me," but Blessing places his Point of Attack within the first moment of *Independence*. Kess's return, seen as the curtain rises, will throw off any fragile equilibrium in the Briggs home and change it forever.

The opening exposition is supplied by the youngest sister, Sherry, three weeks away from graduation and ready to head with her boyfriend to the big city, who greets Kess's return with indifference. According to Sherry, Evelyn volunteers her time at the former mental hospital where Kess once had her committed. Sherry also reveals that virginal Jo dated an unimposing and square gent by the name of Don Orbeck who proposed marriage once he realized he had impregnated her, but Jo turned him down, not wanting to leave Mom alone and not sure Don really loved her. Sherry concludes her piteous tale with the news that Don is now dating Heidi Joy Duckly, who she describes as "this blonde dwarf you wouldn't believe."[45]

The plot of *Independence* holds no surprises. Given the title and situation we quickly guess Jo will find a way to break free of her mother, but the strength of the play lies not in its plot but in its characters, none of whom are cute or cuddly; indeed, they are not only wounded, but wounding. Blessing wrote of them: "I don't know if I've ever written characters who feel more real to me than the Briggs women.... The emotions ... are what is truly real in them and what will continue to be."[46]

Jo, the main character, makes many changes on her emotional and physical journey, but is it the classic protagonist's journey from ignorance to knowledge? She moves back and forth rather than straight ahead. She shades the truth and retreats into lies. Even Hamlet hems and haws, feigns madness, lies to Ophelia, sets sail for a side journey to England, and takes four more acts to finally fulfill the ghost's command.

In the end, Jo also boldly does the deed and leaves her mother, but, in going from Mom's house to Kess's apartment is she really breaking free? And is Mom *really* crazy, or do her daughters just need her to be?

Scene 2 introduces the didactic side of Kess, now instructing Jo in exercises for her injured neck, the meaning of old English ballads, and promising an improved reading list after having caught her sister reading *Noble Incest*, which she characterizes as a "drugstore novel," adding, "We'll see if we can't find you something better."[47] When Kess invites Jo to move to Minneapolis to live with her, Jo replies: "I can't leave Mom. How can you even suggest it?"[48] Jo introduces the theme of people as objects, foreshadowing the role of an object, the heirloom cameo, later in the play: "Is that the only reason you came down? To try and steal me away from Mom?"[49]

Kess sees the issue as one of independence and Jo meeting her own needs for once:

> KESS: Shouldn't people sometimes ... change who they need?
> JO: Mom's done that.
> KESS: I don't mean Mom, I mean you.
> JO: (a beat) We're getting off the point.
> KESS: What do you need from Mom?
> JO: Nothing. I help her. She doesn't help me. O.K.?
> KESS: Something. You get something out of it.[50]

Then Jo turns the tables to suggest Kess move back into the family home, the likely goal behind her earlier phone call for help. Kess makes the connection quickly and asks: "Is that why you asked me down here? To steal me away from my life?"[51] reinforcing the people-as-objects motif.

But Evelyn is busy as a succubus, stealing Jo's life, disparaging both her own husband and Jo's ex-beau, Don. "Sometimes," she says, "a man comes into your life and you think it's the answer to your problems, but you always find out it's not." She then moves in for the kill:

> I'll be glad when Sherry's gone.... Then it will just be you and me. Won't that be fun? We'll have Kess and Sherry visit now and then, of course. But mostly it'll be us. I rely on you. So few people in the world can really be relied on.[52]

Adding creepily a little later in the same conversation: "I think you and I have a special opportunity—one that a mother and daughter rarely get. We have the chance to give each other something far more valuable than a cameo.... Our lives."[53] But Evelyn, who seems so powerful is, in fact, utterly dependent upon her daughters. As Durbin writes:

> Evelyn is the dependent one. She is completely dependent on Jo.... Evelyn does not want to be alone because she has never been alone.... Her over-dependence on her daughters, first Jo, and then Kess, smothers them and drives them away from her.[54]

Blessing raises the stakes to life itself, two lives in fact. Inside Jo is a baby she and Don conceived. Don proposed marriage but Jo turned him down because "it would have been selfish. To marry him and leave Mom all alone?"[55] But if Jo stays with Evelyn the audience knows her life and that of her child will be lost forever.

Sherry functions as comic relief for the first half of the play but hides a family skeleton. She sleeps with guys at the bar where she works and builds crowd-displeasing sculptures in the back yard. Then we learn that, pregnant and unwed at 15, Sherry was forced by Kess to give the baby up for adoption. She tells Kess, speaking of a wound still fresh years later: "You had to pry it away from me with a stick!"[56] No one, it seems, is independent in Independence, Iowa.

Act 1 literally crashes to a close. As Jo awaits a visit from Don and announces herself ready to accept if he should propose again, we hear Evelyn hurling dishes in the garage. She staggers in, bleeding, and Jo sends Don away, calming Evelyn and locking the prison door on her own life sentence: "I sent Don away. He's gone. He's all gone."[57]

Act 2 serves to free Jo, at least as much as she can be freed. In a series of set pieces, Blessing sketches in the small and failed attempts the family makes at reunification. In Scene 1, Kess and Evelyn play Scrabble, which serves to demonstrate Kess's intellectual superiority. But when Kess dares to speak of her own sexual orientation and the perils of growing up lesbian in rural Iowa, Evelyn heads to the bathroom where she can put Kess out of sight and out of mind, explaining, in words Kess could have used to describe herself, "Nature just suddenly called."[58] It is a much-requested scene even today, Blessing told me, for actors across the country.[59]

In Scene 2, the family gathers to reenact a kind of mad tea party, hoping, in Kess's words, that "it's more important to go through the motions of being a happy family than it is to actually feel like one.... The more we act like a normal, happy family the better chance we'll become one someday."[60] Naturally, it all ends in disaster when Evelyn lets slip the news that Don is engaged to someone else and ends in a chilling prediction from Evelyn:

> Your baby is going to live right here with us—her mother and her grandma. Just the way I did when I was a little girl. And she's going to be every bit as happy and well-cared for and loved as I was. Doesn't that sound nice?[61]

Actually, it sounds horrific and the audience is now ready to support Jo if she can just summon the courage to leave.

To do so, Jo has to go a little crazy herself. In Scene 4, she tells Kess how she found herself following Don's intended bride for four hours, from town to town and shop to shop. The oddness of her actions scares Jo, who realizes it is just the type of thing her mother would do: "Mom should be driving this car. I should be Mom doing this. Then I thought, 'I am.'"[62]

Jo begs Kess for the offer she once made to let her live with her in Minneapolis: "We can't save Mom. Save *me*."[63] "All women," wrote Oscar Wilde in *The Importance of Being Earnest*, "become like their mothers. That is their tragedy." Jo seeks finally to escape this tragedy through flight.

In the penultimate scene of the play, Evelyn smashes the cameo, a family heirloom, one she has variously promised to Jo and to Kess as rewards for their devotion. Jo asks, "How could you do that?" and, Evelyn answers, presaging what she had planned for any daughter who remained in her home and reducing familial relations to ownership and control: "Because it was mine."[64] Destroying the heirloom symbolizes the destruction of familial bonds that Evelyn foresees in Jo's departure. The next morning the final short scene of the play finds Jo leaving to live with Kess. Jo hugs her mother, who allows the hug but does not respond in kind. Jo's final words to Evelyn are ambivalent: "I could call you when I get up there. This afternoon, I mean. I think I will. Should I?"[65]

Clearly, Jo is taking a step towards independence (ironically, in *leaving* Independence, Iowa) but it's an uneasy baby step, and her future is unknown. As Blessing told me: "We don't know what will happen eventually with these characters. The play shows only one step."[66]

Independence was one of three winners of the 1984 Great American Play Contest at the Actors Theatre in Louisville. The critics, however, thought otherwise. *Variety* called it "a searing, humorous play.... The plot is minimal but covers an emotional map the size of a western territory."[67] Elias Stomac, writing in *Drama-Logue*, commented that "many diverse elements shine separately though they never coagulate into a uniform piece."[68] Don Shirley, writing for the *Los Angeles Times*, said of a 1990 production of *Independence* that "theatregoers will be struck by how obvious it all is."[69] And Lawrence Enscoe, at the

L.A. Daily News, inveighed against this "clichéd, hackneyed, shallow piece of midwestern gothic."[70]

But the public embraced the piece and it even played in French in Paris, in 1995, and Montreal, in 1999, as *Liberty,* and in German in Berlin in 1996— quite a leap for a drama set in the American heartland. After seeing the Paris production, Blessing wrote:

> *Independence* is certainly one of my most emotional plays, and therefore, perhaps more universal than others. I wondered at first why a company in the most cosmopolitan city in the world would be interested in a play set in rural Iowa but was amazed at how natural it felt. To watch these women clash in such elemental ways before an audience with whom I could never hope to communicate directly was one of the most rewarding experiences I've had in theatre.[71]

The play clearly spoke to basic human values and relationships: siblings sorting out their rivalries, children escaping their parents' authority, women struggling to make their way in a patriarchal society, individuals battling the conformity of small-town life. These are human, not just American, challenges and the play succeeds without limitations of time or place.

Polly Warfield, in *Drama-Logue,* pegged it a "Critic's Choice," writing:

> *Independence* is equally gutsy, equally intense, intensely female. It also deserves to be a winner.... This play is a tragedy peopled with characters determined to behave as though they are in a comedy and almost succeeding.[72]

Bruce Feld, in his review of *Independence* at the McFadden Place Theatre in Hollywood, wrote:

> *Independence* teaches us that the small battles that are waged in dysfunctional families across the nation may actually outweigh, in terms of thunder and pain, that little fracas with England we celebrate every July 4th.[73]

The last best word may have come from Marion Ross, who played Marion Cunningham (often called "Mrs. C") on the long-running (1974–1984) ABC television show *Happy Days.* While essaying the role of Evelyn in *Independence* at the Burbank Theatre, she said of her character: "She's like Mrs. C. gone bad. [The play is] like a mirror. Everybody winces."[74]

(Blessing co-authored with his first wife, Jeanne Blake, a "TV film treatment" of *Independence* in 1996,[75] which was never filmed, and which I discuss in Chapter 10.)

Riches

Blessing followed *Independence* with *Riches,* a tale of marital breakup. I love *Riches,* a wild two-hander that somersaults us through the angry dissolution of a marriage on the 21st anniversary of its loving inception in just three scenes and 90 minutes of non-stop dyspeptic action. Premiering at the Humana Festival in 1985 as *War of the Roses*, Blessing later changed the play's title when the movie of the same name, starring Michael Douglas and Kathleen Turner, arrived in 1989. Ironically, both scripts followed the escalating violence of a divorce. The movie, however, is a comedy of the blackest hue, while the play, though funny in moments, is deadly serious. Unfortunately, movie and play titles cannot be copyrighted and are frequently appropriated by later authors. Blessing faced the same predicament with his 1989 play *Cobb* when the 1994 feature film, bearing no relation to the play, took the eponymous baseball player Ty Cobb as its central figure.

Riches began life as Act 2 of *Marjorie*, a play Blessing wrote in the 1970s, produced at Iowa in 1979, and "was produced once in Minneapolis."[76] In fact, *Marjorie* shows Blessing experimenting with both form and content. In that play the slowly evolving feminism of the eponymous main character comes to life as three different actors portray her at different stages of her life, a technique Blessing returned to in *Thief River* (see Chapter 7). Blessing loosely based *Marjorie* on his own wife's first marriage and Jeanne Blake both directed and played the character Marjorie in middle age. Blake told the *Minneapolis Star* and *Tribune*:

> This play is a more serious [referring to the character in *Nice People*, who left her husband] view of a woman starting over. But it's not my play. It is about how women escape into marriage and then escape out of it…. Her husband can't understand. He hasn't done anything wrong. If there were a tangible reason it would be much easier. When he's blameless and it's a matter of a woman finding her own way, it can be very sad.[77]

By and large, the critics didn't like *Marjorie*, one critic writing, "The play is utterly plausible and lifelike. But it goes nowhere."[78] David Hawley, in the *St. Paul Pioneer Press*, wrote: "There's a pat, simplistic quality to it, along with the sense that this is sentimentality posing as deep[ly] probed understanding."[79] But Carla Waldemar, in the *Twin Cities Reader*, called *Marjorie*'s "[use of different actors for same character at different stages of life] a provocative tour de force. When it comes to giving Marjorie substance as an evolving woman, it misses."[80] Blessing kept the idea of multiple actors for his future effort and went to work rewriting *Marjorie*. In one revision, *A Nearly Perfect Weekend*, his characters are two couples, the long-married Riches, their longtime friend, his new, younger wife, as well as his ex-wife. Then he tried it as just one woman, Marjorie, and one man, Ben, at a hotel in Red Wing in a production at New Dramatists in New York City in 1984. A year late it became the play we know today.

Not everyone shares my love of the play. In fact, the worst, and truly most vicious, of all the reviews I read of Blessing's plays, was for *Riches*. Kevin Kelly, veteran theater critic for the *Boston Globe*, seemingly conflated his dislike for the play with his dislike for the playwright:

> What is this unexplainable squabble? What it is is a hack playwright trying for a surreal resonance from, say, the likes of Albee and Pinter and going tone deaf in the process. "War of the Roses" is drivel ... honesty has nothing to do with Lee Blessing's technique since rational observation of how persons act and interact with each other is beyond his ability, "War of the Roses" is a sham.[81]

Sometimes you scratch your head and ask a critic: "Did you see the same play I saw?" *Riches* never conjures shades of Edward Albee and Harold Pinter and their Theater of the Absurd until the very end. The play is hyper-realistic rather than surreal and those of us (perhaps a majority of audience members and readers, perhaps everyone except Kevin Kelly) who have ended a marriage or any long-term relationship under unhappy circumstances marked by anger, guilt, regret, rejection, fear, etc., will see that Blessing has captured realistic feelings among realistic characters. Did Kelly see another play, or did the theme, perhaps, strike too close to home?

I love the script because it reads like an overheard conversation rather than invented dialogue, and I was not surprised when Blessing told me the idea for the play came from his own first wife's stories of her previous marriage.[82] And we can hear again the sad echo of that reality in Blessing's own angry divorce 15 years later from the woman who told him the story. In fact, I love *Riches* because it is the story of the end of my own marriage as well.

The power of *Riches* lies in its verisimilitude. The characters slowly emerge out of their actions like sculpted figures being revealed, chip by chip, from a block of marble. They do not *tell* us who they are but *show* us their inner lives through their words and actions.

Blessing takes the audience to Red Wing, Minnesota, to the St. James Hotel room of Carolyn and David Rich. The town, named after a Sioux chief and with a population of 15,000 (in 1985), and a hotel, built in 1875, are real. We can say the Riches exist as well because we all know married couples like them.

The Riches aren't rich, as their name implies, but seem rather normal to all appearances: middle class, middle brow, seemingly happily settled into a long-term marriage, trying to recapture some of the magic of their long-ago honeymoon in the same hotel.

At the beginning, David is fretting that they haven't gotten the exact same room as their honeymoon suite and seems anxious to recreate the details, where Carolyn sat, what they said, as if repetition could recapture an earlier time and now-fading feelings. Carolyn expresses impatience with David's sentimentality and is anxious to go down to dinner with an old friend and his new, and much younger, partner. When they learn the new woman is still in the shower, cleaning up after sex (they assume), David suggests they have sex as well, but Carolyn demurs without rancor, and nothing seems overly amiss. When David asks how he's been as a husband for the past 21 years Carolyn responds not unkindly, but not enthusiastically either: "Fine. You've been fine."[83]

An easy out to break up a marriage might be infidelity, boozing, money, or sexual dysfunction, but Blessing doesn't spring for an obvious answer; relationships are, after all, more complicated than that. What happens, he asks, when a relationship dies but no one murders it?

When David offers Carolyn an engagement ring, saying: "It's for the next twenty years.... It's to thank you for all the good years we've had so far,"[84] Carolyn tells him she wants a divorce. This unexpected news sends him into a torrent of questions to find out if she is unhappy, addicted to alcohol or drugs, or having an affair. But the best explanation she can offer: "I don't know why I have to leave you but I do.... I can't stay in a relationship just because there's nothing wrong with it"[85] is simultaneously unsatisfying and unanswerable.

David, a 45-year-old advertising account executive, and Carolyn, 41, who has some unspecified work outside the home, are the parents of a 19-year-old son who is away at college. In other words, they are neither unusual nor unfamiliar. We don't learn particulars or details of their lives, but they are not ciphers or stereotypes, just middle-aged people stripped down to the raw emotions of the moment as their seemingly tightly woven and richly decorated lives unravel into a tangled ball of cheap thread on the hotel floor.

As Scene 1 closes, Carolyn packs a bag to leave, but David seizes it, refusing to let her leave; he finally agrees to let her go if she will only explain why. Scene 2 begins an hour later with David on the phone to their son, Kevin, attempting to project an air of normalcy. Carolyn is at work with a pencil and paper, listing the reasons she is leaving. She comes up with a list of two items: "You seem smaller to me"[86] and "I don't like your nose"[87] and adds the equally unenlightening judgment: "It's me, not you."[88] Every man in the world has heard these four words from a woman. No man has ever believed them or understood them.

The play climaxes in physical violence. David slaps Carolyn ... twice. She knocks him over with a surprise lunge and kicks him while he's down. He twists her by the ankle and brings her down, scrambles on top of her and hits her hard, until she loses consciousness. When he goes to the bathroom, Carolyn recovers consciousness and clubs him with a book. Scene 2 ends with each of them passed out, David in the bathroom and Carolyn on the bed, surrounded by broken glass and overturned furniture.

Scene 3 comes at dawn. Beaten and bloodied, they shuffle about the room

2. The Estrogen Plays

Riches: Carolyn (Cara Duff-MacCormick) and her husband, David (Paul Collins), resort to physical violence after decades of a seemingly happy marriage. Actors Theatre of Louisville (Kentucky); 1986, photograph by Richard C. Trigg; courtesy of Actors Theatre of Louisville.

Riches: David and Carolyn Rich (Paul Collins and Cara Duff-MacCormick) sit, exhausted, after a wedding-anniversary brawl. Actors Theatre of Louisville (Kentucky); 1986, photograph by Richard C. Trigg; courtesy of Actors Theatre of Louisville.

without a word of dialogue, ultimately finding themselves in bed together. They hold the engagement ring. They clasp hands and, as they look at their joined hands the lights fade to black. What comes next: a rapprochement? divorce?

No.

The hotel is trashed; the bathroom mirror remains splintered on the floor while the exterior window lies in shards on the street below. This physical destruction is complete and symbolizes the end of the marriage. They will painfully move on in separate directions.

For me, the silent and seemingly peaceful third scene is a brief lull between storms. Things have been said that cannot be taken back or forgotten. Blows have been struck and bodies and egos are irreparably bruised. The Riches are used to each other after 21 years of shared living and they can share a bed and even hold hands in a superficial solidarity and mutually shared fear of the future, but this relationship is over. David has foretold their future at the end of Scene 2:

> We're going to have a lousy divorce. We're going to fight over the house, the furniture, the cars. I'm never going to pay alimony.... I'm going to date other girls.[89]

We may argue that life, matrimony, and individual egos are each absurd, but not this play. *Riches* is a highly detailed chronicle of realistic domestic turmoil. As such, it packs an emotional punch for every couple who sees it. And it makes a prescient foreshadowing for the author himself, who based it on a story told to him by his then wife, Jeanne Blake, his frequent collaborator and often the director of his early plays, about her own first marriage.

Critics united in opposition to the play. F. Kathleen Foley in the *Los Angeles Times*, wrote:

> Lee Blessing's "Riches" takes a stab at the psychological slash and splatter of marital warfare but rather than lacerating leaves only an occasional flesh wound.... [The play] is largely a non-event. Based on a strained premise and filled with reiterative interchanges that strike one as emotionally false.[90]

You have to wonder about critics. Lisa Grider and Marilyn Muljat, in *Easy Reader*, wrote:

> If theatrical productions are supposed to stir the soul and touch the senses, then *Riches* does its job. Unfortunately Lee Blessing's production not only beats the soul but also pummels the senses. We have three words to say to Lee Blessing: "Get over it!"[91]

However, in the same article they declare that the film *War of the Roses* was adapted from this play.[92] When you get your facts wrong it's hard for us to trust your opinions.

Riches remains my favorite Blessing play.

Eleemosynary

Blessing was warming up with the first three plays in this quartet, stretching his skills and honing his talent. The resulting final play, *Eleemosynary*, a 90-minute one-act, achieves classic status and marks the author's march from beginning playwright to mature writer. Once again a play without male characters, *Eleemosynary* with its focus on three generations of oddly skewed family matriarchal dynamics, with simple staging, and non-linear, non-naturalistic storytelling moving back and forth in time and even back and forth between life and death. In Hayley Barnes's analysis, the play jumps through multiple dates: April 1969, May 1971, sometime in 1973, 1975, 1976, 1977, September 1981, March 1982, May 1982, June 1982, June 1984, September 1984, January 1985, and February 1985,[93] though not in chronological order.

Eleemosynary touches an emotional and theatrical chord with audiences that has kept it almost continuously onstage somewhere in the world ever since its inception in 1985, Blessing's most produced play, both on campus and off.[94]

Blessing told me about its origins:

> I've mentioned elsewhere that my early plays had few female roles, so I decided to people *Independence* and *Eleemosynary* solely with women—if only to boost my confidence that I could write them. I felt very successful with the experiment in both plays, and both have been done a great deal in colleges and high schools, presumably due to the predominance of women in these venues.
>
> The play came together in a strange way. I was invited to write a ten-minute play by the Playwrights' Center in Minneapolis in 1982 or so. I knew I wanted to write women, and I'd just written a play with three sisters and their mother, so I thought it would be good to do three generations. I was writing a lot of poetry then ... and I proceeded to put this ten-minute play together the way I might put a poem together, looking for disparate elements I could blend together into a fiction that somehow felt "real."
>
> A poet friend of mine had in a journal long lists of "unusable" English words—words most people don't know, like "dysphemism," "peripetry" and ... well, "eleemosynary." Words that might be smuggled into his work—one-to-a-poem, say—in hopes a reader might have enough energy to get up once and consult a dictionary. I looked at these words and thought: Spelling Bee, the only logical dramatic venue where many of them could be used at once. As far as the wings and platform are concerned, that came from watching a short documentary on PBS called *Gizmo*, which featured early films of failed inventions and their inventors. There's a remarkable couple at the end, one of them wearing a pair of wings, who think that by running downhill, flapping the wings and thinking the proper, Classical thoughts, flying will be possible. The results are predictable. Anyhow, I jammed a few of these things together and made a ten-minute scene, which everyone liked. It corresponds roughly to Scene 1 in the present play.
>
> In 1985, Park Square Theatre in St. Paul commissioned me to turn it into a full-length [play]. So at that point I had to decide how these women got to that very odd point in the first place. It became a very feminist piece, about struggling for an equal position in society and how badly the struggle itself can warp a person, making it almost impossible to love in a normal way. It's also, of course, about the generational "sandwich": a woman unable to show love to her daughter but able to love her granddaughter with the greatest ease and naturalness.[95]

A feminist play, in that it grapples with the challenges of being an intelligent and independent woman in our modern society, *Eleemosynary* (not unlike, say, Caryl Churchill's *Top Girls*, in 1982, though more accessible) looks at mother/daughter relationships. Where Shakespeare introduced two sets of twins to double the laughs in his *Comedy of Errors*, Blessing gives us two sets of mothers and daughters (in just three characters) to multiply the conflicts.

The three characters are: Dorothea, a 75-year-old woman of means; Artie (Artemis) her 30-something daughter; and Artie's 16-year-old daughter Barbara (renamed Echo by her grandmother Dorothea almost as a mark of ownership).

Echo, a spelling bee champion, opens by explaining the meaning of the play's title: 'Eleemosynary: of or pertaining to alms, charitable"[96] invoking the audience's own charitable indulgence in considering these odd women. We quickly see that Dorothea has suffered a stroke which has rendered her speechless, but Echo shows us film of a younger Dorothea trying to coax a teenage

Artie into flying down a steep hill with an experimental pair of homemade wings, the play's major prop. Traumatized by childhood events like this, Artie leaves two-year-old Echo with Dorothea (was this a charitable or selfish act?) and flees her own mother's emotional control while seeking a life of her own. Echo's commitment to competitive spelling seems both a way to win her grandmother's approval and to bring her mother home, a task that takes 14 years and Dorothea's final illness.

As Blessing used country music in *Nice People*, here he uses spelling bee words and their meanings as a *leit motif*. In addition to eleemosynary, we learn words like "limicolous" (dwelling in mud), "dysphemism" (an unpleasant or derogatory term; the opposite of "euphemism"), and "autochthonous" (an indigenous inhabitant of a place).[97] Sometimes, the words serve as a commentary on the action or theme (as with eleemosynary) and sometimes they are there to show Echo's love of language, a love of words the playwright admittedly shares.[98]

Along with words go the freighted names: the Greek goddess Artemis was the daughter of Zeus and Leto, the twin sister of Apollo, and the protectress of the hunt and wilderness as well as childbirth and virginity. By changing her name from Artemis to the masculine and vulgar Artie, she subverts her mother's power and declares her resistance. Dorothea's revenge is to turn Barbara into Echo, a beautiful nymph in Greek mythology famous for repeating the words of others, not unlike a spelling champion.

As Blessing multiplies the characters' conflicts (Dorothea v. Artie, Artie v. Echo, Echo v. Dorothea, Artie and Dorothea v. Echo, Echo and Dorothea v. Artie), he also doubles the symbolic conflicts: these women not only struggle for independence in a male-dominated world but also struggle for their own identities within their matriarchal family. The play is the story of the raveling and unraveling and re-raveling of their complex relationships and is simultaneously a family drama and a social drama, and, ultimately, a story of forgiveness.

Eleemosynary is a comedy as well as a drama. Dorothea chooses to be an eccentric "like choosing to be a Lutheran"[99] because "no one holds an eccentric responsible."[100] She entertains everyone not in her immediate family by experimenting not only with winged flight but also with "communication with the dead, spontaneous combustion, astral projection."[101] She utters delicious lines, including: "You don't have to smoke but it makes you more powerful. The person you're with knows that while you do need oral gratification you don't necessarily need it from them."[102]

For Dorothea, odd behavior is a rational choice to escape a stultifying marriage to a man "who didn't know what to make of me, except a wife."[103] Yet in her own struggle for freedom, Dorothea, part feminist model and part "she monster," has no qualms when it comes to oppressing others, including her own daughter. When Artie flees home following an abortion forced upon her by Dorothea at age 18, Dorothea tracks her down. Artie flees again because, only away from Dorothea's overbearing personality can she be herself. Dorothea tracks her down again years later when she is married and pregnant, and buys a house down the block. When Artie's husband dies in a car accident soon after, Dorothea swoops in to care for the bereft mother and her child. Artie flees to an academic job in Europe and leaves Echo with her mother and doesn't see either of them again for over a decade.

Artie's telephoned suggestion of spelling competitions, a gambit to give these two intimate strangers something to talk about, forms a new bond to her now-teenaged daughter. Artie calls regularly and they practice Echo's words together. Echo realizes that spelling binds them and resolves to be the best speller in the country. By the time she reaches the National Spelling Bee finals, with Artie and Dorothea in the audience, sweet Echo has transformed into a competitive bully, cruelly scheming to win at any cost. Ironically, she wins the contest by spelling the word eleemosynary, the spirit of charity she no longer values as she bludgeons her young opponent with her knowledge hoping that

> although she cannot control the way her grandmother behaves or where her mother is, she can learn the spelling bee words. She can memorize them and regurgitate them for an audience of adoring fans; perhaps if she can control these words and this bee, she can control her own future. If she "wins the approval" of the judges at the bee by actually winning, Echo thinks that she can win the approval of her mother.[104]

Unfortunately for Echo, her mother and grandmother are repulsed by competitiveness:

> ARTIE: Echo was a little different than I thought she'd be. I mean, she was terrific and everything, but she seemed so ... desperate.
> DOROTHEA: She was frightening, is what she was. More frightening than anyone I can remember. Oh, Hitler and Mussolini were worse, certainly, but from them you expected it.[105]

Dorothea's stroke brings Artie and Echo together physically and her death begins their emotional reunion. But, first, Artie tries to palm Echo off on her brother Bill and his "normal" family. Echo runs away, back to Artie, convinced she can make Artie love her. And, in the end, she does.

Eleemosynary is a tender, heartbreaking, and heart-healing play. Audiences feel that. Adam Langer, writing in the *Chicago Reader*, called *Eleemosynary* "a small gem ... a marvelous evening of theatre."[106] *New York Times* critic Frank Rich (never a Blessing fan and writing a year after savaging *A Walk in the Woods*), wrote:

What we get instead of emotional or intellectual depth are words, lots of them.... When "Eleemosynary" induces restlessness, as it does at least half the time, it's because the writing, not the acting, lacks the human reality that might root the play in the theatre or in the audience's psyche.[107]

However, Lawrence Bommer, in Chicago's *Windy City Times*, wrote:

Unfortunately the characters' conflicts and emotions (and all the subtexts that explain them) remain always on the surface, ultimately on the verge of being explained to death. It leaves little for three excellent actors to do but flood us with their prefabricated feelings in a reverse game of "tell but don't show."[108]

Perhaps it is too much to point out Bommer's misuse of the term "subtext," which, by definition, cannot "remain on the surface. It is either present (below the surface) or it is not. Bommer is correct that, in fact, *Eleemosynary* contains little subtext and that many critics would say that the more subtext there is in a play, the better the play.

But let's turn this around a bit. The great German playwright and critic Johann Wolfgang von Goethe (1749–1832) suggested we ask three questions in judging a play (or any work of art):

1. What is the playwright trying to do?
2. How well has he or she done it?
3. Was it worth doing?[109]

In *Eleemosynary*, Blessing set out to write a multi-generational play consisting solely of female characters. His aim was to present flawed human beings (the only kind there are, really) confronting each other's failures and the way they had damaged each other and finding some reconciliation and forgiveness at the end. He accomplished this goal by creating believable and entertaining characters and putting them through a series of interpersonal conflicts. Since much the same theme is shared by a majority of novels, movies, and plays, we have to accept it is worth attempting.

Does Blessing telegraph his punches? Yes. But they do pack a wallop. Does Blessing neatly tie up all the loose ends? Yes. But we're emotionally satisfied that he does. Is the play simple? No. Simplifying? No. Blessing complicates the action and the characters every chance he gets. Does he have something to say? Most assuredly. Is it worth saying? Yes. Is it said well? Yes, again.

And for these reasons, *Eleemosynary* remains part of the Great American Playbook (to borrow from the more commonly known Great American Songbook) of popular standards that is performed regularly just because it *is* popular and continues to speak to generations of young people. In her BFA thesis, South Mississippi College student Hayley Barnes described her stint in performing as Echo in a September 2011 production at the Hartwig Theatre in Hattiesburg,

Mississippi. To Barnes, *Eleemosynary* "is an exploration of strong women and how they can make a difference in their own lives and each other's."[110]

And *Eleemosynary*, with its all-female cast, led indirectly to one of Blessing's most controversial plays, *Patient A*, also about a unique and polarizing woman, Kimberly Bergalis, as we shall see in Chapter 5.

Chapter 3

On Fields of Dreams

> *Oldtimers Game*
> *Cooperstown*
> *Cobb*
> *Fantasy League*
> *The Winning Streak*
> *For the Loyal*

Lee Blessing told me:

> It's rare that sports make a good play. Sports doesn't sell to theatres, maybe because theater people didn't excel at sports. And, of course, theater and sports are competitors for the audience's entertainment dollar.[1]

Despite this, he has returned to sports, usually baseball, as the subject or backdrop for five plays and a screenplay. Sports are inherently dramatic since someone must win and someone lose and the final result, or climax, often hangs in the balance dependent upon the action, heroics, or failure of a single character. A skillful author can easily move the audience to root for one side and against the other.

Baseball is quintessentially American and so it also

> happens to be a handy parallel world in which we can view a lot of attitudes and values that we live by, whether we want to believe it or not, and see them under a microscope.[2]

Blessing also happens to love sports and especially the teams of his native Minnesota. He was 12 years old when the Washington, D.C. Senators moved to Minneapolis to become the Minnesota Twins. He "imprinted" on the Twins and their players, including future Hall of Famers Harmon Killebrew, Bob Allison, and Tony Oliva. The Twins remain his team, as do the Minnesota Vikings in football. He went so far as to a name a character in *Nice People* after Twins' second baseman Rob Wilfong.

Oldtimers Game

Blessing turned from his first success with westerns (*The Authentic Life of Billy the Kid*) to sports with the *Oldtimers Game* at the Sixth Annual Human Festival of New American Plays in 1982. His all-female casts (The Estrogen Plays of Chapter 2) came after. The play was revised, rewritten, and reproduced until it found its current, published title, *Oldtimers Game*. Here, on a baseball farm team, love of the game takes a backseat to careers that are either ascending or ending. As Blessing told critic Owen Hardy:

> On a triple-A team the point is not to stay where you are. The player is either headed up—to the major leagues—or down—and out of professional baseball forever. For me, it's an instantly nostalgic event. It creates a world where you see the ballplayer in every stage of his career, a career which ends at 40.[3]

Set entirely in the team's locker room, *Oldtimers Game* brings together an odd collection of current and former Otters playing out a lackluster season on the one day of the year big-league owner Mr. Thompson visits for the annual oldtimers game. The gang of current players includes an up-and-coming black star, Sut Davis, the clubhouse clown and practical joker, a catcher recently sent down from the Big Leagues; Harly Nix, the Latino shortstop who has spent ten years in the minors; Jesus Luna; and the alcoholic manager, Cal Timmer. As Sut tells Harly and Jesus, he has his heart set on getting to the show:

> Man, you got to get to the majors. Down here they pay you the minimum, they tell you what to do, they fucking own you.[4]

An equally colorful collection of former Otters have returned to join this fractious crew. The oldtimers include Old John Law, a 65-year-old former pitcher and Hall of Famer, a star in the baseball firmament; Jim Nealy, now doing broadcast work after an injury forced him off the field; and Crab Detlefsen, who had a brief sojourn in the Big Leagues and now works as a part-time scout. Problems grow with the arrival of the owner, Mr. Thompson, a newcomer to baseball who made his money in advertising. Thompson seeks to shake things up. As he tells the players and their manager, Cal, the former owner didn't make the grade:

> He'd lost his capitalistic edge. He had failed to inspire a winner. That's what an owner does—he inspires. I'm going to inspire you. I'm going to be an inspiration for every man in this organization.... Unless, of course, you don't want to be inspired. In which case I'll fire you.[5]

Thompson arrives with Dave Pearl, a former Otter but now a real major leaguer from the Dodgers, in tow. The minor leaguers greet him with pride, mixed with envy. Thompson reveals he has fired his L.A. manager and is promoting Cal in his place. Sut, anxious to move up as well, badgers Thompson for a decision until they tell him it all depends upon his improved fielding, which will be judged at today's game. The present day Otters have no faith in Cal's coaching abilities:

> JIM: Nobody likes him. Nobody respects him. He's an average judge of talent and he's out of touch with most of his players. (*Pauses*) And you're right. He'll make a perfect big-league manager.[6]

Act 1 closes as Crab discovers Old John quietly changing out of his uniform, having also changed his mind about playing in the game.

> CRAB: Why's you come today if you weren't going to play?
> JOHN: Because I ... love baseball. It's the people I don't like.[7]

While we might share this sentiment after meeting the current and former Otters, their coach and their wacky new owner, Crab talks Old John out of leaving with the first real words about baseball that reveal a love of the game:

> It's not the people you're here for. Is it? It's the game.... We'll go out there and doff our caps, and do everything we used to do, only clumsier—and if people want to bother us and talk to us, well, we'll just let 'em, and we won't hear a word they say. 'Cause we came to play baseball.[8]

Act 2 brings us back to the locker room three hours later, after the game was called on account of rain after a single inning. Harly and Jesus are losing at cards to Crab. Old John lies down, trying to help his aged back recover from fielding a bunt. Meanwhile, Cal and Thompson continue a meeting in the manager's offstage office, making everyone outside nervous. Harry, Sut, and Jesus hang around, hoping for another chance to impress the new owner and win a trip to California. With the desperation of the real estate salesmen in David Mamet's *Glengarry Glen Ross*, they start to turn on each other. Thompson tells them he and Cal are wheeling and dealing, trading players and changing rosters:

> THOMPSON: I'll tell you what. Cal and I are going back into that room. We're going to switch some rosters around. We're going to move some people up, some people in, some people out, some people down. You will be one of those people.[9]

Crab puts their plight in perspective:

> It's the minors. They still run it the same way. Nothing works, everything hurts, and nobody gets paid enough. When you're here all you want is to be somewhere else. And when they don't want you somewhere else anymore, you're dying to be right back here.[10]

The day suddenly gets even worse when Dave Pearl returns from hitting flies to Sut, who wanted to impress Thompson with his glove work, having already hit a homer off Old John, and reports that Sut tore up his knee chasing a fly in

Oldtimers Game: **Former pro ball players (Michael Kevin, left; Ray Fry) return to the scene of former glory. Actors Theatre of Louisville (Kentucky); 1982, photograph by Richard C. Trigg; courtesy of Actors Theatre of Louisville.**

the rain-soaked outfield. When Thompson and Cal reenter the locker room, unaware of Sut's injury, they share the news, now sadly ironical, that they have decided to bring Sut back to California with them. They have also decided not to bring Harly up; in fact, they'll release him. Jesus, however, will be going to the majors: a reward for the dubious accomplishment of not complaining during his ten years in the minor leagues.

The play climaxes with Thompson's unchallengeable decisions. As the antagonist, he has separated the sheep from the goats, not on the basis of character or ability, but from a capricious and ill-informed whim reinforced by the power of his considerable wealth. Harly, the locker-room clown, attractive underachiever, more bark than bite, as close to a protagonist as we have, now cleans out his locker in utter dejection: "Who's gonna let me *play*? Who's gonna pick me up at thirty-goddam-*four*?!"[11] In despair he slams his bat against the locker and then heads for the manager's office, smashing things along the way. Before we know it, a brawl is on. Sut and Harly go at it and, by the end, everyone else, trying to separate them, has fallen into a writhing, punching heap on the floor.

Sut begs for the chance to prove himself, desperate to head back onto the field with his injured knee, while his teammates beg him to reconsider. Old John starts swinging the bat Harly sawed off to stop Sut from damaging his future with injury upon injury. In the denouement, Thompson breezes out to his private plane, Jesus, bereft of wife and children, heads for the local watering hole to celebrate. Cal takes Sut to the hospital for X-rays, leaving Harly, Crab, and Old John alone in the locker room. Old John ducks out. Harly and Crab head out to dinner as lights fade to black.

> CRAB: Where's the best place to eat in this town?
> HARLY: Nowhere.
> CRAB: Then let's go there.[12]

Oldtimers Game uses baseball as a backdrop, but we see no ball played onstage and the subjects, rather than sport, are really the various oddities of personality, ambition, the crassness of money, capitalism which reduces all to commodities, old age, and mortality. These fairly stock characters: the jaded old-timer, the new kid, the sensitive wiseacre, the self-satisfied rookie, the boss with more money than brains, inhabit every vocation.

The critics, by and large, enjoyed *Oldtimers Game*.

Richard Stayton, in the *Los Angeles Herald Examiner*, enthused:

> We don't care to think about those who toil forever in the obscurity of the minor leagues. But baseball losers are exactly who playwright Lee Blessing wryly celebrates in "Oldtimers Game".... What makes Blessing's play a winner is its implication that even our fabled heroes, for all their deification, are secretly losers.[13]

In the *Los Angeles Times*, Dan Sullivan wrote:

> "Oldtimers Game" has its innings particularly when the guys are busting up the clubhouse, but some infield practice wouldn't hurt.[14]

And William Mootz, in the *Courier Journal*, said:

> Blessing's wily, cantankerous and altogether irresistible comedy.... [The play] flows so naturally, provides so many laughs and occasionally pulls so shamelessly on our heartstrings that it tempts one to accuse it of being facile.... But Blessing writes with a roaring energy. His ballplayers are of real flesh and blood.... We get to know them well[15]

Cooperstown

In 1993, Blessing's script for a TV-movie on baseball players aired as *Cooperstown* and could be understood as another side of *Oldtimers Game* or *Cobb*, but with a happy ending. The movie starred Alan Arkin, Graham Greene, and Ed Begley, Jr. Charles Haid, an actor and director best known for his role as Officer Andy Renko on the television series *Hill Street Blues*, directed. As he told *Drama-Logue* (in words that echoed Blessing's in talking about *Cobb*): "It's about coming to terms with your own life. And I made this film for my father. As a matter of fact, I made this film for everybody's father."[16]

Not available today from Netflix and rarely rebroadcast on commercial television, I haven't been able to view *Cooperstown*, but the plot synopses I've read run like this: Harry Willette (Alan Arkin), as a retired pitcher, learns that his Native American battery mate, Raymond Maracle (Graham Greene) has been elected to the Baseball Hall of Fame, but died just prior to notification. Willette, with regrets for his past actions and jealousy of Maracle, drives cross-country to the induction ceremony, with his catcher's spirit as company. Also along is a meditating nephew and a hitchhiking woman who is a baseball fanatic. Willette, a sort of rehabilitated Ty Cobb, learns from the error of his ways and honors both his non-white teammate and the warm and fuzzy traditions of the national pastime. It sounds like the anti-*Cobb*. *Entertainment Weekly* called *Cooperstown* "very charming and schmaltzy."[17] John O'Connor, in the *New York Times*, wrote, "Not much that happens in 'Cooperstown' can't be spotted at least two miles down the road."[18] However, the *Los Angeles Times* called *Cooperstown* "captivating,"[19] and the movie garnered major awards. Blessing, nominated for the CableACT award for 1994, won the Humanitas Prize for 1993 for his screenplay. Alan Arkin won the CableACT award for best actor in a movie or miniseries.

Cobb

In *Cobb*, without schmaltz or sentimentality, Blessing uses baseball to examine racism, capitalism, egotism, success, and even the divisive policies of the Reagan years.

And, he has said, this is about *family*:

> In some ways *Cobb* is my father's play because a lot of things Cobb bought into, men of my father's generation bought into as well. My father was a self-made businessman. He worked very hard and long hours believing in the American dream.... [Cobb's tragedy] is he didn't see that for everything he gained he was giving up something very, very central in his life. And he ended up with a ruined marriage and children who were estranged, [and was] really quite a lonely man in his old age.[20]

As Blessing told me: "My dad was a much nicer person than Cobb but, like Cobb, he was a person making [his] way in the world without the best education."[21]

As he did in *The Authentic Life of Billy the Kid*, Blessing turns here to reconsider the life of a real person, Tyrus Raymond "Ty" Cobb. He was born in rural Narrows, Georgia, in December 1886, and died in Atlanta in July 1961. "The

Georgia Peach," as he was known, played the outfield for the American League Detroit Tigers from 1905 to 1926, hitting for a lifetime average of .367, the highest career batting average in major league history. Over his 25-year career, Cobb led the American League in batting 12 seasons, including six consecutively, also a record. In all, he set 90 baseball records in his career, 15 of which still stand. His record of 4,191 hits stood until Pete Rose broke it in 1985. The first player voted into the Baseball Hall of Fame, many consider him one of, if not *the*, greatest player in baseball history. Through stock market investing he also became the first baseball millionaire while still a player.

He was simultaneously, quite possibly, the most hated man in the sport. Disdained by opponents, disliked by his own teammates, distant from his children, another record Cobb held for many years was for being ejected from 38 games in a single season. He terrorized other players on the base paths, often sliding into base with his spikes high, spikes he had made a show of publicly sharpening prior to the game. "I wonder," mused Lloyd Richards, the African American *Cobb* director, "what it says about our values that those spikes were in the first exhibit in the Hall of Fame?"[22] Cobb also assaulted at least three Black people off the field and once entered the stands to beat a heckler who, due to an industrial accident, turned out to have no hands. His angry demeanor was often traced back to his experience as a child when his mother fatally shot his father, who possibly suspecting his wife of infidelity, crept past her bedroom window. Cobb's mother claimed she was shooting at a presumed burglar and was acquitted.

The play, set in an otherworldly limbo, or a dreamscape, over a 100-year span, features three iterations of Cobb: The Peach, 20-year-old Cobb, energetic and still an idealist; Ty, the angry adult and realist; and Mr. Cobb, now dead, as the bitter old man fashioning his own myth. Each is played by a different actor, just as Blessing used multiple actors to portray a single character at different stages of life in his plays *Marjorie* and *Thief River*. Rather than offering separate monologues, the three Cobbs interact onstage at the same time. One wonders if these three manifestations represent a single consciousness, symbolic of Freud's ego, superego, and id? The fourth character is 30-year-old Oscar Charleston of baseball's Negro Leagues, and known as "the Black Ty Cobb." Blessing also adds as projections backdrop pictures of actual baseball players from the early 20th century.

Once again, Blessing gives us a character who is already dead, Mr. Cobb here, Kim in *Patient A*, Michael at the end of *Two Rooms*, and Billy in *The Authentic Life of Billy the Kid*. Mixing dead characters and characters from the past is similar to that used in earlier plays and yet different, chosen specifically to suit this play's content. As Blessing told me:

How do I decide what structure to use in a play? That's always subject to whatever I determine the action of the play is—which is to say, what its climax is intended to be. I'm a bit troglodytic, in that I tend to think all plays have climaxes—most especially those not intended to have them. So I try to choose the structure that best serves a play's climax. This means I have to determine the play's climax before I write the play, which is sort of like trying to jam lightning up my ass before the storm clouds even form.[23]

The play is non-linear. Plays often unfold in a linear, chronological manner. Since we experience life in a linear progression this underlines the seeming "realism" of such plays. Non-linear plays jump backwards and forwards in time, like our dreams or our memories. This adds a non-realistic element that prepares us to accept the usually unacceptable, like characters who are already dead or the interaction of characters who never actually met. A second category of non-linear plays which end where they began, and so are circular in nature, like Eugene Ionesco's *The Lesson* or *The Bald Soprano*, for example, we classify as both non-realistic and as Theater of the Absurd.

Inspired by Charles C. Alexander's biography of Cobb (*Ty Cobb: Sport in American Life*, Oxford University Press, 1984), Blessing covers the high and low points of Cobb's life through the onstage interaction of the Georgia Peach, Ty, and Mr. Cobb. As in his previous use of a published book for his play *The Authenticate Life of Billy the Kid*, Blessing's research shows in the events and anecdotes they recount, beginning with Cobb's mother's killing of his father, through the physical fights with several black people and Cobb's beating of the crippled heckler in the stands. Such events, however, are not acted out but rather recounted by Peach, Ty, and Cobb as Blessing uses the disagreements between the three to create some dramatic tension in what amounts to storytelling, interrupted by conflicts between the storytellers. The stories are entertaining, certainly, but Aristotle's description of drama as the "imitation of an action" here becomes talk *about* action, and not drama. Sometimes, all three personas of the single Cobb character egg each other on like a Greek chorus, as in this retelling of Cobb's fight in the stands:

> TY: He called me a ... a ... "half-nigger."
> PEACH: And up I went—over that railing. Hell, I'd a jumped over the Earth to get that man.
> MR. COBB: Twelve rows!
> TY: Twelve rows!
> PEACH: I went like a shot!....
> TY: I was bigger than him. I was stronger than him, and dammit, I was better than him! I punched him. I threw him down ... and someone suddenly screamed, "Stop it! He has no hands!"
> PEACH: And I never paused. I just kept kicking!
> TY: I shouted back—
> MR. COBB: *I don't care if he has no feet!!!*[24]

However, by adding the "black Ty Cobb," although the two center fielders may never have crossed paths in real life, Blessing focuses the story on racism, which he has called "the major element of the play,"[25] and the capitalist system, within which racism functions as a key structural support. And Ty Cobb himself stands in for entire countries and political systems:

> I see Ty Cobb as a real archetypal American. Puritanical, he channeled all his creative energy into being the best ballplayer and into being a multi-millionaire so that he didn't have any left over for more human aspects of life. He was very, very bitter. But he was driven to be the best.... Countries think in this vein—being the best instead of being a member of a community, a community of nations.[26]

Cobb represents American capitalism in the early 20th century, along with other unpopular capitalist contemporaries like John D. Rockefeller or John Pierpont Morgan, and is symbolic of American power in what *Time* magazine publisher Henry Luce heralded as "The American Century," in 1941. In words that any prominent industrialist of the time might have endorsed, Mr. Cobb, speaking of sports, says: "At the turn of the century I took a rustic, folk art form called baseball and applied the science of warfare to it."[27] He also boasted, "Before me, baseball was a virgin. When I was through, it was American."[28]

It takes a fan, like Blessing, to celebrate the innate beauty of the game:

> PEACH: Whenever I walked into a ballpark, it was like fallin' in love for the first time—again and again.... And the feel of the glove and the bat—these objects were always there.... They were tools you used, but they were also a part of your body. They made me feel more natural, more physically complete.[29]

But for all his love of the game, Blessing sees the sport clearly:

> Everything you read and see on the screen about baseball is sentimentalized. I refused to fall into that trap.... For more than 50 years baseball was one of the most, if not the most, nimble expression of the color line in America.... It is so easy to forget the realm of [black] baseball that wasn't documented.[30]

Barred from white baseball teams, black athletes began forming their own teams as early as 1859 and fielded the first organized all-black league in 1887 and played their own Black World Series beginning in the 1920s. White baseball began integration with the addition of Jackie Robinson to the Brooklyn Dodgers in 1947, and the Negro Leagues ended as separate entities in 1948. These black teams had their own stars, though they often played on subpar baseball diamonds before sparse crowds and with little publicity outside their own communities. Many of their best players were known by the names of their white correlates: Josh Gibson was the "Black Babe Ruth," Buck Leonard was the "Black Lou Gehrig," and Oscar Charleston, who often hit over .400 in multiple seasons and played centerfield, was known as the "Black Ty Cobb." As his character says in the play:

They never remembered no Oscar Charleston. Just the "Black Cobb." Kind of strange, having your fame with another man's name on it.[31]

Though Charleston and many other black stars are now in the Hall of Fame in Cooperstown with the white players, very few ever got the chance to compete against them and statistics and records on black players are spotty and incomplete at best. To this day we do not know how good they were or which were indeed better players than their white counterparts. Charleston taunts Peach with avoiding playing black teams in fear of being shown up.

> CHARLESTON: 1915, 1922 and 1923. Three different years ... your Tigers played exhibition games against teams I played on.... You could have been there, and you never were. When you did that you cheated yourself out of something for all time.... You'll never know if you were better.... And say goodbye to your record book. Without us in your league, the record book doesn't exist.[32]

In the end, *Cobb* functions as a morality play: The greatest player to ever play the game died alone, despised by his peers, alienated from his children and former spouse, alcoholic, clutching a paper bag filled with money, in a Georgia hospital bed. Only two fellow ballplayers attended his funeral. His hometown opened a Ty Cobb museum, which later closed for lack of visitors.[33]

As Blessing told a reporter:

> For all the pains he [Cobb] took to become the best ballplayer of his era he shared with his whole generation a lack of understanding that you need to work that hard to succeed in personal relationships too ... that has been at the heart of a lot of trouble with this society for years.[34]

"The play ... asks," said Blessing: "What's the meaning of the life of a human being?"[35]

Reviewers weren't buying it. Blessing's *bête noir* at the *New York Times*, Frank Rich, who had hated *Riches* and *A Walk in the Woods*, wrote:

> Mr. Blessing knows how to talk baseball in the form of flavorful theatrical dialogue.... It's when Mr. Blessing steps from the specifics of Cobb's story to grand themes that "Cobb" becomes intellectually shallow and dramatically inert.... Poor Cobb! Mr. Blessing is going to have to give this promising play more drama and less preaching."[36]

Malcolm Johnson, in *The Hartford Courant*, was even less kind: "Bleak 'Cobb' strikes out as drama ... a lifeless, preachy, monotonic 'Cobb.'"[37] George Weinberg-Harter, in *Drama-Logue*, piled on:

> *Cobb* is purely presentational.... Finally it seems that all this triplicity is merely an unsuccessful attempt to prevent what is mainly a monologue from becoming as boring as in fact it is.... Indeed there's no perceptible dramatic progress or development.... Dull as dishwater.[38]

The *Coast Dispatch* got nastier:

Ultimately, though, the play fails because there is no drama to get us interested. Perhaps that is why there is no intermission—nothing would bring us back in for a second act.[39]

But critics were not of a single mind. *Variety* commented: "[*Cobb* is written] with soaring vigorous elegance that rises to heights of poetry."[40] A year later, the show business bible called it "generally fascinating."[41] Margaret Spillane, in the *New Haven Independent*, wrote, "If theatre's purpose is to illuminate society's compelling and dangerous myths, then 'Cobb' is amply doing its job."[42] Bill Hager, in the *San Diego Tribune*, celebrated the play:

> If you like theatre, you'll like "Cobb," if you like baseball, you'll like "Cobb." Blessing's concept is a bold and difficult one, but director Lloyd Richards and a major league cast belt it out of the park.[43]

Opening in New York in 2000, *Cobb* almost closed prematurely. Word got out that the production was in financial trouble. Oscar winner Kevin Spacey had seen the play and called the artistic director at The Melting Pot Theatre to say: "You can't close it, it's too good. How much would it cost to keep it open?" The director told Spacey the amount and "I got a check the next day."[44] In spite of these kind words we can see that the play's major problems include a heavy-handed message, a one-dimensional character in Oscar Charleston, who has no motivation apart from enraging Ty, Peach, and Cobb, and the static nature of the drama which allowed for little, if any, action.

Three years after the play, a movie biopic, also titled *Cobb*, premiered. Starring Tommy Lee Jones as the troubled baseball legend, the script was based on a biography by Al Stump. Once again, as in the play *War of the Roses* (which Blessing retitled *Riches* to avoid confusion with the movie), Blessing found Hollywood breathing down his neck. It also happened when the Lebanon kidnappings that formed the subject for Blessing's *Two Rooms*, birthed the TV-movie *Forgotten: The Sis and Jerry Levin Story*. In that case, Marlo Thomas, of Lebanese descent, negotiated briefly with Blessing and then chose a different script, yet with a similar theme. In *Fortinbras*, Blessing imagined Hamlet appearing on a television set eight years before director Michael Almereyda did the same in his 2000 video-within-a-film version of *Hamlet*, starring Ethan Hawke. When I asked Blessing about those brushes with Hollywood, he replied:

> The coincidences you note are, I believe, just that. Every writer has these experiences of real or imagined "something in the *zeitgeist*" moments. I don't think they mean much. The sad part I suppose is that people know the three films you mention far better than my plays.[45]

Fantasy League

Launching Mile Square Theatre in Hoboken, New Jersey, in 2003, artistic director Chris O'Connor hit upon a novel idea for a fundraiser: a festival of short plays about baseball. As he explained:

> Baseball, America's national pastime was officially born on June 19, 1846, when the New York Baseball Club defeated the Knickerbockers 23–1 at the Elysian Fields in Hoboken. The first playwright I asked to write, Lee Blessing, happily agreed. A passionate fan of the game, Lee gave the event instant cache and others quickly jumped aboard.[46]

Since its beginning, Mile Square has birthed some 48 ten-minute baseball plays. Blessing's contribution, *Fantasy League*, takes a ten-minute romp through marital relations and, while the dialogue centers on baseball, this field of play hosts a battle of the sexes. Identified as only "Husband" and "Wife," our characters joust around a bed where Hubby recovers from a nasty fall following an unsuccessful reach for a heavy "Abstract of Baseball" on a top shelf of his den. The wife tries to help him keep up with his fantasy league though newspapers and Internet notes seemingly lovingly tendered.

Though his league is a fantasy, Husband takes it a little too seriously. When his ace pitcher develops a blister on the index finger of his pitching hand, Wife assures him: "It's not the end of the world, dear." Husband reacts strongly:

> It's worse! You know how much I have down inside bets alone? Beckett could be out for two starts! I gotta have him. He's my rock, my stopper, my ace in the hole![47]

In fact, one player after another on Husband's fantasy team has succumbed to injury, or so reports Wife. Not even a proffered Lorna Doone cookie assuages his pain. The roll of bad news reflects Wife's own injuries, psychic though they are:

> Why would I torment you? Haven't I always supported your hobbies? Didn't I say, "Go ahead, dear—transform the sweetest downstairs room we have, the one with all the light, into a cramped library of baseball trivia?" Did I complain when you stacked books to the ceiling, creating a death-trap of votive sports arcana? No. "Go ahead," I said. Spend your spare time peering into a computer, emailing your fellow no-lives, betting on the Delusional League.[48]

Tensions have built over the years:

> WIFE: And who let you spend your last three vacations driving around to major-league ballparks with your buddies?
> HUSBAND: I have to see the players! I have to look 'em in the eye! How can I make an intelligent draft otherwise?
> WIFE: I understand. After all, it is the one thing that gives you pleasure.[49]

Slowly light dawns over Marblehead:

HUSBAND: I always knew you resented this. This whole Fantasy Baseball thing. You think I use it to hide out from you, don't you? Well, I'll tell you something—I *do*! You think Pujols is bored? He should try life around here! I can't believe I married a woman who wasn't a baseball fan.[50]

Hubby loses all:

WIFE: In fact, you want to know what the *real* news is? I've called up some of the wives—you know, of your Fantasy League buddies?—and we're going to the ballpark. You know what we're going to do? Fantasize—real, real hard. There's all sorts of men on a ball team. All ages and colors and sizes and ... there's players and coaches and batboys, not to mention umpires. We may fantasize all night, if you know what I mean. And when we're done fantasizing there, we're going to take a road trip—all over the country.[51]

A horn honks outside and Wife departs as she sings: "Buy me some peanuts and Cracker Jack, I don't care if I ever get back..."[52]

Ouch!

The Winning Streak

I attended the Eugene O'Neill Memorial Theater Center in Waterford, Connecticut, in the summer of 1999. Founded in 1964 by George C. White, the O'Neill, named for the playwright Eugene O'Neill, the only four-time Pulitzer Prize winner for drama (*Beyond the Horizon, Anna Christie, Strange Interlude,* and *Long Day's Journey into Night*) and a Nobel Prize winner for Literature, is a beautiful former private estate bordering Long Island Sound. The center pioneered new play development for many dramas and musicals that later appeared on Broadway.

The National Critics Conference ran simultaneously at the O'Neill with the National Playwright's Conference. I'd won an American College Theatre Festival/Kennedy Center Critic's scholarship that year. Not, mind you, the national critic's award that came with a free ride to the O'Neill, but an ACTF Region VIII award that required me to pony up some of my own money as well. I got to study theater criticism with Dan Sullivan, theater critic at the *Los Angeles Times* for 20 years, and Michael Feingold, theater critic at the *Village Voice* for over 30 years, and see and review staged readings by both established and emerging playwrights. One treat I remember was sharing a table, just the two of us, with the O'Neill's artistic director Lloyd Richards, one of the first African Americans to direct a play on Broadway; he had earlier won the 1960 Tony Award for Best Direction of the play *A Raisin in the Sun*, the first play by an African American, Lorraine Hansberry, to appear on Broadway. Richards had furthered the careers of such theater luminaries as August Wilson, Wendy Wasserstein, Christopher Durang, David Henry Hwang, and ... Lee Blessing. Blessing was there that summer, too, as he had been in 1984 and 1986, with a draft of his newest work, *The Winning Streak*, then a nine-scene play mimicking the usual nine innings of a baseball game.

The O'Neill "process" involved a week or so of work on a new play with a professional director and actors, culminating in a staged reading. The morning following the reading, open to all and critiqued in reviews written by those of us in the Critics' Conference, the playwright would sit center stage (often wearing sun glasses to mask his/her reactions) as all the other O'Neill participants sat in the benches of the outdoor amphitheater. The playwright sat and listened to the criticism, but could not respond. It could be a brutal experience, but it was one that Blessing endured, and returned to, many times. *The Winning Streak* made it into full production a year later. *Cobb* had gone through the same process a decade earlier, and Lloyd Richards had directed its premiere as well.

But where *Cobb* used baseball as context, history, symbol, and historical reality to explore American exceptionalism, racism, and capitalism, the game of professional baseball in *The Winning Streak* seems little more than colorful backdrop to what is, finally, a story of father and son antagonism and reconciliation. In the end, our main character could as easily be a retired truck driver or an accountant as a big league umpire. But dramatic events in Blessing's own life foregrounded the baseball metaphor.

As Simon Saltzman later explained in *TheaterScene*:

> It was ... in 1998 that playwright Lee Blessing was told that his father was diagnosed with lung cancer. The prognosis was not good—six months at the outside—for the senior Blessing, who was living in retirement in San Diego.
>
> "The one thing I noticed was how quickly the disease was disabling him," says Blessing, who, although he was living in Manhattan, was spending more and more time with his father. The other thing that Blessing noticed was how the San Diego Padres, in the midst of a winning streak, gave his father the will to get up and see another day. "It gave him a lifeline as it also gave me the idea for my play *The Winning Streak*."
>
> Just as Blessing knew how much watching the Padres meant to his father, he knew it was also the time for him to confront and work out certain issues with him. Blessing makes it clear that the characters and the issues in the play are not the same as those he faced with his father. However, he explains that the reunion and the process by which the father ... and the son he never knew, get to know and understand each other are similar.
>
> "The reason that I love this play, about two men who were going to forge a bond that lasts, is that it gets farther down the road in that regard than I was able to go with my father." Blessing admits that he was determined that his characters would have the kind of resolve that he didn't have with his father.[53]

The published play contains a dedication: "For Frank Blessing, 1915–1998." So this is a personal, not a political, play but one to which men especially can relate. Most of us who are fathers and most of us who are sons, and most of us who are both fathers and sons, can probably list two dozen issues unresolved in our own relationships. The particulars often devolve down to forgiving our fathers. So it is for Ry and Omar in *The Winning Streak*.

Complications reign. Ry, in his thirties, is the product of a one-night stand and has not seen his father (or progenitor, really) before. Omar, retired baseball umpire, curmudgeon, and sadly solitary man in his sixties, never married or had children he knew about. Ry, employed as an art restorer, "a sissy job" in Omar's estimation, who always wondered who his father was, has tracked him down to an unnamed city in the American Midwest, which sounds a lot like Chicago. Omar, for his part, accepts Ry's intrusion into his life, or so he says, only because his favorite baseball team (think the historically cursed Chicago Cubs, who have not won a World Series since 1908) are on a possibly record-breaking winning streak tied to Ry's arrival, and dependent, says Omar, on Ry's continued presence:

> OMAR: Hey, be proud. A lot of folks would love to be as lucky as—
> RY: I'm not lucky! I grew up without a father! I am not lucky.... Is that why you called me back after saying you never wanted to meet me? Because your ball team started winning?
> OMAR: They're not just winning, they're on a streak. This is serious.[54]

So, we do not like Omar as we see him manipulating his son for his own rather marginally significant ends. But we are rooting, perhaps we are conditioned to root for, a reconciliation, the kind few of us, including Blessing, have had with our own fathers.

Omar exceeds many fathers, I hope almost all, in the sheer disgust he can inspire, as when he tells Ry: "It's not like I was trying to bring you into this world! You're a fucking accident! God, I regret the day I made you!"[55] Or, later: "You're lucky for the team; that's it. Everything else about you is a total disappointment. You got too much education, a faggy job..."[56]

Omar seems enchanted only by baseball, whose games he listens to on radio rather than attend in person due to yet another superstition: that his presence is bad luck:

> I hate everyone associated with it [baseball]. Owners, agents, players—pre-adolescent bastards every one of 'em. Makes me wish I was at the Pearly Gates. Yer out! Yer out! Yer OUT!!! I'll tell you something, though. The minute I retired?.... It all changed like magic. You couldn't see their faces anymore. They weren't a bunch of shit-heads any more. They were uniforms, caps, gloves, bats, helmets. All perfectly arranged around a diamond. That's what seduces us in the first place. That diamond, opening out forever.... Only infinite game.[57]

Baseball is, after all, America's game and, though now surpassed in fans and revenue by football remains with Mom and apple pie a symbol of America's strengths and weaknesses. Luckily, for dramatic effect, Omar has another weakness: late onset lupus which, since he is not taking his medications, could prove fatal. Ry decides to stay with Omar: "I want to take care of you."[58] It turns out, in facts that stretch credulity, that Ry has neither the wife nor the son he claimed to have. In addition, he has already lost his job due to a "lapse," that destroyed a priceless drawing:

> And while I was working on it, suddenly it hit me: this little noise I kept hearing in my head.... It was the sound of an empty life.... And it distracted me.... I knocked something over.... A very harmful chemical. And it—really instantly—destroyed the Rubens. Forever.[59]

Two failed lives intersect here. And stick. Though Ry declares nears the end: "I'm sorry I had to have a father at all,"[60] Blessing engineers what reads like the only tender moment of what had been a hard-boiled play:

> Almost against his will, Ry sits down. Neither man moves. Finally Omar reaches to turn on the radio. Ry puts his hand on Omar's, stopping him. Ry's hand rests on Omar's for a long moment. Then, carefully, Ry's hand moves to the radio and turns it on.... Ry and Omar look at the square. Then, at exactly the same moment, they look at each other. Lights fade to black.[61]

Ry's revelations are too late, too extraordinary, and ultimately unbelievable, betraying the crusty tone of the play. It's too stereotypically neat to be emotionally satisfying and no willed suspension of disbelief can swallow this emotional flip-flop as much as all of we fathers and sons want it to.

    By and large, the critics were not kind. Bob Rendell, in *Talkin' Broadway*, wrote:

> The 90-minute, one-act play proceeds at a pace which makes it feel more like the period of three weeks during which it elapses as we learn precious little about Omar and Ryland. What we learn is unsurprising and of little interest.
>   Author Lee Blessing appears to have created a play conforming to an outline that he would present to the students in a basic playwriting class. It seems clear that both Blessing and George Street [Theatre] are just marking time with *The Winning Streak*.[62]

Mike Schulz, in *River Cities' Reader*, opined:

> Lee Blessing's *The Winning Streak*, currently at Davenport's Nighswander Theatre, is one of those shows that could easily read better than it plays.
>   Yet while Blessing writes clever dialogue and displays a shrewd understanding of familial dynamics, *The Winning Streak* is the type of play that, if it isn't *perfectly* cast, can be hell to sit through; the witty badinage can feel oppressive in the sledgehammer style of Neil Simon, and the insights can feel tacked-on and maudlin. (And there isn't enough going on visually to distract you *from* the dialogue.)[63]

    In the *New York Times*, critic Naomi Siegel took up the baseball imagery:

> At the risk of metaphor overkill, Lee Blessing's new play, "The Winning Streak," concerning the emotional reunion of a retired major league umpire, Omar, and his long-lost ille-

gitimate son, Ry, is neither a grand slam wallop nor a game-ending strikeout. Instead, it's a series of looping Texas leaguers that, ultimately, doesn't deliver the goods.... Mr. Blessing fails to chalk up a victory in this start.[64]

In 2000, Blessing directed a fully staged production of *The Winning Streak* at the Ensemble Theatre of Cincinnati. "It was the first time I had ever directed a play and I don't think I want to do it again, especially since it is so time consuming. I would rather put my play in the hands of someone I trust."[65]

For the Loyal

Blessing loves baseball and has used the game as a setting or backdrop for four or more plays, a screenplay and several TV scripts, but he also follows football, from the NFL's Minnesota Vikings to top college teams and in one play he used the gridiron rather than the diamond as a backdrop for a headline play that raised enormous moral issues.

In November 2011, state police arrested former Penn State assistant football coach Jerry Sandusky and charged him with committing sex crimes against numerous young boys over several decades. A jury convicted Sandusky and sent him to prison for 30 to 60 years. The scandal grew as the press revealed a cover-up at the highest levels and led to the firing of both legendary football head coach Joseph "JoePa" Paterno, winningest coach in NCAA Division 1-A football history during his 55 years at the school, and Penn State University President Graham Spencer. Hired to investigate the crimes, former FBI director Louis Freeh reported that the university had betrayed its principles in pursuit of football revenues. A graduate student who stumbled upon Sandusky acting inappropriately with a boy in the team locker room, and his courageous decision to report what he had seen, led to the unraveling of crimes and cover-ups by the team and the university.[66]

The shocking headlines led to a book, *Paterno* by Joe Posnanski; a documentary by Amir Bar-Lev, *Happy Valley*; a planned HBO film directed by Brian De Palma, with the working title "Happy Valley," starring Al Pacino as Joe Paterno, with John Carroll Lynch as Jerry Sandusky (though production went on hiatus after financial difficulties); and a play by Lee Blessing, *For the Loyal*, which premiered at the Illusion Theater in Minneapolis, April-May 2015.

However, Blessing sets his play in the early 1990s in the graduate student housing apartment of Mia and Toby, at a major unnamed state university in the Midwest, and at no time refers to Penn State, Paterno, or Sandusky. He focuses instead on the universality of the issues and the implication that the scandal could have happened anywhere—it could be happening *now*, anywhere, since perpetrators and enablers maintain a conspiracy of silence. For Blessing, the play marks a return to themes of pedophilia and sex crimes first visited in *Lonesome Hollow* in 2007, and a return to plays with a sports theme, though previously that sport had always been baseball.

The play starts with a bang. Toby tells his very pregnant wife, Mia, that he has witnessed "a sex crime"[67] between an underage boy and Assistant Coach Carlson, and that Head Coach Hale warned him not to tell anyone. People worship Coach Hale, we learn, for turning around a sport program "on a slab, being corpse-raped by the NCAA."[68] But telling Mia what he has seen angers Hale and places Toby between divided loyalties:

> TOBY: I'm sorry.
> MIA: He didn't break his word to me.
> HALE: Really? Did he promise to protect you? Was that a vow? 'Cause he's not protecting you now. I'm the one protecting you.[69]

Hale takes full credit for the team's success, which translates, again in highly sexualized language, into triumph for the college and the state:

> Things are looking bright, though. People in this state have their pride back. Hell, they've got their balls back, and they thought no one could do that for 'em. Yeah, there may be better feelings in the world, but right now I sure as hell can't think what they are.[70]

Assistant Coach Carlson played a key role in this turnaround but carries baggage and claims his own sense of victimization:

> CARLSON: I know the rumors. What can I say? I like kids. Like being around 'em, helping 'em. No one sees that, of course. They look at a man my age around boys, and they only think one thing. Amazing anyone even tries to become a Boy Scout leader, priest, whatever. All the prejudice you face.... They judge you every minute of the day, and they judge you when they really don't know.
> MIA: They don't?
> CARLSON: Hell, no. Nobody knows what's in my heart.[71]

Hale arranges for Carlson to resign without scandal or other penalty and for Toby to advance in his place.

> HALE: Mitch, you're the best offensive coordinator I ever worked with, but you're a fucking child molester. It breaks my heart, but I've got bigger fish to fry. The lives of hundreds of people depend on this program. You understand that?[72]

The success of the lucrative university football program is more important than punishing or stopping a child molester. Hale spells it out for Toby:

> All right. No one speaks of this again. (To TOBY) If you do, I guarantee your career will end before it starts and you, your wife and your little prospect [Mia's unborn child] there will probably starve. Are you completely clear on that?[73]

Hale lays out his plans quite explicitly in words reminiscent of the Catholic Church's handling of pedophile priests:

> Tell you a secret? I'm almost glad this happened. We needed to get rid of Mitch. This way, he won't squawk. You can't change somebody like him. All you can do is make him someone else's problem.[74]

Talk of a cover-up horrifies Mia and Hale's plans for a quiet departure for Carlson go seriously awry when Mia picks up a gun and shoots him in her bathroom. As the apartment morphs into a sort of limbo (reminiscent of those in *Cobb*, *The Authentic Life of Billy the Kid*, and *Courting Harry* in which the players are populated by the dead), Mia confronts the coach she murdered:

> MIA: Like ... why did I ... trade my life for yours?
> CARLSON: Just now, you mean? Is that what you did?
> MIA: You were a criminal.... Now I am.[75]

Mia seeks some understanding of Carlson's fantasies and crimes to justify her own crime, but he walks away. Still in limbo, she finds Carlson's young victim on a bus heading out of town. Now her actions seem neither noble nor effective.

> MIA: I wasn't thinking at all. I couldn't let him out of the house, that's all, Carlson. If I did, he'd—
> THE BOY: He'd what?
> MIA: Get away. Forever, maybe.
> THE BOY: And that'd be bad, right? 'Cause he's so evil and shit?
> MIA: Yes.
> THE BOY: Carlson gave me money. Gave me a bunch more when he put me on the bus. You never gave me a thing. All you did was shoot him in the head.
> MIA: He was a predator.
> THE BOY: So's the guy I'm going back to. Gonna shoot him?[76]

Mia has the deceased Carlson assume the roles of the athletic director and then the university president. Each wants Carlson gone; neither wants to involve the police.

> CARLSON: Well. Then I guess ... we're ... good, right? No harm done.
> MIA: What about your soul?
> CARLSON: My...?
> MIA: Your soul. What about it?
> CARLSON: I don't think we need to trouble the police about that.[77]

In fact, when Toby and Mia do visit the police—still in limbo and played by the same actors portraying Coaches Hale and Carlson—we learn Mia's motivation for murder: growing up, she suspected a childhood friend was being molested by her father. The friend denied it until she killed herself after having sent Mia a letter saying it had all been true. Mia took the letter to the police, but with the girl dead, the mother refusing to talk, and the father gone, the police claimed to have no case. The exposition covers Mia's motivation and another of her monologues explains that she had a gun, the one used to shoot Carlson, in the house at Toby's suggestion following news of local home invasions.

A jump ahead 15 years brings news that Toby has remarried and that neither he nor Mia's son have visited in over a year, though Mia's release from prison is approaching in a month. Toby has taken Carlson's old job as offensive coordinator under Coach Hale. Mia remains unrepentant:

> What other solutions were there? Calling the police? The university? Calling his wife?... Wouldn't have worked. Nobody wanted to believe it. Nobody. If he'd blown a boy in the City Hall atrium, they would have called it a halftime show. If I'd picked up the phone, Toby would have been fired. Carlson would have gone right on screwing kids. Now at least Carlson's in hell and those kids are safe.[78]

Mia harshly judges all those who kept silent, who covered up Carlson's crimes, telling Toby during a prison visit:

> You're the one who should be in here! You, not me. You're the one who saw! You saw him, and you did nothing![79]

For the Loyal: A grad student's wife (Anna Sundberg) confronts a powerful football coach, Mitch Carlson (Garry Geiken), and the boy (Michael Fell) he molested. Illusion Theatre, Minneapolis, Minnesota; 2015, photograph by Aaron Fenster; courtesy of Illusion Theatre.

She also judges Carlson, who still haunts her dreams:

> MIA: I wish I could burn your birth certificate, every record there ever was of you. Everything you created to convince people that you were good, or had even an atom of good to offer the world.
> CARLSON: I did plenty for the world. (*He places his hand on the playbook*) This. Helping kids. I did a lot more good than bad.
> MIA: That's what makes the worst kind of evil: thinking you're mostly good.[80]

Mia briefly imagines an alternate future in which Toby never told her what he saw Carlson do, in which their first child, one of three, grows up to play football, in which Carlson goes to coach somewhere else and continue his predations, and Mia now works for Coach Hale in a bigger and better football program. A program to which Coach Carlson wants to return.

Prior to Mia's release from prison, her son (the same actor plays "The Boy," sometimes as Carlson's victim, sometimes as Mia's son) visits to tell her he does not want to see her again; he has even told his classmates she died. Carlson appears to show Mia, using The Boy, her son, how he recruits new victims, perhaps even her own child.

We flash back again to the world where Mia only thought about grabbing a gun and killing Carlson. Toby has his promotion. He has bought into Coach Hale's program:

> TOBY: If you could've heard Coach Hale at Froggy's tonight—He was inspirational. He really was. All he asks is just a little belief, a little faith, a little—
> MIA: Loyalty?
> TOBY: Exactly...[81]

As the play ends, the last words we hear are Toby singing the school fight song, from which comes the play's title:

> Victory is ours throughout the land.
> Steadfast and strong we'll always stand.
> Proud of our warriors, we form a crew
> For the loyal, the brave and true.[82]

As Toby sings, Mia exits, touching her pregnant body with one hand and, with the other, the letter from her molested friend who had killed herself.

Blessing packs *For the Loyal* with more issues than you can shake a script at. Do we owe our loyalty to families or to our jobs and supervisors? Did Carlson sin by being loyal to his twisted desires rather than to his own wife? Are pedophiles irredeemable and deserving of death? What should be the penalty for covering up for pedophiles in college sports, the Catholic Church, or elsewhere? Did Mia's murderous act constitute a crime or a necessary sacrifice? By killing Carlson and going to jail, Mia has deprived her own son of a mother: is this a form of child abuse? What are our responsibilities to step forward and report suspected child abuse when the end result may cost us a job, our reputation or even our lives, or ruin the lives of others?

Form follows content here. Mia's existence in two alternate lives, one where she shot Carlson and one where she did nothing co-exist, giving shape to our own moral choices: what happens to us when we act on our convictions, and what happens when we do not?

In another context, an interviewer asked Blessing: "What kind of theater excites you?" He replied: "Theater which can genuinely make me think and feel—which is to say, theater which most audiences find off-putting."[83]

For the Loyal makes you think ... and feel.

In its single production at Illusion Theatre in Minneapolis, the critics, as usual, provided mixed reviews. Dominic Papatola, in the *Pioneer Press*, wrote:

> But for a play that attempts to analyze the powerful and seemingly impenetrable dynamics of major-college sports in the face of scandal, *For the Loyal* botches the handoff and fumbles the ball.[84]

David and Chelsea Berglund had the following to say in their column "How Was the Show?"

> Ultimately *For the Loyal* hamstrings its conversation in neglecting its characters for the sake of its ideas. In doing so, it fails to engage at a level worthy of its weighty subject matter. Of course, compared to the exploitative properties common to television procedurals, this show respects rather than sensationalizes, and in that, it should be commended.[85]

Arthur Dorman, on the website "Talkin' Broadway," added:

> Blessing raises important questions, and draws out possible answers in ways that are both playful and disturbing. In the end, we are no closer to definitive answers, but we have a much greater sense of the complexity and ambiguity that confound society's efforts to put an end to abusive behavior. *For the Loyal* is a well-written, sharply performed play, as valuable for casting light on social challenges as for its dramatic merit. On both scores, it deserves to be widely seen and discussed.[86]

CHAPTER 4

A Walk and a View

A Walk in the Woods
A View of the Mountains

Nearly every play review, interview, and article about Lee Blessing begins by noting that he authored *A Walk in the Woods*, often mentioning the awards it garnered, including his nomination for the Pulitzer Prize. No doubt he knows it will be cited in the first sentence of his obituary no matter how many more plays he writes. With its international success and enduring presence, that fate seems not just fitting but altogether acceptable to a unique career built, in part, upon making political abstractions dramatic and stageworthy. As Blessing himself acknowledged, although he had been writing plays for ten years: "Until 1987, when *A Walk in the Woods* was nominated for a Pulitzer, no one in New York took any notice of me."[1]

A Walk in the Woods

The idea for the play began modestly:

In 1985 the *New York Times* wrote that playwrights were not dealing with contemporary politics. I had visited the USSR and studied Russian [and taken many Russian Literature courses in college]. The idea for *A Walk in the Woods* came to me as I was driving home one night from a production of *Riches* in Louisville. I switched on the radio and there was speculation about who would succeed Andropov [Yuri Vladimirovich Andropov, head of the KGB, 1967–1982, and General Secretary of the Communist Party and so head of the Soviet Union from November 12, 1982 until his death from renal failure on February 9, 1984] and I began to think more about ways to dramatize the relationship between our two countries. [*A Walk in the Woods*] became the most explicitly political play I'd written. It did so well that I began looking at newspaper front pages for ideas and the next play I wrote like this was *Two Rooms*.[2]

Blessing told the *New York Times*:

> In late 1985 I decided to take a new direction in my playwriting. Previously I had been writing plays on family relationships, including *War of the Roses* [later *Riches*] and *Eleemosynary*. I decided to try a political play. I really wasn't into writing about a historical event but rather about a personal encounter. The walk [in the woods] fascinated me because it was one of the few times when diplomats took the initiative and tried a plan of their own.³

As Blessing also told me:

> I wrote the play in the fall of 1985, a couple years after the original "walk in the woods" occurred in Geneva between American negotiator Paul Nitze and his Soviet counterpart, Yuli Kvitsinsky.... I completely fictionalized the negotiators, reversing their ages, and centered the play's theme around the effort to find a human basis for learning to trust. A number of years earlier I'd done a tour of the Soviet Union, where I'd had the experience of making friends with a Soviet man. This actually startled me, since I'd grown up during the Cold War, when the worst was usually assumed of all Russians. I suppose this experience opened me to the strategy of Botvinnik demanding friendship from Honeyman as a price for good-faith negotiating. I quickly decided the play should be in four scenes, each one matching a season of a single year. One of the real surprises to me was how strong a "character" the countryside itself became. Nature, simply by being the context for these talks, developed its own "voice," so to speak, delivering a constant, silent rebuke to the arrogant militarism which had occasioned disarmament talks in the first place.⁴

The play took on a life of its own, first national, then international:

> The play was accepted by the O'Neill Playwrights Conference, and before it went there was workshopped at both New Dramatists and the Playwrights' Center in Minneapolis. It was extremely well received in each of these venues. It changed in a few ways, particularly at the O'Neill, where Michael Feingold proved a very valuable dramaturge, but in general the play has never changed greatly from the form in which it was first written. The Yale Repertory Theatre asked to do the play, and Des McAnuff was asked to direct. It was our first collaboration. He also acquired the right to produce the play again just a couple months later at La Jolla Playhouse, his own theatre, in the summer of 1987. From there it went to Broadway, opening in February 1988. Des directed all three productions, with the only significant changes being the cast. Yale, La Jolla and Broadway all sported different casts, as it happened, with the Broadway cast consisting of Sam Waterston and Robert Prosky. Reviews for the play, in all these avatars, were overwhelmingly positive, and it set box-office records at both Yale and La Jolla. Later it went to London's West End in a separate production featuring Sir Alec Guinness and Edward Hermann. Still later the Broadway cast was invited to do the play in Moscow at the Pushkin Theatre in early 1989, just as the Soviet Union was in the process of crumbling. It was an amazing time.... I was very pleased indeed with the play.⁵

Actor Sam Waterston, who starred in the Broadway run, touched on the play's unusual accomplishment in an interview with the *New York Times*:

> The idea of a two-character play about arms control set in a hillside in Geneva would have been unthinkable, but here it is.... The road to theatre hell is paved with high minded plays that aren't brought off but this one touches on the emotional part of a serious theme.⁶

We cannot underestimate Blessing's monumental achievement. He dramatized the undramatic: negotiating is all talk, posturing, and canned arguments while the subject, MIRV, ICBM's throw weight, confounds any layperson. The stakes, human survival versus nuclear destruction, never loomed higher in any other play. Blessing distilled the issues, fears, and hopes down into a single relationship, that between nuclear arms negotiators Andrei Botvinnik, for the Soviet Union, and American John Honeyman, meeting alone in the woods outside Geneva. He modeled it on a true story: American negotiator Paul Nitze and Soviet delegate Yuli Kvitsinsky went for a private stroll outside Geneva in 1982, made a deal, and then saw their own governments kill it.

Blessing took the incident and, with artistic license, changed it to his own ends. He reversed the ages of the principals: making the American negotiator younger and the Soviet older than his counterpart, and whereas the actual walk in the woods occurred on a single day, July 16, 1982, when "the two men sat on a log in the rain and hammered out a plan for real arms reductions,"[7] Blessing set the play among the four seasons, creating a circular play. Absurdist plays (e.g., *The Bald Soprano*, *The Lesson*) usually utilize a circular plot (though in reality they have no plot *per se* and simply end where they began). While *A Walk in the Woods* is realistic in style, its subject, nuclear Armageddon, is existentially absurd.

Blessing took the name Honeyman from an old college friend, and Botvinnik from an actual Russian chess champion[8] to create an odd couple, of sorts: the cynical, wisecracking, big-hearted Russian and the pragmatic, focused and businesslike American. He gives the Russian most of the good lines and makes us like him, quite a trick at a time when we Americans thought those barbaric Slavs, whom most of us had never seen or met, might be happily incinerating us at any time in a surprise nuclear attack.

Blessing built the action in four scenes over the four changing seasons. He employed nature as a third character in the play:

> In the best productions, the outdoor set has truly become another character. Birds sing, insects chirp, leaves fall, fog creeps, sun shines, shadows lurk—and men like these could make it all disappear. In a sense it's like watching two potential murderers discuss the fate of a bound victim.[9]

The first scene opens in summer. Botvinnik and Honeyman enter and find a bench. Botvinnik explains that he wants to be friends; Honeyman, however, wants to retain a formal relationship:

> BOTVINNIK: Formality allows many things, but it does not allow friendship.
> HONEYMAN: I think formality—
> BOTVINNIK: Formality is simply anger with its hair combed.[10]

Botvinnik requests they address each other by first names, though Honeyman fixes on the work rather than the relationship: "What I'm saying about friendship is that it takes us away from the central point.... Mutual commitment to the hard work of negotiating a treaty."[11]

Blessing wisely never lets the details of any possible treaty get in the way of focusing on the budding friendship and what it represents. Though the negotiations between Nitze and Kvitsinsky concerned so-called Intermediate-Range Nuclear Forces (INF) and U.S. plans to base these missiles in Europe, ever closer to the Soviet Union, Blessing asks us, in the persons of Botvinnik and Honeyman if, to paraphrase Rodney King, "Can't we all just get along?" not in any simpleminded fashion but in a deep commitment to avoid Mutual Assured Destruction (MAD), in which the U.S. and the U.S.S.R. stockpiled tens of thousands of thermonuclear missiles and bombs close at hand to ensure the death of all life on earth. Blessing, who steeped himself in the details of nuclear arms, but kept these details out of the play by and large, chose a scientific, and absurd, image to ground his writing: the

> term "nuclear fratricide." It referred to having so many missiles trained on the same target that the explosions of the first to arrive would actually destroy the ones landing seconds later. I have to admit I thought of this image many times in the months of [writing *A Walk in the Woods*].[12]

Trying to make peace, the characters discover, holds its own absurdities and humor:

> HONEYMAN: My question about whether or not you agree we shouldn't be friends.
> BOTVINNIK: Ah, Well, my answer is, of course, that I agree with you.
> HONEYMAN: You agree?
> BOTVINNIK: Yes.
> HONEYMAN: That we shouldn't be friends?
> BOTVINNIK: Yes.
> HONEYMAN: That's not what you said before.
> BOTVINNIK: But then I didn't know your view. Now I do and I want to agree with you.
> HONEYMAN: You want to agree with me?
> BOTVINNIK: Yes.
> HONEYMAN: Why?
> BOTVINNIK: Because you are my friend.
> HONEYMAN: I can't be your friend. That's my whole position.
> BOTVINNIK: Yes, and I agree.
> HONEYMAN: You can't agree.
> BOTVINNIK: But I do.
> HONEYMAN: You're contradicting yourself.
> BOTVINNIK: I know. But I will go to any length to keep a friend.[13]

4. A Walk and a View

We soon learn Botvinnik suffers from Sjogren's syndrome and must use eye drops to combat the dryness. Blessing researched the disease and used it as yet another humanizing detail to this oddly appealing Russian we have encountered.[14]

Scene 1 ends in bickering and Scene 2, set two months later, in fall, begins on a similar note, though this time, we learn, Honeyman has suggested the walk. Honeyman berates Botvinnik for stalling negotiations while Botvinnik assures him the Soviets cannot make a move until after the forthcoming U.S. elections. He proposes that since the serious talks are not progressing, they instead should have a "frivolous" conversation. The author, through Botvinnik's words, questions our reality. As Botvinnik says:

> I hear certain words—whether I say them or someone else says them—words like "detente," "human rights," "Star Wars," Central America," "readiness," "early warning," and I feel like I am falling away from the Earth. I can see the Earth—the entire planet, like I am a cosmonaut. And it is falling away from me. We are both simply ... receding into the dark."[15]

We build instruments of mass death and the other "reality," the reality of our fragile grasp on life and our planet, slips right out of our hands. For Honeyman the answer lies in making a deal. He tells Botvinnik:

> We have no choice. If we don't believe in our, albeit, weak efforts to save ourselves, then everything dies.... If we fail now, history itself will disappear. Time will stop. There won't be any right way to think or feel, because there won't be anyone here to have thoughts or feelings. There will be no *here*.[16]

If Botvinnik will not go home and lobby for their proposal, Honeyman threatens they will never be friends. And for that proffered friendship, Botvinnik agrees, as Act 1 ends.

Act 2 opens with both men meeting again on a gloomy day in late winter, after months indoors in negotiations and consultations in their home countries. We learn that the Soviets have rejected their own plan after the American president (Ronald Reagan in the real-life events, though he is never named in the play) prematurely announced the details publicly. They fear acceptance now makes them appear to be agreeing to an "American peace." This leads them to return, like Alice, through the Looking Glass, with words both surreal and sad:

> BOTVINNIK: Neither of our countries can afford to be second in the quest for peace.
> HONEYMAN: What quest for peace? At this rate there is no quest for peace.
> BOTVINNIK: But there's the quest for the appearance of the quest for peace.[17]

In the end, the proposal failed for lack of trust:

> BOTVINNIK: We don't trust the safeguards.
> HONEYMAN: There are checks on the safeguards. Verifications.

BORVINNIK: We don't trust them.
HONEYMAN: Andrei—
BOTVINNIK: Even if there were checks on the checks on the checks, we couldn't trust them.
HONEYMAN: Why not?
BOTVINNIK: Because we don't trust *you*.[18]

Botvinnik explains that they will continue negotiating without ever agreeing on a treaty while scientists develop more and better weapons, controlled by computers, not humans, and when war comes he and Honeyman will die in the woods in mid-sentence: "Right between the words 'arms' and 'control.'"[19]

At this moment of despair, Honeyman leaves behind his government's script and proposes he and Botvinnik make cosmetic changes in the already-rejected treaty they previously negotiated and ask their governments to reconsider it privately. In a leap of faith, trust, and friendship, both men agree, though neither knows how their leaders will react or how their own careers may suffer.

The final scene, Act 2, Scene 2, finds the two men back on their bench, six weeks later. It is now springtime and Botvinnik picks a bouquet of wild flowers for Honeyman. Both governments have rejected their plan … again. Honeyman now better understands Botvinnik's cynicism:

HONEYMAN: He [the U.S. president] looked me straight in the eye and said, "Don't try so hard." Don't *try* so hard.
BOTVINNIK: It was only a euphemism.
HONEYMAN: For what?
BOTVINNIK: For don't try at all.[20]

In fact, Botvinnik—Andrei Lvovich Botvinnik—has been recalled by his government. He is leaving Geneva and their friendship. As he tells Honeyman:

I have served for many years here by doing absolutely nothing. Now it is time for a new man to come and do absolutely nothing. In this way we achieve continuity of results.[21]

Honeyman protests: "My God—we've established a process, the two of us. If you're replaced, that's all gone."[22] Botvinnik reassures him (though not us) with a vision of failed negotiations stretching to the end of time:

You're smart, tough, charming. You can say no almost as well as me. They will keep you here a long time. And after long enough, you will be like I am now.[23]

And then he speaks a political truth borne out by history: "Every treaty we have negotiated has been followed by an unprecedented arms buildup…. There will always be new weapons building."[24] Honeyman clings to hope: "Hope for progress, for good faith, for enough time."[25] Botvinnik and Honeyman share a final thought:

BOTVINNIK: Our time together, John, has been a very great failure. But—a successful one. Shall we go back?
HONEYMAN: Let's stay a while.
BOTVINNIK: Really? Do you want to? What do you want to talk about?
HONEYMAN: Nothing.[26]

Lights fade to black ... and we contemplate our shared future.

Blessing accomplished several extraordinary things with his play. He created a Soviet character likable and entertaining enough to be invited into our homes at a time when Americans often saw Soviets as a threatening undifferentiated mass of ideologically driven killers. He made the arms race a topic of everyday discussion and convinced each of us that, as citizens of this country, we not only had a stake in this debate but also a say in its outcome. Nuclear war, Blessing seems to say, is too important an issue to leave to the politicians. People of goodwill—Honeyman and Botvinnik, he argued—could reach an agreement if only our respective governments would get out of the way. Rarely does a play, or any work of art, both empower and energize people in this way.

As Blessing told me:

> The whole intent of the play is to show the almost existential pressures on two people in this position. After all, what are they (and we) to expect if they fail? They're officially there to stop the arms race, and are, thus, "responsible," in a sense, for the life of everyone on the planet. The oppressive sense of what might happen if they don't succeed suffuses the play. As for getting into the heads of these two men, my experience with making a friend [Mikhail Pridat 'Ko] in Moscow in 1971 during the Brezhnev era helped immeasurably. I realized he was someone I would have made friends with had I met him anywhere in the world. So I felt free to conceive this sort of a Soviet citizen and free to let him want what he wants. I'd studied Russian in college, and had, of course, visited there (including a six-week, twelve-city student tour), so I felt relatively confident that I could avoid stereotypes.[27]

By personalizing the issue, Blessing moved the discussion from the War Room to the living room. Dr. Elaine Scarry, Cabot Professor at Harvard University, points to the disenfranchisement of the people and their elected representatives in Congress as nuclear decisions concentrate in the hands of the executive branch of government:

> [These weapons] are utterly incompatible with governance.... [Nuclear weapons] put the population completely outside the realm of overseeing our entry into war—or having a say in their own survival or destruction. We have to choose between nuclear weapons and democracy.[28]

Today, nine nations stockpile nuclear weapons, making the world even more unsafe than it was 25 years ago. As Dr. Scarry pointed out:

> Even a nuclear exchange between Pakistan and India, with 0.015% of the world's nuclear arsenal would leave 44 million people dead immediately and one billion likely to perish in the following month given the effect on food supplies.[29]

Even former Secretary of Defense Robert McNamara, who led the American War in Vietnam in the 1960s, later realized: "U.S. nuclear weapons policy is immoral, illegal, militarily unnecessary and dreadfully dangerous."[30]

A quarter-century ago, people around the world entered the debate about the future of our planet. *A Walk in the Woods* reached Broadway in February 1988 and stayed for 136 performances. Portraying Andrei Botvinnik was Robert Prosky, a Polish American actor of renown. (Prosky essayed a remarkable 130 roles, including Willy Loman in *Death of a Salesman*, during his 23-year stint at the Arena Stage in Washington, D.C.; he is best known, however, as Sergeant Stan Jablonsky on NBC's acclaimed police drama *Hill Street Blues*.) Sam Waterston, another well-respected actor, played John Honeyman. (Waterston has appeared in such films as *The Great Gatsby* [1974], *Interiors* [1978], *The Killing Fields* [1984], *Hannah and Her Sisters* [1986], as well as on television for several seasons as District Attorney Jack McCoy on NBC's *Law and Order*.)

A Walk in the Woods became a phenomenon discussed not solely on the theater pages but on the front pages as well. The *New York Post* even printed a photo of Katharine Hepburn leaving the theater after seeing the play.[31] Only a year earlier Blessing had told the *San Diego Daily Transcript* that

> nobody gets to Broadway with serious dramas—Broadway is about musicals, comedies, imported plays. A serious play is the hardest thing to get on Broadway.[32]

He proved himself wrong.

A Walk in the Woods became the first-ever Broadway play co-produced by Americans and Russians, opening in May 1989 with the Broadway cast and directed by Lloyd Richards at the Pushkin Theater in Moscow. The cast performed the play 11 times in Moscow, with simultaneous translation on cassette. The Soviet Premier Mikhail Gorbachev attended with his wife, Raisa.

Regional theaters (in Seattle, Chicago, St. Louis, Phoenix, and Portland) offered productions. Theaters mounted productions in France, Germany, Sweden, Spain, the Netherlands, Greece, South Africa, Israel (in Hebrew and English), Norway, Canada, Belgium, and Switzerland, as well as in Vilnius, Lithuania.[33] The play traveled to London's West End, with Sir Alec Guinness returning to the stage after a long hiatus, as the Russian negotiator, and Edward Hermann as the American. On May 10, 1989, it aired on PBS's *American Playhouse* and aired on May 26, 1988, on ABC's *Omnibus*, hosted by Beverly Sills. Translated into Russian and German, the script sold thousands of copies. The original Broadway cast also performed for the U.S. Senate and House of Representatives and invited foreign diplomats, in a production arranged by Senator Sam Nunn, chair of the U.S. Senate Armed Services Committee, and performed in Coolidge Auditorium at the Library of Congress on May 23, 1988, at the

4. A Walk and a View 75

time when the Intermediate Range Nuclear Forces Treaty was being debated in the Senate, which passed the treaty four days later. The treaty eliminated nuclear and conventional ground-launched ballistic and cruise missiles with intermediate ranges, defined as between 500–5,500 km (300–3,400 miles). A Broadway revival in 2014 starred Kathleen Chalfont as Soviet negotiator Botvinnik, although this time as negotiator *Irina* Botvinnik. Blessing approved of the casting:

> In recent decades more and more women have reached the highest echelons of government in western developed nations. People like Angela Merkel, Hillary Clinton, Janet Yellen and Christine Lagarde routinely wield responsibilities, which not long ago belonged only to men. Given such developments, it seems to me informative rather than jarring to re-envision a character from my play as a woman rather than a man.[34]

The character of Botvinnik, wise, funny, engaging—even likable—worried some people. John Podhoretz wrote in the *National Interest*:

> Blessing's decision to make a high ranking Soviet official the hero and voice of wisdom in his play is a rather disturbing innovation.... Those who represent the interests of Soviet dictators are excused from bearing responsibility for anything bad that happens inside the Soviet Union.[35]

Indeed, Podhoretz got part of the playwright's strategy. As Blessing told one critic:

> One of the reasons I wrote the play was that growing up in the '50's and '60's in the Midwest, I had this set of assumptions about what the world was like. I was so surprised to go to Russia and find that there were people who would have been my friends at anytime, anywhere.... There are individuals worth knowing on any side.[36]

Botvinnik gets all the good lines and, as one writer noted: "Stereotypes are reversed. The Russian is the wiser, more relaxed, warm and friendly person while the American is suspicious and stolid."[37]

(I visited the Soviet Union in 1985, and again in 1987. I went with a head full of stereotypes and suspicion. Landing at Moscow's Sheremetyevo International Airport seemed like a landing on the "dark" side of the moon. As I toured Moscow, Leningrad, Volgograd, and Irkutsk, I kept reminding myself: "These are Soviet pigeons and these are Communist cats." They seemed a lot like the pigeons and cats at home. The people, the old ladies in the street, the priests in the Russian Orthodox churches, the *shammus* at the synagogue, and even the officials in the Kremlin seemed, to my great surprise, like people I knew in Los Angeles and New York. *A Walk in the Woods* brought this simple idea home to thousands of Americans just as ignorant as I.)

Victor Zvezden, Deputy Representative of the U.S.S.R. to the United Nations, in a letter to Jeffrey Richards, press agent for *A Walk in the Woods*, wrote:

Lee Blessing (right), with dramaturge Michael Feinberg, working on the production of *A Walk in the Woods*. Eugene O'Neill Theatre Center, Waterford, Connecticut; 1987, photograph by and courtesy of A. Vincent Scarano.

> ... I think it was the first time I saw an unbiased and non-distorted image of a Soviet man, in particular of a Soviet diplomat, in an American play or movie.[38]

That caused some conservatives problems. The prolific theater critic and director Robert Brustein wrote in the *New Republic*:

> He [Blessing] displays an obstinate pessimism about transactions between governments as opposed to the possibilities of positive dealings between men of goodwill, perhaps in liberal delusion that long-standing ideological conflicts are merely the result of misunderstanding ... rather than the consequence of genuine differences.[39]

Another conservative saw it differently. In a letter to actor Robert Prosky, who portrayed Botvinnik on Broadway, U.S. Senator Alphonse 'Al' D'Amato, Republican from New York (1981–1999), wrote after seeing the play:

> Dear Bob,
> So often here in the Capitol we talk of players in the game of politics. Scenes are set, arguments made. But it is the artist/playwright who elevates the game with careful, spare language, the actors who provide rhythm and trained voices, and give us needed insights so that hopefully we can perform our jobs better.[40]

After a tape of the televised version of *A Walk in the Woods* was sent to him in Geneva, Ambassador David J. Smith, head of the U.S. Delegation to the Negotiations on Nuclear and Space Arms with the Soviet Union, wrote to

David Davis, the president of the Public Television Playhouse: "Thanks again for *American Playhouse*'s role in improving U.S.-Soviet relations."[41]

A Walk in the Woods won the American Theatre Critics Award and *Time* magazine listed it as among the ten best plays of 1987.[42] Nominated for an Antoinette Perry "Tony" Award in 1988, it lost to *M. Butterfly* by David Henry Hwang. Nominated for the Pulitzer Prize in Drama in 1987, it lost to *Fences* by August Wilson.

Reviewers, nationally and internationally, raved. *The New Yorker* said:

> One of the many pleasures the play affords is watching the molds crack as the characters deepen and, above all, connect.... *A Walk in the Woods* ... is indeed a play of ideas and it is written with wit and polish."[43]

Marshall Rine wrote in the Gannett Westchester papers: "*A Walk in the Woods* while not the best play of the year, is the most important."[44] Dan Hulbert, in the *Atlanta Journal*, wrote: "Perhaps only George Bernard Shaw could pull off a play so outwardly uneventful, so dependent on the polite expression of ideas."[45]

Harry Bowman, in the *Dallas Morning News*, called *Walk* "pungent, thoughtful and highly intelligent—not a standard ingredient for today's plays."[46]

Reviewing the West End production, Michael Billington, in *The Guardian*, called the play "polished, witty, and humane."[47] Welton Jones, in the *San Diego Union*, wrote: "'A Walk in the Woods' is a splendid new play, a tapestry of ultimate human realities woven with threads of eloquence, honesty, and passion."[48]

However, Frank Rich, in the *New York Times*, who just a few years earlier had earned himself the sobriquet The Butcher of Broadway,[49] was scathing:

> Like his two characters, Mr. Blessing is an earnest foe of the arms race, frustrated by the intractable political games superpowers play with the destiny of mankind. But as a piece of theater, "A Walk in the Woods" is the esthetic equivalent of Switzerland, and not only because its setting is "a pleasant woods on the outskirts of Geneva." The play at the Booth [Theatre] fudges the distinctions of actual international politics and arms negotiations, choosing instead to telescope the messy, life-or-death conflict into a sentimental relationship between two likable envoys. Because the candied antagonisms of that relationship are more reminiscent of "The Odd Couple" or "I'm Not Rappaport" than harsh reality, Mr. Blessing has made a subject as volatile as the bomb seem as pleasantly cool— and as safely remote—as his neutral forest setting.[50]

John Podhoretz, writing in the *National Interest*, calculated just how cruelly Rich's critique hit home: "The nation's most powerful theater critic, Frank Rich of the *New York Times*, was immune to the play's charms, and his less than positive review probably cost Lee Blessing a Pulitzer Prize."[51]

Interestingly enough, Mel Gussow, also at the *Times* and who had himself expressed a distaste for several of Blessing's earlier plays, contradicted his colleague in his own *New York Times* review: "This is the fourth play I've seen by Mr. Blessing ... and the first one that approaches a substantial theme with commensurate skill."[52]

Blessing's greatest play, *A Walk in the Woods* features fully realized characters and sparklingly funny dialogue. If that was not enough it enriched a substantial, perhaps the most substantial, international political dialogue of its time. It moved its audience to reconsider its preconceptions about our supposed "enemies" and made the esoteric debate over nuclear weapons breakfast table fodder while empowering citizens' peace movements on multiple continents. You cannot use that description for any other American play of the last century.

A View of the Mountains

Twenty-six years later, Blessing revisited one of those who walked in the woods; the only time he has returned to a character from an earlier play in a sort of sequel. "I wanted to look at the continuation of a particular character over time," he told me.[53] Now in his sixties and retired to his estate on the Hudson, John Honeyman, the American arms negotiator we left in Geneva in *A Walk in the Woods* is still negotiating but this time with his son rather than a representative of the Soviet Union. The stakes, though, remain high.

Blessing has this to say about *A View of the Mountains*:

> I don't think of it as a direct sequel. It brings the character of Honeyman forward 25 to 30 years into the future, when he's more or less retired, remarried, with a new son, working for a think tank ... he's been on the sidelines for a while.... I became fascinated with the personal side of his life ... the relationships that he left back in the United States; the things that caused his son to become disaffected. Going to Geneva, it turns out, had a significant effect.[54]

We remember Honeyman as the idealistic and pragmatic negotiator convinced his country had dispatched him to parlay with the Russians in Geneva to end the arms race and save humanity from a Third World War that could end in nuclear apocalypse. From his Soviet counterpart, Andrei Botvinnik, we saw Honeyman learn to loosen up and value personal relationships for more than their political uses as their unlikely friendship blossomed over a year's worth of private walks in the woods. Honeyman slowly realized that his own government wanted him to fail in the negotiations even as they wished to pay no more than lip service to his work. Honeyman's experience might be simplistically labeled as a journey from nationalism and a belief in American "exceptionalism" (the faith that the U.S. stands as a beacon on a hill to a benighted world, or as Gwynn, his daughter-in-law, says: "God made America. If it needs fixing, God's the one who'll fix it."[55]) to cynicism about governments and a newfound faith in humanity across nationalities. That newly minted and idealistic Honeyman, unfortunately, disappears in *A View of the Mountains*.

The last two decades, we learn, have not treated John Honeyman kindly. Divorced after his first wife and he each caught each other in extramarital affairs and now remarried with a teenage son, the retired Honeyman finds himself estranged from the adult son of his first marriage, who has built his conservative political career by publicly rejecting both the Honeyman name and every liberal idea for which John fought. That son, Will Branch, a Tea Party darling and junior senator from Tennessee, stands on the cusp of real political power, never achieved by his father, about to be chosen as the vice-presidential running mate of the Republican nominee for president. Honeyman, hating the idea that his own flesh and blood might inflict conservative values and policies on our nation if he should stand a heartbeat away from the presidency, decides his duty requires him to remove his son from politics by any means necessary, including blackmail.

The first of six scenes in the play show us how far Honeyman has fallen from his idealistic past:

> ISLA: [Honeyman's wife]: Some sons hate their fathers.
> JOHN: I know.
> ISLA: ...it's nobody's fault.
> JOHN: It's my fault. Absentee father, simple as that.
> ISLA: I wouldn't take all the blame. You certainly didn't give Will his politics.
> JOHN: No. He got those from Satan.[56]

But more than a character study of an aging Honeyman returning to our stage, the play aims to critique Tea Party loonies. Insert names Rand Paul, Ted Cruz, or Sarah Palin for Will Branch, and, again, the bad guys—or girl, in this case—get all the good lines. Gwynn Branch, Will's wife and the power behind the throne they are erecting, is our Lady Macbeth. She makes a unique first entrance in Scene 2, running an anti-bugging device over not only the walls but Isla and John as well. When Will protests that "Gwynn, sweetheart, we're with family," she replies:

> We're with your father, whom you hate, and your stepmother, whom you've never met but also hate. I know exactly who we're with.[57]

Gwynn—slim, trim, using short skirts and sex to land Will—is simultaneously mean as a rattler. She suggests that video-game-playing teenager Andrei, Will's half-brother, will make a "good drone pilot,"[58] tastes her hosts' food for poison, insults them to their faces, and then asks them for a campaign donation. She "gnaws her cracker like an angry squirrel,"[59] curses like the proverbial sailor, and threatens to name the mountain nearest to the Honeyman estate in honor of George W. Bush just to spite her in-laws. Best of all, she threatens her husband: "Tell me the truth right now, and I'll help you fix it. If you don't, I'll grind your testicles to powder."[60]

Will and Gwynn have arrived for a visit we learn, without their usual retinue, in response to a message from John: "Will, I have something you can't afford to ignore. Get up here right now."[61] The two loathe each other so deeply that only a political threat could bring father and son together again. One weakness of this premise is that we are told how the relationship ruptured (the divorce, the affair, etc.) as exposition. But since we never see the relationship as anything but toxic, never see the two even think of trying to repair it, let alone attempting a reconciliation, then we cannot feel their pain nor take sides as each seeks only to hurt the other. We neither like nor sympathize with either.

The characters allude to the earlier play but it seems so removed from the present because nothing links it to the past.

> WILL: ...little Andrei Honeyman...
> JOHN: Remember who he's named after?
> WILL: Sure. The dead commie you used to play patty-cake with in the woods.[62]

They spend a page of dialogue debating the efficacy of arms negotiations and then rehash other slights, real and imagined, until finally John asks: "Is that why you rejected me? Because of a stupid affair?" Will's bloodless response does not satisfy:

> God, no. I rejected you long before that. Nothing you stood for made any sense to me. Going through life afraid all the time? Constantly begging a brutal enemy to be "civilized"? That's what you did for a living. Even when you did manage to get home you couldn't hear a different point of view.[63]

Politics alone has torn these two asunder? Then, truly, we can have no hope for finding common ground among political opponents, Democrat, Republican, Socialist or Tea Partyer, a direct refutation of what we learned in *A Walk in the Woods* when capitalist and communist built upon a shared humanity to at least *try* to save the world.

Has the writer lost all hope? Blessing said the play was inspired

> by national campaign cycles more than anything. I was working on it just before the 2012 election, and the polarization of the electorate was rather stunning. Basically we've got two countries that don't know how to talk to each other—and may not have any desire to.[64]

Does he doubt Sarah Palin and Hillary Clinton could take a few walks around the park and find any common agenda for helping humanity? Does he think the Tea Party today threatens the Republic more than the Soviet Union did thirty years ago? Instead of hope, Blessing gives us cynicism: a father, who does not love his own son, must stoop to extortion to get him out of politics, even though he recognizes another crazy politician will assuredly take his place and the right wingers will still win the national election. The once-idealistic negotiator who discovered the shared humanity of his Soviet counterpart now decides to bludgeon his opponent into abject surrender and humiliation and destroy any humanity they share.

The instrument of attack is scandal and the hypocrisy that accompanies it. Back in high school, Will, who now adheres to a right wing social agenda, had a homosexual affair. Afterwards the rejected young man killed himself. Will denies responsibility but knows he cannot admit the facts:

> WILL: It's just the letter, right? Let me buy it.
> JOHN: You still think I need money?
> WILL: I can't quit my career!
> JOHN: But that's my price.[65]

I feel dirty quoting this. Could you blackmail your child? I couldn't. However, I love Gwynn's horrified response to news of the letter: "A *boy*?!! You fucked a *boy*!!?"[66] Will knows publication of the letter means an end to his career:

> WILL: I'm a Republican about to be in a national race. There *is* only one sexual orientation.
> ISLA: So ... you never need to be with men?
> WILL: I need to be Vice-President, that's what I need.[67]

Hypocrisy abounds on all sides: Will denies his sexual feelings and fronts a Party dedicated to denying rights (job discrimination protections, marriage) to people like himself. On the other hand, John, paying lip service to liberalism, democracy, and free choice, wields the letter like a deadly rapier. The struggle becomes physical: Gwynn sends Will off for twine so she can tie Isla and John up and search the house for the threatening letter. Isla jumps on Gwynn, and beats her with a shot glass, Gwynn elbows Will in the nose as he tries to pull them apart. As the four sit disheveled and bleeding, young Andrei enters to ask, "What are you doing?" In as good a metaphor as we are likely to have for today's version of raucous and obscene political debate John answers: "Talking politics."[68]

Scene 6 wraps up the conflict. Andrei, returning to his home to gather up another video game to play while staying at a friend's house, has heard and recorded the whole brouhaha on his inexpensive listening/recording device from Radio Shack. John promises Andrei all new equipment in exchange for destroying the evidence. Will accompanies Andrei to his room. As they leave,

Andrei asks him, "Are you going to be the first gay Vice-President?" To which Will can only respond: "My God."[69]

Isla emerges as the sane one of the bunch, urging John to give Gwynn and Will the letter and end the affair.

> ISLA: Oh God, John, Let it *go*! We have no respect for them on any level, we detest what they stand for. They're the last people on earth we want to see coming up the drive. Don't you see what that makes them?
> JOHN: Family?
> ISLA: Exactly. You don't extort your own family.[70]

Isla, who had no previous knowledge of the letter or John's plans for its use, threatens to divorce him if he does not surrender the letter, which he finally does. Gwynn, having chewed the scenery, now tears the letter into little pieces and eats it as the play ends.[71]

A View of the Mountains works as satire and comedy. It's red meat for conservatives and liberals alike, unfair to all involved, and may lead to fisticuffs in the aisles while, unlike its predecessor, *A Walk in the Woods*, it will not advance rational political debate in this country one iota.

Some critics rejected the play for what they perceived as its nastiness. Bob Rendell wrote in "Talkin' Broadway":

> Blessing is only interested in presenting a lurid depiction of the pure evil of those with whom he disagrees.... It does promote a rigid political agenda and demonizes those opposed to it. Just how worthy is that?[72]

On the other hand, Ken Jaworowski, in the *New York Times*, liked it:

> Despite some rough edges, *A View of the Mountains* is an easy enough play to like. Over its 75 minutes this political satire ... raises a couple of questions, launches a few zingers and features a plot twist or two. Not everything here succeeds. But taken together, enough works to make it all worthwhile.[73]

But I think Blessing came closest to the truth when, speaking of *A View of the Mountains*, he told Tom Chesekin, "The Asbury Pulp":

> There are times when theater must attack the audience, rather than being some bourgeois ritual designed to make you feel safe and warm. This play asks a lot of questions. At its best, theater makes the audience ask the hard questions of themselves.[74]

The characters rarely reference the somewhat enigmatic title of the play. Yes, the Honeyman estate features a view of the Catskills, but do they stand for more than scenery? Gwynn has the longest speech of the play in which she speaks of the role of mountains in past human history. People ascend mountains to talk to God, she says, and that they were also God's telephone. Had the best reception apparently.... When you're up a mountain whispering in the Great Celestial Ear, no one but you can hear what He says back ... you can come back down and tell people what to do for the rest of time.[75]

In *A Walk in the Woods* Blessing showed us two men, conscious of their frailties, struggling to save humanity and seemingly failing. In *A View of the Mountains* he warns us not to trust those who reject their frailty and claim omnipotence. The view from the mountains may be exhilarating and yet delude us into ideological certainties that diminish our humanity. While we have reduced some nuclear stockpiles, he implies, we have never reduced the human hubris that may still lead us to Armageddon.

CHAPTER 5

The Headline Plays

Critics and readers know Blessing for his plays on contemporary issues from nuclear disarmament (*A Walk in the Woods*) to the AIDS epidemic (*Patient A*) to the war in Afghanistan (*Wood for the Fire*) but his approach is quite different from the "ripped from the headlines" trope exercised by the television shows like *Law and Order*, which exploit recent events for "up-to-the-minute" relevancy to enliven stereotypical cop dramas. Blessing doesn't use current events as backdrop for a plot or to stir up partisan emotions. Not a polemicist or political infighter, he explores issues and takes the audience along for the ride, delving deeper into stories that may have disappeared after a single news cycle to examine possibilities and alternatives. When it comes to serial killers (*Down the Road*) he asks not just "Why do they kill?" but what part of our own, seemingly normal, psychology is vulnerable to their appeal. In *Lake Street Extension* he examines the issue of personal and societal redemption within the context of a Central American massacre. In *Going to St. Ives* he looks at the Hippocratic Oath and the moral equation of committing a single murder to prevent thousands. In *Two Rooms*, his first headline play following *A Walk in the Woods*, he humanizes the human toll of Middle East politics and in *Seven Joys* he burlesques the impotent power of the nuclear club. *Patient A* and *34th and Dyer* can be read as investigations of grief and fear nurtured by extraordinary evil. *Whores*, I would argue, through comedy, eroticism, and visual fireworks, directly indicted U.S. government policy and helped to change it. Blessing is, as Elias Stimac wrote in *Drama-Logue*, a "playwright whose concern for the times he is living in is reflected in his works."[1] And yet his primary concern always stays with the conflicted human beings within those treacherous times.

Within each chapter I've discussed the plays in the order of their production.

5. The Headline Plays

Two Rooms
Down the Road
Lake Street Extension
Patient A
The Rights
Going to St. Ives
Chesapeake
34th and Dyer
Whores
Wood for the Fire
Seven Joys

Two Rooms

Two Rooms, originally titled "The Quality of Tears," dramatizes the rash of kidnappings in Lebanon of 96 foreigners from 21 different countries during the period 1982–1992, by groups protesting either U.S. aid to Iraq in its war with Iran, or Western aid to Israel in its occupation of the West Bank and Gaza. This involved such prominent Western hostages as Dr. David Dodge, president of the American University of Beirut; Presbyterian minister Rev. Benjamin Weir; Terry Anderson, correspondent for the Associated Press; and Anglican Church envoy Terry Waite, who went to Beirut to negotiate hostage releases and then found himself abducted and held prisoner for five years. Eight of the hostages died in captivity, struck down either from untreated illnesses or murdered by their captors. The growing list of captives and their lengthy detentions became nightly staples of the national news, even as Lebanon devolved into bloody civil war and Israel invaded. On October 23, 1983, attackers drove a truck bomb into the American barracks at Beirut International Airport and killed 241 U.S. Marines. On February 26, 1984, the last Marines left Beirut. Eighteen days later the CIA station chief there was kidnapped on his way to work. In August 1985, as the families of the hostages begged their government to do something, President Reagan decided to secretly trade missiles for hostages in what became known as the Iran-Contra scandal that also covertly funded the illegal U.S. Contra war against the government of Nicaragua.

Terry Waite, in Lebanon representing the Archbishop of Canterbury to negotiate the release of four kidnapping victims, joined their ranks in 1987, and spent nearly five years in captivity. In his account of that time, he recalls the cries of other prisoners being executed and thought he might be next:

> They came into my cell and told me I had five hours to live. I actually went to sleep. The body shuts down to give you some respite from what is happening.[2]

After allowing time for prayers and a last letter to family his captors put a gun to his head: "I could feel it.... Then they dropped the gun down and just said, 'Another time.'"[3] He survived. When the series of kidnappings ended, two captives, Peter Kilburn, a librarian at the American University in Beirut, and CIA agent Bill Buckley had been murdered.[4]

Against this backdrop of events in the Middle East, and following the success of *A Walk in the Woods*, Blessing received a commission for two more plays from Des McAnuff,[5] managing director at the La Jolla Playhouse in southern California. The two commissions, in consecutive years, topics unspecified, served simultaneously as a blank check to the playwright to write about subjects of his own choosing and a challenge to come up with "something" for a production. The result: *Two Rooms* and *Down the Road*, explore fear, murder, matrimonial despair, and existential pain.

Blessing told the *Kansas City Star* that

> after *A Walk in the Woods* ... I was looking for another issue that tends to haunt people for months and years at a time in the front pages.... With *Two Rooms* what I became interested in ... as I wrote was the role of the government and the media and the interaction that they had with the lives of the people who were directly affected by the hostage taking.... We end up in a position that for Americans is very frightening which is a feeling of helplessness. So I think that aspect of it is always going to be current because Americans really have a hard time waking up from that dream of security that they have.[6]

As Blessing told another reporter, there were specific reasons to choose such a grim and forbidding topic:

> After *A Walk in the Woods* he [Blessing] became concerned that humor came too easily to his style ... so he purposefully removed that "tool" of his craft to see if he could make do without it. The four works that followed—*Two Rooms, Down the Road, Cobb*, and *Lake Street Extension*—he fondly refers to as "my tetralogy of pain."[7]

The Lebanon hostage story did not lend itself to a simple telling since the actual kidnappers were often unidentified and the foreign policy maneuverings of our own government and those of other countries like Iran, Lebanon, Saudi Arabia, and Israel remained covert. Clearly the CIA was involved as were the clandestine services of other countries like the Soviet Union, whose diplomats were also kidnapped. Then the tale raveled off into President Reagan's decision to trade missiles for funding a covert and illegal war in Nicaragua and charges that the U.S. invasion of the tiny island of Grenada, in 1983, just days after the deadly Marine barracks bombing in Beirut was designed to draw attention away from a public outcry seeking to ascertain blame for putting largely unarmed U.S. military personnel in harm's way. Such a sprawling story called for a 700 page novel more than a two-hour play.

So Blessing decided to put the focus on just four people caught up in the geopolitical crisis: Michael Wells, a 30-year-old educator kidnapped in Beirut; Lainie Wells, Michael's 30-year-old wife trying to move heaven and earth to free her husband even as she struggles to maintain emotional ties to her missing spouse; 30-year-old reporter Walker Harris; and 40-year-old Ellen Van Oss, a U.S. State Department representative to the hostages' families.

Blessing paired the minimal cast with a minimal and practically bare set, the stage divided in two to represent simultaneously Michael's cell and a room in Lainie's home. Slide projections of bombed-out buildings, teenagers with automatic weapons, and weeping women served to show the effects of the Beirut fighting. He broke the two acts into four scenes each, but each scene is itself separated into smaller scenes in the style of French scenes, where a new scene commences each time a character enters or exits the stage rather than waiting for a change in setting or time. Blessing kept all the violence offstage, eschewed the intricacies of the political contest (conflict between Israel and the Palestinians and Hezbollah, between Shiite and Sunni Moslems, etc.) and focused not just on the hostages but on those they had left behind, those who were physically free and yet suffered their own confinement as emotional prisoners of events. He placed the emphasis not on action but on an exploration of feelings. It became, not unlike *A Walk in the Woods*, an international political story condensed to the lives of just two people, a story of the powerful versus the powerless, governments, and, in this case, the kidnappers versus the hostages and their loved ones.

As Blessing said:

Two Rooms I felt needed to be all about the imaginative potential of a nearly blank space. Blank for virtually being empty rooms and not an empty stage. What could come into that room? What could be kept out? In many ways it was one of the most impressive features of the play. It's easy to envision the empty....[8]

The play opens with lights up on Michael on one side of the stage. He is blindfolded, unshaven and handcuffed. Only a mat on the floor marks this as a space for sleeping, for living, for captivity. Writing letters to his wife, Lainie, in his head he speaks them aloud, telling us a year has passed since his kidnapping. These mental letters will never be sent but provide the audience with an understanding of his fate and his inner life. Michael's kidnappers are never seen, never speak. He tells us:

Their voices are so young. I'm sure it's a delusion, but sometimes I think I've had one or two of them in my class.[9]

Lights go down on Michael and up on Lainie on the other half of the stage. She talks out loud to the husband she cannot see and who cannot hear her as she rearranges his home office into a bare cell. She says:

> Michael's here. I can't explain it, but for me he is.... The moment I come in I feel ... the warmth of his body. The rest of the house—everywhere else—is cold.[10]

By creating her own physical space of isolation and loneliness, Lainie feels closer to the husband she imagines inhabiting a space as spare as hers.

Two characters turn up regularly to invade Lainie's solitude. One is Ellen Van Oss (note the name Van Oss: the O.S.S., Office of Strategic Services, was the World War II precursor to the U.S. Central Intelligence Agency), the State Department employee assigned to "handle" Lainie. She speaks in an unfeeling and bloodless bureaucratize, an Orwellian reinterpretation of language:

> The important thing is to maintain cautious optimism. Advised hope, I call it. We're hopeful but we're advised. We're not unintelligent. We recognize the reality of the situation, then we inject hope. Into that reality. Because without hope there can be no foreign policy.[11]

Ellen is not a nuanced or likable character.

Lainie's other visitor is Walker, a reporter who initially sees Lainie and Michael as little more than fodder for his newspaper and who urges Lainie to speak out publicly in opposition to the government approach of keeping quiet, arguing that Ellen and her superiors care more about policy than individual lives. Note the name "Walker." Is it meant to remind us of William Walker, the 19th century American "filibusterer" who invaded Nicaragua and briefly ruled there as "President" and link it to the 1980s U.S. war to overthrow the Sandinistas?

A struggle ensues for Lainie's "heart and mind." Oss tells her: "You're a potential embarrassment. In the world of international politics that can be serious."[12] Walker, who seemed more sympathetic at first, closes the first act by breaking his promise to wait for Lainie's permission to write about her, forcing Lainie into a public role, pitting her against Ellen's attempt to keep her quiet.

Ellen opens Act 2 with a long-winded and unconvincing explanation of why the terrorists hate us:

> Think of it—enormous numbers of people all over the world hating Americans.... Why? ... To reject what they can of the Western world—which floats before them as an unreachable illusion both detested and desired.[13]

This sounds like the simplistic explanation we heard after 9/11: "They want what we have." This serves as one of the few attempts any of the characters in the play makes in terms of trying to explain what is happening to Michael, and Lainie, in foreign policy terms. (Contrast this silliness with, say, the detailed presentations of the historical and poetical roots of terrorism to be found in the play cycle *The Great Game: Afghanistan*, also discussed in this chapter.)

> But, remember, this is a play about emotions, not politics. And Blessing underlies this with references back to nature much as he did in *A Walk in the Woods* but this time nature is more threatening, "red in tooth and claw."[14] Lainie tells Ellen of the cuckoo bird which hides its egg in warblers' nests where it masquerades as a warbler to kill its nest mates as, she says "God looks on.... With approval."[15] Michael tells Ellen, in what seems to be a dream, about the brine shrimp which lie dormant in dry desert lake beds until a downpour makes them briefly come alive only to slip again into the mud as it dries waiting to come alive again. Says Michael: "You get out of the United States you see a lot of that. Whole cultures waiting to be alive."[16]

Events move rapidly. Ellen and Walker report action we do not see onstage. Terrorists take 23 Americans captive at an airport terminal in Crete. Lainie goes on national TV with a picture of Michael and his colleague and fellow captive Mathison. The terrorists' demands are met and the Americans in Crete are released. Mathison is also released. (Because of Lainie's appearances?) In a small town in Italy, government forces gun down a terrorist resisting arrest. Perhaps in retribution, Michael's kidnappers kill him. The play ends with Lainie refusing to attend a planned ceremony as Michael's body is returned to the U.S. and threatening to burn any official letters of condolence; asking Walker and Ellen to leave. In the final moment Lainie and Michael, a ghost, a dream, a memory, are alone together. Their brief farewell closes with another nature story. The male African hornbill, Lainie tells us, walls up the female bird in the hollow of a tree after mating.

> LAINIE: After the eggs are hatched he breaks down the wall again, and the whole family is united for the first time. You see? It hasn't been a prison at all. It's been ... a fortress.
> MICHAEL: Their devotion, you mean?
> LAINIE: Their devotion.[17]

As she strokes his hair the lights fade to black.

Two Rooms is a 1990s kind of tragic love story: Romeo and Juliet torn asunder by geopolitics beyond their ken or power. In the end, their story gives us an inkling of the pain of our ordinary fellows caught up in extraordinary situations. As Blessing told Dana Bourke:

> The public isn't told much of what really happens. The individual citizens are expected to bear the brunt of pain and sacrifice while bureaucrats work hard not to be embarrassed or outmaneuvered. The relief of human suffering is a very low priority, especially compared with the furthering of a foreign policy agenda. The media are manipulated at nearly every turn and are usually happy to be thus used.[18]

While Bourke, herself, sees archetypes used throughout *Two Rooms* with Michael as all hostages, Lainie as all hostage families, Walker as the self-

Two Rooms: In her own home, Lainie Wells (Catherine Koons) attempts to form a psychic bond by recreating the room in which her husband, Michael (David Johnson), is being held hostage in Lebanon. Theatre Alliance, Washington, D.C.; 1992, photograph by Susan Johann.

aggrandizing media, and Ellen as the government that doesn't care about individuals,[19] the strength of the play lies in Blessing's ability to make Lainie and Michael, at least, particular and individual. Unlike *Patient A*, also discussed in this chapter, which relies upon fact and figures and highlighted its author's distance from and ambivalence to its controversial protagonist, *Two Rooms* takes us into the shared experiences of a human relationship where the scenes of Lainie stroking[20] Michael's hair, for example, are too intimate not to strike a deep emotional chord with audiences. And Michael's death strikes the final tragic coda to the affair.

Though Michael dies, and so goes on a dramatic journey from life to death, Lainie strikes me as the real protagonist of the play who struggles throughout, though unsuccessfully, to save his life. Though we do not encounter her before the kidnapping of her husband, but rather meet her a year after the three-year ordeal begins, we gather from her interactions that she is traveling a profound inner journey of her own, developing a new inner strength and maturity in navigating the machinations of her government, the self-serving media, and an uncaring public. Ultimately alone, she struggles to maintain her relationship, her love for her spouse, and her sanity.

As late as opening night in Minneapolis: "It [the play] changed so much, that.... Blessing still did not know whether Michael would be killed or released."[21] However, his death provides a sense of realism and finality to the relationship as death does in Shakespeare's *Romeo and Juliet* while remaining true to the dangers and toll of the times. While many hostages survived long imprisonments to return to their grateful families, countless civilians died in mass and individual acts of terrorism. Michael's death robs the play of a happy and, therefore I think, forgettable ending. The audience has witnessed a tragedy in parallel with all the deaths society witnessed at the time. Written a decade before the September 11, 2001, terrorist attacks on the World Trade Center and Pentagon, *Two Rooms* is both descriptive and prescient of the civilian costs of an ongoing "War on Terrorism." The videotaped beheadings of Westerners by ISIS in Iraq and Syria in 2014 reach a mass audience for which Blessing created an emotional context in *Two Rooms*.

Following the production of *Two Rooms*, TV actress and producer Marlo Thomas, herself of Lebanese descent, met with Blessing with the idea of turning *Two Rooms* into a TV-movie, but Lee and his agent decided not to move forward with the project.[22] Though sometimes misidentified as being based on Blessing's play, Thomas's ABC TV-movie, starring herself and David Dukes, entitled *Forgotten: The Sis and Jerry Levin Story*, directed by Roger Young, and broadcast in 1991, was based on a different script recounting the 1984 kidnapping of the CNN Beirut Bureau Chief in Lebanon who escaped his captors in 1985. Television undoubtedly demanded a happy ending.

Critics generally liked *Two Rooms*. *Time* magazine chose it as one of the ten best plays of 1993,[23] writing several months earlier that "no American playwright uses factual material more imaginatively than Lee Blessing."[24] Pamela Somners, writing for the *Washington Post*, praised the "precise and evocative language and also its faith in the audience's imaginative faculties."[25]

Mel Gussow, a critic for the *New York Times*, wrote admiringly as well:

> Mr. Blessing is sure-footed in paralleling the wife's isolation with her husband's. With an exercise in his imagination, the playwright brings the couple into varying degrees of proximity. In her mind, the wife visits the husband and each speaks what might normally appear in a letter.[26]

Gusso added:

Moving back and forth between a prison in Beirut and his wife at home, the playwright artfully explores the shared stoicism that unites the characters and the external forces that keep them divided.[27]

Other critics expressed unhappiness with the static nature of the play, as this critic for *Variety*: "The first act, with strong, we're-all-in-a-trap overtones of Kafka and Sartre, abounds with narrative but plods with inaction."[28] Dan Sullivan, after seeing the play at the La Jolla Playhouse in 1988, wrote in the *Los Angeles Times*:

> The plot is full of problems, possibly because the play feels as if it's still in an early draft. Where, for example, are the couple's parents and friends throughout this crisis? Has the wife chosen to isolate herself from them? (That would be interesting.) Why, if the journalist is such an opportunist, does he overlook the golden opportunity to stage a confrontation between the wife and the government when her husband's remains are shipped back to the states? ... *Two Rooms* is an idea play but the idea has only been roughed out so far.[29]

Dueling critical reviews seem the norm with new plays, and audiences and readers make the final judgments. The writer for *Variety* speaks of inaction but means inaction on the stage. Offstage, people are murdered, hostages released, and deals made. Think of *Oedipus Rex*, where we are told, but never see, the murder of the King, the suicide of the Queen, or the blinding of Oedipus. It strikes me that the "inaction" on the stage perfectly parallels the inaction to free the hostage and the toll this takes on his family, living in a kind of emotional limbo made physically apparent in Lainie's empty room, stuck within a state of fear and helplessness, unable to do anything to save a loved one. The reference to Sartre's *No Exit* is apt, I think, set as it is within one room where three people relentlessly torture each other emotionally as they do little more than sit, stand, pace, and talk. Their hell is remarkably similar to the hells of Lainie and Michael, where the absence of action is the source of their pain.

Blessing was also taken to task for raising questions but not providing answers. Walter Jones, writing in the *San Diego Union*, said:

> If there is in this play a concrete suggestion for solving the problem of American hostages in Lebanon it gets lost amid the anguished rhetoric and frustrating complexities.[30]

But is Jones confusing a playwright with a president? It is exactly because the situation was complex and frustrating that no one seemed to have an effective answer at the time and President Reagan's plan, to sell missiles to Iran, nearly brought down his government.

Is it a playwright's job to be answering questions politicians can't? Blessing himself indicated his goals for the play:

I think it makes people pay that much closer attention to issues that they might not otherwise have thought much about. As Americans we don't like to think about things in general. We'll have a convulsive need to talk about an issue and the media features it and people talk about it and then it disappears. I think that when you get out of this country you get a wider perspective. I think because of our history, because of our geography that Americans tend to be a bit provincial in the way that we look at the world. It makes it very difficult for American foreign policy to be flexible.[31]

Blessing correctly reminds us that the playwright's role is to make us think and feel. Answers and solutions ultimately come from us. *Two Rooms* won the Hollywood *Drama-Logue* Critics' Award for Outstanding Achievement in Theatre in 1989.

Down the Road

Blessing followed the tragic/political play *Two Rooms* a year later with his second commission from the La Jolla Playhouse, the equally dark and disturbing *Down the Road*. Again the two main characters are husband and wife, in this case Dan and Iris Henniman. Again the stage is divided into two rooms: a sparsely furnished motel room and the interview room in a maximum security prison. Again it is a play about victims and perpetrators, powerlessness and power. Again the subject is one we'd rather not deal with: a sort of domestic terrorist, a serial killer. Blessing tells the story in a single act of 22 short scenes, switching back and forth from the motel to the prison.

Blessing based the play on actual serial killers, including Ted Bundy, but his focus is not on the slaughter but on our societal reaction: "Our strongest cultural response to people like Ted Bundy seemed to be the buying of souvenirs. I thought that needed addressing in a play."[32] You will no doubt remember that Ted Bundy (to quote popular culture as found in Wikipedia)

> was an American serial killer, rapist, kidnapper, and necrophile who assaulted and murdered numerous young women and girls during the 1970s and possibly earlier. He confessed shortly before his execution to 30 homicides committed in seven states between 1974 and 1978.
> Bundy was regarded as handsome and charismatic by his young female victims, traits he exploited in winning their trust. He typically approached them in public places, feigning injury or disability, or impersonating an authority figure, before overpowering and assaulting them at more secluded locations. He sometimes revisited his secondary crime scenes for hours at a time, grooming and performing sexual acts with the decomposing corpses until putrefaction and destruction by wild animals made further interaction impossible. He decapitated at least 12 of his victims, and kept some of the severed heads in his apartment for a period of time as mementos.... He received three death sentences.... Ted Bundy died in the electric chair at Raiford Prison in Starke, Florida, on January 24, 1989. Biographer Ann Rule described him as "a sadistic sociopath who took

pleasure from another human's pain and the control he had over his victims, to the point of death, and even after." He once called himself "the most cold-hearted son of a bitch you'll ever meet." Attorney Polly Nelson, a member of his last defense team, agreed. "Ted," she wrote, "was the very definition of heartless evil."[33]

I, or Wikipedia in this case, may have already told you all the facts you need to know about *Down the Road*. The details of his murders that William Reach relates to his interviewers are all based on actual cases that Blessing read about, although he did not interview such a killer himself. The research affected him:

> Every detail in the play has been done in real life.
> I've never been so paranoid as when I was doing the research because what's frightening about serial killing is the randomness of it.... After you've read three or four books about serial killers you end up triple locking the door and then you wonder if that's enough.[34]

So, why write a play about a monster? Because, moving beyond Wikipedia and the headlines, you have something new to tell us ... or make us feel. Blessing wants to investigate why American society has seemingly more serial killers than ever, why they fascinate us so, and what the killers, themselves, are really after.

The set, again barren and claustrophobic as in *Two Rooms*, serves this theme:

> *Down the Road* had to be about a serial killer who had already been caught, tried and sentenced I thought, since I wasn't interested in any of the usual suspense-generating devices that support crime stories.... So he had to be in prison [at the outset]. The kind of interview room that the interviewers of Ted Bundy found in a rural Florida prison—and the bleakness of the nearby motels—seemed the natural locations for the play. It also seemed natural to bleed the two areas into each other more and more as the play went on, and that's what I finally decided to do—a process not really complete until the Louisville production. Thus, the disintegrating state of mind of the writers could be reflected in breaking down the stage convention.[35]

Into this bleak landscape, Blessing introduces Iris and Dan, a young married couple with a mission: to fulfill a book contract about imprisoned serial killer William Reach. Iris is the seasoned crime reporter; Dan, the novice. Their goal is to write the book, gain fame and fortune, and raise their hoped-for children in a safe and happy life shared for years to come. Reach, however, has other plans for them.

Ironies abound: Iris and Dan are trying to create a new life; Reach has taken innocent young lives. Iris and Dan conceive a baby girl in their sojourn in the nondescript motel room. Reach's victims were all girls, one as young as ten. And what of the future of their own unborn child, could it grow up to be a victim, or even a killer? To keep Reach cooperating, so that they might complete their book, Iris and Dan must be accommodating, polite, and sensitive to a monster from whom they would ordinarily flee, even as he lures them in deeper and deeper with hints that he might reveal new crimes and victims, new exclusive details to make their book a bestseller.

The play opens as Iris and Dan unpack, moving into the bare motel room that will be their new home for several months. Iris, looking out the window, notices a rusting water heater sitting on the porch of a house across the street. Conversation returns to this water heater in Scene 3 and again in Scene 10, when Iris muses:

> There's a woman sitting next to the water heater. Middle-aged, shapeless house dress.... I believe she serves the water heater in some way. Perhaps she's the high priestess.[36]

Near the end of the play Dan hires junk men to remove the water heater. This disturbs Iris: "I liked the water heater."[37] It also foreshadows the seeming end of their own relationship. What is a rusty water heater doing in a play about a serial killer? Is it a symbol of decay, uselessness, ugliness? For when Iris and Dan report on their walks around the vicinity of the motel all they see are a "car dealer, gas station, tire store, muffler shop, gas station, McDonald's.... 'Oblivion World,'"[38] as if the bleak landscape were itself malevolent or at least inciting, in its ugliness and sterility, of an antisocial state of mind. Blessing had his special reasons for having the characters fixate on the water heater:

> No one knew what to make of the water heater in *Down the Road*, which is what I wanted. I set out to create an uncomfortable, not exactly entertaining experience and I think the play does that rather well. Unlike works like *Silence of the Lambs*, which tend to treat serial murder as no more than the next fascinating wrinkle in the colorful (and $$$ entertaining $$$) world of crime in America, I wanted to think about [what] this very fundamentally different criminal development said about who we might be becoming. I thought if an audience thought I was out to entertain them, then the point was lost. Dan and Iris are in a horrible place, just as we are. Part of what happens is that they fixate on the irrelevant but irritating details of the environment—because it's still better than thinking about why they're really there.[39]

Iris and Dan enter this environment to tell the story of a sadistic murderer, further their careers and, hopefully, make money on the resulting book. But William Reach is a man without redeeming qualities.

> IRIS: Why did you kill her?
> REACH: I don't know."
> IRIS: How did you kill her?
> REACH: Stabbed her ten times. Strangled her with a nylon rope, nearly severed her head from her body.
> IRIS: What did you do then?
> REACH: Cut off her head, took it home, set it on a table, stared at it.
> IRIS: Then what?
> REACH: Had sex with it.[40]

With horrific details like this we can see Reach exploiting his interviewers to have a captive audience, as Iris and Dan, in turn, exploit Reach for material for their book. But one can ask: Is Blessing exploiting the horror to titillate a theater audience even as he condemns the mass media for exploiting the serial killers to build an audience of their own?

Blessing is taking aim at the media here, as he did in *Two Rooms* and as he will again in *Fortinbras*:

> Of course the media have too much influence over people. Why? Because we grant that influence to the media. We're still staring at TV like a bunch of stunned apes, and before we wake up, CD-Rom technology will have us enthralled even more [this is 1995]. Any intellectual knows that tossing the TV out the window and severely limiting one's belief in what's printed in the newspaper will greatly enhance one's sense of self-worth, security and basic intelligence—not to mention one's sense of obligation to one's fellow man. The media more and more are used to scare us into sitting passively in our own homes and keeping out of the way of those who really make the decisions in the world. But apparently we like it that way because we keep watching instead of thinking and interacting.[41]

This is not to say that Blessing doesn't leaven the deadly serious with humor:

> DAN: You cut her head off....
> REACH: Yes. Put it in a plastic bag, threw it in the trunk of my car.
> ....
> DAN: You ... took the head home?
> REACH: I had to stop and see my therapist.... I had my last session with the therapist that day.
> DAN: And you drove there, with Melanie Bryce's head in the car's trunk and had your last session with him?
> REACH: That's right.
> DAN: What did he say to you that last day?
> REACH: He said he thought I'd made real progress.[42]

Audiences and critics might expect several things from such a play: insight into the motives of serial killers and, even, suggestions on how to prevent them. Blessing seemed to agree that he was about solving a social problem, telling one interviewer:

> In some ways it's my most Ibsenesque play. It's a play that points fairly forcefully and clearly towards an issue that it has some concern about—and that's essentially the American tendency to simply co-opt some of the worst behavior in its society and to celebrate it, rather than to sit and analyze it and reflect on it and try to change it so that it lessens. We tend to have somebody like Ted Bundy revealed to us and instead of really learning much we simply turn him into a folk myth.[43]

Blessing throws out a few ideas. For example, Scene 14 is given over to Dan's contemplation of the Interstate Highway System. Begun by President Dwight Eisenhower in 1956, the Interstate now encompasses over 47,000 miles of connected paved highways. Dan muses:

5. The Headline Plays

Down the Road: Serial killer Reach (Mark Shannon) shares sensational stories of his crimes with writer Iris (Bernadette Sullivan). Actors Theatre of Louisville (Kentucky); 1991, photograph by Richard C. Trigg; courtesy of Actors Theatre of Louisville.

> Getting lost on the largest engineering project in the history of the world ... no limit to where you can go. In the decade of the 1950s before the completion of the Interstate, there was only one case of serial murder reported in the United States. In the whole decade, just one. Now—one a month.[44]

Later, in a newspaper interview, Blessing continued his character's thought:

> There's something about the interstate [highway] system itself—the fact that it allows such ease of travel. You can literally travel from one jurisdiction to many jurisdictions away before police even know a crime has been committed. So it provides opportunities for certain kinds of crimes which just weren't there before.... There's something about the world of the interstate, which is so impersonal. It's a place that in a sense isn't even there. And we use an enormous amount of land in this country and we sort of make it disappear into a non-world of cloverleafs and interstate highway. So no one's really there when they're there. And a lot of the serial killing that has gone on in the last two or three decades has been associated with that kind of travel.[45]

He also offered:

> Some people have suggested that murder is America's form of revolution. Just because there aren't political revolutionary movements it doesn't mean there isn't a lot of anger, dislocation, and alienation in this society. Why does it [serial killing] increase so much if it doesn't have social causes?[46]

In another interview, he explained his original intent in writing the play:

> It's sort of Hitchcockian [*Psycho*?] that a lot of my ideas hit me in the shower. The water was splashing over me when I began to wonder what produced a serial killer like Ted Bundy. I was interested in the kind of killer who might seem outwardly sane, even charming, an everyday man. *Silence of the Lambs* piled it on with two outrageous serial killers. You'd never get into a car with either one. Reach, my protagonist, would fool you.... In real life, sensationalism sells.[47]

In fact, no one knows what turns a person into a serial killer like Ted Bundy. Childhood abuse, broken families, psychological deviancies, low self-esteem, drug abuse, etc., all may be found in the lives of individual murderers but are also found in the lives of people who become productive members of our society, even people who are empathetic and altruistic.

"Sensationalism sells," said Blessing and he pursued that issue of the media and celebrity within *Down the Road*, as he explained:

> A person can be a wonderful basketball player, for example, but unless he's NBA caliber society doesn't care about him. I think that sends a subtle message to a society—that unless you're on top of the world you're not in the world at all.[48]

Or, as Iris explains in the play:

> IRIS: Unless you succeed—unless you're really famous—you don't exist.... Before he started killing people, there was no BILL REACH. There was "Hey, you." ... the only way out [of anonymity] was to become a monster.
> DAN: By that criterion, almost anybody could become Bill Reach.
> IRIS: Maybe anyone could.[49]

Maybe. But they don't.

In the end, Iris quits the project, disgusted with Reach and with the possibility that their own book might inspire more atrocities by people seeking fame like his, while Dan remains, tantalized by the chance Reach will describe a new killing he hasn't previously disclosed and so guarantee the book will become a bestseller. The quest for fame and money wins again.

Drama-Logue observed: "Lee Blessing is a playwright whose concern for the times he is living in is reflected in his works."[50] Critic Peter Vaughan disagreed: "Lee Blessing's *Down the Road* is little more than a social observation masquerading as a play."[51] Greg Evans wrote in *Variety*:

> With "Down the Road," Blessing again shows his superiority at presenting an intellectual yet emotional look at the various facets of a twisted, virtually unsolvable issue. And if the play's success is measured by how much it disturbs emotions and stimulates discussion, "Down the Road" ranks as a major achievement.[52]

Sylvia Drake, however, in the *Los Angeles Times*, thought:

> He [Blessing] raises the hard questions and when he can't answer them, he aborts the play. Why do serial killers kill? Someone has yet to provide the answer.[53]

Clive Barnes, in the *New York Post*, wrote:

> ["Down the Road"] is an apparent attempt to exploit the current vogue in novels and TV dramas for true-life crime stories.... "Down the Road" has much more in common with those newspapers that neatly mix piety and hypocrisy, showing how shabbily sleazy the tabloid opposition is by repeating all their shabby, sleazy details. Thus, like the playwright, they stand to cash in as they opt out.... The unnecessarily obscene details of Reach's murders can have no purpose other than that of titillation, and the play leaves a singularly nasty taste behind it.[54]

Darryl H. Miller, in the *Los Angeles Daily News*, stated the obvious without offering a personal judgment: "With *Down the Road* Blessing once again demonstrates his gift for using the theatre to address current events."[55]

What are we left with? The water heater leads nowhere. Perhaps this is symbolic since the play doesn't take us anywhere, either in terms of new ideas or even questions. We know the pitfalls of celebrity and we know we live in a celebrity-crazed society. My own college students want to be both rich and famous but invariably choose celebrity over money when I ask them which they want more. Once upon a time people became famous for what they accomplished. Now celebrities are famous for being famous. And, in our violent society perversity is another route to fame.

When I've asked those same students to write a list of ten things they want to do before they die a few include "kill someone," though they tell me they choose this not for fame but to "see what it feels like." This may not be a more comforting answer but it is a scarier one—and one you won't find in this play.

There are no heroes in *Down the Road*. Clearly, Iris is the protagonist, the central character who takes a "journey from ignorance to knowledge" and makes a life-defining decision in the end to walk away from money and celebrity. But the play is ultimately unsatisfying, and having sat through the (verbal) gore, misogyny, violence, and perversity, we'd like a little more of a payoff. The overall feeling for some will be the desire for a hot soapy shower to wash it all away while wondering if this is exactly the effect Blessing was intending.

Oddly enough, *Down the Road* was performed in tandem with *Riches* at A Company of Angels, April 8, through May 21, 1999, a weird juxtaposition of emotions and themes, billed as an "Evening of Two Lee Blessing Plays." Movie actor Eric Stoltz (*Mask* [1985], *Pulp Fiction* [1994], and the outstanding *The Waterdance* [1992]) added star power, or celebrity, as Reach, in a New York City production in June 1993.

Lake Street Extension

For well over a hundred years the U.S. government has meddled in South and Central America, to murderous effect. For an historical overview see *The Open Veins of Latin America* by Eduardo Galeano, a *tour de force* indictment of events mostly unknown to our countrymen; for more recent events, my own book *Nicaragua: A New Kind of Revolution* stands among many. During the 1980s, I worked to send humanitarian supplies, including wheelchairs, to the victims of U.S. intervention in El Salvador and Nicaragua and visited with fellow clergy throughout Central America to aid the hundreds of thousands of people made refugees by the policies of, first, President Carter and then President Reagan, which aligned U.S. military and economic aid with some of the most regressive regimes in our hemisphere, like the 30-year Somoza dynasty in Nicaragua and the government "death squads" in El Salvador.

Some of those refugees fled to the United States, where the government worked to deport them back to the killing zones they had narrowly escaped. A "sanctuary" movement grew up in U.S. churches to protect these people, sometimes whole families, who had already seen friends and associates murdered in their native countries. I organized the sanctuary movement in Los Angeles beginning in 1983, and, enlisting Unitarian Universalist, Catholic, and Protestant churches, as well as a synagogue, provided physical shelter to these exiles for up to six months in our houses of worship. At times, exiles slept on the couch in my home or the homes of colleagues. The United States government considered "sanctuary" a criminal offense.

Lake Street Extension, a 90-minute one-act, is a play about those times. Blessing's inspiration, if that word can be applied to mass murder, was the El Mozote massacre in El Salvador. As Blessing told one reporter:

> During those days in December 1981 nearly 800 men, women, and children were murdered in the village of Mozote and surrounding settlements in a remote part of El Salvador. The unit accused of this atrocity—the Atlacatl battalion—was in part trained by U.S. advisors and supported by U.S. military aid. When news of what happened at Mozote was reported, the Reagan administration refused to acknowledge that it even occurred.[56]

Author Mark Danner added a first-person account of the mass murder in his report "The Truth of El Mozote":

> Rufina could not see the children; she could only hear their cries as the soldiers waded into them, slashing some with their machetes, crushing the skulls of others with the butts of their rifles. Many others—the youngest children, most below the age of twelve—the soldiers herded from the house of Alfredo Márquez across the street to the sacristy, pushing them, crying and screaming, into the dark tiny room. There the soldiers raised their M16s and emptied their magazines into the roomful of children. When they

reached the playing field, "there were maybe thirty children," he says. "The soldiers were putting ropes on the trees. I was seven years old, and I didn't really understand what was happening until I saw one of the soldiers take a kid he had been carrying—the kid was maybe three years old—throw him in the air, and stab him with a bayonet. They slit some of the kids' throats, and many they hanged from the tree. All of us were crying now, but we were their prisoners—there was nothing we could do. The soldiers kept telling us, "You are guerrillas and this is justice. This is justice."[57]

I heard stories like this, of other Salvadoran towns and villages, from the refugee families passing through our sanctuaries to what, we hoped, were safer lives.

So how does a playwright put such horrors on stage? Blessing does it with another troubled and troubling threesome, as in *Down the Road*, giving us father, son, and foreign refugee, each with a terrible secret. In an unnamed northern U.S. city, Fuller, 50 years old and a convert to religion, is attempting to atone, or maybe just deny, his abuse of his own son. That teenage son, Trace, now "turns tricks" as a male prostitute to survive in an abandoned hotel and periodically returns home to remind Fuller he has not forgiven him. When he returns this time, however, Trace discovers in his old basement bedroom Gregorio, who seems to be running from the Salvadoran military but is really a soldier himself. Blessing once referred to the work as "a horrible little play about three men in a basement."[58] In this basement, the lowest level of a home not unlike the lowest level of our existences, also known as hell, three souls, not unlike those in Sartre's *No Exit*, torture one another, changing sides, ganging up two against one, until each is bloody and broken.

Pederasty works as a metaphor for U.S./Salvadoran relations here. The U.S. acts like the big brother, or "Tio Sam,"—Uncle Sam—to the smallest country in our hemisphere, working its will, deposing and imposing governments, investing and divesting in sugar, bananas, and railroads and snuggling close to the landowning oligarchy of "Fourteen Families," leaving 95 percent of the people landless, hopeless, and poor. In a sexual as well as economic sense, American soldiers had their way with them. Maria Irene Fornes uses a similar allegory in her play *The Conduct of Life*, 1985.

Molestation by a single man symbolizes the victimization of an entire country. As Blessing said:

> A number of my plays, which deal with political issues, tend to find very personal stories ... almost parables to illustrate some political point. This one may be more that way than any of the others.[59]

Secrets get teased out slowly in *Lake Street Extension*, the name of the road on which Fuller's house fronts but which once bore the grandiose name The Great River Road, a grand title for what Trace calls "a butt killing piece of crapped out asphalt.... Now we're just Lake Street Extension. Not anything. Just here."[60] While it doesn't work very well for a play title, offering little insight and less attraction for an audience, it may function symbolically, categorizing the downward progress of the three characters and the country they inhabit falling from the lofty perch of the imperial ambitions they once claimed.

Here Blessing touches on themes of innocence, redemption, confession, and sin. The fact that the play consists of 13 scenes reinforces the sinister atmosphere. No one is innocent, but each seeks the innocence they might once have claimed although now have lost.

> FULLER: Leave him [Gregorio] alone. He's innocent.
> TRACE: The other night you know what some guy said to me? We were having sort of a—business meeting—and he said in Japan women pay doctors like a hundred thousand bucks to get their virginity put back. For their weddings. That's innocence, man. That's valuable stuff.[61]

Fuller has taken in a refugee and plans to go to El Salvador himself to help the victims of that war seemingly as an act of atonement. Most of us hope our errors, sins, mistakes allow for forgiveness and yet Blessing saddles Fuller with the seemingly unforgivable crime of child abuse. As Blessing said:

> Fuller has molested his own son over the course of many years, but having stopped that and turned over a new leaf, he now tries to live in a morally upright way—helping along the way a Central American refugee. Still he has to face the question of whether there's any real way he can atone for what he's done in the past.[62]

But going to El Salvador is also running away, leaving Trace and the house, the victim and scene of his crime, behind.[63] Complicating the situation, as a playwright ought, Blessing reveals that Fuller not only abused his son, he, himself, was abused by his father, making him both victim and victimizer. His allegorical description of that abuse in Scene 6 is perhaps the most moving part of the play:

> My father's hands.... I tried believing that his hands were different from each other. That one hand was bad and one was good. The right hand, the bad hand, would hit ... do the other things.... Then I tried believing my father's hands were separate from him.... I followed his voice into the deepest silence I ever knew.[64]

Ironies abound. Fuller cannot make a complete confession of his crime to his minister or to Trace, his victim, the only person who has the power to forgive him. And Trace wants blood:

> What would it take for me to forgive you—even a little bit? What would I need to hear you say? "Trace, please kill me for everything I did to you." Maybe.[65]

Oddly, Gregorio senses a kinship with Fuller: "I am a man like you"[66] and makes his own confession. He is not an "innocent" refugee. He joined the Salvadoran

Lake Street Extension: Fuller (Joe Sharkey, left) confronts Trace (Keith Brush), the son he abused as a child. Signature Theatre, New York City; 1992, photograph by Susan Johann.

army, collaborated with the CIA, participated in torture at interrogations, and was forced into killing peasants at El Mozote. "You think I could tell this to a good man?" asks Gregorio,[67] relieved that, in Fuller, he has found a man as guilty as himself to whom he can confess.

But when Fuller learns the truth about Gregorio he feels no solidarity in shared guilt and secretly sets the wheels in motion to have Gregorio arrested as a murderer. When they discover Fuller's treachery, Gregorio and Trace flee together. In the final scene, a Fuller monologue delivered ten years after the story we have seen, we learn that Trace has disappeared for all this time and that Gregorio was arrested and deported to El Salvador, where his body was found on the beach a year later with a bullet hole in the head. Things appear grim. But we can see positive signs. The Salvadoran fighting has stopped. The mass graves are being excavated at El Mozote. Fuller has confessed his sins to his pastor, and every week he looks for Trace. Maybe, maybe, truth, even redemption, can follow evil and mendacity.

Gabrielle S. Kaplan, in the *Chicago Reader*, wrote:

Drawing a parallel between the abuse a father inflicts on his son and the abuse a fascist government inflicts on its people, Blessing shows how the personal is political without ever becoming preachy. Fuller is the father who can't come to terms with the fact that he molested his son but is now a born-again Christian who wants to help the rebels in El Salvador: Blessing shows the hypocrisy and naïveté of Americans who see things in black and white. His portrayal of sexual abuse is fair and accurate, not judgmental: Fuller's imagistic monologue about his own father's hands reveals how the cycle is perpetuated.[68]

Anne Kelly-Saxenmeyer, in *Backstage*, called *Lake Street Extension* a "contemplative drama,"[69] and Julio Martinez, in *Variety*, described it as a "gripping collision of three misshapen lives."[70] But Mel Gussow, in the *New York Times*, gave the play a poor review, as he often did to various Blessings plays:

There are too many crosscurrents of deceit and revenge and too few glimpses into the psychology of the characters. The play is crushed under the weight of the plot, most of which happens offstage. Additional damage is inflicted by the character of the father ... who is presented as an altruist trying to forget, but not to atone for, the sins of his past.... The horrific events might find a parallel in Life, but taken in such cursory form they become unreal. At crucial points, the dialogue is unintentionally laughable, as in the father's crass response to his son's story of being raped as a child by the father's employer: "I could never let that happen to him by a stranger."[71]

However, Blessing's art reflected life, as read in the headlines of those times: "Father Molests Son," "Peasants Slaughtered in El Salvador," "Churches Open Sanctuaries to Central American Refugees." But his art gave those headlines substance and feeling for American audiences far from the front lines of these battles.

Patient A

Patient A, a ninety-minute one-act, a form in which Blessing often works, examines the complicated AIDS landscape, personal and political, of the 1990s in which 23-year-old, blonde, attractive college student Kimberly Bergalis, a self-professed virgin, contracted AIDS, not from sexual relations, drug use, or a blood transfusion, but from her gay dentist, Dr. David J. Acer, and died in 1991. Dr. Acer extracted two of Bergalis's molars in December 1987, a few months after he had been diagnosed with AIDS. She, along with five other of his patients, tested positive for the same strain of AIDS as their dentist and she won a $1 million dollar judgment against his estate after his death. Bergalis weighed just 47 pounds at her death in Fort Pierce, Florida, on December 8, 1991, and the inexorable, heartbreaking and very public decline of this once-vibrant young woman over just two years transfixed the nation.

In an open letter published in *People* magazine, Bergalis wrote:

I have lived to see my hair fall out, my body lose over 40 lbs., blisters on my sides.... Do you know what it's like to look at yourself in a full-length mirror before you shower—and you only see a skeleton?... Now I shower with a blanket over the mirror.[72]

Shortly before her death she testified before Congress, a frail wasted figure in a wheelchair, in favor of a bill, denounced by civil libertarians, to require mandatory AIDS testing of all health care workers and to bar those testing positive from performing invasive procedures. The bill, "The Kimberly Bergalis Patient and Health Care Providers Protection Act," co-sponsored by 26 Republican representatives and endorsed by leading homophobes Jesse Helms and Pat Buchanan, would also have allowed doctors to test their patients for the AIDS virus without their consent.

When Bergalis referred to herself as suffering from AIDS unfairly because "she hadn't done anything wrong," claiming to be a virgin and denying intravenous drug use, while simultaneously implying that other, equally ill victims had "done something wrong," she drew to her side right-wing politicians and conservative religious leaders who were quick to condemn the gay men and IV

Patient A: Kimberly Bergalis (Robin Morse) struggles with a diagnosis of AIDS and an early death; she is flanked by Lee (John de Vries, left, representing the play's author, Lee Blessing) and Matthew (Richard Bekin), a gay man suffering from AIDS. Signature Theatre, New York City; 1992, photograph by Susan Johann.

drug users who made up the vast majority of AIDS sufferers at the time.[73] This was a time when an AIDS diagnosis was tantamount to a death sentence, and many blamed the victims for their suffering. One commentator called Bergalis, "The Willie Horton of AIDS," recalling the fear-inducing Republican ads of that furloughed black rapist that were used so effectively to sink the Michael Dukakis presidential campaign of 1988.[74] As dramatic as it sounds, the metaphor doesn't work particularly well since now this white (not black) heterosexual woman had become the poster child for anti-gay activists to stigmatize people with the same disease as her.

The play is set against a backdrop of a worldwide epidemic. The numbers are staggering: 36,000,000 dead worldwide since 1981,[75] and 636,000 dead in the U.S. alone.[76] In the year of the play's 1993 premiere, there were 41,920 AIDS-related deaths in the U.S.[77] To write about a single death set against this carnage and to devote a play to a statistical anomaly (a nonsexually active heterosexual woman) like Bergalis seemed insensitive to some.

Making the play even more controversial, Blessing wrote it on paid commission from Kimberly's grieving parents; her mother, Anna, was a public health nurse and her father, George, served as finance director for the city of Fort Pierce, Florida. For the first time in writing a topical play, Blessing risked offending his usual liberal political sympathizers. AIDS activists and many of his fellow playwrights, gay themselves, feared Blessing would produce an antigay play and land on the wrong side of the culture wars. The *Village Voice* reported: "In the fall of '91, Larry Kramer [author of the play *The Normal Heart* and co-founder of the Gay Men's Health Crisis] told the *New York Times*, "If he [Blessing] writes something sympathetic [to Kimberly Bergalis] it will be flying in the face of what everyone in the theatre stands for."[78]

No wonder then that Blessing told me of the play: "It's a challenge to explore something so politicized" and that he sees it not as a political statement but as "an exploration of grief."[79]

First things first, though: what a great and unusual idea for a family to memorialize a child by commissioning a play about them. Certainly from the Renaissance onward, as the focus of art expanded from solely religious subjects to include human endeavors as well, wealthy patrons (the Medici of Florence come immediately to mind) had retained artists (Donatello, Botticelli, and Michelangelo) to include their own recognizable faces in frescoes and paintings destined, first, for churches and, later still, for private homes. Today, I suppose, anyone with sufficient funds can hire an artist to paint their portrait. But a play? And, with someone who enjoyed her own 15 minutes of fame, why not seek out the Lifetime Movie Network or *People* magazine to tell their daughter's story? Kimberly's father, George Bergalis, explained their thinking:

We wanted her story to be told and we weren't doing it for the money. We thought a playwright would have more freedom of expression to do what was in the best interest of Kimberly Bergalis and not be subject to the influencing factors of who's paying for what.[80]

Bergalis worried that a TV-movie or feature film "would be too commercial."[81] The Bergalis family retained Blessing on the advice of the family lawyer, Robert Montgomery, who had recently seen a production of *Eleemosynary*, Blessing's play about three strong-willed and misunderstood women (discussed in Chapter 2), and met the playwright at the Florida Stage in West Palm Beach, where his wife, Mary, served on the Board of Trustees.[82]

The first questions I asked [wrote Blessing] was what kind of play do Kim and her family want? When the answer came back, "Whatever play you write" I knew I could accept the commission.[83]

Guaranteed complete intellectual and authorial freedom, Blessing stressed the difference between being commissioned (as he had been commissioned to write plays several times in the past, and would be in the future, by theaters that specified neither subject nor content) and being retained (like a lawyer who is sometimes referred to as a "mouthpiece").

The Bergalis family gave Blessing the mandate, paid their money (the amount has never been revealed) and got out of his way, giving him complete freedom to write the story in whatever manner he chose. In fact, the family didn't see the script or the play until "they sat in the audience on opening night"[84] at its public premiere and only then pronounced themselves satisfied with the result.

To research the play, Blessing interviewed Kimberly and her parents and read her journal. He first met her in a hospital in April 1991 as she received a blood transfusion and a spinal tap. He admitted he was "so spooked he couldn't touch [her]." He later attended her funeral.[85] As he told one critic: "I've never been so personally involved with a subject and subject matter."[86] It took Blessing two years to research, write, and produce the play. He wrote:

The fact that my politics were not the same as the family's—nor the same as those of their strongest critics—left me with no idea whether anyone would respond favorably to the play. My hope all along had been somehow to raise the material above narrow and acrimonious debate over the public policy issues surrounding her case and create a portrait of a society struggling to do what's most humane in the face of an inhumane tragedy.[87]

And, for the first time, Blessing made himself a character in his own play seemingly to objectify his personal conflicts about the case. The style is reminiscent of *Eleemosynary* in employing numerous monologues and three characters: Kim, Lee (the middle-aged playwright), and a gay man, Matthew, who also suffers from AIDS. Like the main character in his play *Cobb*, two of the main characters here, Kim and Matthew, are already dead as the play begins. As Blessing did in real life, the playwright character we see onstage, the only living character, must negotiate the politics and emotions of the polar extremes of the controversial case. "I realized most people in the country were pretty much in between both sides of the issue," said Blessing. "Since that was the point of view I shared, I was a good candidate [both to write the play and to be a character therein]."[88] The play is his way of working out his own, and, perhaps, his country's, ambivalences and confusion regarding the subject of AIDS. Given that his own brother had died in a car crash at age 20, Blessing was no stranger to the trauma and unfairness of early death.

Blessing's approach in *Patient A* could be called postmodernist or poststructuralist. Unlike modernist theater, against which it reacts, postmodernist theater demonstrates the inability to represent Truth. Aristotle's 2,500-year-old definition of drama as "the imitation of an action," in his *Poetics*, becomes redefined as the *approximate* imitation of one of *several* possible actions. Truth becomes subjective, even unknowable; we see only individual truths and various possible realities. This drama then raises more questions than it supplies answers. In *Patient A* the audience is exposed to the multiple "truths" of Kim, Lee, and Matthew and must choose among them for its own understanding of the issues. Because truth is a chimera, the playwright seeks new ways of searching it out through multiple viewpoints, partial texts, and discordant experiences as the audience, often addressed directly, stitches together its own truth and becomes, in a sense, an actor in the play. Such a postmodernist play often becomes metatheatrical, making no effort to hide its artifice and self-consciously commenting upon the manufactured quality of its presentation. In such a play we can call forth dead characters who know they are dead, like Matthew and Kim, and insert "real" characters, like the playwright himself. Blessing chooses a postmodernist approach here to avoid taking sides, to appear nonjudgmental and to facilitate dealing with and understanding conflicting ideas.

However, in spite of not wishing to choose sides in the controversy, it can be argued that he stacks the deck from the beginning, titling the play for Bergalis, as Patient A (the CDC's designation for her to protect her anonymity as they investigated how she got AIDS), while juxtaposing a single well-known heterosexual victim against a fictional gay victim with no real personal story who must represent tens of thousands of men like himself, as well as numerous other characters within the play and then ending the play with the characters speaking the single name: "Bergalis."[89]

It's also difficult to write powerfully out of one's own unresolved inner conflict and ambivalence. Blessing sidesteps this issue by opening the play with that ambivalence demonstrated before the audience. The opening stage directions have the playwright character Lee instructing Kim to lie down on the stage "parallel to the audience line," while he explains

> LEE: if you have an actor lie feet first to the audience, then it's a tragedy. But if you have her life head first—
> KIM: Should I do that?
> LEE: No, no. If you have her lie head first, then it's a comedy.... The position itself preconditions us.
> KIM: But you've got me lying sideways. That's not anything, right? I mean not tragedy or comedy.... Why, I'm not neutral?
> LEE: ... I know you're not. But I am.[90]

The playwright's distance from the central conflict is reemphasized a bit later when the two dead characters reprove his opinion:

> MATTHEW: And who are you to judge?
> KIM: Yes, who are you?
> LEE: Nobody.[91]

Lee (this is the character's name and solidifies his role as a stand-in for the author of the same name) also weaves quotations from the Andrew Marvell poem, "The Nymph Complaining for the Death of Her Fawn," about the loss of innocence, throughout the play, although Kim struggles to understand how the poem relates to her. At Lee's urging she tells the story of her illness, diagnosis, and suffering. Lee interjects statistics on the AIDS epidemic and tosses various moral/political questions to Kim and Matthew. He is the ethically sensitive Everyman trying to reconcile personal pain and public policy.

Lee (in a true story about Blessing himself) raises his personal loss to illustrate the conundrum:

> My brother died when he was 20. Many years ago. It was a one-car accident. It was an old car, no seat belts. The kind of seat belts that would have saved his life were still years away, though the technology had been there for decades. We as a society were sacrificing maybe 10,000 people a year this way. It really wasn't a big enough number to change our public policy. He's been dead for over 25 years. And each year, on April 16th, though I don't plan too, I notice it's his birthday again. Someone dies every day, of something.[92]

It's a jarring summation: society (who *does* make public policy?) decides a certain number of seatbelt-less automobile deaths are acceptable but a single death, of a brother, can never be forgotten by his surviving sibling. We see the conundrum, but seemingly absent are anger or a call for political change. The mere presentation of an issue (what to do about AIDS transmission) featuring lots of talk and no action onstage seems devoid of human conflict, the very soul of drama.

The Bergalis family expressed satisfaction with the play, Kimberly's father, George Bergalis, saying: "He [Blessing] addresses the different sides of the issues without taking a strong position one way or the other and people have to decide for themselves."[93] Bergalis also saw the advantages of having his daughter's story told by an outsider:

> I think [spectators] should leave the play with a lot of deep thinking to do, a lot of soul searching to do, but I don't think anybody could leave the play being offended by it. If we had done the play ourselves we probably would have been more critical of people whose irresponsible conduct caused harm to Kim. We would have offended people.[94]

Reaction from the gay community was mixed. While *Patient A* was produced at the Freedom Stage, Washington, D.C.'s professional Gay and Lesbian Theatre, the *Washington Blade*, D.C.'s gay and lesbian newspaper, first threatened not to cover the production, later relented, and finally gave it a negative review.

Straight critics were a bit divided as well. William A. Henry III, writing for *Time*, said: "[Blessing's] appetite for moral complexity has never been more challenged and his incapacity for settling for mere indignation has never been more welcome than in *Patient A*."[95]

Also supportive was the usually dissenting Mel Gussow of the *New York Times*:

> In this play.... Mr. Blessing eventually makes an asset of his own equivocation. In indirect fashion, he manages to depict the full complexity of the Bergalis story. The audience comes to share the playwright's criticism of the cowardice that surrounded her, as she is taken up by the news media and health care officials and put aside partly because she is so atypical.[96]

However, J. Wynn Rousuck, theater critic for the *Baltimore Sun*, saw the play as more of an educational lesson than a drama:

> "Patient A" attempts to shed light in the darkness, though it does so in a fairly didactic manner.... "Patient A" is ultimately more debate than drama.... But the script's structure is obtrusive in and of itself. Blessing's approach admirably avoided turning Bergalis' story into yet another docudrama, but even AXIS' [AXIS Theatre] best efforts cannot keep it from becoming a soapbox, however noble.[97]

And Alvin Klein, Gussow's fellow critic at the *New York Times*, had this to say:

> Mr. Blessing's play, steeped in conscientiousness, is thinned by a lack of focus, a self-conscious attempt to be evenhanded, and little sense of a playwright's urgency.... Throughout, "Patient A" remains a play about a playwright searching for a way to write a play.... By the end, Mr. Blessing has not found the voice to theatricalize the tragedy of Kimberly Bergalis, or the resonance, or "something that's evocative".... "Only equivocal."[98]

As a then-topical story, *Patient A* certainly works to raise issues of public policy and demand answers of its audience in ways a newspaper cannot. It briefly contributed to the national dialogue, as contemporary theater occasionally can. However, from the date the play was commissioned to its first performance, the AIDS landscape shifted: new drugs and treatments meant that an HIV positive diagnosis was no longer a death sentence and "Kimberly's Bill" of mandatory HIV testing had been defeated in Congress, even as Kimberly Bergalis, herself, has now been, sadly, largely forgotten. As "an exploration of grief" it comes so heavily loaded with yesterday's politics and expositional, but now out of date, information that the humanity of the deceased is entombed in amber like a Cretaceous Age insect, beyond human feeling.

The Rights

For many years I kept notes I had taken or collected about *The Rights* in a computer file labeled "the unknown plays" since Blessing left the title off his own list of plays he had authored and because little about it could be found in production and it was never published. An early draft lies in a box at the Ransom Center at the University of Texas and I had looked through it on my two-week-long visits to these archives. As Blessing told one critic in 2001:

> I think I've written about 20 or 21 plays since that have been professionally produced. And that's been oh, 20 years. So it's been about one a year. Those are the plays I'll admit to, of course. There are others that I wouldn't let anyone see.[99]

Years later, he told me when I inquired about *The Rights*:

> *The Rights* (even though it was produced by the Ensemble Theatre of Cincinnati, 1994 [directed by his then-wife, Jeanne Blake]) was such a failed play that I put it in a drawer and then I lost the drawer.[100]

The plot certainly holds potential: when a planned reality television show about the illegitimate daughter of Prince Charles falls through, the producer travels home to his own screwy family living in a Frank Lloyd Wright house, outside New York City, and decides to put them on TV instead. The two-act play looked at the depths to which the U.S. public will sink for entertainment, especially if the story can be sold as "true." Chris Jones, in *Variety*, enjoyed the production he attended:

> For all its disconcerting inconsistencies and stylistic oddities, "The Rights" is ultimately quite a provocative and amusing piece of work.... This will probably remain a whimsical sidetrack within the growing Blessing canon.[101]

Critic Michael Kape, on radio station WABE-FM, liked it, too:

> *The Rights* is a high energy, high speed, wickedly funny exploration of just how Hollywood exploits the strange but true stories of humanity for upcoming movies of the week ... a truly wicked, blazingly funny look at [Reality TV].[102]

Blessing rewrote *The Rights* under the appropriate title *Rewrites*, which premiered in March 2001 in Chicago at the Dolphinback Theatre Co., a small non-equity venue, where the director, Ellen Larabee, was writing her PhD dissertation on Blessing's work, and was produced yet again, the following month, at Denison University, where Blessing was then teaching. Blessing seemed a bit surprised to see the play onstage again, telling the critic for the *Chicago Tribune*:

> If a theater puts on a play that hasn't been as successful as the others, I can always say, "How nice. They picked the slow child."[103]

Perhaps *The Rights*—or *Rewrites*—will someday escape its drawer and return to the stage.

Going to St. Ives

Blessing offers a funny story behind the writing of *Going to St. Ives*:

> [When he did *A Walk in the Woods*] A couple of actresses who were at the O'Neill in 1986 said, "You know you should write a play like that for women sometime." ... It interested me that they said that. Sometimes women (in terms of political plays) get shorted a little bit in terms of focus and roles. So, I said I would get on that, and eight years later I thought of an idea. And a mere two years after that, I actually came up with this play. Right on schedule.[104]

Going to St. Ives is a two-act two-hander, set in the present. Act 1 takes place in the eponymous St. Ives, a small town near Cambridge, England; Act 2 is laid in a central African nation. The play offers female characters only: Dr. Cora Gage, a Caucasian eye surgeon with a husband and a recently deceased son she refuses to discuss, and May N'Kame, an imperious African woman, the mother of a self-styled "emperor"; May suffers from acute closed-angle glaucoma and has traveled to England to undergo corrective surgery.

Emboldened by the prominence of her patient and against her scruples, Cora pleads with May to intervene with her son to win the release of four doctors condemned to hang in May's country. Cora argues that they acted honorably:

> CORA: Refusing to work in situations of torture, refusing to revive—
> MAY: Other traitors ...
> CORA: ...Thousands of people have been murdered. Thousands. And the world knows.
> MAY: But the world doesn't care.[105]

To intervene on their behalf, May wants a reward, to know about Cora's dead son, accidentally shot by teenage thugs, black like May as it turns out, as the family drove to a sports arena in L.A.

5. The Headline Plays 113

May says she will help the doctors if Cora does something for her. But, first, she asks:

> MAY: Tell me why you became a doctor...
> CORA: I love life. I love to discover life, to save it. I love to see it stay.
> MAY: I want you to help me kill my son.... If you want four doctors to live.... I want to poison him. I need your help.[106]

Unfortunately, modern Africa calls forth a host of possible tyrants we might imagine as May's son: despots like Charles Taylor in Liberia, Robert Mugabe in Zimbabwe, Siad Barre in Somalia, Mobutu Sesse Seko in Congo, and Muammar Gaddafi in Libya, most trained by their often equally bloodthirsty former colonial rulers, Britain or France. Most memorable of all, however, remains Idi Amin Dada, with his flair for the dramatic. Trained by the British, Amin came to power in Uganda in a military coup and created for himself the rank of Field Marshall. He killed opponents left and right, throwing some into rivers as food for the crocodiles, though we might remember him best for humiliating white diplomats, people not unlike Dr. Cora Gage herself, as we see them in 1970s photos bowing down to Amin or carrying him in a litter above their heads as Africans were once forced to carry their colonial overlords. May's son could be any one of them.

Now May asks for help in killing her own son from a doctor who believes she is responsible for her own son's murder and who, upon entering into her healing profession, swore a Hippocratic Oath, which includes the phrase: "I will utterly reject harm and mischief."

> CORA: I can't kill him. He's a human being.
> MAY: There you go again, making snap judgments.
> CORA: Someone—someday—will judge him in a court of law.
> MAY: After how many more are dead? He won't change. He'll kill until he's forced out. You could save many lives today... [107]

Going to St. Ives asks many questions rather blatantly: can it be ethical to kill one person to save many? Can mothers ethically kill their own offspring? Can a white doctor from a former colonial power intervene to change the course of a black nation's future? Are today's black tyrants merely the excellent students of their one-time white masters? For what are we responsible when unspeakable crimes take place a continent away? And, finally, can women who differ in their experience, skin color, politics, and nationality become friends?

Convinced by her new acquaintance of the necessity of taking action, Cora hands over the poison to May at the end of Act 1. As Act 2 begins, six months have passed. Cora flies to Africa to visit May who, having killed her son, is under sentence of death by the new regime. (Blessing spares us the exposition around the murder of the emperor and the rise of new but seemingly equally ruthless leaders, or how they caught May after she used what Cora prescribed as an undetectable poison.) May describes her recent trial as

> farcical. A parade of former servants, all bribed or terrified of prison.... I was convicted of killing people I never knew existed.[108]

Cora tries to convince May to flee to the airport with her in a car waiting outside under a government promise of safe passage. All May needs to do is sign a confession for the crimes she has already been convicted of committing. The government wants the confession, it being in Cora's words: "Another chance to vilify your son's regime."[109] May refuses to confess to crimes she did not commit. For her part, Cora's life has unraveled since her fateful decision to supply May with the poison. She has stopped practicing medicine, since she is no longer "unmurderous,"[110] and her husband is divorcing her for her actions. More than anything, Cora thinks she needs to rescue May to save her own collapsing life, even to entice her back to the security and comfort of her home in St. Ives, a suburban, and foreign, white world May rejects. But May, feeling that in giving birth to a monster she herself shares in his crimes, is ready to pay the ultimate penalty for her "crime." At the end she suggests Cora not return to England and the safety, boredom, and predictability of St. Ives, but that she relocate instead to … Africa.

> MAY: Everyone wants a doctor here, you know. You could save a great many lives....
> It would give you peace.
> CORA: It would serve you right.[111]

The play ends in silent action, stage directions:

> (*May smiles quietly and sips her tea, Cora stares at her a moment then sips her tea as well. They stare across the garden. Unconsciously their cups rise and fall in unison.*)[112]

In *Going to St. Ives*, as in most of his plays, Blessing violates the cardinal rule of writing fiction: he consistently tells rather than shows. We never see the emperor. We never see an atrocity onstage. All we ever see are the two characters, May and Cora, talking. The height of their action is lifting a cup of tea. Ignoring Aristotle, who defined a drama as the imitation of an action, Blessing gives us talk *about* the action. It works not only because the talk is fresh and fast-paced, giving actors a chance to inhabit intriguing characters, and, here, May catches our eyes with her African dress and our ears with her complex wordplay and teasing and sometimes insidious manner, but with the playwright's ideas.

For all the questions Blessing slings about the stage the one the audience is finally left to grapple with describes the space most of us fill in this world; the place of not-so-innocent bystanders. Tyrants rise and fall in Uganda,

5. The Headline Plays

Liberia, and Zimbabwe. Civil wars rage in Somalia, Congo, and Sudan. Genocide takes literally millions of lives in Rwanda, Darfur, and the Central African Republic. And we, in the words of Cora's newly awakened conscience, ignore it all:

> I see my neighbors as they really are now: moving around in a kind of immunized dream—a great communal coma. Africa means nothing to them.... You pick up a newspaper–"More horrors from the third world? Next page." Then I go home from shopping among these strangers I've known for years—all utter strangers now. And I think, "I should ring someone." And then I think, "But who?"[113]

We see Cora and May make their choices with their eyes wide open. After the play *our* eyes are open. What choices shall we make? Blessing asks.

Critics get so many things wrong, it seems. Consider Jeffrey Borak's review in the *Berkshire Eagle*:

> Lee Blessing's dense, oppressively cluttered play ... ultimately ... buckles under the weight of its formidable verbiage and polemics, leaving us, in the end, with two highly skilled actresses in search of a play.[114]

Or Charles Isherwood in the *New York Times*:

> Mr. Blessing is a fluid, articulate writer with a knack for domesticating seemingly unruly subject matter. In "Going to St. Ives," he wraps the knotty moral issues at hand in a pleasingly neat, dramatic package.... Mr. Blessing doesn't go in for the impassioned polemics, and fearless dramatic sprawl.... But this level head is not exclusively an asset. The play's structural and thematic niceties, the careful manner in which Mr. Blessing sets up unexpected correspondences between the lives of his two disparate characters, for instance, are intellectually pleasing, but they also impart a hollow, manufactured quality.[115]

Yet another critic, David Finkle, in *TheatreMania*, somehow missed most of the play's salient details, perhaps when he was nodding:

> The dilemma(s) faced by Gage and N'Kame are so challenging that audiences can't avoid becoming absorbed by them. Moreover, the doleful conclusion that Blessing draws about their prospects is honest; he doesn't suggest a bright future for anyone committing questionable acts, even for what might appear to be the right reasons, and no one watching the ambiguous outcome is likely to disagree. However, the two noble ladies do an awful lot of talking about what to do next. In the second act, particularly, their somber têtes-à-têtes can begin to set patrons' heads nodding. Also, unless I missed N'Kame's explanation, at no time is the reason why she's ostensibly doomed made clear. Was the undetectable poison detected after all, or does the subsequent regime simply consider her a partner in her son's atrocities?

He gets it partly right in the end:

> Though N'Kame declares Blue Willow [the china pattern of the tea set in Cora's home] "synthetic trash, designed to charm ignorant, middle-class customers," Lee Blessing's play isn't. It's strong tea for the intellectually equipped.[116]

Matthew Murray, on the "Talkin' Broadway" website, must have been nodding as well when he noted:

> There's a funny, engrossing, and topical play currently being presented by Primary Stages.... Unfortunately, it's only the first act of Lee Blessing's latest endeavor, *Going to St. Ives*. After intermission, the play gets hopelessly lost on its journey, but until then, it's quite a memorable trip.... Blessing deftly crafts an hour of fine drama.... But the second act ... dampens the first act's impact with its thoroughly conventional and democratic treatment of the consequences of Cora's actions. Everything fresh in the first act here seems unduly stale and irredeemably familiar.... The first act seems so complete a story in itself that when a colleague asked me at intermission why the play even had a second act, I had no answer to give him.[117]

At least Larry Murray, on the "Berkshire on Stage and Screen" website, hit the target succinctly:

> While *Going to St. Ives* is not Lee Blessing's most famous work ... it is nevertheless one of his most thought provoking.[118]

The play takes its title from a riddle it quotes:

> As I was going to Saint Ives,
> I crossed the path of seven wives.
> Every wife had seven sacks,
> Every sack had seven cats,
> Every cat had seven kittens,
> Kittens, cats, sacks, wives,
> How many were going to Saint Ives?[119]

Cora lives and practices in St. Ives, a real town in Cornwall, of course. But the title signifies much more. Only one person was going to St. Ives in the riddle. All the wives, cats and sacks were passed coming from the town. Why were they leaving? What were they fleeing? May tells us: "I used to imagine I was the one going to St. Ives—the only one with courage enough to encounter whatever monstrosity dwelt there."[120]

Have we, asks Blessing, the courage to go where monsters, and monstrous choices, dwell?

Chesapeake

In 1999, Vassar College, in upstate New York, premiered Blessing's *Chesapeake*, unique as his only one-character full-length play, an extended monologue in two acts, in which a single actor tackles multiple characters, including a dog. It also ranks as one of his most hilarious political satires.

The target is anti-art politicians and their opposition to the National Endowment for the Arts (NEA), an independent body of the U.S. government, created in 1965, which offers support and funding for artists, museums, etc. President Ronald Reagan attempted to abolish the agency as early as 1981 and it came under attack again in the late 1990s from conservative, Republican, and fundamentalist Christian groups. They targeted particularly lurid examples of what they considered blasphemous or pornographic art, like Andres Serrano's "Piss Christ," the homoerotic photographs of Robert Maplethorpe, and performance artists Karen Finley, Tim Miller, John Fleck, and Holly Hughes, who became known as the "NEA 4," after their grants were vetoed on the basis of subject matter rather than artistic merit. The "NEA 4" won their case before the Supreme Court in 1993. As a consequence, the NEA, bowing to Congressional pressure, ceased funding individual artists. Blessing himself had won NEA grants in 1985 and 1987, so he knew whereof he wrote.

However, NEA support for "controversial" projects continued as a campaign issue with the opposition led by Republican senators James "Strom" Thurmond, South Carolina, and Jesse Helms, North Carolina. Blessing's antagonist in *Chesapeake*, Senator Therm Pooley, is widely believed to be based on Strom Thurmond. In the play, Pooley experiences a sort of conversion experience over his own divided inner feelings in ways that are ironically prescient of a secret revealed about Senator Thurmond following his death in 2003, four years after *Chesapeake* premiered. This committed segregationist had voted against all civil rights legislation and actually ran for president in 1948 on a states' rights platform opposed to civil rights. But six months after his death we learned that, at the age of 22, he had fathered a mixed-race daughter with his family's 16-year-old black maid. The woman remained unacknowledged for over 70 years, although Thurmond contributed to her education and support and occasionally visited with her through the years. This hypocritical gap between personal life and political expediency, the inner war of strongly held but contradictory beliefs, is a part of *Chesapeake* as well.

But the story also includes themes of defending the value of art, personal growth, and forgiveness. Many "points of attack" exist for a playwright to tell such a tale and Blessing chose perhaps the oddest and most inventive: a performance artist named Kerr kidnaps Senator Pooley's dog, a Chesapeake Bay Retriever, accidentally kills himself and the dog, finds himself reincarnated as a sibling of his canine victim and converts Pooley to his cause on the floor of the Senate.

Did I mention it's a comedy?

Kerr flees the South as a young man to become a performance artist in New York City, aping the "Futurists" of a hundred years before who assaulted their audience in hopes of generating an emotional reaction, any reaction. "Art," he tells us, "is an act of will.... A form of domination.... Art was there to confront all smugness and unoriginality in society, to upset everybody's applecart."[121]

Kerr develops a signature act. Using a grant from the NEA, he recites the Biblical "Song of Songs," filled with erotic imagery, while inviting the audience to remove his clothing. He ends his act, nude onstage: "It was not Las Vegas, or some Times Square peep show, it was art," he avers.[122] Back home, Therm Pooley, running for the Senate, seizes on Kerr as a "purveyor of filth disguised as art,"[123] and rides the public's upended applecart all the way to the United States Senate. Determined to make his revenge itself an act of art, Kerr dognaps Senator Pooley's Chesapeake Bay Retriever, Lord Ratliff of Luckymore, to transfer the dog's loyalty from Pooley to himself. However, through hilarious misadventure, both man and dog drown.

Kerr's death ends Act 1 but not the play, for in Act 2 he returns as a Chesapeake Bay Retriever himself. "I was dead," says Kerr, "—and I was a dog.... So this was my hell. To be my enemy's dog... —that's not hell. I was in a position to cause him the kind of pain and terror a mere artist could only imagine!"[124]

But Kerr's dreams of revenge run up against two elemental forces: a dog's own thousand-year-old inbred love for its master and a human being's ability to forgive. In the Pooley home, doggy Kerr discovers both the hypocrisies of his moralistic antagonist who, trapped in both a loveless marriage and an equally loveless affair, seems downright pitiable even as he treats his dog with great tenderness. "I felt something," Kerr tells us, "that seared me to my core. I felt sorry for Therm Pooley."[125]

Manipulating the senator's computer keyboard with his ungainly paws, Kerr pecks out his message, which Pooley takes as a Christian miracle: "God wants federal support for the arts."[126] More craziness ensues. Pooley speaks in favor of arts funding on the Senate Floor. In response, the majority leader keels over from a heart attack. Mistress and wife band together to kill Pooley. Doggy Kerr saves the senator and, at the end of this lengthy "shaggy dog story," filled with connected but unlikely events, twists, turns, and cliffhangers, senator and dog reunite, rescuing high culture and reinforcing the old saw that a dog really is man's best friend.

The critics, by and large, laughed. Chris Jones, in the *Chicago Tribune*, wrote:

> Lee Blessing's very amusing little play *Chesapeake*.... There are plenty of other laughs in this ironic show—which surely is Blessing's funniest piece of work to date. *Chesapeake* is, for sure, a little long and it sags some in the middle of the second act, when Kerr finds himself in very strange circumstances. It would be better, for sure, if the amusements were contained in a single act.... But to Blessing's great credit, *Chesapeake* can be enjoyed by people who don't give a darn about whether or not the NEA gets re-authorized or whether those feisty senators from the Carolinas knew whereof they spoke.[127]

Max Fischer, in the *Milwaukee Journal Sentinel*, wrote that the play is

> as topical today as it was when it debuted in 1999 ... numerous twists in the increasingly bizarre and loose-limbed second act—which caps a two-hours-plus show that could easily lose a third without missing a beat.
>
> The core worth preserving involves a tried and true Blessing theme: whether people who seemingly share nothing [in common] might somehow learn to communicate.... *Chesapeake* reminds us that if we actually want to move ahead, we must walk there together—even if it takes a dog to first save us from ourselves and point the way forward.[128]

Tim Treanor, in *DC Theatre Scene*, added:

> "Chesapeake" becomes an exercise in the storyteller's art, which is to say that it doesn't sound like "art" at all, but like something out of real life—some fantastic story that a good friend tells you over a beer or two at the local bar. You are riveted by the story despite its implausible facts because of the insight it gives into the human spirit. With each line, the story sinks deeper into shaggy-dog absurdity; and with each line the human and emotional truth becomes clearer, like the lucid water in the middle of the Chesapeake Bay.... The ultimate benefit of art is that it helps us understand how to be a human. The additional benefit that "Chesapeake" gives us is that it helps us to understand why the struggle to be human is worthwhile.[129]

34th and Dyer

During September 9–11, 2002, more than 150 theater artists gathered at Town Hall, an historic performance space dating from 1921 in midtown Manhattan which seats approximately 1,500 people, to commemorate the first anniversary of the 9/11 attacks on New York and Washington, D.C. On the agenda were three days of performances, skits, and songs in a unique benefit performance for the New York Children's Foundation, for children directly affected by 9/11. Borrowing a quote from Shakespeare's *The Tempest*, organizers called it "Brave New World." Producer-writer J. Dakota Powell helped put the program together because:

> I lost friends and a relative at the World Trade Center that day. And I lived only ten minutes away from the World Trade Center. I felt powerless ... that terrorism had changed our lives, even if we didn't realize it had. I also felt that there had to be a way for the theatre community to respond to the events. I was—and am—convinced that theatre could really reflect what was in our psyches. My mission was to unite artists in this effort.[130]

Participating actors included Ethan Hawke, Amanda Peet, Edie Falco, Stanley Tucci, Julianna Margulies, Fisher Stevens, Cynthia Nixon, Marisa Tomei, John Turturro, Liev Schreiber, Sam Waterston, and Amy Irving. Playwrights and composers involved included Christopher Durang, John Guare, Beth Henley, Tina Howe, David Henry Hwang, Arthur Kopit, Alan Menken,

David Rabe, Alfred Uhry, Lanford Wilson, Stephen Sondheim ... and Lee Blessing.[131]

Blessing's play *34th and Dyer*, acted by Cynthia Nixon (of *Sex and the City* fame) and by Keith Nobbs (stage, television, and film actor perhaps best known for his portrayal of Joey Ice Cream in the TV series *The Black Donnellys*) appeared on September 11, 2002, the first anniversary of the attacks on New York. As Nixon explained her involvement: "They talked to me. They mentioned some of the playwrights involved and I said, 'Great I would love to be part of it.'"[132] Although I was unable to obtain a copy of this unpublished short play, critic Robert Simonson, in *Playbill*, tells us:

> The play takes place on the street corner named in the title, where a freshly recruited (read: post–Sept. 11 [and recruited perhaps to replace someone killed in the attack]) police officer is trying to keep an eye out for suspicious characters. He is distracted, however, by the chatter of a teacher on her way to work. The talk begins in a friendly, even flirty, manner but it soon becomes clear that the woman has responded to the terrorist attack in a sad and frightening way.[133]

She imagines how she would avenge the city by killing Osama Bin Laden:

> And I'll squeeze the trigger oh so slowly and half his head will smash against the wall. A whole section of his skull with that matted hair and blood and brain. The innocent brain but not so innocent as mine. And his body will tremble for a moment and then flop around like someone in a religious ecstasy and then he will stop and he will be dead.[134]

We have all become savages.

Robert Dominguez, in the *New York Daily News*, called the play "witty."[135] Bruce Weber, in the *New York Times*, credited it with "raising questions about the nature and delusion of innocence" and then commented on the theatrical marathon, its goals and challenges:

> My reservations about certain works and performers notwithstanding, there was something valiant going on. All of the artists taking part in "Brave New World" are aware, I suspect, that the events of a year ago remain too resonant and complex for clarity, but they attempted it anyway because all of us ache for it so badly. We may feel from time to time that we indulge our artists too much, but we also ask a great deal. In this case, they really stuck their necks out on our behalf.[136]

Whores

With *Whores*, Blessing inserted himself into the struggle for justice around a particularly vicious political crime, the murder of three North American Catholic nuns, Ita Ford, Dorothy Kazel, Maura Clarke, and one social worker, Jean Donovan, who were beaten, raped, and murdered in San Salvador on December 2, 1980, by five members of the National Guard of El Salvador, which the United States had armed and trained.

5. The Headline Plays 121

Whores: General Casanova (Shawn Elliot) cavorts with two prostitutes (Catherine Curtin, left, and Maryann Urbano), who remind him of the nuns his troops murdered in El Salvador. Contemporary American Theater Festival, Shepherd University, Shepherdstown, West Virginia; 2003, photograph by Stephanie K. Patterson; courtesy of Contemporary American Theater Festival.

As retired General Raoul asks in *Whores*:

> Have you ever pulled a body out of wet clay? Have you ever pulled four corpses out of a common grave?
> They were all shot in the back of the head. One had her face blown off.
> ANGELIQUE: I remember that! That was a movie of the week when I was in college. I cried so hard. It made me want to be a nun.
> RAOUL: Yes, it was a good movie of the week. All part of the system, I thought. All part of the crying and forgetting. We had graves of wet clay, you have movies of the week. They help us cry, say too bad and *move on*. Why aren't we moving on?![137]

The murders, combined with the assassination of Archbishop Oscar Arnulfo Romero (March 24, 1980), the murder of six Jesuit scholar/priests, their housekeeper and her daughter (November 16, 1989) on their college campus in the capital, as well as the massacre of 800 civilians in the countryside by the Salvadoran Army at El Mozote on December 11, 1981 (a key event in Blessing's earlier play *Lake Street Extension*, 1992) eventually turned U.S. public opinion against the war and led to a peace agreement between the Salvadoran government, supported by the U.S. under President Reagan, and the guerrillas of the Farabundo Marti National Liberation Front in 1992.

The war ended, but a search for justice continued. The five soldiers convicted in the murders of the nuns claimed their orders came from higher up, and government files, declassified after the fighting, backed up their claims. Oddly enough, the two government officials, both generals and former ministers of defense, Jose Guillermo Garcia and Eugenio Vides Casanova, had retired to Florida where relatives of the murdered brought suit against them under the Torture Victim Protection Act. In the year 2000 the generals finally faced their accusers in a West Palm Beach court room. Blessing read the trial transcripts and got angry.

Whores fits right into this real-life tale of justice delayed and, finally, justice served. But why that title? Might one general's name, Casanova, have given Blessing the idea for his play's scenes revolving around the shooting of a porn movie? Or could the larger idea—realized in *Lake Street Extension*—that Uncle Sam acts like a child molester in his 200-year-long maltreatment of his "little brown brothers" in Latin America (56 U.S. coups, invasions, interventions, police actions, etc., since 1890),[138] make him think someone was screwing someone else? Or was it the simple horror of the event, that women who had put aside their own sexuality to serve their church should face the ultimate indignity of being sexually violated before being murdered?

As Blessing told one critic:

> One of the biggest hurdles I faced in dealing with this material is the great wall of denial in this society concerning the obscenity of violence. Violence has for so long and so effectively been sold as a commodity in the culture that there is almost no violent act that can fully evoke revulsion in modern audiences. I chose instead to use sexuality as the shock force in this play. It all takes place in a man's mind [as in *Cobb*], after all. Men are supposed to think of sex every seven seconds.... We are not inured to viewing these sorts of things as members of a theatre audience. Sexual elements still have the power to frighten, disgust, and outrage us.[139]

Whores unwinds as a pinball fantasy, complete with flashing lights and pulsating music, in the general's mind as he sits in Florida, mentally entertaining four whores each a decade older than the other. The opening no doubt shocked some in the audience as Miou-Miou, dressed in a nun's habit, approaches Raoul:

> MIOU-MIOU: Do I arouse you?
> RAOUL: Of course you do.
> MIOU-MIOU: That's good, because we're a service order—[140]

They then simulate sex on stage,[141] followed by a blackout.

The whores are alternately lawyers, TV producers, dance instructors, and those four murdered nuns. Lights onstage quickly go up and down between short scenes and the effect for the audience is of a collage or a mind's microbursts of memories ... or a nightmare. We jump back in time and space between the past and present, between Florida and El Salvador, where the whores pluck dead chickens while the voice of the martyred, and recently beatified, Archbishop Romero is heard on the radio.[142]

Blessing always adds humor to the most serious subjects as when the general introduces himself: "My full name is Raoul Raoul. General Raoul Raoul Raoul Raoul ... de Raoul. In Central America we have long names."[143] And defending himself from charges of fascism he offers in his defense: "We were not fascists! We never got one train to run on time!"[144] Another running gag has each character unable to remember their country of origin and the name "El Salvador" never passes their lips or appears in the script. With this omission Blessing reminds us of the U.S. syndrome of recurring political amnesia, as we forget our history of interventions and then wonder why those in Iran (our support for the tyrannical Shah Pahlavi and the CIA overthrow of Premier Mohammad Mosaddeg), and Cuba (numerous invasions and occupations by U.S. troops, 1898–1959), and Santo Domingo (the U.S. invasion of 1965 or the occupation of 1916–1924), and Chile (CIA coup of 1973 and the brutal Pinochet dictatorship) and, etc., and, etc., harbor feelings against us to this day.

Of course, Raoul sees it differently: the U.S. as an inconstant ally (bemoaning the loss of aid following the murders of the nuns):

> Your FBI, how I want it. Your CIA—I could make love to it. Not that you don't share. You give us secret advisors, teach us how to interrogate prisoners, their wives, their children—how to keep them barely alive, in a state worse than death, in cells too small to *sit*, feeling cockroaches run up and down their bodies all night. You bring us to the very brink of full control, and then ... *then* you deny you ever touched us and *take away our helicopters!* Why? Why do you undo all our good work? No wonder we're bitter. No wonder our soldiers lash out. You never let us *finish the job.*[145]

Or, as Raoul later tells the audience, in perhaps his best line: "You sent us rifles and nuns. You are the least consistent people on the face of the earth."[146] Like Bush at the Hague in *When We Go Upon the Sea*, Raoul is alternately defiant and pleading: "They can't convict me.... Because Ronald Reagan said it was all right."[147]

> RAOUL (addresses audience): You don't prejudge me. How can you? We're on the same side. World democracy is a team effort, right? And you own the team. We don't complain. On the contrary, we spend our lives reading the fine print of your foreign policy. We read between the lines, too. "Lift up the world's poor," you say. But we know you're not serious. There are far too many of them. "Manage the poor." That's what you mean. "Keep them from rising up, from moving around— from moving to Florida." And we do. We keep them poor, we keep them ignorant, we keep them *off your back.*[148]

For the audience is Raoul's jury; America must judge itself.

In "real life," Generals Casanova and Garcia faced jurors not for killing the nuns or even for ordering their murders but with responsibility for those crimes under the doctrine of "command responsibility" which holds that, as commanders, they should have known and stopped abuses by troops under them. Since they tolerated those abuses and failed to punish offenders, they also could be held accountable for their crimes. But, in 2000, a Florida jury refused to hold them accountable. The families filed an appeal and won a verdict against the generals in the amount of $54 million. Another court overthrew this judgment on appeal in 2005. Blessing began writing *Whores* in 2001 and settled on a final script in 2004. But the story did not end there and has not ended yet.

I see *Whores* as an agit-prop (agitation and propaganda) play on the order of the Federal Theatre Project, or a Brechtian "learning play" or an Augusto Boal "headline" play, each written to illustrate and correct a social problem. In *Whores* we get an angry Blessing, pissed off at murderers who go free, and the society—his society, our society—which countenances their crimes. The whore, Josette, describes the crimes under examination in unforgettable and heartrending language:

> You beat four women, strip them, rape them—how can you be sure what anyone said? Just a few more groans and cries, soaked up by the night. The sergeant leaves, drives off to make a call. When he comes back you tie them up, put a gun to the back of their heads, one after another, and pull the trigger. One. Two. Three. Four. Blood flies everywhere, but it's the jungle, so nothing gets dirty. The rain will wash it off the leaves. Scores of tiny animals will lick it up and be nourished. Ants will clean it from their feelers, accepting the protein as one more gift from a universe of mystery and miracles.[149]

Ita Ford, Dorothy Kazel, Maura Clarke, and Jean Donovan committed their lives to improve the lot of their brothers and sisters wherever they suffered in the United States, Nicaragua, and El Salvador. They committed no crimes, harmed no person, and obviously did not deserve their horrendous fates. General Raoul, on the other hand, is a different kind of Catholic, and elicits no sympathy. He tells us:

> I would remind you, Mary, Mother of God, that whatever sins I may commit, I fully intend to make a deathbed act of contrition that allows me to crawl into your lap in Heaven, right next to the Baby Jesus. And I warn you, I *will* fight for the best teat.[150]

(The villain's concern for the afterlife and the author's search for a sense of justice, often in juxtaposition to religious beliefs, arises again for Blessing when he considers the swindler Bernie Madoff in his later play *A Users Guide to Hell*, discussed in Chapter 9.)

When Blessing finished *Whores*, Raoul (General Casanova) felt confident of vindication, telling Carmencita:

5. The Headline Plays 125

If they convict me, what are they going to do? Prosecute General Westmoreland or Lieutenant Calley [My Lai massacre commander]? What happens when some other country tries an American under these same laws for murdering dirty, flea-bitten natives in a part of the world you wouldn't even piss on? International law is a joke. It's simply war in a courtroom. Those with the most power win.[151]

As *Whores* closes, Raoul celebrates his court victory, telling the audience, as he engages in that most American pastime of mowing the lawn:

Finally I am one of you! Finally I am as innocent as you are! Thank you, neighbor! I have passed all obstacles! I have worked a miracle!.... I am living proof the system works!.... There's an orderly lawn at the end of death's road![152]

Whores made people angry, as it aimed to. It angered some for its burlesque of Catholicism (though Blessing leavened in Islam, Hinduism, and Judaism, as well in *A User's Guide to Hell Featuring Bernard Madoff*). The Catholic League opined in its journal *Catalyst*:

While mainly an anti–American satire, *Whores* is also intentionally offensive to Catholics.... It would be instructive to interview the people who are attracted to this kind of play. We have a hunch: none would admit to being a bigot and all would consider themselves tolerant. Par for the course.[153]

Years earlier, some Protestants raised much the same objections about Blessing's play *Independence* (also, perhaps not coincidentally, featuring four female characters):

The play contained profanity, took God's name in vain, blasphemed the name of Jesus, presented sexual promiscuity, premarital sex, adultery, and homosexuality, conservative Christians complained in an ad in the Asheville [NC] *Citizen-Times*."[154]

Robert Daniels, writing in *Variety*, also objected on grounds of taste:

Though *Whores* is advertised as a black comedy, the audience at the performance reviewed sat in stony silence with wide-eyed disbelief at the blatant barrage of irreverent humor. While political injustice deserves to be recognized, it is not well served by such abstract, sloppy satire ... such a blatant display of tastelessness on the boards.[155]

Critics were right to be outraged. Audiences were equally right to be outraged. The playwright wrote because *he* was outraged as well ... at our government's support for terror and murder, at the deaths of four gentle women, at the ease with which bloody-handed generals found comfort in Florida retirement, and every fact of the case Blessing described, every ribald story he included, every satiric thrust at government and religion aimed to outrage reader and audience and move them to action. Surprisingly, Blessing gathered all his information, ideas, and outrage from his imagination and research rather than from firsthand experience. As he told me: "I've never been to anywhere in Latin America except Cancun, Mexico, one Christmas."[156]

Raoul (I mean, General Casanova) did not, in fact, spend his golden years in peace. Though court verdicts of human rights abuses were overturned by appeal in 2005, the appeals court studied new evidence and then overturned their own earlier opinion, reinstating the civil penalties. General Casanova forfeited over $300,000 of his own money. With a change in administrations in Washington, D.C., the Department of Homeland Security initiated deportation proceedings against both Generals Casanova and Garcia in 2009. In 2013, a federal court ordered both generals deported to El Salvador to stand trial. Judge Horn, deciding the case, minced no words in his decision:

> "These atrocities formed part of General García's deliberate military policy as minister of defense." He added that the general "fostered, and allowed to thrive, an institutional atmosphere in which the Salvadoran armed forces preyed upon defenseless civilians under the guise of fighting a war against communist subversives."[157]

The case continued its path through the courts. On March 11, 2015, The Board of Immigration Appeals ruled, according to the story in the *New York Times*, that General Casanova "can be deported from the United States because he participated in or concealed torture and murder by his troops" and that General Casanova "had a direct role in the abuse and killings of civilians because of his 'command responsibility' as the top military officer." He became the highest ranking official prosecuted. "Among other crimes, the board found that General Vides [Casanova] was directly involved in covering up the role of National Guard troops under his command in the rape and murder of four American churchwomen in December 1980."[158]

General Casanova's conviction came in spite of his testimony that during his term as commander, he was "consistently and uniformly led to believe that his conduct was consistent with the official policy" of Washington.[159]

When I emailed Blessing a link to this *New York Times* story, he responded: "Love seeing this!"[160] The next month we saw what had once seemed unthinkable: on April 8, 2015, the United States Government, after a 16-year legal battle waged by the families of his victims, deported General Casanova to his native El Salvador. There, the former defense minister may face criminal charges.[161] Once again I emailed the *New York Times* link to Blessing and he wrote back: "Thanks. It's a red-letter day."[162]

I concur with the judgment of Bob Rendell in "Talkin' Broadway":

> Lee Blessing's *Whores* is an exceptionally provocative and promising new play. It is unusually theatrical and ribald for a play which engages the mind with strong political and social commentary.... A superior work that can be highly recommended.[163]

Wood for the Fire

The Tricycle Theatre in London mounted three continuous days of plays about the U.S./U.K. war against the Taliban in Afghanistan at their theater in London, April 17–19, 2009, attracting great critical and public attention and snagging an Olivier nomination for all involved. Tricycle commissioned original one-act plays from playwrights in both countries and assigned them to specific eras in Afghan history to cover the Western colonial period 1842–2010. Tricycle had previously done similar theatrical/political work concerning the troubles in Northern Ireland and the U.S. prison at Guantanamo, among other subjects.

In summer 2010, Tricycle took the series of short plays on tour to the United States, performing at the Shakespeare Theatre in Washington, the Berkeley Rep, the Guthrie in Minneapolis, and the Public Theatre in New York. When American author J. T. Rogers withdrew his one-act play from the London revival and the U.S. tour to turn it into a full-length play, Tricycle commissioned a new play from Lee Blessing, *Wood for the Fire*, which was included in the revival and tour and the published anthology of 13 plays, under the title *The Great Game: Afghanistan*.

In February 2011, the U.S. Defense Department, led by the Joint Chiefs of Staff (with private funding from the Bob Woodruff Foundation and the British Council), presented a special two-day Washington, D.C., performance of *The Great Game: Afghanistan* free to military officers and veterans as an educational experience, a "primer on Afghanistan for serving soldiers, veterans and politicians,"[164] a unique example of theatrical and military cooperation. One U.S. soldier, about to be deployed to Afghanistan, said the play cycle "'offered a personal connection' to the information he has been studying" while a British naval officer felt the plays get "across how difficult it is to make progress there [in Afghanistan]."[165]

This collection of plays, formerly onstage and now in book form, constitutes more a political event than dramatic literature. The short one-acts are didactic and filled with historical information based more on exposition than character development or plot twists. Several are little more than dramatized lectures. The repeated theme is the mad violence and wastefulness of foreign intervention in a land the Great Powers (successively Britain, Russia, the Soviet Union, and the U.S.) never understood or appreciated. The "Great Game" of the title, introduced into literature by Rudyard Kipling in his novel *Kim*, refers to the historical British/Russian rivalry to control Central Asia, and so, the land approaches to India, the greatest jewel of the British Empire. As a piece of anti-war theater, in fact, as an anti-war statement, *The Great Game:*

Afghanistan leaves an audience feeling that their governments have, for centuries, futilely sacrificed blood and treasure for naught in Afghanistan.

As Blessing told me:

> What I love about this cycle is that each playwright could work quite independently of the others. Nick had pointed me to a wonderful source, a book called *Ghost Wars: The Secret History of the CIA, Afghanistan, and bin Laden, from the Soviet Invasion to September 10, 2001* by Steve Coll, and most of the background information I needed could be found there. But Nick [Nick Kent, artistic director for the Tricycle] emphasized that he wanted each of the playwrights to write a play first and foremost, in whatever style we wished, and not a mundane history lesson. So there's a great variety of approaches in the plays, and the overall effect is more one of feeling a century and a half of tremendously important history rather than reading a report on it. The cycle does what I think theater ought to do to an audience vis-à-vis a significant political issue. It forces us to think and feel about it in more complex ways than we have before.[166]

Blessing's contribution, *Wood for the Fire*, follows Owens, the CIA station chief in Islamabad, Pakistan, as he negotiates with the commander of the ISI (Pakistan's Inter-Services Intelligence Agency) to pay a personal visit to the front lines of the Afghan insurgency against the Russian occupation and to meet firsthand the mujahedin fighters the U.S. is covertly supplying with weapons. General Akhtar, the ISI Chief, wants to keep Owens out of the loop so that all of the CIA money and weapons are funneled through, and controlled by, the Pakistani government, which has its own agenda in Afghanistan and in arming to oppose its traditional enemy, India, which, inconveniently, happens to be a U.S. ally.

In reality, the head of the ISI during this time was a General Akhtar Abdur Rahman, a close confidante of the Pakistani president Zia ul Haq, who came to power through a coup d'état. The two men died together, along with the U.S. ambassador to Pakistan and 30 others, in a suspicious plane crash in August 1988.

Owens finds himself "hoodwinked"[167] by Akhtar when he is taken to a fake guerrilla camp. Owens's more cynical deputy, Karen, tries to talk him into just going along with Akhtar to keep their CIA bosses happy. Owens, however, feels the need to press the flesh with real guerrillas and sets out for an unauthorized motorcycle trip to the border with mujahedeen commander Abdul. The next thing we know, Owens is removed from Pakistan and Karen is negotiating serially with both General Akhtar and Abdul, promising Akhtar more weapons than he can imagine (KAREN: Triple everything. GENERAL AKHTAR: Wood for the fire! Wood for the fire!)[168] while alienating Abdul by sending him to the ISI for his munitions.

The May 2011 killing of al Queda leader Osama Bin Laden by U.S. forces in Abbottabad, Pakistan, in a compound just a mile from an elite Pakistani military installation seemed to publicly confirm long-held suspicions that the Pakistani ISI manipulated rival Afghani forces to thwart a final U.S. victory in Afghanistan while keeping billions of U.S. dollars and weapons flowing into its own hands. In that scenario, *Wood for the Fire* predicts events in that part of the world as clearly as his fellow playwright Tony Kushner in *Homebody/Kabul*, which Kushner began writing in 1997 and was in rehearsal when the 9/11 attacks occurred. In *Homebody/Kabul* an Afghan character chillingly says to a British woman whom he thinks is American, "You love the Taliban so much, why don't you bring them to New York! Don't worry. They're coming to New York!"[169]

Today, U.S. forces are preparing a 2014 exit from Afghanistan after fighting our longest war, to no clear conclusion. The future may hold further civil war in Afghanistan and continued meddling from Pakistan versus Indian- and Iranian-funded guerrillas while facing its own insurgency from militant Islamic groups and tribal leaders previously supported and controlled by the ISI. It's all wood for the (continuing) fire.

At the conclusion of his "A Defence of Poetry," Shelley writes:

> Poets are the hierophants of an unapprehended inspiration; the mirrors of the gigantic shadows which futurity casts upon the present; the words which express what they understand not; the trumpets which sing to battle, and feel not what they inspire; the influence which is moved not, but moves. Poets are the unacknowledged legislators of the world.[170]

Perhaps today, playwrights are the unacknowledged prescient political soothsayers (as opposed to politicians or legislators) of the world. Years from now students interested in our era will be reading *The Great Game: Afghanistan* and *Homebody/Kabul* rather than the speeches and books of our current political leaders, Bush, Obama, etc., who seem to have been wrong about everything regarding that part of the world.

Critics generally liked *The Great Game: Afghanistan*, with Erik Haagensen, in *Backstage*, calling it: "Epic in scope yet intimate in characterization, the show is smart, absorbing, and deeply affecting." Writing in the *New York Times*, Ben Brantley averred: "Seeing all three sets of four plays in one day, I was seldom bored or impatient, even if only a few of the individual works meet the standards usually asked of first-rate drama...." While David Gordon, at NYtheatre.com, wrote: "This mammoth, day-long, meticulously acted three-parter is probably the most fascinating production currently in town." Elisabeth Vincentelli made the point in the *New York Post* that the "show would have made the jump from very good to memorable if it had committed to theater as much as to education." And Matthew Murray, in Talkin' Broadway, found it "ambitious but arid.... It wants to condense everything we know about a flash point of two centuries' worth of conflict into a single package, without much concern about the results' overall theatricality."[171]

Given its emphasis upon education over theatrical or literary values, *The Great Game: Afghanistan* recalls, to some extent, the "learning-plays" of Bertolt Brecht, which he called *Lehrstücke*. Written in Germany between 1929 and 1934, these six plays—including *The Measures Taken, The Exception and the Rule,* and *He Who Says Yes*—Brecht reacted against the long-held notion that the theater was reflective, a mirror held up to nature, arguing that "art is not a mirror held up to society, but a hammer with which to shape it."[172] However, Brecht believed people learned by doing, and designed the *Lehrstücke* to impact the participating actors by forcing them to wrestle with moral/political issues. *The Great Game: Afghanistan* harkens back to an even older teaching model: the lecture, the illustration, or the monologue which seeks to instruct a largely passive audience. Some would see it as preaching to the choir, certainly, but at a time when most of the public either supported the war or remained ignorant of its costs, *The Great Game: Afghanistan* made a statement and rallied the antiwar movement to a theatrical communion, enhancing their energy to finally make the U.S. war in Afghanistan untenable. *The Great Game: Afghanistan*, for Blessing, "does what I think theatre ought to do to an audience vis-à-vis a significant political issue. It forces us to think and feel about it in more complex ways than we have before."[173] At the production for military veterans in Washington, a Department of Defense spokesperson commented: "There is an assumption that the arts and our men and women in uniform are from different planets. It's not the case. We're all in this together."[174]

So, can a play make a difference politically? When I asked Blessing about that production for the military he seemed less optimistic: "Can the Army be educated? The leadership, unfortunately, never seems to get the message."[175]

Seven Joys

Blessing teamed up with the Tricycle Theatre of London again in 2012, having worked with them earlier on *The Great Game: Afghanistan*, in 2009. Like the earlier effort, this involved a sort of anthology of short plays around a particular subject, in this case the Atom Bomb. As Tricycle's artistic director, Nicolas Kent, described the project's explicitly political origins and goals:

> Two years ago Baroness Shirley Williams (then advisor on Nuclear Proliferation to Prime Minister Gordon Brown) asked me why, as the final decision for the Trident renewal programs was approaching, the theatre was not tackling the nuclear weapons debate. These plays were conceived out of that conversation and challenge.[176]

Five plays (including Blessing's *Seven Joys*) premiered in London on February 9, 2012, and five additional plays opened a week later. Oberon Books published all ten (plus an additional Russian play) in *The Bomb: A Partial History*, in 2012. The two halves of the anthology are titled *First Blast: Proliferation (1940–1992)* and *Second Blast: Present Dangers (1992–present)*, including nuclear weapons development by Iran and North Korea. The short one-acts are meant to be seen on consecutive nights or, on weekends, in an afternoon and evening of a single day.

A quick Internet search under the terms "most exclusive clubs in the world" brings up names like the Alfalfa Club, the Bohemian Club, the Hurlingham Club, and Cercle de Lorraine, places I'd never heard of but which not only cost thousands of dollars to join but require sponsorship by existing multimillionaire members. However, a more exclusive club exists that began with just one member and now includes merely 14. You have to spend billions, bankrupt your citizenry and frighten your neighbors to join: the nuclear weapons "club," as it has been referred to for many years. Founded by the U.S., with the attacks on Hiroshima and Nagasaki in 1945, and joined by the U.S.S.R. in 1949, this club later allowed entry to France, China, India, Israel, and Pakistan. North Korea snuck in and has resisted expulsion. Belgium, Germany, the Netherlands, Italy, and Turkey are sponsored secondary members because they host U.S. nuclear bombs within their borders. The U.S. and other members brokered a deal just this year (2015) to keep Iran, which had tried to sneak in, out of their club for the next ten years. Only one member ever disaffiliated: South Africa joined in the 1980s, and then resigned by dismantling its nukes in the 1990s.

Blessing takes the "conceit," the surprising literary metaphor that allows us to see reality in new ways, in *Seven Joys*, by literally making the nuclear club a real gentlemen's club, with a stage dominated by leather club chairs, where each of the five characters represents a nation capable of ending life on our planet through the planned, or accidental, use of nuclear weapons.

As the play begins, silence and serenity reign at the club. The only member, Cal, an American, enjoys his status as the sole resident. His British servant, Henry, takes care of his needs. But others envy his solitude. "Admissions to the club," says Henry, "everyone wants to get in. Especially Slava [the representative of Russia]."[177] As Cal explains:

> CAL: For the first time in history a club like this exists. And people are afraid....
> HENRY: Yes, sir. Yes, they are.
> CAL: They're afraid of what I might do.
> HENRY: Yes.
> CAL: 'Cause I could kill them. By the millions. Like that. For the first time in history.[178]

Bully that he is, Cal enjoys lording it over Henry, reminding him of the U.S. role in World War II: "Because I did save you. Without me you'd all be saying, 'Please fuck me in the ass' in German right now."[179] Time advances, and soon Slava enters, representing Russian admission to the club. Slava brings along Wei, as his Chinese cook who, beneath a traditional robe, wears the uniform of the People's Republic of China. The club expands. Ominously, Wei mentions serving Korean food.

Each new member of the club cements his admission by producing a glowing egg-like object, the size of a goose egg, representing The Bomb, their very own thermonuclear weapon. We get a taste of how close they come to using them when Cal and Wei get into a physical fight on "kim chee night,"[180] a culinary metaphor for the 1950–53 Korean War that brought Korea, China, Russia, and the U.S. to the brink of nuclear destruction.

> (CAL *picks up his glowing egg.*)
> WEI: I dare you to use it!
> CAL: I will use it!
> SLAVA: (*picking up his own glowing egg*) And I will use mine!
> (*A standoff.*)
> WEI: No kim chee for you.[181]

The solution, says Cal to Henry: "I'm getting a bigger egg!"[182]

Soon a sexy Frenchwoman in high heels, Marianne, named no doubt for the national symbol of the French Republic and a portrayal of the Goddess of Liberty, arrives with a small force de frappe to break up the exclusively male club. Poor France dedicated itself to an independent nuclear strike force in the 1960s so that they no longer had to rely on the U.S., which had proven such a fickle ally in frustrating their abortive invasion of Suez in 1956.

Blessing writes:

> CAL: I had no idea you wanted this, um ... frap, thing, Marianne.
> MARIANNE: Really? I've been complaining about it for some time. You didn't hear me?
> CAL: How could I? You were outside.
> MARIANNE: And now I'm inside. Can you hear me now?[183]

When Wei takes dinner orders we hear them all quite clearly:

> MARIANNE: I'll have four hundred active warheads, split between submarine-launched and medium range air to surface missiles.
> SLAVA: Tonight I'm very hungry. Forty-five thousand warheads—mostly active.
> WEI: Ooh, that's a lot. Will you want a doggy bag?
> SLAVA: No. And I want multiple delivery options.
> WEI: Very well. And you?
> CAL: (*Of Slava*) I'll have what he's having.
> WEI: Some big eaters in this club.[184]

Indeed, they're eating us out of prosperity and safety, as Cal and Slava seem to agree:

> CAL: It *is* costing us an arm and a leg
> SLAVA: And the other leg.[185]

They move to slightly smaller eggs. But the moment passes. The U.S. helps India join the club, so China helps Pakistan get in. And Iran knocks on the door: Britain sold them nuclear technology when the Shah ruled. Wei adds a slightly larger egg for China. Wei lectures his fellow club members:

> All of you try to control the flow of technology, but it's a losing game. Ultimately every weapons system in history has become available to anyone who can pay for it or steal it. You constantly try to keep nuclear weapons out of your enemies' hands without ever asking why they have become your enemies.[186]

The play ends with a knock on the door. Someone new wants to join the club. More knocks are heard at the door. Then a drumbeat of knocks. The final stage picture chills: *"Lights fade until only the glowing eggs are illuminated."*[187]

In a few brief moments Blessing captures decades of nuclear insanity and manages to hit some of the subtler notes as he focuses attention on the racism, oppression, and machismo that accompany the arms race.

Critic Philip Fisher, in the online "British Theatre Guide," singled out *Seven Joys* for praise, writing: "*Seven Joys* is one of the day's highlights. Lee Blessing has written a satire on this very serious subject and it works a treat."[188] Sarah Hemming, in the *Financial Times*, agreed: "There's a sharp satire from Lee Blessing." She refers to the cycle of plays as "a vivid, serious examination of one of the most pressing issues of our time."[189]

Charles Spencer, at the *Telegraph*, wrote:

> Not all these short plays, with a total running time of five hours, are first-rate, but there isn't a complete dud among them, and the best pieces are superb examples of powerful one-act drama.... One leaves the theatre thrilled, chilled and deeply fearful about what the future may hold.[190]

Unfortunately, I can find no evidence that the plays from *The Bomb: A Partial History* ever made their way to American shores because, as Michael Billingot wrote in the *Guardian*: "The Tricycle has once again started a debate that our politicians would prefer to suppress." He meant British politicians, but his words apply equally to those of the United States.[191]

CHAPTER 6

The Race Plays

Black Sheep, Flag Day, and *Perilous Night* constitute, Blessing told me: "What I call my 'accidental Trilogy' about race relations in this country."[1] "I didn't want to write plays about black/white relations because it's a huge topic that does not go away. But I hoped the plays might engender a few epiphanies," he said.[2] And when I suggested that audiences might actually hate such explorations, Blessing told me: "They will if I'm doing it right."[3]

Black Sheep
Flag Day
Perilous Night

Black Sheep

Most families have a black sheep. In the case of the Winship family (parents Nelson and Serene, both in their fifties, and their adult son Max), their so-called black sheep is an extended relative, Carl by name, the sole black member of a white family. Like the stereotypical "black sheep," Carl just got out of prison. A one-act play in 21 short scenes, *Black Sheep* slides through the water (a recurring metaphor) like a dream of a play; or, more accurately, a nightmare, reminiscent of August Strindberg's *A Dream Play* (1902) or his *The Ghost Sonata* (1907), or Edward Albee's *A Delicate Balance* (1966), all disturbing dramas of The Theatre of the Absurd. Though, unlike Blessing, none touched the third rail of American society: the highly electrified subject of black and white relations.

The play's anarchic style came, Blessing told me, from his experience teaching playwriting at the University of Texas at Austin, where new styles were not embraced and "where Ibsen was a swear word. So I was challenged to write something formally different."[4]

The Winships stand apart from most other American families in another way as well: they have more money than they can ever spend. As patriarch Nelson explains to Carl: "No matter how much money we dispense there always seems to be more. Like some sort of great fountain.... The dynamics of capital."[5] Look at their family name, Winship. Did they "Win" the economic lottery? Did their "ship" come in? Nelson's wife, Serene (the "serenity" of great wealth, perhaps?) recalls nights making love to her husband on the vast rolling lawns of their estate. The newly arrived Carl now resides there, in the guesthouse. Nelson believes his family's great wealth is part of God's plan, as surely as Shakespeare's Henry IV saw his own kingship as part of God's plan:

> There's a reason we are who we are and that a place has been reserved in the order of things for us. Our place. Inviolable.... Think of it: the world without great wealth, without the holders of great wealth. I mean, what on earth would be the point? The money flows through us, you know. We're the stewards of the money.[6]

But "uneasy lies the head that wears a crown" wrote Shakespeare in *Henry IV, Part 2* (Act 3, Scene 1), and, like Henry, Nelson finds the holding of great wealth leads to fear and anxiety. His rich friends seem to be disappearing, succumbing to accidents, as if the very order of nature were under attack, "some sort of divine retribution," in Serene's words, "a supernatural culling of the rich."[7]

Both Nelson and Serene, while feigning "post-racial" attitudes, and yet accusing each other of racism, attempt to talk Carl into killing the other and their son, Max, for good measure. Max, once an aspiring filmmaker, now works as a for-hire movie critic, supplying hyperbolic catchphrases for soon-to-be-released films, telling Carl:

> I write stuff like "Extraordinary!" "Pure adrenaline!" Crap like that. They run my stuff before it opens. By the time the shitfest actually comes out, I'm already on to the next one.[8]

Max gets by as an Orwellian cog (think *1984*, where "War is Peace"; "Freedom is Slavery"; "Ignorance is Strength") in the cultural media/celebrity machine, hyping crap as if it were sliced bread, devaluing language like a skilled politician, creating nothing of value and selling that nothing for something. Sadly enough, Max applies the same faked vocabulary to his own life, shouting, "Hugely entertaining ... packs a wallop" while making love to Elle or masturbating by his lonesome[9] until they become the only words he has.[10]

Carl decides: "Max's problem is he could never learn how to be rich."[11] Max's other problem is Elle, his sexy, though untouched (by him), girlfriend who may be having an affair with his dad and, later, Carl, while starring in films like *All the President's Hookers,* in which, she tells Carl, "I was the slutty one."[12] Max and Elle ask Carl to kill Nelson and Serene for them. Everyone has murder on their minds; Serene calls them "the most homicidal family since the Borgias,"[13] and all see black sheep Carl as their bespoke assassin.

This stew mixes race, sex, and capitalism in a mordant take on American society at the dawn of the new millennium. Water imagery (perhaps signifying the amniotic fluid of birth, or death by drowning) recurs on almost every page: "pool" and "poolside," for instance, are referenced nine times,[14] the lake 14 more,[15] while each character relates a dream they've had.[16] Carl finally announces that it's all been a dream: "Ever since I came to this house I've had ... strange experiences. Couldn't figure out what it was. Then one morning I woke up and it hit me. I'm dreaming it all."[17] Time to reread Strindberg.

Reality bites when Carl describes the crime for which he was sentenced to prison at the age of 15: the murder of his white half-brother:

> He said he was the real son and I was the coon son.
> He tried to make me say it. He put the gun against my head and told me to say "coon." That I was a coon. I was crying.... When I wouldn't say it, he started poking the gun barrel against my head.... I grabbed his hand and the gun ... the gun ... went off. Right through his chest.... There was lots of blood.... I shot him eight more times.[18]

The threat of black violence haunts the qhites, especially those who are rich. What if the men and women who were once slaves got the upper hand? But note, that while we sympathize with Carl as a victim of racism, Blessing seeks complexity over such simple responses. How much sympathy can we feel for Carl when he tells us, "I shot him eight more times."[19] Like Bigger Thomas in *Native Son,* Richard Wright's 1940 novel, Carl's violence goes well beyond mere self-defense.

Carl went to prison, and his parents never spoke to him again. Now he is the undefinable "other" haunting the dreams of an unmoored family bound together only by their wealth and the absence of melanin in their skin. The very rich, Carl knows, as did F. Scott Fitzgerald, are different from you and me. Fitzgerald wrote: "They think that they are better than we are."[20] Carl says "[They have all] the time in the world. Only rich people can afford to do it like that."[21] While each character commiserates with Carl's lost youth in prison and opine that he never should have been tried as an adult at age 15, Nelson, undoubtedly thinking of his own arrested development, adds: "They should never try anybody as an adult."[22] In fact, we find no adults in *Black Sheep.*

The trademark Blessing humor surfaces often, as when Serene says, "Carl's practically a member of the family," to which Carl retorts: "I *am* a member of the family."[23]

In Scene 19, murders abound: Carl drowns Serene, Max strangles Nelson, and Elle poisons Max, and yet, somehow, in Scene 21, the final scene of the play, we find Nelson, Serene, and Elle eating breakfast together and all three share that they had "the strangest dream last night."[24] Nelson assures all concerned: "A dream is the mind talking to itself."[25] Elle has had a call from her agent to appear in a remake of the 1953 Japanese classic *Ugetsu*, a black-and-white film filled with dreamlike apparitions. Perhaps not coincidentally, *Ugetsu* is the video Serene brings home in Scene 7.

Just then, more African carvings arrive in barrels, much as they did at the opening curtain, but, this time, Carl is wheeling them in while wearing a deliveryman's uniform. When Nelson and Carl unpack the barrel: "*Max's dead, naked body—falls headfirst out the bottom. His corpse is wet.*"[26] All stare, but no one reacts emotionally. They close with the following comic patter:

> SERENE: I have a tape of that movie, you know. *Ugetsu*. We should watch it.
> ELLE: Sounds nice.
> SERENE: It's a ghost story. I watch it all the time. Over and over.
> NELSON: Wonder how Max would've reviewed it?
> ELLE: Dazzling.
> NELSON: Riveting.
> SERENE: A barrel of fun.[27]

And then the final line of the play:

> NELSON: I had the strangest dream last night.[28]

So, what do we have here? The critics didn't see much:
Wrote Markland Taylor in *Variety*:

> Playwright Lee Blessing says "Black Sheep," his recent exercise in dated black comedy, is about doubt. But there's no doubt it's a very minor, mostly pointless outing replete with déjà vu by a scribe capable of such perfectly good plays as "A Walk in the Woods" and "Cobb".... Blessing has created no actual characters, projects no clear point of view and has certainly failed to write a play with a voice of its own.[29]

In "CurtainUp: The Internet Theater Magazine of Reviews, Features, Annotated Listings," Elyse Sommer wrote in an undated column:

> Even when the earnest Blessing gives vent to his comic impulses he does not abandon his trademark Blessing Op-Ed page to stage sensibility. With his comic mask in place, he also tends towards abstraction that is more precious than profound and generally over-spiced with bizarre twists. His monodrama, *Chesapeake*, was a case in point; so, I'm afraid is *Black Sheep*, his latest venture into comedy.... *Black Sheep* feels and looks edgy but shoots itself in the hoof with well-meaning but painfully transparent ideas.[30]

In "Gail Sez," Gail M. Burns wrote in 2002: "This is the strangest play I have seen since I was in college,"[31] but she meant it in a good way.

Let's dig a little deeper. Blessing never put fingers to computer keys without an idea and a purpose. He leaves us lots of clues. The repeated water imagery speaks of birth, death, and rebirth. Characters repeatedly reference Kenji Mizoguchi's 1953 award-winning Japanese film *Ugetsu* (or *Ugetsu Monogatari*), a tale of ghosts and broken dreams and misplaced ambitions. Not surprisingly, *Ugetsu* opens with a panoramic view of a lake its characters will cross and re-cross during the film, a lake of mysterious possibilities, not unlike the lake fronting the Winship estate.

The play also literally plays with the sense of reality of readers and audiences to move us into a surreal realm, the oft-referenced dreams each character experiences, where we might ponder realities, like race and capitalism—thoughts we otherwise bar from our everyday contemplation. In an era when the rich grow richer (they "win," their "ship" comes in, they have "more money than they can spend" because their invested capital keeps reaping returns without the inconvenience of having to lift a finger). But the rich wear the golden crown uneasily. It is a "delicate balance" (à la Edward Albee), to be tormented by unseen but imagined fears like Nelson's oft-expressed suspicion that his rich friends are disappearing mysteriously, one by one. Race also upsets the balance. Will the poor, the black, the brown, ever get angry enough to shoot rich white people not once but nine times, as Carl did his half-brother?

The surreal dream in *Black Sheep* is the obverse nightmare of Dr. Martin Luther King's "dream" in his speech at the "March on Washington for Jobs and Freedom" in August 1963. In this dark, *Black Sheep* specter, *everyone* judges Carl by the color of his skin and not by the content of his character. In fact, the playwright affords him little character at all. Little white boys and girls do not join hands with little black boys and girls as brothers and sisters, as King had hoped. Perversely, those that are *actually* brothers and sisters in *Black Sheep* join their hands only to murder each other. Before an Obama presidency ushered in dreams of a post-racial America, *Black Sheep* insists race determines destiny and America's unresolved racial divide portends a violent future. White police shootings of unarmed black men in 2014 in Ferguson, Missouri (Michael Brown), Cleveland, Ohio (Tamir Rice), Bastrop, Texas (Yvette Smith), Houston, Texas (Jordan Baker), Iberia Parish, Louisiana (Victor White), Beavercreek, Ohio (John Crawford, III), Los Angeles (Ezell Ford), St. Louis (Kajieme Powell), Brooklyn (Akai Gurley) and Phoenix (Rumain Brisbon)[32] have proven his point. As *Boston Globe* critic Scott Heller wrote in an understatement: "'Black Sheep' is provocative stuff."[33]

Flag Day

Flag Day returns us to some previous Blessing play structures, using two plays written separately but yoked to run together, à la *Nice People Dancing to Good Country Music*, which combined that original one-act with *Toys for Boys*, written later. Also, as in topical play *Patient A*, where he added himself as a character named Lee, here we have a writer named Adam as a likely stand-in for Blessing himself. As in *Black Sheep*, viscerally vicious interactions of white and black people drive the drama.

Blessing calls *Flag Day* "a play in two plays," the one-act *Good Clean Fun* followed by the one-act *Down and Dirty*. While the two plays (or acts) share none of the same characters, producers may choose to employ two of the same actors from the first play so that audiences see the continuity of theme. The white actor who appears as Hewitt in *Good, Clean Fun* reappears as the dying Rex in *Down and Dirty*, while the black actor who plays Denby in *Good, Clean Fun* is seen again as Vandell in *Down and Dirty*. Performed together, the plays take the flow of racism from place to place, year to year, and person to person, through these linked actors.

Good, Clean Fun plunks us down in "an anonymous corporate office."[34] The spare set, undifferentiated by city or state, lets us know we are facing a universal, rather than a specific, situation.

At curtain's rise, we discover Hewitt, a white man in his forties, at work on his desktop computer; his colleague, Denby, a black man in his twenties, enters late for work. Nothing seems out of the ordinary until Denby pulls an egg timer out of his drawer and sets it ticking while he relates the cause of his tardiness: a nasty encounter with two white policemen who pulled him over and drew their weapons for his "crime" of D.W.B. ("driving while black"). His recitation ends as the egg timer dings.

Hewitt pulls out an egg timer of his own and tells Denby how two men, "both black,"[35] carjacked and beat his cousin. The ding of the egg timer ends Hewitt's account. It falls to Denby, then, to provide the necessary exposition: their CEO introduced the idea of using egg timers, believing it better to create a safe space for the direct expression of racial stereotypes and stupidities rather than have employees dance around such unavoidable issues and feelings. Denby says their boss, Standpipe, told him:

> We look each other square in the eye and say, "I don't like you. Don't like your music, your TV shows, the way you look, the way you talk. I just don't like you." But, Mr. Standpipe said, "We do it with discipline. We do it with this (*tapping his timer*)."[36]

Where, an audience wonders, will this go? Can name-calling really be compartmentalized, given and taken, without upsetting relationships and without leading to violence? Hewitt and Denby trade information on a corporate project, but soon they each have the egg timers out again and offer stories of personal racial animosity or humiliation. We gather the timers have a dual purpose: the man employing it has the floor while his companion must remain silent, so they, in turn liberate themselves and oppress the other. Standpipe has given them, Denby says, the "the rare and golden opportunity to share our innermost fears and hatreds."[37]

But Hewitt, we learn, is chafing under Denby's role as their project manager, and feels free to criticize him. Denby retaliates by upping the ante, regaling Hewitt with tales of how Hewitt's wife, Sandy, now much prefers her life, and lovemaking, with Denby, managing to explain before the timer dings: "And yet I stretched her. Performance-wise."[38] Hewitt rages as the insults become more personal and he learns Denby has impregnated Sandy, but continues to obey the ritual of the egg timer even, as Denby tells him: "Anyway, you should be getting the divorce papers today."[39]

Flag Day: co-workers Hewitt (Lee Sellars, left) and Denby (Albert Jones) come to blows when their employer encourages them to express their "true" feelings about race. Contemporary American Theater Festival, Shepherd University, Shepherdstown, West Virginia; 2004, photograph by Ron Blunt; courtesy of Contemporary American Theater Festival.

Animosities escalate and epithets fly. Denby challenges Hewitt to call him a "nigger."[40] Denby quotes the boss: "Seek out the subtle positives this program offers. Find a way to turn your anger into good, clean fun."[41] Hewitt accepts the challenge: "You fuckin' nigger," he says to Denby.[42] This finally leads to the violence we've been expecting, as Denby grabs Hewitt, only to release him when the egg timer dings again. Denby and Hewitt revert to ordinary office demeanor:

> DENBY: I do believe we are going to be on time.
> HEWITT: Never a doubt.
> DENBY: Work together, win together.
> HEWITT: Efficiency equals equality.[43]

As the play ends, "*The sound of scores—hundreds?—of egg timers emanates from down the hall.*"[44] Everyone offstage, it seems, is behaving just as Hewitt and Denby have, and with similar results.

The play's overall title drips with irony:

> *Flag Day* is a day for all Americans to celebrate and show respect for our flag, its designers and makers. Our flag is representative of our independence and our unity as a nation ... one nation, under God, indivisible. Our flag has a proud and glorious history. It was at the lead of every battle fought by Americans. Many people have died protecting it.[45]

Hewitt and Denby, each American, represent the disunity and clear divisibility of our country along the fault line of black/white relations, the same fault line that divided us at our country's (and flag's) birth over two centuries years ago. While the Continental Congress created our national banner in 1777, and President Harry Truman chose June 14 as the national celebration of Flag Day in 1949, racial animosity, unlike slavery and legal segregation, continues to be observed. As events in 2014 remind us (as if we need reminding)—the police shooting of Michael Brown in Ferguson, Missouri, or that of Trayvon Martin two years earlier in Sanford, Florida, by a Neighborhood Watch coordinator—there is no "good, clean fun" here.

Act 2 (or play 2), entitled *Down and Dirty*, moves us from near-violence to actual homicide and lets us see the flag we are celebrating. It's based on, or inspired by, the real-life case of a woman in Fort Worth, Texas, who, on October 26, 2001, hit a homeless man as she drove home, under the influence of alcohol and the drug Ecstasy, and parked her car in the garage as the man bled to death on her windshield over the next two to three days. The driver was a black woman, and the victim a white man. The gruesome details inspired episodes of *CSI* and *Law and Order* on TV and two feature films, *Stuck* (2008) and *Accident on Hill Road* (2009). In Blessing's play, the monstrously self-absorbed driver is named Dot; the hapless victim is named Rex. According to the stage directions:

> Rex [floats] above and slightly behind her [Dot], lodged in a smashed windshield. His eyes are closed; he emits regular, soft groans.⁴⁶

Beneath the dying man, his assailant relaxes with a beer and berates his noisy groaning:

> DOT: Shut the fuck up! I'm tryna think.
> REX: What are you thinking about? I'm bleeding.
> DOT: What I gotta do?! Beat you to death?⁴⁷

In the midst of this grotesque situation, the subject of race rises to the surface. Rex tells Dot her name is not "very black"⁴⁸ and Dot later pokes fun at the comatose victim: "It's black enough now, isn't it? Only it's you, not me—big ol' black dot, right in the middle a' my windshield!"⁴⁹

Dot's friend Vandell—also black—advises Dot on how to dump the body and avoid the police. When she goes into the house to rest and leaves him alone in the garage with Rex, he evinces no interest in aiding the victim. When Vandell wanders off, Adam, who is white, enters. Seemingly a time traveler, he informs Rex of his impending and agonizing death, having already read his obituary. Is Adam another symbolic name, drawn from the Bible's first man and here representing allegorically all men (and women)? Or is Adam the playwright who is creating these "facts"?

Morning, in Scene 2, finds Adam and Dot together in the garage, and Scene 3, that afternoon, brings Vandell back as well, this time carrying a large American flag with which to celebrate Flag Day. It seems that Dot always celebrates the holiday by flying the flag because, she claims, without irony, "I happen to be a patriot!"⁵⁰

When Vandell learns Adam is a writer, creatively dealing with a real incident of homicide in which he views race as the center of the story, he says:

> And now you're trying to sell your impressions of black folks? Making a little money inventing a bunch of us and getting us to talk funny? Having us commit a bunch of crimes?⁵¹

This speech reminds us of the complaints of the gay AIDS victim in *Patient A*. The character of the writer is an outsider—a disease-free male. In *Flag Day*, the writer is white, educated, not marginalized. He serves as a mediator, or buffer, moderating and mitigating the raw reactions of the other characters. He deflects their anger from us, the audience, to him. He is literally not a *dramatis personae* because, though present at the drama, he knows the future, but he does not move the action forward, creates no conflict, and evades any resolution. When Dot tries to suffocate Adam with a plastic bag after learning he is descended from a slave ship captain, she ultimately relents. A mere character can't harm the author, after all.

Dot references the real 1998 murder of African American James Byrd in Jasper, Texas, dragged with chains behind a car by white men until his body fell apart, and Adam asks her: "Could you have done it if he'd [Rex] been black?"[52] Dot replies: "I ain't hit him 'cause he's white. But I ain't savin' him neither."[53] Racial violence begets racial violence as it has for 500 years in America since Europeans dragged the first African slaves off ships (in what is now South Carolina) in 1525. To punctuate that history and reinforce Rap Brown's dictum, "Violence is as American as cherry pie,"[54] and leave us with an unforgettable final stage picture, Dot, when Vandell tells her Flag Day is over, takes down the flag and drapes it over dying Rex's head; America's national symbol temporarily serves as a shroud for the many victims of racial violence. The play's final words belong to Vandell (vandal?): "Won't be long now."[55]

The *Washington Times* called the play

> a raw-edged, cringe-inducing exercise in good old-fashioned theater of cruelty.... "Flag Day" is a frank, powerful, insightful commentary on the still-poisoned status of race relations in this country.... Unexpectedly balanced and provocative, "Flag Day" will have audiences peering deeply into their own souls long after they have left the darkened theater.[56]

An uncredited review in *Potomac Stages* differentiated between the two halves of the play:

> Oh, what fun is "Good, Clean Fun"! Lovers of sharp, flashy dialogue and high concept scenes will revel in the exchanges between the black supervisor and the white subordinate who reveal more and more about their relationship with each start of their egg timers.... After such a strong start, "Down and Dirty" turns frustratingly facile.[57]

Anyone who tackles racism in America earns kudos in my book for both perception and courage. Few Caucasian playwrights take the chance, though black writers have built an *oeuvre* around the subject, perhaps because they tackle it daily in their own lives: think Lorraine Hansberry, Amiri Baraka, Ed Bullins, Lynn Nottage, Langston Hughes, Suzan-Lori Parks, and, of course, August Wilson. Where is the corresponding list of white playwrights? We have Tracy Letts (*Superior Donuts*) and David Mamet (*Race*) and...? In *Race*, Mamet has his white character say: "There is nothing. A white person. Can say to a black person. About Race."[58] Too many white playwrights seem to agree. But racism is not a black problem. Racism, as Blessing makes abundantly clear with his blatant flag symbolism, is an American, black and white problem.

In raising the race issue, however, some might take Blessing to task for offering no solutions to perhaps the most violent ongoing division in American society. This hardly constitutes an indictment when America's collective intelligence has failed to solve the problem over a period of hundreds of years. When did a work of art solve any social problem? Perhaps we might better ask, how do these plays add to our national conversation on race, a conversation that recognizes the issue and gropes for solutions rather than denying the oppressive ongoing existence of racism in what some would like to believe is a "post-racial" era of racial harmony ushered in by the election of America's first black president.

I do fault Blessing, however, for a lack of evenhandedness as this white playwright creates black monsters onstage who quite outdo their white counterparts in evil. In *Good, Clean Fun*, the white Hewitt's racism, sense of entitlement, and superiority reveal a nasty person we'd rather not share a dinner table with. But he merely talks and blusters. Denby fights white racism by action, not talk: seducing and impregnating Hewitt's wife and throwing those actions in his face whenever he can. In *Down and Dirty*, the two white characters, Rex and Adam, whine and lecture. But Dot is a cold-blooded killer. To make black people the most reprehensible characters onstage in each play can only reinforce a white audience's own underlying racism. And Blessing's audiences are overwhelmingly white, as he knows.

The contemporary poet Stephen Dobyns (coincidentally, like Blessing, a graduate of the Iowa Writers Workshop), wrote in reference to William Wordsworth's lyrical expression of grief:

> Only through art do we come to appreciate his emotional state as we engage in an act of imagination that makes the poet's experience our own. The social function of this within the society is that it forges links between us.[59]

Applied to *Perilous Night*, Dobyns's words speak to a racial empathy and solidarity found there, though not in Blessing's two previous plays on the topic of race in America.

Perilous Night

Blessing subtitles *Perilous Night*, written in 2007, revised in 2008, and produced in 2013, *A Play in One Breath*, though the reference is not as clear as *Flag Day*'s subtitle, *A Play in Two Plays*. Perhaps he points to a timelessness of the content, or the rush in which it passes.

He sets *Perilous Night* in a private mental-health facility. The time, he tells us, is "Eternity—which is to say, the present,"[60] an undifferentiated limbo he has visited before in *Cobb* and *Patient A*. The title itself takes us back to *Flag Day*, with its echoes of the "The Star-Spangled Banner":

> Oh, say can you see by the dawn's early light
> What so proudly we hailed at the twilight's last gleaming?
> Whose broad stripes and bright stars thru the perilous fight...[61]

6. The Race Plays

Here Blessing purposefully mangles the third line even as so many singers publicly muff the lines to our national anthem. Blessing references the flag, but something (race relations) is off-key. In the script, the introductory quotation taken from the 1948 presidential campaign of the late South Carolina Senator and segregationist Strom Thurmond, who appears under another name in Blessing's play *Chesapeake*, prepares us for the worst:

> All the laws of Washington and all the bayonets of the Army cannot force the Negro into our homes, our schools, our churches and our places of amusement.[62]

Mocking the senator's sentiment, Blessing *does* force the Negro into our place of amusement, the theater, in the person of Harriet, a young black inmate. Harriet opens the play by bursting into the room of an older white woman who is silently embroidering with imaginary needles and styles herself "Her Royal Majesty Queen Elizabeth III." Harriet seeks to hide from a young white attendant by the name of Samuel, whom she calls her "boyfriend."

Harriet styles herself a teacher of history and shares with Elizabeth her rather optimistic view of human evolution:

> History's the study of whence we've come. It's how we look back from our current heights down the long glittering staircase of human achievement.[63]

Elizabeth, citing a multitude of man-made disasters, explains that her reign will come 257 years in the future and that her presence in the here and now is the work of dreaming and "certain powerful drugs."[64] In the future, she reveals, women run the show with the help of male *castrati* and "things are far calmer in our time. So much more gets done."[65] Samuel's repeated appearances at Elizabeth's window, as he seeks Harriet up and down the corridors, clearly hints at a much less calm, and more male dominated, present day.

Elizabeth and Harriet continue their discussion of utopians past and dystopias to come; Harriet arguing for diversity of races, religions, while Elizabeth describes a monocultural future, from whence she is visiting. When Harriet examines the piece Elizabeth is embroidering, her "device," a symbol of her royal reign, she finds a surprise:

> HARRIET: It's so ... simple, Just a pair of...
> ELIZABETH: Balls, yes. A human scrotum. Stylized, of course. Hairless, since that is the fashion of our time. How do you like it?
> HARRIET: It's a very nice ... scrotum.
> ELIZABETH: Suspended in air. Floating impossibly on a golden field, with three tiny drops of blood beneath. See how bright they are? Most difficult to find this shade of red.
> HARRIET: What's the blood for?
> ELIZABETH: Natural by-product of castration.[66]

At this point, anyone who knows their Chekhov ("If in the first act you have hung a pistol on the wall, then in the following one it should be fired. Otherwise don't put it there.")[67] knows that even imaginary embroidery needles and blood droplets introduced in Act 1 foreshadow serious bloodletting before the play ends. On cue, Samuel, the attendant, enters Elizabeth's room. Harriet has hidden in the bathroom. It is clear, we are told in stage directions, that "*Samuel doesn't want to enter.*"[68] He enters cautiously, keeping a distance from Elizabeth as in fear of this seemingly sweet and harmless old lady. He delivers the requisite exposition in snippets: he is hunting for his keys which Harriet has taken, he "loves" Harriet, Elizabeth's family pays the institution a lot to put up with her, and that another attendant may have come to grief at her hands. Harriet exits the bathroom and explains that she ran because of something dreadful that another attendant, Carver, did to her black roommate Annabeth. When Samuel leaves, locking the two women in the room together, Harriet reveals the cliffhanger that ends Act 1: she is pregnant.

Following the intermission, lights come back up at the "same instant"[69] in time. Blessing quickly works in a theatrical and self-deprecating joke:

ELIZABETH: And who was this Mr. Lincoln?
HARRIET: President of the United States....
ELIZABETH: And how did Mr. Lincoln die?
HARRIET: He saw a terrible play and shot himself.
ELIZABETH: A fate all too common, even in our day.[70]

And only here, in Act 2, do racial issues overtly enter the play for the first time. In Harriet's warped retelling of history, amiable Africans became slaves to Europeans because they were the "most agreeable people on earth," but notes, rather astutely, that "without slavery the world economic model could not make sudden and enormous strides." However, civilization degenerated so swiftly at Harriet's own birth that the previous peacefulness shattered and even Harriet and her own mother were raped by white people.[71] Harriet's baby, she tells Elizabeth, hers and Samuel's, a black and a white parent, will set "the world back to the way it originally was."[72]

The immediate impediment to this rosy future is the white attendant, Carver, whom Harriet has seen that night sexually abusing and suffocating another patient, also black, the unseen roommate Annabeth. We learn that, in the past, the brutish Carver, in trying to locate and confiscate Elizabeth's embroidery tools, held the poor woman's head under water to force her cooperation. But when he slipped on the wet bathroom floor and fell unconscious, Elizabeth used the very same needles and tiny scissors to partly castrate him. He lost a single testicle. Carver (note the name), armed with a knife, now threatens a little carving of the Queen. Carver brags of his membership in a fascist-sounding "Brotherhood." Clearly, both the patients and the attendants in this asylum live their days in separate fantasies. Carver departs to prepare for some sort of escape with Samuel, after having locked Elizabeth and Harriet in together again. Revelations, or exposition, flow freely: Harriet seduced a shy Samuel; she knows her child will be female; Elizabeth, in reality the scion of a local wealthy family, gave birth as a teenager to a black child which she disposed of and then went mad from the guilt; Samuel and Carver are members of the "Brotherhood of the Perilous Fight," misquoted by the rather dim Samuel as the "Brotherhood of the Perilous Night," and conjuring images of the racist Aryan Brotherhood prison gang.

Action replaces exposition when Samuel and Carver return to Elizabeth's room and Carver severely beats Samuel for impregnating Harriet and blabbing about the Brotherhood. Harriet's hope to birth a half-black, half-white baby to heal the world constitutes Carver's worst racial nightmare of miscegenation. He seems a true son of the South and of Senator Thurmond. His escape plans include only Samuel and himself: having already killed Annabeth, he now plans to kill Harriet and Elizabeth. But when he decides to rape Harriet prior to departure, Elizabeth stabs him in the eye with a hidden and very real embroidery needle and Harriet ties him up in the bathroom and finishes the chore of castration Elizabeth began prior to the beginning of the play. Finally, Harriet escapes this hellhole alone but into what kind of future an audience can only imagine.

The author's choice of setting is inspired: blinded by ludicrous ideas of race, Americans have made their entire country an insane asylum. Racial prejudice has driven us mad. Like some of the clinically insane faced with an unacceptable reality, we also react by choosing to live in a constructed "reality" we find more accommodating: Elizabeth's future reign of a monoculture filled with only white people, Carver's fascist vision of racial war, or Harriet's world of interracial peace and love that brings us only:

> beautiful little children the color of sandy-brown beaches who all went to college and got elected to Congress, where they made kinder and kinder laws until no one could remember why they made laws at all, since there was no longer any crime.[73]

Reviews were mixed. Nick Huyck, in *City Pages*, wrote:

> As much as *Perilous Night* offers a sometimes compelling and funny take on our society's obsessions and blind spots, there are some breakdowns in the script—of both clarity and storytelling.... It makes for a sometimes compelling, sometimes confounding, and often uncomfortable piece of theater.[74]

Lisa Brock, in the *Minneapolis Star Tribune*, said:

> "Perilous Night" is not without flaws. Nimbus' production, however, makes the most of the play's strengths, including nimble wit, layered characters and some plot twists as intriguing as they are unexpected.[75]

And Michael Opperman, in *Aisle Say Twin Cities*, added:

> *Perilous Night* is a Maroushka doll of sinister revelations. There are points that strain the seams of the fourth wall with exposition that doesn't know where else to be; this puts a burden on the actors to stay in the momentum of a scene while delivering information. The play itself requires notable world building for audience comprehension and the *dramatis personae* orchestrate that well. The play and the production are ambitious and provide plenty to talk about over wine or coffee afterwards.[76]

But what would we ask of any theater than that, in Huyck's words, a play be both "compelling and confounding?"

On November 14, 1960, a six-year-old girl named Ruby Bridges walked, head down, carrying her lunch box between four tall U.S. deputy marshalls as she became, under court order, the first black student to attend William Frantz Elementary School in New Orleans, her iconographic photo appearing on the front pages of newspapers around the globe and inspiring a Norman Rockwell painting, "The Problem We All Live With," for the cover of *Look* magazine in January 1964. As she walked, jeering crowds of segregationists unfurled Confederate flags and shouted profane insults. One woman threatened to poison the child, and another proffered a coffin with a black baby doll inside. Each and every white student in the school withdrew and teachers resigned, leaving Ruby Bridges as the only student. Some 54 years later, the city of New Orleans unveiled a statue of the child at her former school. Said Ms. Bridges on that occasion: "You almost feel like you're back in the sixties ... race is a very hot topic."[77] Norman Rockwell's painting of Ruby Bridges now hangs in the White House. Lee Blessing needs to keep writing plays about race in America.

Chapter 7

Love Is All There Is

Blessing's obvious forte is writing dialogue that is believable, hilarious or touching by turn, and sometimes lacerating. Since what we know of a character on stage we can learn only by what they say, what others say about them, and what we see them actually do, playwrights lack the easy reliance upon the interior narratives of the novelist or the voiceover of the cinema. They must rather build or destroy a relationship before our eyes within but a two-hour (or less) span. This chapter's plays explore love, fear, and hate among our fellow creatures. In *A Body of Water* Blessing asks what relationships survive when memory dies; in *Lonesome Hollow* he looks at how power corrupts human intercourse, in both senses of the word, and in *Great Falls* his road trip balances adolescent growing pains and parental fears. *Thief River* shows us the conflict inherent in a love suppressed by society, while *Into You* dissects violation and revenge. *The Scottish Play* exposes jealousies and infighting behind the seemingly functional but ultimately superficial community created in theater. *The Roads That Lead Here* pokes fun at our attachments to things rather than people, and *Uncle* has fun with the cycle of love and lust over the last 100 years. In each, Blessing asks, why in desiring love so much do we so often destroy our own dreams of happiness?

Thief River
The Roads That Lead Here
A Body of Water
The Scottish Play
Lonesome Hollow
Great Falls
Into You
Uncle

Thief River

Set entirely in an abandoned farm house in the Midwest, and with its action spread over the month of June in three different years, 1948, 1973, and 2001, *Thief River* traces the development of two main characters, Ray and Gil, who become lovers, and four ancillary characters. The play calls for six actors in all, each playing two characters. Confusingly, three actors portray Ray at different stages in his life, at 18, 43, and 73, while three others portray Gil, also at ages 18, 43, and 73. The 12 brief scenes move back and forth through time. Blessing first experimented with this technique in his play *Marjorie,* which was produced just once, in 1984, and never published. The time shifts and the doubling of actors thoroughly confused one critic, John Simon, who wrote:

> I seldom could tell who was doing what to whom, or when, or where, or why.... After a while I gave up and just watched Mark Lamos's overheated staging that rendered Blessing's vehemence with incremental hysteria the way I would watch a Chinese martial arts movie without subtitles.[1]

Though this sounds damning, Simon did manage to finally figure things out:

> Blessing, who here comes out of his usual blandness, writes lively dialogue that flexibly encompasses many modes, from the wry to lyrical, from erotic to spiritual, and that—once you can follow it—keeps you involved.[2]

"Usual blandness?" Where has John Simon been?

Though the title, *Thief River,* sounds allegorical, conjuring up images of a natural force that steals (thieves) time or love, or life, there is a real town, Thief River Falls, in Minnesota, Blessing's home state, which locals refer to as Thief River, population around 2,000. And while

Lee Blessing, at a rehearsal for *Thief River*, Guthrie Theater, Minneapolis, Minnesota; 2002, photograph by and courtesy of Michal Daniel.

this may seem an odd locale for a gay love story Blessing seems to be tapping into the zeitgeist once again (as when *Riches* preceded the movie "War of the Roses" or his play *Cobb* preceded the movie of the same name) for it predates another more famous rural gay male love story, *Broke Back Mountain*, released as a film in 2005, though written by Annie Proulx in 1999.

The play opens in 1948, the night of the local senior prom. Gil enters, bloody and bruised, tearing off his clothes, after a night of tangling with Lewis, a macho heterosexual who both attracts and attacks him. Gil's revenge, taking a shot at his tormentor and wounding him in the hand, leads him to seek sanctuary in the abandoned farmhouse, where Ray finds him. Unfortunately for them, the seemingly vacant farmhouse houses Harlow, awakened by the ruckus and demanding the gun at the point of a straight razor. As the three characters freeze, a 40-year-old version of Ray enters to set the scene. Ray's father built the house immediately after his service in World War II, but the war-damaged vet shot Ray's mother and himself as soon as he finished it. No one has ever lived here, and Anson, the father's friend, raised the orphaned Ray. Scene 1 ends with 40-year-old Ray 2 referencing Gil's wounds and how Anson won't allow him to see his old friend.

On this mysterious note from 1948, we shift without pause into Scene 2, thrusting us forward into 1973. A 40-year-old, and scared, Gil 2 enters the farmhouse with Perry, Ray's father-in-law. Perry tells us that Gil turned up unexpectedly at Ray Junior's wedding rehearsal and that Gil's much younger lover, Kit, disrupted the rehearsal. Confused yet? A lot can happen in 25 years.

Kit cuts quite a figure, crawling on the floor, camping it up and telling stories of his childhood: "We were poor. So poor we had to *eat* cow manure. For us, cow pies were really pies."[3] Gil, now employed as a travel writer, has returned to his rural roots after a 25-year absence. Weekly, for those 25 years, Ray wrote Gil letters, explaining, "I cannot be with you," and always adding, for the sake of mixed messages, "I love you, Gil."[4] Gil 2 has come because Ray 2 stopped writing. Ray 3 enters the scene to tell us "I still love him,"[5] and explain why he still chooses to remain in a heterosexual marriage with Molly.

Scene 3 whisks us into 2001, as Ray 3 and his grandson Jody visit the old farmhouse that, Ray tells us, he has not visited in 17 years. Reese, researching his family tree and related, by marriage, to Harlow, also shows up. Front and center is a funeral urn. Blessing lets us wonder whose ashes it contains and, as the men carefully navigate creaking floorboards, who might fall to the floor below.

Scene 4 takes us back to the play's opening in 1948 as Harlow holds that straight razor to Gil's throat and terrorizes him as he waits for Ray to find the gun he wants. Homophobic Harlow claims to have killed five "faggots"[6] and plans to kill both Gil and Ray, a plan only thwarted by Anson's appearance, wielding a shovel and knocking Harlow unconscious. What happens next in this bloody stage picture has to wait while the next scene takes us to back 1973 and Scene 2, as Ray 2 and Gil 2 ruefully discuss what a shared life could have been or still might be in a small apartment in New York.

> RAY: Where'll I put my personal things?
> GIL: Personal things?
> RAY: You know—wife, son...⁷

Gil declares his love for Ray and, while Ray reciprocates the feeling, he will not leave his wife, his son, or his respectable "life."⁸ Scene 6 zips us back to the end of Scene 3 in 2001. Now Gil 3 joins Ray 3, Jody, and Reese, and promptly kicks over the urn of ashes, which constitute, we learn, the final resting place of Harlow. Under court order, all have gathered to conduct a ceremony for the murdered miscreant. We also learn

Lee Blessing, at a rehearsal for *Thief River*, Guthrie Theater, Minneapolis, Minnesota; 2002, photograph by and courtesy of Michal Daniel.

that Ray answered a newspaper ad placed by Reese, confessed to the killing 53 years after the fact, named Gil and Anson, as his accomplices, and exited the closet, all at the same time. While Jody can accept his grandfather's homosexuality, Reese's own homophobia recalls that of Harlow himself. Acceptance advances, but change is uneven.

Back to Scene 7 and Anson, Ray 1, and Gil 1 stand over the unconscious Harlow back in 1948; homophobia pulses through Anson's veins this time, as he threatens Gil's life if he ever "touched" his grandson.⁹ Ray answers yes for him, and Anson asks: "More than once?" Ray responds: "Last fall. All winter."¹⁰ Seeking to "protect" his grandson's good name, social standing, etc., Anson decides to kill Harlow. We hear a shot. Gil 2 enters to tell us:

One bullet. One hole, one hole in the ground, and then—no holes at all. Nothing. The fields went on forever. No one in sight. And, for miles and miles, no one who'd ever heard of Harlow.[11]

Scene 8 takes us back to 1973 to complete Scene 5 between Gil 2 and Ray 2. Just as we see Ray weakening and accepting Gil's offer to visit for a 25-year-delayed tryst in the city, Perry bursts in to announce that Ray Junior is beating up Kit offstage. In the next scene, it's 2001 again and we're back to Scene 6 with Ray 3 and Gil 3, as the two men, now in their seventies, compare life's wounds: Gil's lover, Kit, died of AIDS; Ray's wife, Molly, died without knowing the truth about her husband; Ray suffers the aftereffects of a stroke; Gil nursed and then buried friends felled by the AIDS epidemic; Ray lost his farm, lost all contact with the son who could not accept a gay father. This time, Ray proposes that the two old men live together in the town where they grew up, but Gil is having none of it and delivers the most touching speech in the play:

> You didn't say, "Gil, I still love you. I always have, but I was a coward. I was afraid to act on my love. I preferred a life of lying to everyone around me. I was a fool and so I got half a life, and I sentenced you to the same." You didn't say that. You just said, "Well, we're both alone." ... We're born alone, Ray, we die alone. And every minute of our lives is a chance not to be alone anymore. But it takes a lot.[12]

Scene 10 snaps us back to Scene 8 and Ray Junior's beating of Kit, who is now being tended to by Gil 2. Kit admits he gave Ray Junior a letter from Ray to Gil, describing their last time together. Now Gil, Ray, and Perry all fear Junior will take that letter to Ray's wife, Molly, and his life, as he has known it for 25 years, will end. In Scene 11 we travel back to 1948 and the aftermath of Harlow's murder. Anson, who shot Harlow to save his grandson Ray's reputation, swears them all to secrecy for the crime, advises Gil to turn himself in for shooting Lewis and threatens to kill Gil if he ever comes back to their town. While the shooting of Lewis served as the Inciting Incident, here the murder of Harlow—even though we learn of it only late in the play—works as the Point of Attack, having set all of the previous/past/future actions of the characters in motion. Now, when Gil asks Ray to leave town with him, Ray makes his fateful choice to stay: *"I have to have my life!* Gil? I have to have my life." In response, Gil tears the razor from Anson and slashes his own neck in despair. Ray and Anson pick Gil up to rush him to a hospital.

Scene 12, the shortest and last of the play, finds Gil 3 and Ray 3 as they stood at the end of Scene 9. Ray 1 and Gil 1 stand motionless in the room as well. Gil 3 and Ray 3 leave, having discussed the possibility of Gil visiting again in the future. As they exit, the final tableau is of Gil 1 and Ray 1, together as in 1948, as the lights slowly fade. The final stage picture juxtaposes the unknown future and the known past. While Gil 1 and Ray 1 had their lives before them,

Thief River: Two midwestern men (Bard Goodrich, left, and Alex Podulke) struggle with their gay identities over the course of a forty-year period. Guthrie Theater, Minneapolis, Minnesota; 2002, photograph by and courtesy of Michal Daniel.

filled with promise, potential and a multitude of possibilities, the audience has seen their lives unfold on stage in a mixture of loss, denial, pain, and, yet, hope remains.

If placed in chronological order the scenes of the play would be Scene 1, Scene 4, Scene 7, Scene 11, Scene 2, Scene 5, Scene 8, Scene 10, Scene 3, Scene 6, Scene 9, and, finally, Scene 12. Why has the author chosen to tell his story out of order? Form, they tell us, should follow content. Does it do so here? Interestingly, another critic agreed with John Simon that the nonlinear nature of the play was simply confusing. Bruce Weber, in the *New York Times*, found it gimmicky:

> *Thief River* is the kind of play that teaches you how to watch it; you have to absorb its structural parameters before you can follow it precisely. There is no warning that the changes of scene mean changes in time, and there seems to be no pattern to the changes.... Nor are there any overt signals that the actors in one scene are playing the same characters as different actors did in the scene before.... All of this makes the storytelling more interesting than the story.[13]

Certainly a playwright, especially one like Blessing, who hates to repeat himself, constantly searches for both new content *and* new forms: telling different stories in different ways. In *Thief River* the experiment works on several levels. The passage of 52 years allows us the scope to see how social attitudes about sexuality have changed—and how they haven't. I performed my first same-sex wedding as a Unitarian Universalist minister in 1978 when every state in the country banned such marriages. In 2014, 35 states offer legal gay marriages and only 15 still bar them. In 2015 the Supreme Court ruled them legal in *every* state. One of the first public demonstrations for gay rights took place on July 4, 1965, in Philadelphia, a watershed moment, now immortalized in a public mural downtown, in a country that has struck down anti-sodomy and other discriminatory laws. In *Thief River*, Gil 3 and Ray 3 inhabit a world in 2001 that Gil 1 and Ray 1 might never have imagined in 1948. But homophobia and homophobic violence remain real, as personified by Lewis, Harlow, and Anson in 1948, Ray Junior in 1973, and Reese in 2001. Jody, Ray's loving grandson, the lone straight, none homophobic character, appears only in 2001 and would have seemed unthinkable in 1948 or, perhaps, even 1973.

Blessing endorsed this idea in an interview about the play:

> I don't think the different periods of the play would resonate nearly as much as they do if we saw them successively.... I think that when we move from one to another, back to an earlier period, and forward—in an order that is not completely predictable, we start seeing these people. We are forced to keep making those shifts that society made slowly over 50 years.... I think it is very energizing and helpful to travel that distance very quickly back and forth. I think it helps us realize how far we've come, and how far we've yet to go.[14]

Because we still have quite a way to go, the play ends on a vaguely hopeful note, with no guarantee of success: Gil refuses to move in with Ray, but offers as almost his final line: "Maybe I'll come up for a visit."[15]

So the play and time tell a tale of past struggle and much present progress. But the doubling of characters tells a troubling psychological tale as well. Four of the actors playing Gil and Ray (Ray 2 and 3, and Gil 2 and 3) also play homophobes of varying intensity. The actor playing Gil 2 appears as Harlow, Ray 2 as Reese, Gil 3 as Perry, and Ray 3 as Anson. At one extreme, Harlow actually kills gay people, Reese sees them as sinners to be prayed for, and Perry and Anson find them socially objectionable and best hidden. Here the playwright reminds us, I think, that within each of us lies a muddled and troubled awareness of our own sexuality. If, as Dr. Alfred Kinsey wrote, the majority of us are neither entirely homosexual nor entirely heterosexual, sexuality becomes a sliding scale between polarities that we negotiate throughout our lives. Heterosexual and homosexual tendencies lie within each of us. And some of us, I think of my childhood when we regularly called kids we didn't like "faggot," also have harbored or may still harbor homophobic feelings. The doubling of actors onstage mirrors our own complex and sometimes contradictory psyches.[16]

The doubling and time shifting work on a third level as well: challenging the audience to figure out who is doing what when and, after an initial period of confusion, making the play interactive as the audience pays attention to puzzle out the clues.

Oddly enough, Blessing originally conceived of the play as a heterosexual love story but at some point shifted his ground ... to our benefit.[17] I agree with critic Kim Surkan, who wrote that in *"Thief River*, Lee Blessing has created an extraordinary portrait of the gay experience in rural America during the past half century."[18]

The Roads That Lead Here

Blessing has written many ten-minute plays, a newer and increasingly popular genre for both theaters and contests looking for fresh talent or seeking to put established writers through the rigor of a strictly limited genre. Theaters often make a night or two of collections of such plays and audiences appreciate knowing that if they find one play unengaging another will take the stage shortly. The Guthrie Theater, in Minneapolis, founded in 1963 by Sir Tyrone Guthrie, has showcased annual ten-minute play fests for many years, and Blessing's play *The Roads That Lead Here* appears in their 2002 published anthology:

Ten-Minute Plays from the Guthrie Theater. The upside and downside to a ten-minute play are the same: they're short. "Brevity is the soul of wit" as Shakespeare's Polonius tells us in *Hamlet*, comedies work best within the limitations of time. When Blessing and other playwrights choose to tackle more serious dramatic action rather than go for the laughs, however, the result often feels unfinished, containing ideas not fully explored and yet worthy of further stage time.

In *The Roads That Lead Here*, more a play of ideas than a comedy, we meet three brothers in their twenties, Jason, Marcus, and Xander, who reunite annually at their father's house to share their contributions to "the project," a nationwide road trip to collect pictures, sounds, and objects from a vanishing America. At play's open, Marcus and Xander are sharing photos of their journeys and the sights they collected, like dried yellow grass in Wolf Point, Montana, and waves in Pensacola, Florida.[19] We soon see that, oddly enough, their photos and notebook jottings (in rather rhapsodic purple prose) concern nature. People, relationships, human artifacts, do not seem to exist for them, or, at least, do not draw their interest or their collecting.

In a few minutes Jason enters following an offstage meeting with "The Eminent," who, to their collective surprise, has promised Jason a 30th birthday present.[20] All three share an unease. The Eminent, whom, we learn, is really their own father, has changed. As Jason relates:

> He said "thirty" in the strangest way. "You're going to be thirty, Jace. You deserve something very special this year." I said my life is already special.... I mean, what other father would help make a project like ours possible?[21]

The project they are working on is about "accumulation." Says Marcus: "The gathering of experience." Xander agrees: "America as we see it."[22] But it seems Dad is no longer attached to the project. Jason tells his brother: "The Eminent says we're not growing up."[23] He asks his siblings: "Do you wonder if we shouldn't be doing more with our lives?"[24]

> MARCUS: *More?*
> XANDER: How could we be doing more? I drive 200,000 miles a year.
> MARCUS: We all do. We have a project.
> JASON: We have a vision.
> XANDER: America without the people.[25]

These collectors do exhibit cases of arrested development. Preteens collect comic books, video games, baseball cards, Barbies, and then outgrow them or become lonely hoarders. And so, Jason relates:

> The Eminent—Dad—said that he doesn't think our project is ... helping us grow. He thinks we should get married, for one thing.[26]

The Eminent—Dad—seems to be right about these three:

> JASON: We're virgins.
> MARCUS: And proud of it.
> XANDER: Yeah!²⁷

And, yet, their screwy mission achieves some level of poetry and mindfulness, even for us:

> XANDER: [We'll have] everything but the people. Everything they don't see, or feel, or hear or smell or taste. Everything they forget about, every day—when they're only thinking about themselves ... a record of love.
> MARCUS: Proof that it's still worthy of love. That no matter how many of them there are, no matter how badly we may behave, it's still here.²⁸

The philosophizing ends quickly as an explosion is heard offstage. Dad is torching their three cars. The road trips, and the play, end:

> MARCUS: What's that sign he's holding up?
> JASON: I can't read it. All the smoke—
> XANDER: It says ... "You're grounded."²⁹

The Roads That Lead Here: Three brothers in their twenties, Jason, Marcus, and Xander (the actors are uncredited), reunite annually at their father's house to share their contributions to "the project," a nationwide road trip they take to collect pictures, sounds, and objects from a vanishing America. Actors Theatre of Louisville (Kentucky); 2003, photograph by and courtesy of Actors Theatre of Louisville.

The Roads That Lead Here delivers some laughs. The three clueless adults stuck in perpetual childhood, the seeming vapidity of their project, and, finally, the destruction of their cars by the very man who sent them on the road in the first place all strike us as funny. But when the actors leave the stage they have walked for less than ten minutes, larger questions remain. Have *we* "stopped to smell the roses?" Have we taken all the sights, smells, feelings, and senses of this great land for granted? Are we so out of touch with our own environment that we can only wonder at the excitement of Marcus and Xander as they stroke the fur of a fisher (a small North American mammal nearly rendered extinct by human pursuit of its fur)? "Wonderful animal," says Marcus. "Underrated," agrees Xander.[30] Have *you* stroked the fur of a fisher? How can an animal be underrated?

In the summer 2012, Blessing left his position as head of the graduate playwriting program at Mason Gross School of the Arts at Rutgers University in New Jersey, rented a U-Haul truck, and moved himself and his possessions to Los Angeles in a cross-country solo trek. As he wrote then:

> [This] makes the eighth time I believe that I've driven part or all of my things either halfway or all the way across America since 1995.
> I've grown rather fond of Interstate 40 in the process, I have to say.[31]

We find traveling history not only in *The Roads That Lead Here*, but in plays like *Great Falls* and *Tyler Poked Taylor*.

A Body of Water

In Eugene Ionesco's *The Bald Soprano* (1950), Mr. and Mrs. Martin compare notes and find they share an address, a bed, and a child, leading them to think they are married and have found each other again. We laugh to think that a married couple could be so clueless about their lives and then the second joke kicks in: as the Martins embrace in happiness, the maid, Mary, informs us that they are, in fact, mistaken and neither are who they think they are. Ionesco challenges our self-satisfied idea that we know our surroundings, the people with whom we share relationships, and our place in the world. Blessing dives into *A Body of Water* to extend the joke and ask if we do, indeed, know anything at all.

His couple, Avis and Moss, who may or may not be married, have no context, no memory, no clue as to who or where they are. As Avis says, sitting in a house high on a hill, at the beginning of the play: "There have to be roads. We must have gotten up here somehow."[32] Moss is not so sure: "We could have been dropped off by a helicopter."[33]

Whose house is it? They think it could be theirs. Maybe it's just one of several residences they own. Why not? Their clothes, wherever they came from, look expensive. They question everything. Avis states: "We don't know that we are a couple."[34] They check and find no wedding rings on their fingers, though they do remember waking up that morning naked in the same bed.

> MOSS: Maybe we're just acquaintances. Maybe we don't even know each other that well. We could be houseguests of someone who's ... gone away for something.
> AVIS: And while they were gone—apparently all night—we slept together?
> MOSS: Maybe we have loose morals.[35]

It gets pretty funny. Moss suggests they inspect each other's naked bodies to jog their memories. And while Moss finds Avis "beautiful," Avis, obtains a pair of tongs from the kitchen and "applies the tongs and inspects, apparently turning his member to various angles" and judges it "like a penis, only smaller."[36] A younger woman, Wren, arrives at the end of Scene 1 to demand, "What in hell's going on?" To which Avis can honestly answer: "We have no idea."[37]

Wren, however, does seem to know what is going on and that unnerves Avis and Moss. Avis suggests: "We should tie her up. We can overpower her." Moss demurs: "I'm not going to overpower anybody."[38]

> AVIS: We don't know who she is. She could be anyone. She could be—
> MOSS: Our daughter.[39]

When Avis and Moss admit to Wren they don't know who they are or who she is, Wren exits and returns with a wallet for Moss and a purse for Avis, telling them, "If you want to know who you are, simply look," and leaves for a "run."[40] Moss lets his imagination run wild: perhaps Wren works for the CIA, he suggests, and that he and Avis "could be material witnesses, international criminals, terrorists—"[41]

> AVIS: Have you heard of Occam's razor?
> MOSS: I think so.
> AVIS: You should get it, and use it to cut your throat.
> MOSS: (*After a beat, quietly*) That's no way to talk to a perfect stranger.[42]

They consider the purse and wallet Wren supplied.

> MOSS: It'll probably jog our memory.
> AVIS: I think our memory already jogged. It jogged away.[43]

Inside the purse and wallet they find picture IDs and discover, to their consternation, their actual names, Moss Sibley and Avis Mecklenburg, which come as a complete surprise. Though they do not share a last name they *do* discover a shared address. Like Ionesco's Mr. and Mrs. Martin, married or not, could the unrecognized Wren be Moss and Avis's daughter?

A Body of Water: The aging Avis (Michael Learned) and Moss (Edward Hermann) wake up each day with amnesia and wonder if they are somehow related. Guthrie Theater, Minneapolis, Minnesota; 2005, photograph by and courtesy of Michal Daniel.

Wren returns with additional explanations: Yes, they are married; no, she is not their daughter. She informs them of their vocations: Moss is a judge; Avis, a director of a center for healing wounds. Both, she says, are on sabbatical; their 11-year-old daughter disappeared from their home five months before and her body appeared two months ago in the thawing lake, the body of water of the title, just beyond their door. Yet neither Moss nor Avis admit remembering any of this.

Wren, probing, doubting, accusing, believes Moss and Avis, the young victim's own parents, murdered her.

WREN: Everyone in the world thinks you did it.
AVIS: The world thinks ... we're murderers?
WREN: *Aren't* you?[44]

So now everyone in the audience is recalling the Jon Benét Ramsey murder case of 1996 when the court of public opinion, but no actual legal court, convicted the six-year-old's parents, John and Patricia Ann "Patsy" Ramsey, of killing the beauty contestant in their Boulder, Colorado, home. But Wren is not a detective nor a prosecutor. As Scene 2 ends, she reveals herself as working for their defense. At this point, for me, the play gets less interesting. We seemingly pass from the impenetrable mystery of *The Bald Soprano* or *No Exit* to the weekly television staples *CSI*, *Criminal Minds*, or *Elementary*. Or do we?

Wren, trying to bolster their defense, leads Moss and Avis through photo albums to jog their memories. They claim no recognition but Wren and, she says, public opinion, believe they are faking their memory loss, a memory loss so complete that every previous day is forgotten the next time they awaken. Given such extraordinary circumstances, can Moss and Avis even believe Wren is who she says she is or that their little girl, if they ever raised one, is gone? Moss wonders: "Maybe we're being set up here."[45] It happens that he's right. In an explosion of anger, Wren admits the charade of a police investigation and now claims she invented it all to break up the monotony of being caretaker to two amnesiacs. She tells them:

> And sometimes I lie—yes, I lie. I make up a whole huge story about a daughter named Robin, 'cause that's what I wished you named me instead of Wren. I work out scenario after scenario, tell you you're physicists or chess champions, or revolutionaries ...[46]

But, can Moss and Avis trust Wren now as she tells them she really is their daughter and, as part of a team of doctors and a caretaker, has been trying for a long time to bring back their memories. Wren explains:

> Like I say, it's sort of a grab bag, depending on my mood. Sometimes I actually like you. I get all bright and sunny, and we spend the whole day pretending to be the most normal family in the world. Other times ... like today ... you don't want to be here. I don't want to be here. But here we are.[47]

But just as Moss orders Wren to leave, she reverts to her earlier story. As their lawyer, she wants to show them morgue shots of the murdered daughter. Scene 3 ends as Moss stares at the photos in shock, and Avis weeps.

For the audience, the mystery continues and deepens in Scene 4, wherein Avis is working a crossword and Moss reading a magazine as they easily recall all the crossword clues they need: "erne" for seabird, "ogee" for curved moulding and "quad" for an extinct South African zebra. As Avis says to Wren—whom she greets as "honey"—"Isn't he good? What a memory." Wren responds: "You're an ace, Pop."[48] Have we returned to a new play?

Moss quickly shatters the superficiality of feigned domesticity when his allusion to having had sex with Avis the night before upsets her equilibrium. He then diverts Avis's growing fear by admitting: "I was pretending."[49] But all of life seems a pretense:

> WREN: Avis, do you believe that I'm your daughter?
> AVIS: You tell me you are.
> WREN: Do you believe Moss is your husband?
> AVIS: I don't know. He seems like it, but ...[50]

In Scene 4, Avis and Moss remember their names, or seem to, or pretend to. But in the last scene of the play, Moss asks Wren once again: "And you say my name is...?"[51] Now, Wren offers a new story of explanation for their situation: "Car accident. Pretty rough one. You and Avis ... went off a cliff one morning, close to here. Right into the lake."[52] But Wren further explains this was no accident: Avis, behind the wheel that day, had left a note, describing how she planned to kill them both after discovering Moss had kept journals, detailing her every foible and smallest mistake.

This sounds plausible, but the playwright has fooled us before. What is really up with these amnesiacs? And why is Wren a serial liar? And what do we make of it when Moss asks when Avis will return from what Wren has told him is a trip to the "Wound Healing Institute," and Wren answers: "She's never coming back?" And when poor Moss asks, "When will I get better?" Wren tells him "I think if you were going to get better, it would have happened by now."[53] Of course, as soon as Moss leaves, Avis returns, and now, Wren tells her that Moss died years ago. Avis protests that they woke up together. "No," says Wren, "you thought you saw him, but you didn't."[54] But *we* saw him.

A Body of Water: Wren (Michelle O'Neill) claims to be many things as she cares for an older woman, Avis (Michael Learned) who cannot remember her life. Guthrie Theater, Minneapolis, Minnesota; 2005, photograph by and courtesy of Michal Daniel.

Moss returns in the next moment and now all three characters share the stage. Moss and Avis know that Wren has lied to each of them. Was she lying about being their daughter? about being their defense attorney? about those gruesome morgue shots? We'll never know, as Wren rushes offstage. "I'm going shopping." she says. "Sorry—gotta run!"[55]

Unfortunately, in the minute left for the play to run, Avis and Moss don't ask those questions. Instead, Avis offers a metaphysical answer to their dilemma:

> I was thinking that maybe this is what happiness looks like. If we could see it, I mean. Does that make sense? Perhaps we're simply caught in ... a state of happiness. And there's no need to get out.[56]

For a moment, we think Avis has hit upon an existential truth. Perhaps we think of the 1999 book *The Power of Now: A Guide to Spiritual Enlightenment*, by Eckhart Tolle, in which he claims we need to avoid thoughts of the past and future and live in the present moment, what he calls the "now." Pop psychology for the masses, the book sold millions of copies in 33 languages, and Oprah Winfrey publicly endorsed it. No one lives more in the "now" than Avis and Moss.

But Moss, in response to these words from Avis, the stage directions tells us, "*covers his face and weeps silently.*"[57] For him, at least, this "now" is a terrible place to be. End play. Meaning? The critics didn't think much of the possibilities and snatched at the lack of conclusion. Charles Isherwood, in the *New York Times*, wrote:

> This sputtering drama about a man and a woman who wake up one day with matching cases of amnesia is ultimately so, er, forgettable that its resolution ceases to be a matter of suspense long before it arrives.[58]

Kerry Reid, in the *Chicago Tribune*, agreed:

> Call it a lack-of-memory play. Lee Blessing's "A Body of Water," ... takes its audience through blind alleys, rabbit holes and more twists than a corkscrew as it unfolds several possible takes on an aging couple's mutual amnesia, only to end up becalmed in its own narrative contrivances.[59]

Though critic Bob Rendell, in "Talkin' Broadway," enjoyed the play:

> Unlike the dark and menacing nihilistic works of Harold Pinter, Lee Blessing strives (successfully) to provide stimulating, accessible entertainment. Are weighty matters such as the unreliability of memory and the mechanisms we employ to cope with loss, betrayal and guilt part of the fabric here? Possibly. There are interpretations which would support such a view. However, whatever weighty matters are introduced, they are made part and parcel of the entertaining game that Blessing has designed for us ... clever and entertaining.[60]

A Body of Water makes its audience work: work to follow the conflicting scenarios, work to trace the progress of the characters, and work to figure out what it all means. Oddly enough, in keeping the audience guessing, it keeps them in the "now." Many of us are willing to do the work required here because we love unraveling a mystery or because we got hooked on the larger issues: relationships between a husband and wife and between parents and daughters, or the struggles many of us will face dealing with the terror of memory loss and the unknitting of decades-long intimate relationships brought on by Alzheimer's Disease, which now afflicts millions of people worldwide, ravaged my own parents, and quite possibly someone you love.

Blessing returns to water imagery for his title here as he does in *Thief River*, *Great Falls*, and *When We Go Upon the Sea*, or as he does in the body of the play in *Black Sheep*. Of course, he did grow up in Minnesota, the "Land of 10,000 Lakes."

The Scottish Play

Athletes are superstitious by nature. The *Curse of the Bambino* followed the Boston Red Sox after trading Babe Ruth to the New York Yankees in 1919. The until-then successful Boston franchise nosedived into an 86-year playoff drought while the Yankees flourished for decades. The Chicago Cubs haven't gone to the World Series since ushers escorted Billy Sianis and his billy goat out of Wrigley Field in 1945 and Billy cursed the home team in return. Players won't change socks, bats, or ball, when on a streak. Theater people feel the same way. When so much seems to depend on chance: does the high and inside pitch get fouled away or crushed for a homer? does the infield grounder squirt though the second baseman's legs for a hit or get turned into a game-ending double play? Does the unknown understudy go onstage at the last minute to flub her lines or wow the critics? does the aging star summon past youth or dodder about the stage? A success or failure onstage or on the ball field rests on inches, inspiration, intangibles, and just plain luck.

Actors say "Break a leg," never "Good luck," which would somehow constitute bad luck, and they keep "the ghost light" burning between performances to keep away bad spirits. But no superstition matches the refusal to say out loud *Macbeth*'s full title *The Tragedy of Macbeth*, by William Shakespeare, 1606. Call it "The Scottish Play," "Mackers," or simply "the play," but never call it by its full name within a theater. If someone slips and says it, that person must leave the room immediately. They must then

> close the door, turn around three times, say a dirty word (or spit, some say), then knock on the door and ask to be let back in. If you can't do all that, you simply quote from *Hamlet*, act 1, scene 4: "Angels and ministers of grace defend us!"[61]

Others believe the play itself brings bad luck; that Shakespeare copied out real satanic curses for his theatrical witches and that real witches cursed him for his impudence. As a direct result, they say, actors have died, productions have failed, and fortunes as well as lives have been lost to accidents, fevers, plague, lightning strikes, riots, and fires. With such a rich, dramatic history, Blessing's take on The Scottish Curse, set at a present-day Shakespeare festival in Bannockburn, Michigan, somehow fails to deliver both the comedic and tragic turns its title promises.

The trouble begins in Act 1, Scene 1, set promisingly enough in "The Dark Thistle, a British-style pub,"[62] as actors, directors, and producers celebrate 30 years of success for the "Northernmost Shakespeare Festival." Blessing writes for a cast of ten, large for him, and yet the characters seem stereotypes and the dialogue stilted. In almost all his plays we see that Blessing has an extraordinary facility with dialogue and language, creating characters who sound real and speak with distinctive voices. Reread *Riches* to feast on the verbal ping pong of two characters moving from daily convention to murderous violence. But *The Scottish Play* Act 1, Scene 1, is chock full of exposition, not action.

We learn that the festival founder, Alex McConnell, seeks to cap his 30-year cultural run by staging *Macbeth*. Artistic director Bill Neil, also a veteran of those 30 years, refuses to do the play based on its history of bringing disaster to theaters and actors. Alex saw this coming and already has the associate festival director, Jack Bonner, ready to take over Billy's position. Learning this, Billy stalks out.

Scene 2 takes place the following May, in the midst of a blizzard. The poster announcing the upcoming production of *Macbeth* is covered in icicles. A fire, caused by a squirrel chewing on a power line, has already destroyed the stage sets, while pipes bursting in the cold weather have flooded the basement and attracted hundreds of frogs who must be corralled and removed. Omens of impending disaster? Worse still, Billy has hung around and taken to sleeping in his office, dedicated to making Jack's life hell. And, yet, the festival secretary, Pewter Piper, who openly declares her love for Jack, can say, "I can't believe we're having all this *bad luck*."[63] Pewter's love for a reformed Jack is unrequited and funny:

> JACK: There was a time in my life, not so very long ago, when I might have taken you up on that offer to kill people for me, or give yourself to me in a frankly sexual way—
> PEWTER: Yes—!
> JACK: But ... but—that was the old Jack. The one who spent too much time over at the Dark Thistle, having too much to drink and messing up his life and the lives of others—
> PEWTER: Mess me up, Jack. Mess me up right now.[64]

While Jack was digging out from under several feet of snow, Billy has stepped in to hire Jack's three ex-wives to play Macbeth's three witches.

Scene 3 brings us the three exes, each an actress and each loathing the other, who quickly get into a slapstick food fight. They can unite, however, over their lingering hatred for their shared ex-husband. One almost feels sorry for Jack. Then Alex arrives with some good news: he has returned with Hollywood film star and heartthrob Path Sanderson in tow to star as their Macbeth and garner national publicity for the production, even though Path has never actually acted onstage before and never read the play, believing, "It's an action-adventure thing, right?"[65] Uh-oh, more trouble brewing.

About this time, as Jack's problems mount and his goal of producing the play seems to be slipping away, the audience begins to discern the author's intent to draw metatheatrical parallels between the play we are seeing, *The Scottish Play*, and the play within the play, *Macbeth*, and between Jack and Macbeth himself. The parallel seems tenuous. Yes, both share a driving ambition to succeed though Macbeth aims to be King of Scotland and Jack wishes only for a successful theatrical production, albeit one that wins national notice. Macbeth gives in to the blandishments of his wife, Lady Macbeth, and together they kill King Duncan. Pewter Piper does tell Jack she would kill for him but we see this only as the hyperbole of the love-struck. Billy says Jack stole the theater from him, as Macbeth steals Duncan's crown, and the witches appear in both plays though they act as the "point of attack" in *Macbeth* and only as comic relief in *The Scottish Play*. Macbeth brings ruin upon himself when he unleashes his inner evil in pursuit of his goal. Jack seems more a hapless victim as events unfold around him. Does our playwright intend a bit of professional revenge based upon his own life in the theater: leading us to think all directors channel an inner murderer?

In Scene 4, a heat wave follows the blizzard, the stage trap door swings dangerously open unexpectedly, the actors at the lodge have fallen ill and flood waters cut off their exit, while reporters arrive to cover Path's stage debut. When Path, a stereotypical self-centered and dumb movie star, who has not read the script, discovers that Macbeth is a murderer he calls for "Rewrite!"[66] When called upon to read his lines he delivers "the single worst reading of Shakespeare they have ever heard"[67] and clears the stage, concluding Act 1.

Act 2 begins with Zita, ex-wife and current witch, handcuffing Jack to his chair for an impromptu therapy session, since she once played a psychotherapist on TV. Though she exits, he remains handcuffed till Billy cuts him free and he dashes off to find his AA sponsor. That leaves Billy hanging around as Path enters to complain about his role:

And Macbeth, I thought, with swords and shit, was a natural. I thought I'd be like, you know, Lancelot or something. Instead, I'm grabbing at knives that aren't there, having guys kill my best friend—what shit is *that*?—not to mention my wife, who kicks my ass for, like, basically the whole play.[68]

To make Path happy and, more importantly, to make Jack *un*happy, Billy suggests Path take another role in the play instead. We learn that the costume shop has exploded, burning all the costumes and props in the latest disaster to strike the "cursed" production. With Billy's encouragement, Path now wants to play a "good guy," Macduff, instead of the villainous Macbeth and with script rewrites worked out with Billy, Path even has a new name for the play: *Macduff*, a new play by Path Sanderson "*and* William Shakespeare. And that is how the writing credit will read—"[69] Path threatens to walk if he doesn't get his way and Jack capitulates, agreeing to act as Macbreath, the new name given the Macbeth character to avoid the curse of saying the character's name in the theater, in the new play *Macduff* while taking on his nemesis, Billy, as assistant director.

In Scene 3 we learn "real" actors are leaving to avoid appearing in the new script where everyone will be wearing togas left over from a production of *Julius Caesar*, following the costume shop disaster. Path's script, it seems, has failed to improve on Shakespeare:

> EDEN: Please don't go back to Scotland. He'll kill you!
> PATH: You're so good and beautiful. But I gotta.
> EDEN: Don't deprive me of your gorgeous eyes and … and hero's lips!
> PATH: Time's up, Babe. Macbreath's days are numbered. I know he killed my partner. Now I gotta prove it.
> EDEN: Oh please, prove it fast. Chop him to pieces. And chop his wife up, too. She is such a bitch.[70]

Finally, in Scene 4, we get to see the progeny of this mad mating of ambition, greed, and star power as the company stages *Macduff* for a preview audience. Jack, literally driven to drink by all that has happened, seeks vengeance by trying to decapitate Path with his prop hatchet as the stage dissolves in fog, missed cues, stumbling actors, and improvised speeches, and Eden falls into and out of and into the witches' cauldron. Before Jack can kill Path we hear the roar of a tornado *and* an earthquake and the lights go out.

The play concludes the next day back at the Dark Thistle, where it began. The anomaly of a tornado and an earthquake occurring simultaneously has destroyed both the theater and the town. But some hope lives on. Path has left. Billy and Alex make plans to reproduce the festival somewhere in Canada, though vowing never to stage *Macbeth*. Meanwhile, Jack has achieved tenuous contact with his alienated teenage son. In the final stage picture, Jack's cell phone rings and then it's lights out. The show must go on.

No mixed reviews this time. The critics universally panned *The Scottish Play*. Steve Oxman wrote in the *Los Angeles Times*:

> Blessing's reputation as a reliable writer, though, takes a significant hit, as this lame effort is so distinctly poor that it's enough to generate a new superstition: Plays about the cursed play are cursed from their inception.[71]

Anne Marie Welsh, theater critic for the *San Diego Union Tribune*, wrote:

> To the list of disasters that have befallen actors in "Macbeth," we can now add this one—"The Scottish Play," Lee Blessing's lead-footed Shakespeare spinoff, perhaps the worst new play ever staged by La Jolla Playhouse.[72]

While Julio Martinez, in *Variety*, commented:

> There is so much action and so much information being introduced that the heart of the production, Bonner's journey of self-reinvention, is not fully realized. The calamities simply overwhelm everything else, leaving all the human agendas in a useless heap.[73]

But perhaps Rob Stevens, in *TheatreMania*, put it best:

> While he has a lot of fun playing with theatrical traditions and laying on the curses, the play feels unfinished, as if something major is missing—such as heart.[74]

Unlike his other romp with Shakespeare, *Fortinbras*, which comments on power politics, media campaigns, leadership, foreign military adventures, and government lies, *The Scottish Play*, like some girls, "just want to have fun," but without anyone to root for or anything to think about, never quite does.

Lonesome Hollow

This dystopic play set in the very near future—or "soonish," writes Blessing[75]—about the criminalization of love, sex, and art and the destruction of intimate relationships, gave me nightmares after I read it. In *Lonesome Hollow*, imprisoned for indefinite terms, with little hope of ever experiencing freedom again, Tuck, who had sex with a teenaged girl, and Nye, who preyed on young boys, inhabit a bucolic, isolated, but ultimately hopeless existence. Can we imagine a society where people convicted, and sentenced, are still incarcerated after serving their sentences? Unfortunately, that day arrived some time ago. In 2007, ironically the year *Lonesome Hollow* premiered, the *New York Times* reported: "About 2,700 pedophiles, rapists and other sexual offenders are already being held indefinitely, mostly in special treatment centers, under so-called civil commitment programs in 19 states."[76] Criminals of all stripes—thieves, swindlers, drunk drivers, even murderers—serve out their terms and eventually reenter society, and yet we often treat sexual criminals, especially when the victims are children, differently, fearing, perhaps in a mixture of old-fashioned Puritan guilt that such crimes are unforgivable and the helplessness of seeing them as too easily repeatable, as, ultimately, irredeemable. Blessing makes the point:

> NYE: Predators ain't the only repeat offenders. Wife-beaters, drunks, drug addicts—you don't keep them past their sentences.
> GLOVER: We like them better.[77]

Why have I classified this as a "Love Is All There Is" play as opposed to a "Headline" play? The headlines scream, certainly, of sexual predation and child exploitation as well as the abuse of civil liberties in combatting them, but the play's real drama lies in a web of relationships that break the heart.

The play opens with Tuck building a labyrinth, a project Nye cannot understand. Tuck explains in words that speak to all of us:

> It's not a puzzle for children, it's a spiritual journey for adults. It requires creativity, intuition. It's for those who choose to walk a spiritual path.... The labyrinth forces us to see in all directions, from all perspectives. That's why it doesn't have walls like a maze.... Nothing's hidden.... Your only foe is yourself.[78]

Turns out that Tuck has miscalculated. His foes are legion and arrive in recurring visitors: Mills, a female lower functionary of the company that runs this prison; Pearl, Tuck's sister, who counsels soul-killing capitulation; and Glover, upper-level manager of the prison farm and Big Brother personified in his callous manipulation of humanity's best impulses.

Mills is most problematic of the three. Willing to taser Nye and reduce him into a writhing epileptic fit for some insignificant back talk but also willing to unbutton her blouse and expose herself to spark an affair with Tuck, her actions seem designed to fulfill the author's plot points and theme rather than as an expression of believable character. Mills, no first name (as is the case with all of the play's characters) functions as the sexy fascist whose totalitarian violence arises from repressed sexuality.

Poor Pearl appears as the greatest victim in her own way, trying to move heaven and earth to free her brother and falling down the rabbit hole after him. Pearl visits Lonesome Hollow on two occasions. Note the title choice from a playwright who loves words:

> TUCK: Lonesome Hollow. Was that really the name of this town?
> MILLS: Both the name and the state of mind. Lonesome Hollow. Two negatives make a positive, I suppose.[79]

Mills explains the rules to Pearl:

> MILLS: NO support of any kind. No acceptance of their past behavior. Any sign of approval of their past behavior may be interpreted as complicity in their crimes...
> PEARL: I have to say your rules are—

MILLS: No comments on the rules. Any criticism for the operation of this facility may be deemed grounds for an investigation into sympathies you may have with the resident you are visiting.[80]

From Pearl we learn that Tuck's books of nude photographs, once openly sold as art, are now banned and merely possessing one is a crime; Tuck's father, we learn, has killed himself in shame. And in a scenario that recalls both the book burnings of Nazi Germany and the twisting of family loyalties seen in the Chinese Cultural Revolution, Pearl urges Tuck to burn his own books on camera as a condition of his release. "Do it, please? It's just a gesture."[81] Her love for her brother drives her abject capitulation and, in the end, this attempt to appease overt evil leads to her own destruction.

Blessing's fiction parallels our own recent reality. Tuck, a fictive art photographer, recalls the real-life case of Sally Mann, whose book of nude photos of her own three children, all under the age of ten, entitled *Immediate Family*, and published in 1992 led to public accusations, but no legal charges, of child pornography.

Pearl describes a fictive world shaped by real-life anti-pornography crusaders like Andrea Dworkin (1946–2005), who claimed that magazines like *Playboy* "in both text and pictures promotes both rape and child sexual abuse."[82] Dworkin campaigned for local legislation, "The Anti-Pornography Civil Rights Ordinance" that proposed to treat pornography as a violation of women's civil rights and to allow women harmed by pornography to seek damages through lawsuits in civil courts. Dworkin and others, like the poet Robin Morgan (*Monster*), saw pornography as causing sex crimes that endangered the lives of all women. "Pornography is the theory; rape is the practice," wrote Morgan.[83] In our time, such efforts did not succeed as science failed to prove a causal link between pornography and sexual assault. The fictive Glover, however, believes pornography, or even otherwise innocent photos of naked adults or children, does lead directly to sexual assaults, telling Tuck: "Men who drool over your books ... go out and do something about it."[84]

Tuck, Pearl, Nye, and Mills are all pitiable human beings and, one must admit, one-dimensional characters. Blessing's villain, Glover, comes to life here, however, and it was he who gave me the nightmares. Claiming to be a therapist to the residents (inmates), a protector to the sexually exploited, and a bureaucrat sympathetic to the paradoxes of the human condition, he easily steps back, drops the mask, and orders the most vicious punishments:

GLOVER: You know what happens if we catch you in the act. You'll lose a hand. You'll lose the use of a hand. We have shots for that too....
NYE: You can't maim us. You ain't allowed to do that!
GLOVER: Of course we are. We do it every day.[85]

Lonesome Hollow: At a special prison for sexual predators, Tuck (Sheffield Chastain, right) seeks spiritual growth through a labyrinth, while fellow inmate Nye (Lou Sumrall) looks on. Contemporary American Theater Festival, Shepherd University, Shepherdstown, West Virginia; 2007, photograph by Ron Blunt; courtesy of Contemporary American Theater Festival.

By the end of the play Nye, like a concentration camp inmate, is reduced to the mere semblance of a human being in a painfully unforgettable bit of theatricality. When last we see him:

> He's not walking, not even crawling. His legs are now as dead as his hands, so he's pulling himself along by his arms with agonizing slowness.[86]

Nye's victimization at Glover's hands in the near future recalls the torture of others in the near past. Alan Turing (1912–1954), the British mathematician credited with decoding Germany's Enigma codes during World War II and shortening the war, as dramatized in the 2014 movie *The Imitation Game*, nominated for multiple Academy Awards, ran afoul of anti-homosexuality laws and, according to the *Daily Mail* was

> convicted of "gross indecency with a male" in March 1952. Instead of prison, he was sentenced to chemical castration—injections of the female hormone oestrogen, designed to suppress his homosexuality. The injections destroyed Turing's athletic frame (he would have run the marathon for Britain at the 1948 London Olympics if it hadn't been for an

injury) and turned him into a bloated monster. In the words of one of his biographers, it also set the diffident genius on a "slow, sad descent into grief and madness."[87]

Propelled by a Calvinist fear that someone somewhere is enjoying themselves, Glover hates humanity, even his own:

> No man's innocent. We all struggle with the same suspect hormones. A picture of a naked girl or boy, no matter how young, can stimulate us. We have to work to make it *not* stimulate us. Those who succeed survive; those who don't.... We're normal men, Nye, which is to say we've got to be watched like hawks.[88]

Glover warns of a totalitarian future when he tells Nye he can have no visitors since "fraternizing with a child molester is illegal." Nye protests: "They can't make visiting your own family a crime." Glover responds: "If you get the people behind you, you can make anything a crime. That's what democracy means."[89]

Melodrama, most often defined as a play, film, or novel in which "the plot is often sensational and the characters may display exaggerated emotion"[90] has a bad name, by and large today. We think of villains twisting their long mustaches while heroines struggle against the ropes binding them to the tracks before an oncoming train. However, a more nuanced definition, referencing structure rather than plot, might highlight the role of the villain, or antagonist, as the engine of action in melodrama. Whereas Hamlet, in that eponymous play, as the hero, or protagonist, moves the action forward by seeking out his father's ghost, spying on his uncle, confronting his mother, pretending to be mad, etc., in *Lonesome Hollow* the *antagonist* moves the action. Glover torments Nye, uncovers the affair between Mills and Tuck, arranges to have Pearl's children taken from her, manipulates Tuck's escape attempt and recapture, and generally orchestrates everything we see onstage.

Villains can intrigue us much more than the rather bland heroes they sometimes confront. Think of Iago in *Othello*, Angelo in *Measure for Measure*, Shylock in *Merchant of Venice*, Richard the III, Lady Macbeth, or the deadly duo of Tamora and Aaron the Moor in *Titus Andronicus*, to confine our examples to Shakespeare alone. Glover embodies mid-level bureaucratic smarminess, denouncing sexual predation even as he drops inappropriate sexual comments about Pearl and asking Tuck about Mills:

> How do you like her tits? (*After a tense beat, laughing.*) I'm just teasing. Classic therapeutic ploy, designed to get a rise out of you. Beneath me, really. Can't help it. I get so bored out here sometimes. But seriously, would you fuck her?[91]

A bit later he expounds upon his value to society:

> I'm the one who protects every small, dreaming head that lies on a pillow tonight. I'm the reason the bedroom door will stay closed, the window will not be raised silently, the car will not roll to a stop beside the playground tomorrow, the nice man will not bend

down to smile in the face of a child—*your* child—and say that Mommy wants her home. I'm the reason there will be no car to hop into, and I am the reason—the *only* reason, clever fellow that I am—that she'll be there when you say grace at the dinner table.[92]

And all Glover wants for this guaranteed security (which, of course, not even he, or any other fascist, *can* guarantee) is obedience and the surrender of our individual consciences and minds. To see a Glover-like character become the hero of the story, check out the 2005 movie *Hard Candy*, where actress Ellen Page, before her break-out role in *Juno*, kidnaps, binds, Tasers, bludgeons, castrates, and drives to suicide a presumed pedophile and walks away scot free, her vigilante crusade for a safer world just begun.

Blessing portrays incarceration at Lonesome Hollow as the final apotheosis of the slippery slope to an illusory "safe" society. As Glover says of Nye:

> We have a clearly perceived goal: Nye. Get Nye. Keep him from moving next to us, changing his name, sliding into the crowd, on to the Internet.... But how do we get him?[93]

Finally, we see that Glover has physically and mentally destroyed Nye (and to some degree Tuck, Mills, and Pearl) in the service of safeguarding us and our children. Nye gets the abject last words: "You know, it really ain't that bad here. Once you know the rules."[94]

The idea that we might all be living in Lonesome Hollow "soonish" made the critics take ideological sides. An unsigned review in the right-leaning *Washington Times* read:

> Lee Blessing's "Lonesome Hollow," ... is less a play than a pompous, paranoid sermon laying out the grim, totalitarian future that today's thought police (who hail, of course, from the religious right) have in store for us.... Mr. Blessing is less interested in storytelling than he is in goading the audience into fearing the implied terrorism of a mythical right-wing morality squad. As a result, "Lonesome Hollow" rapidly deteriorates into a tiresome propaganda vehicle gasbagging to a predictably gloomy conclusion.[95]

Writing for the "Chicago Theater Beat" website, Katy Walsh felt differently:

> Playwright Lee Blessing has spun a fascinating tale of political extremists. The premise is inconceivable and totally believable at the same time. It's uncomfortably powerful.[96]

Great Falls

Want to join Monkey Man and Bitch on a claustrophobic cross country road trip? In *Great Falls* (entitled *Thermopolis* in an earlier version presented in an evening of short plays in New York City in the mid–2000s) Blessing puts a car (literally or figuratively, depending upon the set designer) and its two passengers, a middle-aged man and a teenage girl, on stage and begins with talk of kidnapping, prison, and rape, drawing us in to wonder, who are these people with the funny names, and why are they on the road in South Dakota? The backstory slowly emerges, in part through a phone conversation with Bitch's mother, Monkey Man's former wife. Monkey Man has cajoled, tricked, or wheedled Bitch into the trip on the spur of the moment to talk, think, and work out some relationship issues. When Bitch announces she has named her stuffed jackalope Vicious Penis Destroyer the conflict appears clear and promises to get nastier. One week shy of her 18th birthday Bitch epitomizes teenage petulance, but, clearly, an even deeper anger percolates within.

Of course, the title *Great Falls* acts as more than a place name and symbolizes that either or both characters have or will take a great fall.

The eight short scenes of the play unfold like a roadmap along Interstates 90 and 94. Rather than scene numbers we get place name titles so we can follow the characters' physical journey. Scene 1 is titled simply "Wall" [western South Dakota], Scene 2 "Thermopolis" [central Wyoming], Scene 3, "Yellowstone" [northwest Wyoming], Scene 4, "Anaconda" [southern Montana], Scene 5, "Kalispell" [northwestern Montana], Scene 6, "Great Falls" [western Montana], Scene 7, "Miles City" [eastern Montana], and Scene 8 "Fremont" [outside Omaha, Nebraska]. The trip is circuitous and circular though, and like the evolving relationship it symbolizes, it has a beginning and a stopping point, if not an end. Usually, you can predict that characters who begin a journey with such hostility will end it with hugs and kisses. Let's see.

Bitch lives up to her name, calling Monkey Man (also a name she has bestowed on the man) a "pig fucker."[97] Monkey Man indulges most of her hostility and tries to placate her, buying her cigarettes, letting her choose the motel bed she prefers, suggesting sights to see, etc. He seeks to make amends for past deeds and while she showers out of earshot he rehearses a speech in which he confesses to cheating on her mother, explaining:

> Everyday. I was in pain everyday with her, and these ... lapses, adventures—I don't know what to call them—were a kind of relief that instantly palled.[98]

Bitch breaks this private sexual reverie by raising the stakes when she exits the bathroom topless and later accuses Monkey Man of "drooling" over her.[99] Monkey Man asks her to put clothes on and when he leaves to use the bathroom Bitch calls her mom, showing a slightly softer side, seeming to appreciate the hotel room for the first time and allowing: "He's spending lots of money. I think he's trying to buy my love."[100] But the nastiness returns when he reenters the bedroom in his boxers and Bitch notes: "I can see why she left you.... Can't believe she didn't vomit every time you..."[101]

Monkey Man is recreating a boyhood trip he took with his parents because

Great Falls: Monkey Man (Tom Nelis) and Bitch (Halley Wegryn Gross) confront taxidermy and each other during a road trip. Actors Theatre of Louisville (Kentucky); 2008, photograph by Harlan Taylor; courtesy of Actors Theatre of Louisville.

"I liked my parents best on trips."[102] But Bitch isn't buying it: "Who [do] I hate more. You, or my father?"[103] When they get to Yellowstone National Park, Bitch refuses to leave the car or even look at the Old Faithful geyser as it erupts. Sympathizing with Monkey Man, we agree that "this carries perversity to a whole new level."[104] As he rhapsodizes over the display of nature, Bitch covers her head with a blanket, the better to ignore it all.

Posturings reverse and ebb. In Scene 4, "Anaconda," Bitch calls Monkey Man "Dad," but, surprisingly, he corrects her: "I'm not your dad."[105] As Bitch writes in her journal, we learn that Monkey Man writes novels and poetry and that Bitch used to write poems she shared with him. He cajoles her into reading one now:

> I'm trying to decide
> How big a garbage bag I'll need
> When I trash all your dreams.[106]

There, at the Continental Divide, as large as the divide in their own relationship, Bitch draws Monkey Man out about his philandering and his feelings for her mother and asks a natural question: "If you and Mom were having problems, why didn't you talk about it?"[107] She then adds, surprisingly, "You never gave up on me."[108]

Now we learn that a relative had abused the mother when she was a child and that Bitch was also a victim of sexual abuse.[109] She forces his confession of cowardice in the marriage and the tables turn. Now Bitch will determine where they go; she will also be doing the driving.

She heads for Glacier National Park and while Monkey Man admires the view and reminisces about his own childhood visit, Bitch hits him with another revelation: she's pregnant. We learn a lot, quickly, in Scene 5, "Kalispell": she does not know the identity of the father of her unborn child because two "friends" raped her and her boyfriend beat her up and then had sex with her. Now she wants her stepdad's help in getting an abortion at the next stop on their route, Great Falls (hence the play's title and the symbolic "fall,"—from innocence? from security? from hope?) "I need someone to be there," she tells him.[110] She wants to make a deal: "Do this and I won't cut you out of my life."[111] Bad things do happen to good people, but ... this strains credulity. How many protagonists face this much heartbreak and pain? Tally it up: mother and daughter were each sexually abused as children; Mom was married and divorced twice; Daughter was raped twice and impregnated; Stepdad is alienated from his ex-wife and his stepchildren hate him (Bitch told us earlier that her brother, in a rage, destroyed all photos of Monkey Man); and now Bitch will get an abortion ... on her *birthday*! Blessing stacks the deck and then adds even more tragedy as drama passes into melodrama.

At the abortion clinic Monkey Man breaks down in tears, and Bitch, trying to explain his tears to the receptionist, speaks a truth she has not previously allowed herself to think: "He's fine. He just loves me a lot, that's all."[112] And it's in Great Falls that Monkey Man has the funniest line of the play, to a state trooper who pulls them over, "No, I don't work for a living. I'm a writer."[113]

A few days later, in "Miles City," Scene 7, in a cheap motel room, Bitch suffers fever and pain from the abortion. Ignoring her pleas and insults, Monkey Man finally asserts some parental control and takes her to a hospital. The hits just keep coming, just as they did for Job. Unbeknown to all, Bitch also has chlamydia, complicated by the abortion. Recovering in yet another cheap motel, after the hospital visit, Monkey Man speaks to her affectionately:

> MONKEY MAN: Go back to sleep, sweetie.
> BITCH: I like being your sweetie.
> MONKEY MAN: I like it, too.
> BITCH: I like it, too.
> MONKEY MAN: So do I.[114]

Next day the pleasantries end. We learn that Bitch's biological father sexually abused her and that Monkey Man's marital infidelities destroyed her hopes for a "normal" family life, though she does admit he saved her life in Miles City. In "Fremont," the last scene, they pause just an hour from Bitch's home. It is here that Monkey Man gives her the car as a birthday gift and tells her he will be walking home.

> MONKEY MAN: I've got something in my head. Maybe I'll start writing it. Keep whatever's in the car. It's not important.
> BITCH: Dad—
> MONKEY MAN: Stepdad. Ex. Monkey Man.
> BITCH: This isn't fair.... You're not saying goodbye right.
> MONKEY MAN: No one can. Not in this family anyway. I wish I could do you good without doing you harm. I can't, that's all.[115]

No hugs and kisses here, just a little hope and a lot of despair. He saved her life yet his betrayals ruined her life. We try to love and help others and we fail at least as often as we succeed. We have seen this entropy, "people breaking apart,"[116] in *Riches, Down the Road, Thief River*, etc., and it speaks to verisimilitude and our own hopes and fears better than any sugarcoated Disney-style, happily-ever-after ending.

The critics, by and large, were not pleased with *Great Falls*. Nina Metz wrote in *New City Stage*:

> [The protagonists Bitch and Monkey Man] embark on a road trip that is meant to draw them together. Or offer some kind of closure. Or shed light on who they are as individuals. I'm not sure I actually cared by the end, which is the play's main drawback; plentiful melodrama laced with sarcasm ... but the payoff is zilch and ... [Monkey Man] is never fully realized in human terms. That said, Blessing can write a funny line. His sense of humor does most of the heavy lifting.[117]

Judith Egerton, in the *Louisville Courier-Journal*, thought:

> Blessing's play earns points for examining topics people tend to avoid. However, the playwright has loaded the stepdaughter down with so many layers of emotional trauma, it's hard to find the person behind the brat and the victim.[118]

While an unsigned review in the *Chicago Reader* read:

> Though Blessing's script has a strong emotional arc, he sometimes sacrifices nuance for dramatic effect—particularly in his ending, which wraps up the action too neatly and leaves a bad taste.[119]

Blessing, a stepdad but never a biological father in his own life, has written about parent/child dysfunction before. *Eleemosynary* and *Independence* look at mother/daughter issues; *The Winning Streak* and *A View of the Mountains* tackle father/son problems; while *Nice People Dancing to Good Country Music* examines, in part, mother/son dysfunction, but *Great Falls* stands alone as the only one about a stepfather/daughter relationship and, in the end, is the least successful. Keep in mind that plots and characters do not spring from authors' actual lives but from their creative, imaginative, empathetic minds. Blessing wrote of a serial killer (*Down the Road*) without murdering anyone, of sisters (*Independence*) without having one, of an arms negotiator (*A Walk in the Woods*) without being one. Blessing has said: "Everything you write is you writing about yourself, discovering areas or depths of yourself."[120] That means plumbing your psyche rather than your actual experiences.

Great Falls also succeeds as "theatricality," that visual element of stagecraft that no written fiction can quite duplicate. Though Blessing likes his plays to be read as well as seen, we can see how his visual sense of theatricality develops over the years from his earliest work which relied almost entirely on words rather than images. *Riches* offers a clear, fast-moving script that reads like a short story. In *Nice People Dancing to Good Country Music* the most theatrical event of the play, when Jim tosses Jason over the railing from the second floor of the bar, ends when Jason lands safely *offstage*. In contrast, *Great Falls* offers visual effects, called stage pictures, that stick powerfully with the viewer when seen, a power that can only be imagined when read. The shift in scenes from the car to the cheap motel rooms, the topless Bitch, the inventive scene when Monkey Man and Bitch simultaneously (but separately) talk to state troopers who have pulled them over[121] and, especially, the extended scene at the museum at Glacier National Park when projections of a Rocky Mountain goat and a Bighorn sheep in glass cases standing in for taxidermy exhibits, grow larger, focus from indistinct to clear and then revolve 360 degrees.[122]

Great Falls is not a great play, but we can appreciate what it offers. Perhaps Michael McGregor said it best in the *Oregonian*:

> The yearning at its heart, though—for contact, for comfort, for understanding—is universal. As is the incompleteness it shows of what we can offer each other.[123]

Into You

Set in a house "near a major university"[124] shared by three female roommates, *Into You* takes a look at campus rape, gender relations, and revenge in a plot definitely not for the squeamish. At first glance, the title suggests a saccharine love story (as in "he is into you") that turns out to center on a young woman plunging a blood-filled hypodermic into an unconscious young man.

Society as a whole now pays attention to the issue of campus sexual assault, which was once dismissed as a case of "boys being boys" or women scorned making accusations after the fact. New York's Senator Gillibrand recently called sexual assault on campus an "epidemic."[125]

And, indeed, the numbers paint a horrifying picture:

> A national survey conducted by the Medical University of South Carolina in 2007 found that more than 12 percent of college women had been raped.... The researchers calculated that about 5 percent of college women are raped annually, an estimate that is backed up by separate research by the American College Health Association. That's about 300,000 female students raped every year.[126]

And yet, colleges have done little to solve the problem and a U.S. Senate survey referenced in *Time* magazine found that "only 41% of all universities initiated an investigation into sexual assault claims in the last five years."[127]

A 2015 film documentary, *The Hunting Ground*, makes waves in the mass media as it points out that perpetrators of sexual assault are rarely punished and often remain on campus ... with their victims.

Into You, a short play, written well before such national attention focused on this issue, presents a visceral and unforgettable female response to sexual assault. At curtain's rise, Ter wakes up to find her roommate, Moll, bending over an unconscious and unfamiliar young man in their dorm room. Moll has brought the man, whom she found drunk at a college party, home and, we slowly learn, injected him with some of her own blood. Attacked and raped while drunk at a party some time earlier, Moll has now put some of herself into the unconscious man, knowing that this might include a blood-transmitted sexual disease or HIV. Preyed upon, Moll now prepares to prey on a man, guilty or not; unless being a white male constitutes guilt:

> TER: Molly. Sweetie. What happened?
> MOLL: Nothing.
> TER: Did he do something to you?
> MOLL: No. He was totally out of it. That's why I got the idea.
> TER: What idea?
> MOLL: He was stumbling all over, shit-faced. His eyes were barely open. And his nose was in the air, like he was smelling around for females. Later, when I was leaving, I saw him in the yard puking behind a tree. So I got him another beer and offered to walk him home.[128]

But then something happened and she changed her mind.

> MOLL: I wasn't going to have sex with him. I really was going to take him home. But when I handed him the beer, he groped me. Grabbed my boob—not for support, just 'cause it was there. Don't think it did much for him. He was so drunk, I could have put a potato in his hand; he wouldn't have known the difference. Anyhow, that's when I decided to do it.[129]

Blessing introduces a third conscious character, a lesbian roommate named Lynch, though his reasons for doing so are not clear. Lynch has just been dumped by her girlfriend of a month, Patty, who, she just learned, cheated on her with some regularity. Though she finds some saving grace, as she says:

> Because, to my cosmic relief, *for once*, I'm not being fucked over by a man. And she treats me *worse*. She actually treats me worse.[130]

Moll's angry recollection of her own rape leaves no room for pity now:

> MOLL: They assumed plenty. And they were right. Worked like a charm—I don't remember a thing. One minute I'm dancing at a party, just like tonight, then I feel a little funny—gee, what was in that beer? Then ... nothing. I wake up ... here ... at the bottom of the stairs. And some of my clothes are on, and some aren't. And everything hurts. Everything. And my body knows *exactly* what's been done to it.[131]

Imagine that kind of violation. But Ter demurs.

> TER: You can't just do this. He's a human being. (*As MOLL stares at her*) You can't. It makes you into ... into—
> MOLL: What? Someone who sticks something into someone else just 'cause it feels good?
> TER: Yes.
> MOLL: And doesn't care about the consequences?
> TER: Yes.
> MOLL: So—a man. It makes me a man.[132]

It is time, as Moll says, for "equal treatment,"[133] and we see that the implication of the title *Into You* is the act of "penetrating" human beings against their will in all of its multitude of meanings. Sending the more rational Ter to bed, Moll and Lynch lug the guy out of the house to his new future, as Lynch sees it: "Park bench? Dawn cracking? Puppy licking?"[134] As they carry him out:

> MOLL: He's heavy.
> LYNCH: Dead weight.
> MOLL: I wonder what his name is.
> LYNCH: No, you don't.

And "*lights fade fast as they turn to carry him out.*"[135] Readers might ask, perhaps depending on their gender, has justice been served or have the women simply become as bad as the men?

Uncle

As the play opens, Paul, at his lake-front home, shows his uncle Waring, and us, a wormhole that has opened in his garden, complete with intermittent lights and loud noises, and asks a pedestrian question of this extraordinary event: "Why does everything happen to me?"[136] Paul will not inform the authorities, after all: "I refuse to let this thing ruin my summer! I have a book to finish."[137] Then a creature emerges only to have Paul shove it back into the wormhole. Another emerges, more disgusting than the last, and again Paul disposes of it. Paul cajoles Waring into handling the next one, which he does reluctantly. It screams.

When Waring, quite dazed himself now, leaves to go home, Paul handles alien number four, who seems a tad more human and a tad less dazed than the others. This one speaks and comes bearing gifts: "I bring you an end to all strife. Cures for every disease. Immortality! These are my gifts to your world."[138] Paul shoves this alien back into the wormhole as well, but not before telling it that the book he is working on is about the Anton Chekhov play *Uncle Vanya*. When Paul goes back into his house, the next being out of the wormhole just happens to be.... Uncle Vanya. Sonya follows him. They speak Russian, we are told, but we can understand them.

Paul returns to confront them. He speaks Russian also! Of course, he doesn't believe they are who they say they are: Chekhov's fictional characters from *Uncle Vanya*. But how could *fictional* characters come out of a wormhole, Paul wants to know? Before anyone can explain that, Dr. Astrov also stumbles out of the wormhole, followed by Serebryakov and Yelena. Paul faints at the sight of them, as Scene 1 ends.

Scene 2 takes place two days later. No trace remains of the wormhole. Paul sits in the garden with the five characters from *Uncle Vanya*, whom he happily plans to use to complete his book, which bears the lugubrious working title: "Sonya—Belief, Abnegation, and Self-Sabotage in Chekhov's World: Longing in the House of Obligation," with which he expects to gain tenure at the university. He hopes that by putting these visitors through the scenes of the play he will discover new insights into their characters and actions. After all, they don't have an answer to his rather simple question: "What the hell is *wrong* with you people?... All you do is complain and feel sorry for yourselves."[139] Feeling like slaves transported 100 years into the future, they are miserable: Uncle Vanya wants to know why he is not in the book title; Serebryakov wants Paul to keep his hands off Yelena, his beautiful wife; and Sonya runs off in shame when Paul goads her into attacking her misogynistic father. They all want to go home. Vanya gets particularly angry:

> VANYA: What *are* you?! An imbecile?! A magician?! A demon—*what!!?*
> PAUL: I'm a college professor—!
> VANYA (*throwing him down in disgust*) *Aggghhh*—!! I should have known. (*to SEREBRYAKOV* [a retired university professor]) He's worse than you.[140]

At this point, a reader or audience member might question the basic motivation behind Paul's actions. While academic scholars would like to encounter the characters they are writing about from a long-ago novel, play, or poem, how could such an encounter aid their scholarship? After all, one cannot quote or reference a character outside of the lines they have already spoken in the original work. For example, if Yelena should admit to Paul that she harbors lesbian longings for Sonya, Paul can't announce a new discovery because all the evidence of Yelena we have is what she says and does in the extant play. Why, then, does Paul persist in his metatheatrical shenanigans? Later the same day, in Scene 3, Paul answers that question when he confesses his love for Sonya:

> PAUL: Sonya, ever since I first read *Uncle Vanya* ... I've been in love with you.
> SONYA: You've what?
> PAUL: I love you. You're so strong and good and enduring—
> SONYA: And plain?
> PAUL: I never said that.
> SONYA: Everyone else did. And you got them to.[141]

Paul proposes marriage.

> SONYA: I've know you two days.
> PAUL: And I've known you forever—since I was twelve, anyway. I've loved you all my life. But you were a character, a fiction, an ideal in Chekhov's mind—too pure to be real. Still, I always told myself if I ever met a woman like you I'd propose to her on the spot.[142]

So, perhaps his interest is not just academic! Too bad Paul is *already* married. Good thing his wife has been out of town for two years, doing scientific research in Tierra del Fuego. Knowledge of her distant location does not help Sonya acclimate to receiving a marriage proposal from a married man, however, and she runs out again. Paul follows. This leaves the others to revert to their usual bickering, accusatory form and once again, as in the play bearing his name, Vanya, pining for Yelena, pulls a gun on her husband, Serebryakov. But before he can fire it, the wormhole reappears. All but Serebryakov fear reentering the show of light and sound. Finally, Yelena rolls him into the vortex in his wheelchair but, to his surprise, does not enter after him. The wormhole and Serebryakov disappear. Few seem to miss him, as Scene 3 ends.

Scene 4 finds Astrov, Vanya, and Paul sharing a bottle of vodka. The first two pine for Yelena, the latter for Sonya. They discuss marriage, intimacy, and relationships, albeit cynically. Astrov tries to console Paul: "Honestly, Paul, I don't know why you're complaining. You're rich, you have a wife who's never here.... If that's not complete happiness—"[143] Vanya and Astrov assure Paul that his traveling wife, Paige, is having affairs on her foreign travels and a funny Skype chat follows, with Paige fending off an unseen "friend": "Stop tickling me!"[144] This seems to confirm their suspicions. Paul, they decide, is just like the character "Waffles" (Ilya Ilych Telegin) in their own play, who remains loyal to the wife who has abandoned him. Undaunted by the examples of Paul, Waffles, and Serebryakov, an inebriated Vanya heads into the house to propose to Yelena. He falls over drunk before completing his mission.

A few days later, Scene 5 brings us back to the ladies, as Sonya and Yelena enter from the lake. Yelena thinks they are changing in their new world. She thinks Sonya has fallen in love with Paul. When Paul's uncle Waring runs into the two ladies, their dueling languages get in the way. Waring, rich and dumb, seems a perfect foil for this duo. They work through the final scene of *Uncle Vanya*, but the continuing tiff with Sonya drives Paul to a hilarious meltdown:

> I'm so far behind on my book I'll never get done, and I'll never get tenure, and my wife won't care anyway because for all I know she's being unfaithful with half of *South America*. Not that I give a damn, since I'm clearly in love with you and not her. Not that it matters, since I've blown all my chances with you, and you wouldn't marry me even if I were single and the last man on *earth!* So, please. Please. If I can't have you, and I can't have Paige and I can't have tenure ... let me *please* have Chekhov: my personal sojourn in his beautiful little hell of endless, life-disappointing self-knowledge.[145]

When Sonya stalks off, Paul replaces her in the final scene and reads her final lines from the play, his head nestled, bathetically, in Vanya's lap:

> PAUL: "You've never been happy. But wait, Uncle Vanya. Wait. We shall rest." And I embrace you.
> VANYA: (*as PAUL does so*) This is uncomfortable.
> PAUL: "We shall rest."[146]

But circumstances deny even rest to Paul, as Waring tells him Paige has delegated him to deliver the bad news: Paige *is* having an affair (as Astrov and Vanya surmised) and wants a divorce.

> PAUL Who is it? Who's this lover she's—?
> WARING: A colleague. Fellow lichenologist, mycologist, phycologist—what isn't he? Anyway, they were in a storm together, up on the mountain—
> PAUL: Protecting their lichens, yes.
> WARING: And, to keep warm, they were forced to rub their bodies together in the same sleeping bag for seven straight days.[147]

First shocked and rejected, Paul later celebrates his new freedom, as Scene 5 ends.

The next scene begins shortly after, as Paul Skypes Paige to nail down his divorce and a generous settlement offered by his wife. Things go well until Waring lets slip the news that Paul also has a new love, and arguments ensue. Paul accuses Paige of taking previous lovers:

> PAIGE'S VOICE: What if I have had the occasional lover? You and I are constantly alone. Neither of us is made of stone—
> PAUL: You're apparently made of Silly Putty![148]

7. Love Is All There Is

Blessing writes great marital spats:

> PAIGE'S VOICE: You really are a swine!
> PAUL: You're the one who's humping the fungus licker!
> PAIGE'S VOICE: I told you never to call us that!
> PAUL: Well, if the mold fits—![149]

The wealthy Paige announces she'll not only enforce the prenup, which leaves Paul nothing, but also pressure the university that employs him, and is the recipient of her largesse, to fire him. First shocked, Paul moves to a final reckoning, seeing how he has settled for mediocrity all his life (like certain provincial Russians in certain Russian plays) and declares:

> Take the money. Take the money and my job and do whatever you want. I'm free of it now. Free of the lies we told ourselves about the future. Free of the … nothing … we called marriage. Free of pretending I don't have to exist.[150]

Sonya has heard and seen it all. She kisses Paul … then slaps him and rushes out. Waring, in an understatement to top all understatements, closes the scene with the line: "I can't help feeling this was partly my fault."[151]

The brief seventh scene opens with Vanya and Astrov, now sporting Bermuda shorts and carrying a Starbuck's coffee. Vanya is adapting to his new world. Yelena enters stylishly and somewhat revealingly dressed as well. She looks forward to relocating to Brighton Beach and its large Russian community. She drags Astrov back into the house by his formidable mustache, inspired by the modern women's magazine she has been reading. Waring, suddenly brighter than before, pitches Paul on a new career as a science fiction writer, exploiting the wormhole for ideas and characters, a more lucrative trade than he found in academia.

Finally the time arrives to unite all our lovers in Scene 8. Newly bereft of his moustache, Astrov and Yelena exit together. Sonya proposes to Paul, nicely outlining the challenges of modern marriage:

> SONYA: You think you know who I am when even *I* don't know. You think I'll never change, but all I'm doing is changing. You have no idea if you'll love the Sonya I'm going to become, yet you still want to be my husband. Don't you?
> PAUL: Yes I do, but—
> SONYA: Then everything about our relationship will be a challenge.
> PAUL: Yes, apparently, but—
> SONYA: Don't you see? It will be a lifetime of *work*.[152]

As they kiss, the wormhole reappears. Vanya tries to enter it, with Sonya in tow. Paul grabs her other hand. Vanya pulls his gun on Paul. Sonya wrenches free. Vanya enters the wormhole. Paul sticks his hand in to grab Vanya, who shoots him in the hand but leaves him and Sonya together as Vanya disappears forever.

A brief coda, Scene 9, finds Sonya and Paul alone back at the lake house. Paul writes as a new alien emerges from the wormhole. Sonya takes a photo, leads the creature along a red carpet and kicks it back into the wormhole. They have a new, but challenging life writing best-selling science fiction stories inspired by the wormhole creatures:

> As PAUL writes, he puts his damaged hand on hers. She rests her head on his shoulder. They wait for the next alien.
> The End.[153]

This is very much a work in progress, having received a staged reading at the Arkansas New Play Festival in Little Rock on June 27, 2015. Knowing Blessing, it will evolve through several more rewrites and changes in characters and plots. So anything I write here may soon become outdated.

Blessing has lampooned other authors' plays before, in *Fortinbras* and *The Scottish Play*, burlesquing *Hamlet* and *Macbeth*, respectively; *Fortinbras* aimed at making points about political manipulation of the media and the public, while *The Scottish Play* and *Uncle* skip the brain and aim directly for the funny bone. Since *Uncle* has had only a stage reading so far no critics have weighed in yet. Allow me to be the first. I love *Uncle Vanya* and I love metatheatrical plays, plays that refer us to other plays and plays that take classical stage characters out of their known milieu and plop them into a new place and time, so I am a sucker for *Uncle*. It delivers head-scratching laughs and a chance to revisit our favorite "people," though I always favored Vanya and Yelena over Sonya. Seeing them on stage in our own time is a treat.

Uncle doesn't demand a lot of knowledge of the Chekhovian original, and Blessing supplies the exposition we need. Chekhov's characters stick to their original delineation at first but then the women, at least, change. Yelena tosses Serebryakov away, and Sonya deserts Vanya, unthinkable actions in the original play. Somehow, Vanya himself seems diminished in Blessing's play, which still bears his title, Uncle, if not his name. The play title would seem to reference his importance and yet he really adds nothing to the parody.

And a big question of logic troubles me. Does this wormhole shift time or space, or both? How does it *really* function? What rules govern it if it brings forth actual space aliens both before and after spitting out Chekhov's fictional characters? Why doesn't it bring forth more literary characters than those from a single Russian play? Will the Three Sisters ever appear? or will Prince Hal and Falstaff come along as well? Why do Chekov's characters arrive right after Paul tells us they are the subject of his book? Does the wormhole read minds and deliver the take-out we've ordered like pizza? Within the world of a play, even a fantastical one, certain logical rules must exist, but *Uncle* doesn't play by the rules.

Having said that, more playwrights need to put aliens on stage. They make a great stage picture. Blessing may also be the first writer to put a Skyped marital fight on stage and the interaction of Paul and Paige provides the kind of nasty marital humor I appreciated in *Riches* (see Chapter 2). *Uncle* may be a minor play, but it is a fun play.

Chapter 8

The Rushmore Plays

I call this chapter "The Rushmore Plays" to categorize a series of plays Blessing wrote about U.S. presidents Bush and Reagan, presidents whose faces will probably never appear on that stone monument carved by Gutzon Borglum (1867–1941) in the Black Hills of South Dakota. Four enormous sculpted heads gaze out from Mount Rushmore, reminding us, no doubt, of how low American politics have sunk since Borglum blasted out tons of rock to create this celebration of presidential glory. Blessing finds no contemporary candidates worthy of enshrinement with Washington, Jefferson, Lincoln, and Roosevelt, as he writes about Bush II in *When We Go Upon the Sea* or Ronald Reagan in *Reagan in Hell*; indeed, he makes fun of the whole process of political manipulation in *Fortinbras*, and visits the Black Hills monument for a little gay eroticism at the expense of four lesser Presidents in *Tyler Poked Taylor*.

Fortinbras
Tyler Poked Taylor
Reagan in Hell
When We Go Upon the Sea

Fortinbras

Riffing on Shakespeare and his creations, as Blessing does in *Fortinbras*, has a long and varied history. Most famous is Tom Stoppard's *Rosencrantz and Guildenstern Are Dead*, a 1966 play and 1990 movie. Also, from *Hamlet*, we have *Hamletmachine* by Heiner Muller, 1977. From *Macbeth* we have Eugene Ionesco's *Macbett*, 1972, and Barbara Garson's *Macbird*, 1968. Paula Vogel rewrote the main female character from *Othello*, and changed her from pure to promiscuous to make a feminist point in *Desdemona: A Play About a Handkerchief*, and Edward Einhorn took a character from *The Merchant of Venice* and gave him his own play in 1996, *Shylock*, to examine anti–Semitism.

Mixing lowbrow slapstick and sight gag humor, a dash of sex, and a gaggle of ghosts while injecting the anachronism of a television set on Elsinore castle's battlements, Blessing dished out trenchant political commentary just six months after America celebrated its victory in the first Gulf War, Operation Desert Storm, designed to end the Iraqi invasion and occupation of Kuwait, August 2, 1990, to February 28, 1991. As he told one interviewer:

> That event was very much in my mind as I wrote the play.... It's a commentary, from my point of view, on what presidential politics has become in this country, and perhaps always [has been].... *Fortinbras* is about a young leader who's just trying to be a good young leader and to play the game according to what he perceives as its rules.... I still can't get some images from the Iraq war out of my mind. There was a level of insensitivity to the destruction that was done that boggles the mind. What fascinates me is how quickly people in this nation are able to, are led to forget these images. The whole point of parades was to erase the images of violence.[1]

Picking up Hamlet's tale where Shakespeare ended it, Blessing begins his farce with the entrance of Fortinbras, the young king of Norway who arrives at Elsinore just back from his conquests at the very moment the bodies of Hamlet, Claudius, Gertrude, and Laertes litter the stage. Shakespeare used just two brief appearances by Fortinbras in his play to contrast Hamlet, a man of thought, indecision and self-reflection, with the Norwegian king, a man of action who needs little excuse to lead his army against Poland, while Hamlet cannot bring himself to kill a single man, his own uncle Claudius. Blessing makes Fortinbras his protagonist and gives him a play of his own in a study of political deceit and social manipulation.

Instead of his usual sparse cast (just two characters in *Riches* and *A Walk in the Woods*, or three in *Patient A, Eleemosynary, Down the Road*, and *When We Go Upon the Sea*) Blessing further emulates Shakespeare in his use of large casts, trotting out 15 characters, all but three of whom are familiar to us from *Hamlet*. There's Horatio, set upon getting out the truth about Hamlet's death; Osric, his role enlarged as lackey to Fortinbras; Marcellus and Barnardo, reprising their earlier roles as guards atop the castle turret; and the rather lively ghosts of Claudius, Gertrude, Laertes, Ophelia, Polonius, and Hamlet himself, all of whom arrive to demand their own truths and drive Fortinbras to despair.

Hamlet has the opening lines here at his death scene and closes with his famous "the rest is silence,"[2] but happily it's not for us, and Fortinbras enters with a jarring juxtaposition to Shakespeare's words in offering a very modern

"Excuse me.... Hi, so—God, what's all this?"[3] Horatio gives Fortinbras a quick synopsis of past events as Fortinbras directs the unceremonious removal of the four poisoned and/or stabbed corpses. Unwilling to share the "real" story of so many royal deaths with the public, Fortinbras tells Osric, "I want a full report, ok?... Then maybe I can start to make up the truth."[4] For Fortinbras is the man of action, at least at the beginning, the consummate warlike leader who knows how to govern by deceit:

> FORTINBRAS: Horatio, we've got to have a new story.
> HORATIO: But there's only the truth.
> FORTINBRAS: That's the problem.... We need a story that'll do something for us ... preserve the monarchy.... And most of all, something that will show people how everything that's happened up till now had to happen so that I could become king.[5]

Now set in motion, three plot lines unwind across two acts, exploring the need for the government (in the form of the usurper Fortinbras) to manipulate public opinion, the Norwegian army's conquering march eastward, and the ghosts' needs to redeem themselves in the afterlife. Unhappy with Horatio's true recitation of how Claudius poisoned King Hamlet and, by accident, Gertrude, and how Laertes and Hamlet killed each other dueling with poisoned swords, Fortinbras invents the much simpler story of a Polish spy who killed off a loving and peaceful Danish royal family in an act of international treachery. This fabrication has the advantage of allowing Fortinbras to send his army to the Polish border in reprisal. As a tale of how politicians whip public opinion into a war hysteria with dubious "facts," it well presages the Second Gulf War, which follows the play by two and a half years, in which we invaded Iraq in search of non-existent WMD (Weapons of Mass Destruction). Unlike President Bush, Fortinbras needs to present the public with a Polish spy and, fortunately, has at hand Osric, the accommodating Dane, for the role. Osric, Fortinbras declares, "[Provides] a human face we can all loathe and detest."[6]

Unfortunately for Fortinbras, the Norwegian army not only conquers Poland but continues on, conquering Carpathia, Transylvania, Anatolia, the Trans Caucasus, and Persia, ignoring the king's commands to return to Denmark. As Horatio tells Fortinbras, "You're winning,"[7] and yet when his army approaches India, on the cusp of making Fortinbras, like Alexander the Great before him, ruler of the known world, they throw themselves into the Indrus River and drown. So great empires rise and fall.

But all around him, Fortinbras is besieged by the ghosts of Denmark past. Polonius returns first but transformed from the former gasbag of limitless unnecessary words into a silent specter, unwilling to share a syllable. Ophelia, once Hamlet's chaste *inamorata*, returns to give Fortinbras the best sex of his life, telling him: "Did you know women don't reach their sexual peak until after they're dead?"[8] Gertrude and Claudius are there, more lustful than ever, not daring to even look at each other for fear of sinning, yet contrite for their former sins and committed to virtue.

The *pièce de résistance* is the return of Hamlet himself, star of that other guy's play, but now reduced to a black-and-white figure trapped in a television set, not unlike Hamlet's father's ghost, played by Sam Shepard in Michael Almereyda's 2000 modern-day take on *Hamlet*, who appears on a video monitor in that film nine years later. This allows Ophelia to savor her revenge, using the remote control to shut off the TV and silence Hamlet. "God, that felt good," she tells us.[9]

Fortinbras: King Fortinbras (Keith Reddin) discovers that women reach their sexual peak after death, as the ghost of Ophelia (Samantha Mathis) returns. Signature Theatre, New York City; 1991, photograph by Susan Johann.

Here characters are transformed from their former, Shakespearean selves. Fortinbras, man of action and few words, is now given to frequent soliloquies, like Hamlet, and offers this insight into the political minds: "Kings don't make mistakes, anyway. They reassess policies."[10] Finally, Horatio, merely an observer in *Hamlet*, now put off by Fortinbras's lies and his nonchalant cruelty in accidentally hanging Osric as a spy, stabs him, and kills himself, turning almost every character in the play into a ghost by the final curtain.

Fortinbras reminded me of Alfred Jarry's 1896 scandalous burlesque *Ubu Roi*, which also features an invasion of Poland and the murder of a Polish king, referencing Shakespeare's *Macbeth*, *Hamlet*, and *Richard the III*. Like *Fortinbras*, *Ubu* is a farcical meditation on power and greed and abuse of power featuring physical oddities, scatological language, and puns to make its similar points about the greed and selfishness of modern man. Blessing updates the tale by mixing in the contemporary connection of political power with the manipulation of the media, the government's corrupt commitment to lies to win popular support for military action.

Blessing explained how he wedded form to content in an interview:

> In all the plays up until *A Walk in the Woods* I'd used humor so much I wanted to see what it was like to do a couple of plays where I wasn't allowed to. With *Two Rooms* and *Down the Road* I picked subjects you really can't make jokes about, very truthfully anyway.... It was more a shift to certain kinds of themes and dealing with them in a serious way where I couldn't rely on having a facility to write humor. It's very relaxing now to go back and write something where I can go for the laugh. And comedy is one of the best passes to saying something serious.[11]

And he lets Hamlet explain what he hopes is the immortal power of the truth:

> If you pass through a desert, wandering, lost, you might leave a little cairn of stones. No one will ever find it. You, yourself, will die miles away, your body will disappear. Even the cairn will be buried, in time, by the sand. But somehow you want it to be there, the little mark, deep in the enormous heart of that wasteland. It may never be found, but it exists. Because you existed. That is how the truth works.[12]

There, in the Kuwaiti desert of *Fortinbras*, stands Blessing's little cairn of stones. But a cairn seen far and wide. *Fortinbras* was translated and produced in Japan as well as in regional theaters across the U.S.

The critics, as usual, were divided on Blessing's play. *Time* magazine listed it as one of the ten best plays of 1991.[13] Michael Phillips, in the *San Diego Union*, wrote:

> It seems to make more and more sense as you go along. The point of the play is to explore possibilities—that's what the stage is for. So, in a way, I'm not alarmed if I'm seeing something and large sections of it are mysterious to me or if I don't know quite how they plug in or where they are going.... It's a matter of getting rid of things that don't lead anywhere.[14]

Jeff Smith, in the *San Diego Weekly Reader*, called the play "almost wall to wall funny, though murky metaphysics in the second act dull its witty sheen."[15] While Mel Gussow, in the *New York Times*, criticized it for what it was not:

> [The play] is scarcely more than an extended comedy sketch lacking the portent and linguistic complexity of Tom Stoppard's "Rosencrantz and Guildenstern Are Dead." *Fortinbras* operates on a far less ambitious plane."[16]

T. H. McCulloh, in the *Los Angeles Times*, thought: "Something is funny in the state of Denmark."[17] *Variety* demurred:

> But as the play widens and darkens, moving from farce and spoofery to such heavy themes as truth and death, it slows and meanders, staggering to a pallid finish with its points increasingly elusive.[18]

And Sylvia Drake, in the *Los Angeles Times*, seemed both pro and con, calling *Fortinbras* "breezy, breakable stuff" and "a "caviar soufflé,"[19] but asking, "Who needs the politics?"[20] thereby missing, or choosing to miss, the main point ... that we *all* need the politics.

Blessing began writing politically barbed plays with *A Walk in the Woods*. He continued to handle contemporary issues with *Patient A*, *Two Rooms*, *Down the Road*, and *Lake Front Extension* (his "tetralogy of pain") and then returned to the humor of his first outing with this look at Bush I. His plays on Ronald Reagan and Bush II followed.

Tyler Poked Taylor

In late fall 2001, just months after the 9/11 attacks on the World Trade Towers and the Pentagon, the Actors Theatre of Louisville commissioned 17 prominent American playwrights, including Pulitzer Prize winner David Lindsay-Abaire (*Rabbit Hole*, 2007), Deb Margolin (cofounder of the American theater troupe Split Britches), and Lee Blessing, to write plays in response to a single photograph, Lee Friedlander's "Mount Rushmore, South Dakota, 1969." That now-iconic photo, in the collections of the Smithsonian and Metropolitan Museum of Art, can be found at the MOMA website.[21] Actor's Theater produced the series of short plays in March 2002 at the Humana Festival of New American Plays in Louisville, Kentucky, and published them all in a book entitled *Snapshot*, brought out by Playscripts, Inc., in 2003.

The theater's dramaturg, Amy Wegener, described their goals:

> Photographs capture and document a single moment in time and space.... But what, we wondered, lies outside, beyond, behind the photograph? And what stories, memories, or associations does an image or *place* inspire? ... Because we were commissioning these pieces in the late fall of 2001 ... the idea of thinking about American icons and monuments had particular resonance. What is striking about Friedlander's image, also, is that Mount Rushmore is not captured head-on but is instead reflected in the glass of the visitors' center—so that what the tourists are looking at seems to be looming behind them, facing *us*.[22]

The playwrights were allowed to set their plays at the monument itself, or focus on the characters related to the monument, or deal with the monument in more metaphorical or allegorical ways. Blessing set his short play on the Mt. Rushmore observation deck, where we see and hear 18-year-old Loyal, who begins "muttering quietly swiftly to himself—a kind of mantra":

> Tyler poked Taylor Fillmore pierced Buchanan Tyler poked Taylor Fillmore pierced Buchanan Tyler poked Taylor Fillmore pierced Buchanan Tyler poked Taylor Fillmore pierced Buchanan Tyler poked Taylor Fillmore pierced Buchanan ...[23]

Huh? Interrupted by another, though unseen, visitor to the observation deck, Loyal stops muttering to tell them to back off. He returns to his mantra. Once again he stops to address his parents, also unseen, asking them for "a little privacy."[24] Then he returns to his repetitions as these words are transferred to house speakers in the theater and continue throughout the brief play. What's going on here? Numerous mnemonic devices exist for learning the names, in order, of the U.S. presidents. One that has gained popularity is "Will a Jolly Man Make a Jolly Visitor?" This phrase contains eight words, each beginning with the first letter of the last name of our first eight presidents: Washington, Adams, Jefferson, Madison, Monroe, Adams, Jackson, and Van Buren. However, Loyal concentrates on presidents ten though fifteen, not a very illustrious lot at all and among those least likely to be enshrined on Mount Rushmore. In fact, according to *U.S. New and World Report*, at least four (Tyler, Fillmore, Pierce, and Buchanan) of Loyal's named six make the list of ten worst presidents, with James Buchanan rated the very worst of all time.[25]

He also sexualizes the names so that James K. Polk becomes "poked" and Franklin Pierce becomes "pierced," giving us John Tyler having sex with Zachary Taylor, and Millard Fillmore having sex with James Buchanan. Since all the presidents are men and many historians have speculated that Buchanan, who never married and lived for four years with another man (William Rufus King, a senator from Alabama) was gay, we quickly get the idea that Loyal (and we can ask "loyal" to what or to whom? to an American ideal? to the men immortalized at Rushmore?) is indulging in homoerotic fantasies:

> Tyler poked Taylor Fillmore pierced Buchanan Tyler poked Taylor Fillmore pierced Buchanan Tyler poked Taylor Fillmore pierced Buchanan Tyler poked Taylor Fillmore pierced Buchanan Tyler poked...[26]

Loyal tells us his father brings him to Mount Rushmore every year, telling him he can be president someday and also be immortalized in stone. Loyal doesn't buy it: "I knew I was never going to be President. So instead I made love to them."[27] His dreams are detailed: "[Washington] was first. First in war, first in peace and first in my bedroom late at night"[28]; Jefferson: "We'd make love all night long"[29]; Lincoln: "Splitting rails with his shirt off. He'd gleam with sweat"[30]; and Teddy Roosevelt: "Lay weeping in my arms."[31]

The play closes with the repetitive mantra:

> Tyler poked Taylor Fillmore pierced Buchanan Tyler poked Taylor Fillmore pierced Buchanan Tyler poked Taylor Fillmore pierced Buchanan Tyler poked...[32]

Does Loyal, as his name might indicate, stand in for each of we "loyal" Americans, trained to revere, even worship, historical figures of bygone times? Does his obscene ditty, repeated endlessly, and his erotic reveries serve to subvert American civil religion that makes granite faces of once-living men? In the Friedlander "snapshot," the Mt. Rushmore carvings seem to float above the landscape. Tourists stare out and up at them with binoculars and cameras as if inspecting beings, untouchable and inhuman, from another world. Has the American Dream moved beyond reach?

Reagan in Hell

In 2004, Blessing wrote *Reagan in Hell*, a ten-minute play for the Naked Angels theater company, housed in a warehouse on West 17th street in New York City. They later anthologized the play in the book *Naked Angels Issues Projects: Collected Plays*. Naked Angels regularly devoted an evening to short plays grouped around a political issue. *The Collected Plays* features works on all kinds of political topics, from gun control to environmental degradation, and includes short plays by prize-winning playwrights Theresa Rebeck, Craig Lucas, Warren Leight, Will Eno, Kenneth Lonergan, Jon Robin Baitz, and others. Baitz wrote in the anthology's introduction:

> Most of life is compromise, coarsening, and the banking of fires. These plays burn very bright for a very little while. If nothing else, they remind one of how much is still to be done and how the theatre can help do it, at least incrementally. In short increments. This is not nothing.[33]

A political revenge play sure to be enjoyed by all opponents of President Ronald Reagan, *Reagan in Hell* lives up to its title as the 40th U.S. president encounters Clark, a demon, as he enters "Hell, Alzheimer's Division." Here, Reagan faces eternal torment, including:

> You have advanced AIDS. There is no treatment for AIDS in Hell. You will suffer from this condition for eternity.... While in Hell your job will be to sit in that chair taking an eternal shower in the burning shit and vomit of most of the Salvadoran army of the 1980's, as well as much of the Nicaraguan Contra forces from the same period.... A copy of the U.S. Constitution festooned with razor-blades will be rolled into a flaming baton and SHOVED UP YOUR FUCKING ASS!![34]

When Reagan asks: "Are there jelly beans?" Clark replies that

> you'll never be without. They taste like Salvadoran children who've been shot and hacked to death by government forces, then buried in mud for twenty years. Bon appétit![35]

The punishments repulse and sicken us and, yet, seem appropriate both for a real hell (think of the horrible sufferings of Dante's *Inferno*) and for a politician who conducted murderous wars in Central America, broke Congressional prohibitions by covertly arming our supposed enemy Iran with missiles in exchange for money for mercenary armies in Nicaragua, all the while ignoring the AIDS epidemic at home. But Reagan, here, suffers from dementia and is unaware of his sins, reduced to asking for his mommy and his jelly beans; he is a figure more to be pitied than hated. Can we be induced to feel sorry for Ronald Reagan? No, shove that flaming baton up his fucking ass!

When he gets to our 43rd President, Blessing has refined and polished his technique, turning a blunt instrument into a scalpel in a play that he could have titled "Bush in Hell," but was instead called *When We Go Upon the Sea*.

When We Go Upon the Sea

Americans suffered through eight years of George W. Bush as President, 2000–2008: the wars in Afghanistan, which failed to destroy al-Queda and capture or kill Osama Bin Laden, and in Iraq, which failed to discover nuclear or chemical weapons, failed to usher in Middle Eastern democracy, curb the power of Iran, or assure us unlimited oil supplies, but brought us the American torture of prisoners at Abu Ghraib, Guantanamo, and CIA "black sites" in Europe, and the economic recession and stock market crash of 2008.

Blessing, as he told me, first tried to ignore and, only later, to assess that presidency:

> Actually, I tried to live with "W" just as little as possible over those eight years. I consistently turned off his image and/or voice whenever confronted with them. He hadn't won the vote in 2000; he'd simply been awarded the Presidency by a group of right-wing, activist justices on the Supreme Court. Thus I simply didn't consider him all that legitimate. As a writer it was deeply painful to listen to him speak, simply from the viewpoint of usage and grammar. I never thought I'd write a play about him. But in his seventh year or so, I started contemplating (only wishfully, of course) the possibility that someday he might be tried for his various crimes. It won't happen. But in a play I could make the possibility "real" for one brief evening—so why the hell not? I thought. Of course in the play he never actually gets to the courtroom—what a bore that would be—he only gets as far as the hotel suite. If it's not tender, that's because it's been hard for me to have tender thoughts about "W" (or indeed, about Ronald Reagan, whom I've taken to task in at least five different plays). But I do think that "W" is the best "W" he can be, and I guess I admire that about him. I imagine that's why this play gives him a sendoff evening very reminiscent of his partying days at Yale.
>
> I had a great time writing the play.
>
> Piet and Anna-Lisa are Europeans, but they stand for people around the globe who live in total terror of their elected and unelected leaders. Most of us live that way, if we could get ourselves to tell the truth about it. We make compromise after compromise to be sure those who lead us feel safe and secure. After all, when they don't, we are the ones who suffer, not them.[36]

When We Go Upon the Sea comprises one act in nine scenes and opens in a premier hotel suite in the Hague, the Netherlands, with a huge picture window looking out, we are told, on the (unseen) sea. George W. Bush is drinking bourbon as he is waited upon by Piet, a staffer at the hotel for some 15 years, who promises to provide anything Bush would like or need. This night, however, is different from all others; in the morning former President Bush will stand trial for war crimes in the Peace Palace before the International Court of Justice, often referred to as the World Court, the primary judicial branch of the United Nations. Previous famous defendants include Slobodan Milosevic, who led Serbia following the break up Yugoslavia. Milosevic died in custody of a heart attack after five years of trial in 2006 and before a judgment could be rendered. The United States recognizes the World Court on a case-by-case basis (i.e., when it suits our interests) and, most famously, in 1986, refused to recognize a Court decision in favor of Nicaragua, which accused the U.S. of supporting a Contra insurgency and mining its harbors and denied a judgment to pay Nicaragua damages for these violations of that country's sovereignty.

At least one other person has entertained the possibility of Bush standing trial in the Hague—President Bush himself. In 2011, he canceled a planned speaking engagement in Switzerland on what would have been his first trip to Europe since writing in his autobiography, *Decision Points*, released November 2010, that he had authorized the use of waterboarding on prisoners at the U.S. naval base in Guantánamo, Cuba. Bush would have faced both angry demonstrations and at least the threat of arrest on foreign soil.

Amnesty International announced: "Anywhere in the world that he travels, President Bush could face investigation and potential prosecution for his responsibility for torture and other crimes in international law, particularly in any of the 147 countries that are party to the UN convention against torture."[37]

The case of Chilean General Augusto Pinochet, who had overthrown the elected president, Salvador Allende, in 1973 and murdered and terrorized his own people for nearly 18 years, broke new ground for the international prosecution of crimes against humanity. Magistrate Baltasar Garzon indicted Pinochet in Spain on October 10, 1998, and British police arrested him six days later, in London, where he had gone for medical treatment. The British government, over the objections of his confederates, former Prime Minister Margaret Thatcher and former President George H. W. Bush, held Pinochet for a year and a half before finally releasing him back to Chile in March 2000, but only after the United Kingdom's House of Lords voted that some international crimes, such as torture, could not be protected by former head-of-state immunity and helped establish the principle of universal jurisdiction, the concept that certain offenses rise to the level of crimes against humanity and can therefore be prosecuted in any court in the world.

For this reason, a host of former American officials, from President George W. Bush to former Vice President Dick Cheney to former Secretary of Defense

Donald Rumsfeld and former Secretary of State Condoleezza Rice, cannot travel today to most of the countries in the world for fear of outstanding warrants for their arrest.

Bush may never stand in the dock, but Blessing gets him closer to it than we might have imagined in *When We Go Upon the Sea*, a play that conflates politics, colonialism, and sex. And, here, Blessing does it without the exposition and data loading seen in *Patient A* and *Cobb*, eschewing the details of U.S. wars in the Middle East and choosing instead to frame the play in symbols that keep the reader focused on the increasing tone of menace and despair.

He sets the mood early, with a look at the sea. The Netherlands is uniquely a country below sea level. As Piet tells George: "The sea is above our heads, always waiting to get in. It knows someday it will. We know it, too."[38] The threatening sea ultimately overwhelms all human plans and folly, promising both rebaptism and cleansing. Until then, hubris reigns:

> GEORGE: I was once the most powerful person in the world.
> PIET: You were?
> GEORGE: That a surprise?
> PIET: No, no.... I only thought—well, Mr. Cheney—
> GEORGE: What?
> PIET: Nothing.
> GEORGE: That's not funny, Piet, I ran the show.... I ran it and I had no regrets. My only regret is that I never got around to nuking my allies. Now why don't you get your miserable European ass out of this suite?[39]

And regrets are few. Piet tells George that the Tribunal will have questions:

> PIET: The war?... They'll ask if you lied.... Knowingly that is.... So many dead, so many wounded.
> GEORGE: Are you kidding? Couple dead soldiers a day?
> PIET: One hundred thousand Iraqis.... You feel no guilt?
> GEORGE: They killed each other. Instinctive, inevitable. Can't go all over the world keeping folks from murdering each other.[40]

In Scene 2, Piet offers George "a girl.... Strictly for the ruling class."[41] Anna-Lisa enters, "blonde, very well dressed, and beautiful," not a prostitute but a "relaxationist,"[42] whom Piet first calls his wife[43] and then claims to have only been joking.[44] George, afraid he is being bugged or video-taped to be embarrassed in the press, frisks Piet and Anna-Lisa and searches the room, but finds nothing.[45] Piet assures him, "We want to serve you. That's all.... We want to give you one last perfect evening before the rest of your life becomes so ... troublesome."[46] But more than that, Piet and Anna-Lisa identify themselves as "everyman" and "everywoman":

> GEORGE: You're telling me you have no purpose in life except to make people feel better?...

> PIET: The rich. The powerful. Leaders. Yes.... Yes, keeping the leader safe. Earning his trust. Letting him know he's loved. It's completely natural.⁴⁷

In this case the aim to please quickly leads George and Ann-Lisa into the bedroom offstage, from which the audience hears the sounds of noisy sex.

Here lies the major point of the play, reminiscent of the African proverb: "When elephants fight, it is the grass that suffers." We common people, regardless of nationality, are the ones who "suffer" when the great, the powerful, the leaders of nations commanding armies and nuclear arsenals tussle, even, or sometimes especially, when those leaders suffer no injuries themselves. Our only safety lies in placating, or "relaxing" the beasts to prevent their battles.

Soon, as in his earlier college days, George is snorting coke and enjoying the party as Piet offers a Dutch history of both the Old Master paintings on the walls and the colonization of the New World and how the two went together, when they went upon the sea:

> We'd crossed the ocean and colonized the earth. We had the guns, we had disease. What did they have? We had religion.... We painted our new standard of living.⁴⁸

How ironic, then, to learn this year, as Blessing could have not have known, that George Bush, though no master, has taken up painting as well and in April 2014 opened an exhibition of his rather amateurish portraits of fellow world leaders at the George W. Bush Presidential Center in Dallas. His oil paintings of his fellow "elephants," Russian President Vladimir Putin, German Chancellor Angela Merkel, Indian Prime Minister Manmohan Singh, remind us all of who holds worldly power ... and who does not.

But if Blessing's George Bush stands as the latest in a long line of conquest, blood, and violence, he wants us all to know he didn't do it alone—all Americans were his accomplices, as he tells us in his longest speech by far, expounding the second major theme of the play:

> I never did anything without the support of the American people. You know how I know that? 'Cause no matter how far I sank in the polls, no matter how low that number went, they never, never came to get me. They can whine all they want about how much they objected and how they never wanted to go into Iraq and all the rest of that shit. But bottom line, where were the demonstrations? The riots? Students lying in their own blood? There weren't any...⁴⁹

Americans aided and abetted Bush's crimes and it seems ultimately unfair to leave him facing justice in the court dock alone.

Further scenes reveal murky details that may or may not be true: Anna-Lisa fled her country of origin as a war refugee, her family killed in a country far away (the Middle East? the former Yugoslavia?) and she herself was repeatedly raped and turned into a prostitute. Then she met Piet and they married. In the play's present, she comforts, but does not confront, her abuser, George.

Near the end of the play, George sits staring out the window at the sea again and this time we listen to Piet and Anna-Lisa make love in the bedroom as noisily as George and she did earlier. This mounting and unsettling creepiness culminates in George's departure for trial and one last question, though we remain uncertain whether the answer is megalomaniacal or teasing:

> GEORGE: Know what I like about the ocean?
> PIET: What?
> GEORGE: I like to walk on it.[50]

The overall tone of the play reminds me of Harold Pinter's "comedies of menace," as in *The Birthday Party* and *The Homecoming*, where seemingly normal people plunked into mysterious circumstances, among menacing strangers, do inexplicably disgusting, even animalistic, things. In *When We Go...*, some of the writing is opaque and some is "right on the nose," a frequently jarring tone mixing risqué humor, political disquisition, and aural sex.

Searching for the symbolism may have led me off track but I couldn't help but notice the acronym formed by the play's title. The first letter of each word in the title, *When We Go Upon the Sea* forms WWGUTS. Could it be "we (hate) W's guts?"

The mix of politics, symbols, and sex did not please everyone. Jason Zinoman, in the *New York Times* review, called it "A Political Fantasy," but noted:

> The problem with *When We Go Upon the Sea* is not that it's yet another derisive play about George W. Bush.... The real trouble, dramatically speaking, is that this Bush character ... doesn't do anything of interest.... He just generally acts smug.[51]

Andy Propst, writing for "TheaterMania," found it more interesting:

> Blessing's writing is mercifully subtle.... "Sea" avoids the easy and stereotypical jabs, and instead paints a picture of a man quick to temper, use of force, and driven by his sensual nature. It makes for a thought-provoking look at what guides the man's decision-making processes.[52]

Joe Dziemianowicz, in *New York Daily News*, wrote:

> Provocative, no? Yes, if only for a brief moment. This 85-minute play by Lee Blessing, commissioned by the sociopolitical-minded troupe InterAct Theatre Company, is laced with ideas but remains naggingly low-impact.... That roundabout indictment might land with force on audiences if George W. emerged even a little bit enlightened. He doesn't. He's same old caricatured 43rd—power mad with demented notions about walking on water—so there's no takeaway.[53]

J. Cooper Robb, in the *Philadelphia Weekly*, reported:

> In this dark and disquieting play, Blessing isn't concerned with simple Bush bashing. His purpose in "Sea" is to investigate the relationship between rulers and those they rule. Unlike many Americans, Piet and Anna-Lisa worship Bush. He isn't the first powerful and morally questionable leader they've had in the room and they treat him with reverence. They live only to serve rulers who—in their view—shoulder the burdens of power. "You know what I like about the sea?" Bush asks Piet. "I like to walk on it." At the end of Blessing's drama, we are left with the uneasy feeling that perhaps America doesn't want a man of the people in the Oval Office, but rather an omnipotent ruler with an insatiable thirst for power.[54]

The critics focused, laser-like, on the character George W. Bush, but Blessing had larger fish to fry here. The play tackles the long history of Western imperialism, tying contemporary American exceptionalism directly back to the conquest of the so-called "New World" by the English, Dutch, French, and Spanish who went upon the sea to subjugate the Americas beginning in the 15th century. He touches upon inequalities of wealth, an even hotter political topic right now, and class warfare in his references to the "elite" and those who serve. This hotel room reminds us of the Second Empire drawing room in *No Exit*. Is this hotel room in the Hague a stand-in for hell? Certainly each of our three characters inhabits their own hell: George, deposed and ready to face his accusers; Anna-Lisa, defiled and subjugated; Piet, too traumatized to leave the hotel. In "No Exit," the three characters torture each other mentally and emotionally, but here the three support each other in an intimate collaboration that ensures that the political status quo and the violence of war go on. George needs the subservience of Piet and Anna-Lisa. They, in turn, need George, a "relaxed" George, to make a frightening world seem secure.

The play disdains to preach but indicts the audience as much as the war criminal on stage. The tone is dark, the jokes few, and the catharsis postponed.

CHAPTER 9

The Plays of Life, Death and Immortality

People die, we know, but what happens then? Blessing has a penchant for the afterlife, be it heaven (*Heaven's My Destination*) or hell, sometimes with Bernie Madoff and sometimes with Ronald Reagan. Sometimes it's about the act of dying itself, as in *Cold Water* and *Unknown*. Sometimes he takes us to limbo as in *Courting Harry*, or earlier, in *Cobb*, to see what happens. And then he reverses death entirely and gives us a second chance at life in *The Hourglass Project*. Perhaps we only value life because of death.

Cold Water
Heaven's My Destination
A User's Guide to Hell Featuring Bernard Madoff
Unknown
Courting Harry
The Hourglass Project

Cold Water

Cold Water, set on a college campus, flashes by in just ten minutes but leaves us with a lifetime of disquiet. Protagonist August, serving as a teaching assistant at a *"major university,"*[1] delivers a monologue, in which he looks back at a difficult moment in his teaching career as his friends, Russell, June, and Eric bustle around their shared living space, packing up to send August off to war. Blessing doesn't name the war and college students haven't gone off to fight against their will since Vietnam. Eric says:

9. Plays of Death and Immortality 203

We are going to fight for the delicate wasp waist of the Americas. We are going to keep the Caribbean blue and warm and keep the volcanos from exploding.[2]

As the play was written in 1986, we automatically think of the Contra War in Nicaragua and the civil war in El Salvador, both pursued by President Reagan and referenced by Blessing later in the plays *Whores, Lake Street Extension,* and *Reagan in Hell.*

Eric sees war's upside: "Do you have any idea how much money we made after our last successful war? Twenty five years of unprecedented economic growth."[3] Both Russell and Eric rather unself-consciously mingle homophobic slurs into their interactions and we read more references to "fags" and "faggots"[4] than we have in a long time, called forth, perhaps, by the hyper masculinity of war planning.

Amid the tumult, August thinks back to an incident at a seminar he was teaching in 18th century English poetry. He tells us:

I was doing pretty well—making Pope scintillating as he can be for people who've witnessed 20,000 violent deaths on the tube [think video games today] by the time they're 13. I had my kids in a pretty appreciative state of mind, I thought—to the point where they were genuinely admiring the antiquated eloquence of the heroic couplet.[5]

August allowed the students to bring their dogs to class and, on this day, two of them began copulating beneath the conference table: "The male was too big for the female, so she started screaming like horses do when they're shot. That sound froze me."[6] While the students looked to August for direction he just sat there and several of them had to carry the dogs, screaming all the way, to the men's room and douse them with cold water. As August tells us "After that, it was hard to use the word 'couplet.'"[7]

The incident looms large for August as he turns it over and over again in his mind, and his sense of failure from it now motivates his resignation, not just from teaching, but from life. His friends are burning his books, his clothes, his car. In the final lines, Russell asks: "Hey, August—when you light the car [filled with gasoline], you want to be in or out?" August replies "In." and the spotlight on August goes out suddenly.[8] The wages of war and hypermasculinity at home and abroad, seen here as a denial of homosexuality in August contrasted with the naturalness of animal sexuality, in the two dogs, are death, death visited upon our own young in regular waves of overseas bloodletting in Korea, Vietnam, Santo Domingo, Panama, Nicaragua, Grenada, Lebanon, Afghanistan, and Iraq. The image I conjured of August about to self-immolate in a car filled with gas harkened back to the Vietnam anti-war protests of self-immolation by Buddhist monks, begun by Thich Quang Duc on June 11, 1963, and those of four Americans protesting the war at home, Alice Herz,

Norman Morrison, Roger La Porte, and Florence Beaumont, who burned themselves to death between March 1965 and October 1967.

Heaven's My Destination

Blessing undertook this project, a commission from the Cleveland Play House in 2008 to adapt Thornton Wilder's 1935 novel, *Heaven's My Destination*, to the stage, which premiered in April 2009 under the direction of Play House artistic director Michael Bloom. His only, and earlier, adaptation, is *Courting Harry* from 2007, which he adapted from Linda Greenhouse's book: *Becoming Justice Blackmun*. Blessing described adaptation to me as

> nearly as challenging but different from my originals. [The] hardest part is leaving out so many wonderful facts and passages that don't move the play forward but are great in themselves.[9]

He called the adaptation of Thornton Wilder "very faithful" to the original.[10]

Wilder (1897–1975), a playwright and novelist, won the Pulitzer Prize for Fiction in 1926 for *The Bridge at San Luis Rey*, and the Pulitzer Prize for Drama twice: for *Our Town*, in 1938, and *The Skin of Our Teeth*, in 1943. Blessing himself was nominated for, but did not win the Pulitzer for Drama in 1988, for *A Walk in the Woods*.

Set in the early 1930s, in the American Midwest, *Heaven's My Destination* examines a Pilgrim's Progress of faith and character in the person of 23-year-old George Brush, in a time of financial and moral uncertainty. The play opens with a dying George in the hospital, unwilling to accept the ministrations of a clergyman. George tells him:

> I've broken all Ten Commandments except two. I never killed anybody and I never made any graven images. I was never tempted by idols, but I guess that would have come along any day. I'm saying this because I don't like the tone of your voice. I'm glad I broke those commandments. Wish I'd broken more. I made a mistake all my life thinking you could get better and better until you were perfect.[11]

From his bed the play flashes back to the people and places that brought Brush here, beginning as a traveling salesman on a train. He's selling school textbooks but saving souls and giving free advice, leaving a note on the seat of one passenger he saw smoking that reads: "Women who smoke are unfit to be mothers."[12] Blessing uses a chorus of ensemble actors to provide exposition, describe scenes, and share Brush's thoughts.

Though a Baptist, George decides to take a vow of poverty and emulate Mahatma Gandhi. He begins by withdrawing his money from the bank.

Saving up money is a sign you're afraid of the future. And one fear makes another. Think about it. It's almost immoral—everyone lying in bed, wondering what'll happen to them when they get old and sick. Who can have money in a bank and sleep at night? Worrying about this and that, worrying about whether the banks themselves will have troubles—[13]

But this kind of talk gets him arrested and escorted out of town.

George has a unique take on life: he worries that his boss keeps giving him raises while other people are getting laid off; a fine singer, he sings for free at any church that will have him; he doesn't accept the theory of evolution, won't gamble, drink or smoke or abide women who do either. And after spending a night in the barn with the farmer's daughter he considers himself "married" to her, even though he can't find that farm again. That single night means he can never marry another, raise a family, or settle down. These odd notions earn him the scorn of those he meets. As Margie, a woman of practicality, who does smoke and drink, tells George:

> You make me sick! Where do your theories and ideas get you? Nowhere! Live, kid—live! There's no hope for us sons-of-bitches if we stop to argue every step we take.[14]

The long dramatic scene of Act 1 occurs one night as George saves his tent mate, Dick, at Camp Morgan, from committing suicide. The action includes a pretend car chase complete with sound effects of squealing brakes and a tipped canoe in the lake, theatricality reminiscent of the minimalism of Wilder's own plays like *Our Town* and *Sleeping Car Hiawatha*.

At his next stop, a trio of old friends down on their luck trick George into accompanying them to a brothel, passing off the madam and her girls as one large family "in a fine American home."[15] A modern Candide, George blindly discovers moral values in the human cesspool. One of the men finally gives away the joke: "It's a cat house! My God! You're the simplest galoot in the world! You're so simple, you stink!"[16] Angered at the ruse, George makes to fight, but then reverts to pacifism as the "friends" beat the living daylights out of him, while berating him as a "pontificating bastard."[17] So ends Act 1.

Act 2 opens with George recuperating in the hospital, where one of the men who beat him works as an orderly and tries to explain to George why people hate him:

> LOUIE: Learn to drink! That's what you need to do. Leave other people's lives alone. Run around with women. Enjoy life. You're gonna be dead a long time. A long, *long* time! You keep looking for an American home? What a joke! Believe me, all you're going to find is—
> GEORGE: Get away!
> LOUIE: What?
> GEORGE: *Get away!!* If I was like you, I'd *expect* to be dead a long time! I'd rather be crazy all alone than sensible like you. I'm glad I'm *nuts*![18]

Recovered from his beating and with information from a detective agency, George tracks down the farmer's daughter he once had sex with and informs her he considers their actions made them married. She, however, wants nothing to do with this "Crazy ... coot"[19] or his proffered money or wristwatch. George's rose-colored glasses begin to darken:

> I believe there's a God, all right—but why's He so slow in changing the world? Why does He deliberately disappoint people?[20]

And yet he attempts one more act of misplaced "random kindness" when he helps a stickup man find and take a storeowner's hidden stash of cash, promising the storekeeper to repay him out of his own money; all out of a desire to help a criminal get back on the straight and narrow. This escapade earns George a trip to jail, where a fellow jailbird diagnoses George's problem: "You don't want to grow up—that's the trouble with you."[21] We see that George's actions proceed from an unfounded certainty:

> BURKIN: You're full of evasions. You don't give a goddamn for the truth.
> GEORGE: I have the truth.[22]

Rushing back to Kansas City, George reunites with Roberta, the farmer's daughter, and talks her into marriage. They adopt the daughter of one of the men who had previously beaten up George. But all is not well. Roberta wants to leave him and go back to the farm. George tries to live up to his high standards, but finds unhappiness and rejection once again. He asks: "Isn't the principle of a thing more important than the people that live under that principle?"[23]

Finally, George loses his faith. He also loses his health. Alone in the hospital bed of the play's opening, the nurse visits to tell him his old friend Father Pasziewski has died. A note from his old landlady explains that

> it seemed he knew he was going to die and he wanted to give us something to remember him by. So he said to each take a spoon from the dining-room table. He asked me to give you a spoon from him, too. I told him you liked to hear about him, Mr. Brush, and he seemed to have a special feeling about you. It's a terrible pity you never met.[24]

The gift and the knowledge that the old priest remembered him up until the end rejuvenates George. He gets well. He leaves the hospital. He hits the road again, selling text books. But something has changed. In Lockburn, Missouri, he stops for a cup of coffee and encounters a woman reading Darwin's *The Voyage of the Beagle*. In conversation he learns she is intelligent, believes in evolution and hasn't the funds to go to college. George decides to fund her education.

Back on the road, George gets jailed once again, we're told, on another "misunderstanding."[25] But, in a final stage picture, as the play ends, George wordlessly sends a powerful message of hope, holding up to the light the spoon the priest left him.

Its reflection dances throughout the theater—gradually to be joined by scores, hundreds of similar small lights which glimmer in crazy, unpredictable patterns everywhere he looks.[26]

What happened? Somehow this insufferable prig who placed principle over people but who really did operate out of an ethical code detached from self-interest—always ready to give people money as well as advice, always experimenting with lofty ideals, whether from Gandhi or Jesus—learned that love need not be judgmental and that goodness wears many faces and believes many things. The turning point comes when George funds a college education for a young woman reading Darwin, seeing her not as a heathen but as a thinker. He no longer needs to be right. Father Pasziewski, whom he always inquired about but never met, loved him unreservedly, in almost Christ-like fashion, to bequeath him a gift, the spoon. Now George shares that gift with everyone with the reflected light, calling to mind the "thousand points of light" phrase George H. W. Bush's speechwriter Peggy Noonan adapted from C. S. Lewis and worked into his 1988 campaign for the Presidency to describe a society where people, without fanfare or publicity, aid the less fortunate. Oddly enough, the name George Brush in this play must have resonated with Blessing, who excoriated President George *Bush* in his own later, original play *When We Go Upon the Sea.*

Heaven's My Destination incorporates traditions of the *bildungsroman*, the picaresque, Cervantes's *Don Quixote*, Voltaire's *Candide*, and John Bunyan's *The Pilgrim's Progress*, in which a young man goes into the world with a head full of fancy ideas, gets the wind knocked out of his sails, survives all kinds of adventures, and matures into an ethical, caring, and more realized human being. The twist here is that George Brush begins at a high level of ethical discernment best suited to Heaven itself and, in giving up his fealty to abstract principles, discovers a Heaven on earth of human feeling and failing.

The few critics who saw the play liked it. Bob Abelman wrote in the *Ohio News Herald*:

> *Heaven's My Destination* is an intriguing, thought-provoking play that pits a strangely sympathetic hero against an unbeatable foe. It makes for an interesting evening's entertainment.[27]

While Christine Howey in her blog, "Rave and Pan," wrote:

> This Lee Blessing adaptation [is] a mixed bag of amusing moments along with redundancy and some tedium.... The play itself would benefit from a more targeted focus on fewer characters, so that we could get closer to the kind of monomaniacal innocence, and perhaps the vulnerability, that George Brush represents.[28]

Heaven's My Destination deserves more productions.

A User's Guide to Hell Featuring Bernard Madoff

In this play Blessing goes to hell, following his penchant for the afterlife; remember *Reagan in Hell*, *Cobb* in limbo, and Dorothea in *Eleemosynary* speaking to us after death? Like most of us, Blessing clearly has issues with life and death. As he told one interviewer:

> [I wrote *A User's Guide to Hell*] to examine my concept of the afterlife, hell specifically. I chose Bernie Madoff, because I think he would be a pretty universal candidate for hell.... Bernie, as our guide instead of Dante, is consistently surprised, as I think we are, by what is and is not in hell.... This play's serious theme, if it has one, and I suppose it does, is "what is the nature of faith?" and "what do we mean when we talk about religion: is it comforting or rather terrifying?" and "how does each individual make their peace with a sense of an afterlife or no afterlife at all?"[29]

Bernard Lawrence "Bernie" Madoff, born April 29, 1938, and now serving a 150-year prison sentence, hellish enough you might agree, masterminded a massive stock fraud that bilked some 17.5 *billion* dollars out of private investors and charitable organizations in one of the largest financial frauds in U.S. history.[30]

Among the famous victims of Madoff's deception were Hollywood director Steven Spielberg; baseball great Sandy Koufax; actress Zsa Zsa Gabor, who lost $10 million; actor John Malkovich, who saw $2.3 million disappear; and Elie Weisel's non-profit Foundation for Humanity, which lost $15.2 million, almost its entire holdings.[31]

Compounding the tragedy, Bernie's older son Andrew died of cancer, which, prior to his death, he publicly blamed on the shame brought to the family by his father's crimes, and Bernie's younger son Mark committed suicide on the second anniversary of his father's arrest.

Blessing's play opens with loud noises, screams—all the hullabaloo of a typical day in Manhattan, as Verge, Madoff's own guide to hell, much as Dante had Virgil, hurries him along. Building and storefronts surround them with their windows and doors bricked in. As Verge sets the scene:

> VERGE: There's lots of folks around here who remember Bernie Madoff.
> BERNARD: Are they still mad?
> VERGE: A *little*.[32]

People fill this hell, pushing and shoving past Bernie and Verge, unseen but finally heard softly repeating, over and over, "Fuck you!"[33]

"I'm a Jew." Bernie tells Verge. "I don't believe in hell."[34] Bernie also doesn't believe in God and tells us: "Religion's for people who can't face reality."[35] Since this hell looks like Manhattan, Bernie seeks solace when he sees his old door-

9. Plays of Death and Immortality   209

man, Manny. But poor Manny lost his retirement (investing with Bernie) and killed himself. Bernie claps Manny on the arm, and Manny's arm falls off. Good thing he doesn't touch Manny's leg, as many of Bernie's investors lost both an arm *and* a leg.

But Bernie remains unconvinced as to hell's reality, since the pain he encounters seems so petty. Arriving to rectify that oversight, Verge next presents Dr. Josef Mengele (1911–1979), the so-called "Angel of Death," who carried out macabre and lethal experiments at the Nazi death camp at Auschwitz.[36] Mengele offers Bernie a choice of pain to convince him he has entered hell:

> I could inject dye into your eyeballs and make them a different color. That would be fun—for me. And it's very painful. I could castrate you without anesthesia, make you a woman.... If you had a twin—oh, if you had a twin!—I could sew the two of you together to make a conjoined twin. Siamese, we used to say, but man-made. Then you could both enjoy the pain of the blood poisoning and gangrene. Since I am a man of science, I could inject your heart with chloroform—that is real torment—then cut you up and analyze you, piece by piece. And since we are here, we could do it again and again. What do you say?[37]

The doctor practiced those ghastly torments on Jews, Gypsies, Communists, and homosexuals at Auschwitz and offers them to Bernie since he now serves on staff in hell having "suffered enough in life."[38]

"*You?*" asks Bernie. "How—?"[39]

Menegle whines:

> Do you ever stop to see things with my eyes.... They know I suffered. My work was cut short by the end of the war. I had decades more to give to my research.... Let's give you a little pain, eh?[40]

But Mengele escaped punishment for his sins:

> [Thirty-five years after the end of the War, as an old man living under an assumed identity in Brazil] I died of natural causes. In the warm, salt ocean, swimming along in the dazzling sunshine.... You know what I learned from it all? There is no pain. Not for me, anyway. The terrible vengeance, which you think must surely come, simply ... doesn't. You can do precisely as you wish and ... remain unpunished for the rest of your life. Forever.[41]

Is God still on the job? Does one of the greatest mass murderers in history get off scot free? Bernie asks for Mengele to bring the pain to prove the reality of hell. Mengele threatens it, but then slides off stage. In hell, you do not get what you want, it seems.

> VERGE: What did you get from him?
> BERNARD: Nothing. Nothing. He just left me in——
> VERGE: Doubt. You wanted pain; he gave you doubt. The old Is-There-a-God? routine...

BERNARD: *Is* there a God?
VERGE: How do *I* know?[42]

Next up, Verge and Bernard encounter a modern-day La Llorona, here called "Wet Woman," in hell for drowning her own two children, but she bears no guilt because it's all part of God's plan. She tells Bernie:

> I think about God. People say He's all powerful, but they don't see what that means. It means nothing exists without God's approval. Heaven, hell, a place like this, Satan. God could've stopped me killing my kids, but He didn't. He let me kill them. And He's all knowing, too. When He made me, He knew I would kill them. Everything's the way God wants it. I walk in certain joy, knowing that everything ever done by one human to another—is ordained by the Lord. Otherwise...
> BERNARD: Otherwise what?
> WET WOMAN: God wouldn't be possible.[43]

Clearly, Bernie is encountering not people in hell, but theological concepts. Maybe that's hell: a first-year university philosophy course?

Verge and Bernie head for the sewer where Verge can escape the noise that bedevils him. But the sewer confounds Bernie: no punishments arise, no terrors await—they sit surrounded by nothing at all. "I don't accept this. I simply don't. This is not *anything*," Bernie tells Verge.[44] Verge offers a horrific rebuttal:

> And how do you know this isn't the highest purpose we're created for?.... Maybe we're supposed to be shit, lying on top of other shit—lying on all the shit that ever was. Why would that be so far-fuckin'-fetched?[45]

Bernie stamps off, with Verge in tow, looking for "a better version of hell."[46] Bernie aims for Wall Street, but, by mistake, the two travelers hit upon Ground Zero, where they encounter Mohamed Atta, who, we are told, is *"extremely grouchy and sports an obvious erection."*[47] Atta (1968–2001) piloted hijacked American Airlines flight 11 into the North Tower of the World Trade Center on September 11, 2001. Now, he searches hell for his reward:

> Seventy-seven virgins! And an oasis. And good food to eat. And light. And music. And delight in Allah. Have you seen any of these things?![48]

When Atta learns from Verge that Bernie's stolen billions came mostly at the expense of other Jews, he blesses him: "You are my hero. May Allah rain peace upon you."[49] And when Verge proposes that Bernie might fill the bill of a virgin, he pulls down Bernie's pants and sodomizes him. Finally, Bernie experiences the pain he sought.

But Bernie realizes he wants more than mere pain. He wants a punishment befitting his sins, and so he presses on for Wall Street. On the way, they encounter an Incinerated Woman with a tale of woe:

> I was a village girl in India. He married me when I was very young, but he didn't want to pay the bride price. So before they could collect it, he set me aflame. He claimed I died in a kitchen fire—they're common enough. I didn't, though; he murdered me. He had me, then he murdered me. He moved on to another part of India and did it again. And later again. He liked young girls, but he didn't like to pay for them.[50]

Coincidentally, hubby, who relocated to New York, died in the Twin Towers attack and now, Incinerated Woman tells Bernie, he is searching for his god:

> INCINERATED WOMAN: We have many gods. Some are gentle; some terrifying. He will keep on looking until he finds one who understands him.
> BERNARD: But if you can do anything, always assuming that *some* god will find it acceptable, then what's the point of having a god at all?
> INCINERATED WOMAN: (*losing patience*) You're not a Hindu, are you?
> BERNARD: No, I'm a Jew. We gave the world monotheism.
> INCINERATED WOMAN: And you expect thanks?[51]

Arriving at Wall Street, Bernie finds it maddeningly empty and when Verge heads for an exit to leave him there, alone for eternity, Bernie pulls him back, pins him to the floor, pummels him with his fists and kicks him repeatedly in the ribs. When we think, surely he has murdered him, Verge gets up, good as new.

Verge exits through the wall and a "Man in a Dog Leash," actually Bernie's son Mark, enters, explaining that lacking a rope he hung himself with the leash. Mark also exits through the wall, leaving Bernie in tears.

Just then, Josh and Briana rappel down the wall for a visit. A hedge fund manager and a trader, respectively, they stand in awe of Bernie's "accomplishments" and have dropped in to thank him. Josh and Briana have a religion, too. It consists of:

> BRIANA: Profits like clockwork.
> JOSH: Self-regulating markets.
> BRIANA: Ownership society.
> JOSH: A balloon that inflates forever!
> ...
> BRIANA: The dream of endless acquisition.[52]

Briana and Josh idolize Bernie, who shone like a beacon when the market expanded and, just as importantly, served as a distraction when things went south, thus saving the system from basic changes. Like Jesus, "You died for us," Josh tells Bernie.[53] In gratitude, Josh and Briana usher Bernie into heaven, an endless stock exchange floor. Verge explains that the earlier trip through hell was mere hazing, and that *everyone* goes to heaven.

> VERGE: You did good, Bernie. A real child of God.
> BERNARD: Am I?
> VERGE: You bet. Everyone is.[54]

Verge exits to heaven. Bernie pauses, but does not move, as lights fade to black.

Some critics saw *A User's Guide to Hell Featuring Bernard Madoff* as boring, while others enjoyed its philosophical bent. Jason Zinoman wrote in the *New York Times*:

> the play ... makes hell seem a little like the soundstage of a Michael Jackson video. (There's a lot of white smoke billowing through this city.) It's a pretty halfhearted vision, frankly, introducing notions that are never satisfactorily explored.[55]

Carole DiTosti posted in "Blog Critics":

> It is sardonic, riotous and funny, turning propriety on its ear and smacking up against the absurd at every turn.[56]

Diane Snyder, on the "Time Out New York," website, wrote:

> Despite its tantalizing title, *A User's Guide to Hell Featuring Bernard Madoff*, is surprisingly tame.[57]

Wendy Caster, writing for "Show Showdown," agreed:

> The program features a note from the playwright that begins, "*Hell is funny.*" I don't know if that's true, but I do know that the version of hell depicted in *A User's Guide to Hell Featuring Bernard Madoff* is tedious.[58]

Let's take Blessing at his words, quoted earlier: this play examines faith, religion, our beliefs about an afterlife, and how those beliefs impact the morals by which we live our earthly lives. These are the subject of college bull sessions, certainly, but these thoughts also inevitably creep into our mature minds from time to time as we contemplate our lives and our approaching mortality. Blessing entertains, and makes jokes at the expense of several religions, including Judaism, personified by Bernie, Hinduism in the person of Incinerated Woman, and Islam in Mohamed Atta. The lack of punishment for a monster like Josef Mengele also destroys the Christian view of an afterlife of punishment or reward. Blessing acts as an equal opportunity burlesquer of religion. In the end, Verge tells us everyone goes to heaven, historically a Universalist teaching, although this heaven offers such endless boredom that residents often schedule a short vacation to hell to break up the tedium.

Blessing saves for last the redemption offered by Josh and Briana, complete with the American dream of the endless pursuit of wealth. Their talk of a growing market and the "ownership society," proclaimed by President George W. Bush in 2003, have lost some of their gloss in the light of The Great Recession of 2007–2009.

If all our dreams of the afterlife seem so shallow, so open to mockery, what remains? Whistling in the dark with Bernie, Josef, and Mohamed?

Not a clergyman, philosopher, or guru, Blessing owes us no answers, assurances, or comfort. What he *does* owe us as an artist, and what he delivers here, is a romp through our illusions and delusions and a chance to reexamine, once again, the never answered, and never answerable, big questions of life ... and death.

Unknown

In spring 2012, Center Stage in Baltimore, The State Theater of Maryland, founded 1963, began planning its 50th anniversary under the leadership of newly hired artistic director Kwame Kwei-Armah (born 1954). The British import suggested soliciting 50 playwrights to contribute monologues to a celebratory program around the themes "What is your America?" and "Who is your America?" Artists like Neil LaBute, Christopher Durang, Anna Deavere Smith, Lynn Nottage, and Lee Blessing responded. In 2013, Possible Films Company and director Hal Hartley made a feature film of these 50 monologues, available for streaming at Fandor Films.[59]

Each writer offered a three-minute snapshot of their America, displaying the kind of diversity of theme and tone one would expect from such a varied collection of artists. Blessing wrote about a personal experience he had not previously wrestled with in print: witnessing a young man, just a short distance away from him on the train platform, leap to the tracks in front of an oncoming locomotive, as he waited for his train in Manhattan two years earlier.

In the monologue the speaker describes what happened:

> I never saw his face. I'm grateful for that I think, the strange blessing of it, in a way. He was young—could have been a college student, like those I'd just been teaching. Long, curly, dull-blond hair—it blocked his face so much, I thought he was a girl. But when people started talking to the police I realized: it was a boy who jumped down and then stood up in the middle of the tracks, in the middle of a perfect afternoon, a second before the train hit.[60]

As Blessing told *Baltimore Sun* reporter Mary Carole McCauley, the deadly event made him think about life:

> "When you witness something that extreme, you can't help but carry it around with you," says Blessing, 62. For a young person to be that desperate sort of imprints itself on your psyche.... It's also a reflection of the world and the society that we live in. Suicide may be more shocking when it happens in this country, because we have a more elevated lifestyle here. We're not starving in the streets.... Suicide assaults our most fundamental belief that life is worth living.... Those of us who are still walking around tend to think that it is, but it's not chiseled someplace on a mountain. When someone chooses to die, it reminds the rest of us that we're survivors.[61]

Michael Emerson, an actor in theater, television (*Lost, The Practice, The X-Files*), and film (*Unfaithful* and, as the voice of the Joker, *The Dark Knight Returns*, parts 1 and 2) plays the witness.

The monologue concludes:

> This is my statement: He was right next to me. I didn't know him. We never shared a word or a look, but he taught me more than I had taught my students: the lesson of a dark fate and a whispered warning—of what it can mean to be young, on a perfect day, in a free country.[62]

The witness, and we, are left with the unknowns of the title—who was this young man? Why did he jump? What terrible pressures well up within the people near to us that we never see that can lead them to desperate acts? Would we ever do the same? Could we ever face issues so immense that we could kill ourselves? How, each day, do we decide *not* to kill ourselves?

Courting Harry

Could anything sound drier than two judges debating court cases? Even if they've known each other 50 years? Even if the court they serve on is the Supreme Court of the United States? What if their conflicts revolve around the biggest cases in U.S. history, like Roe v. Wade, which legalized women's right to decide the fate of their pregnancies?

The drama resides in the material no doubt, but think for a moment how you would render that conflict as drama on stage. History Theatre in St. Paul, Minnesota, commissioned Lee Blessing to surmount that challenge and he did so engagingly and educationally in *Courting Harry*, the story of the long-standing and ultimately fractured friendship of Chief Justice Warren Burger and Justice Harry Blackmun within the black-robed and confined quarters of the Supreme Court. For material Blessing turned to the biography of Blackmun, *Becoming Justice Blackmun: Harry Blackmun's Supreme Court Journey*, 2005, by Linda Greenhouse, the *New York Times* reporter who won a Pulitzer Prize for her coverage of the Supreme Court in 1998. Greenhouse was privy to Blackmun's voluminous cache of private correspondence as well as inside information relating to his public decisions.

Warren Burger and Harry A. Blackmun grew up in St. Paul's "unfashionable"[63] Dayton's Bluff neighborhood, where their friendship developed. Each was educated at his law school of choice: Burger at St. Paul College of Law, now William Mitchell College, and Blackmun at Harvard. Republicans both, President Nixon appointed them to the Supreme Court, Burger in 1969; Blackmun, 1970. The press dubbed the conservative pair "The Minnesota Twins,"

9. Plays of Death and Immortality 215

after the baseball team and the two seemed ideological soulmates until Blackmun's 1973 authorship of the decision in *Roe v. Wade* divided them politically and personally from then on.

This might seem heavy going for a night at the theater, but the critics loved the result. Graydon Royce, in the *Minneapolis Star Tribune*, wrote:

> Both parties argue their evidence vociferously and then throw themselves on the mercy of the court (us, in the audience). Whose fault was the rift between Harry Blackmun and Warren Burger? Why did two boys who became fast friends ... turn into bitter foes at the end of their long lives?
> Playwright Lee Blessing provides lots of evidence for each man in his superb new play "Courting Harry," but he refuses to tidy up this messy relationship and leaves us with broken hearts and sympathy for two of Minnesota's most-famous jurists... —just what theater should be.[64]

In the *Twin Cities Pioneer Press*, Dominic P. Papatola added:

> This would be terrific fiction if it weren't such a painfully real story. It demands to be seen.
> On balance, Blessing crams a lot of information and a goodly amount of entertainment into [the play's] 90-minute running time. If it doesn't offer the full meal deal of Blackmun's life and legacy, it's still a tasty and toothsome sampler.[65]

Jill Schafer wrote in *Cherry and Spoon*:

> I have to admit, before seeing the world premiere play *Courting Harry* at the History Theatre, I was afraid that a play about a couple of Supreme Court Justices would be dry and boring. I was pleased to find out that it's anything but; it's actually an amusing, engaging, entertaining, and, yes, educational play.[66]

Since 1978, St. Paul's History Theatre has commissioned new works and produced existing plays exploring Minnesota's past in relation to the state and country's present. Asking native son Blessing to write a play about two other native sons and national figures must have seemed a natural. The script has had no productions in other states, nor has it been printed.

Courting Harry begins "several years after the death of Justice Blackmun."[67] In fact, all the characters we meet on stage have already "shuffled off this mortal coil."[68] Blessing has visited this "undiscovered country from which no visitor returns," as Hamlet called death,[69] previously in *Cobb*, *Patient A*, and the visits to hell he made with Madoff and Reagan. Here, President Nixon, stung by the Senate rejections of his last two Supreme Court nominees, Clement Haynsworth (in 1969) and G. Harold Carswell (in 1970), interviews Blackmun, upon recommendation of Chief Justice Burger, with an idea of finding yet another conservative for the Court. "You're sure your daughters aren't hippies?" Nixon asks twice.[70] The (historically accurate) conceit here is that Blackmun has saved every scrap of correspondence, every diary entry for 70 and more years. We are hearing the real dope, the words and thoughts of the movers and shakers.

Blackmun got the appointment but Nixon didn't bargain with the result. As President Eisenhower had once called his appointment of California Governor Earl Warren as Chief Justice "the biggest damned-fool mistake I ever made,"[71] Nixon lived to rue his choice.

Blackmun does not seem to mind Nixon's unhappiness but he mourns his lost friendship with Burger, which they had begun in kindergarten, and chalks it up to the conflicts around "Roe v. Wade":

> WARREN: We agreed on abortion. We voted together.
> HARRY: At first. What about later? When it *counted*?
> WARREN: So we disagreed; it was a matter of philosophy—
> HARRY: You abandoned me! You acted like you had nothing to do with that first decision.
> WARREN: Ridiculous.
> HARRY: Like it was all my idea. The fact is, you made me write it.
> WARREN: I did not.
> HARRY: *Roe versus Wade*. You assigned it to me.
> WARREN: I had to assign it to someone. God knows, *I* wasn't going to write it.[72]

Once so close that Blackmun stood as best man at Burger's wedding,[73] lifelong friends—or "*almost* lifelong"—as Burger reminds the audience.[74] At times the two sound like jilted lovers:

> WARREN: No, *I* should be whipped for helping you.
> HARRY: Helping me *what*?
> WARREN: Helping you *up*. There are things we do for friendship which.... Well. To say it makes us blind is an understatement.[75]

Burger wheedles year after year for Blackmun to join him in a months-long sojourn through Europe, just the two to them:

> WARREN: People think I'm strong, decisive, impervious to the "slings and arrows." How completely I've failed to reveal myself to those who should know what fragile porcelain can reside within a man.
> HARRY (*to audience*) Didn't know what to think of *that*. Would you have gone with him?[76]

And each year, Blackmun declines.

> Overall Burger comes across as a striving and ambitious sycophant who, in the end, rises quite above his abilities to the position of Chief Justice. As he tells Blackmun:
> I suppose you thought you'd have been better? Well, guess what? You couldn't have been considered, because you had done none of the groundwork. People laugh at mediocrity, but I'll tell you something: sometimes mediocrity works harder. When it does, merit doesn't stand a chance. It's called Natural Selection—try to keep up.[77]

In 1972, abortion hit the court docket for the first time. Blackmun sympathized:

Not much hits a human life harder than an unexpected pregnancy. One day you're in the arms of someone you love, or someone you've just met, or someone you're trying to fight off. A few weeks later you may be begging a physician to commit a criminal act. That's how it was, in many places. The state invades your home, your bedroom, your body—it's not yours anymore. Maybe it never was.[78]

That same year Nixon made his opposition to abortion part of his campaign for reelection and raised the heat on the court. In a birth control case, Burger dissented all alone:

> WARREN (*to audience*) Where I couldn't even get Harry to come along with me. (*to HARRY*) I was the only dissenter. You left me out there alone.
> HARRY: No more Minnesota Twins?
> WARREN: We may as well have been the Chicago White Sox.[79]

Burger joined the majority in Roe v. Wade, but delayed the decision until he had sworn Nixon in for a second term. Blackmun wrote the majority opinion and paid for it. He tells the audience: "I had always abhorred abortion. Now, people were acting like I invented it."[80]

Courting Harry: **Justice Blackmun (Clyde Lund) and his aides (left to right: Sam Pearson, Jamila Anderson, and Charlotte Calvert) sort through a career's worth of judicial notes and decisions. History Theatre, St. Paul, Minnesota; 2013, photograph by Scott Pakudaitis; courtesy of History Theatre.**

Courting Harry: U.S. Supreme Court Justices Warren Burger (Nathaniel Fuller, left) and Harry Blackmun (Clyde Lund) let the legal briefs fly during a friendship-ending conflict. History Theatre, St. Paul, Minnesota; 2013, photograph by Scott Pakudaitis; courtesy of History Theatre.

Disagreements between the erstwhile friends increased. Burger felt betrayed:

> WARREN: You made me look like a fool, Harry—the more you disagreed. You were my man. I vouched for you.
> HARRY: I was a Supreme Court justice.
> WARREN: That doesn't mean you couldn't be reasonable![81]

Disagreements turn to hostility. Burger retires. When Blackmun retires, Burger does not write. Burger's wife dies and Blackmun does not attend the funeral. Burger dies and Blackmun writes no more than: "W.E.B. dies" in his diary. Even dead they squabble.

> WARREN: I wonder how much impact you really had, Harry. Hundreds of opinions, yet you'll only be remembered for one. When that's overturned—
> HARRY It's not going to be. It shouldn't be.
> WARREN: Get a grip. Your legacy's already being dismantled.[82]

Nothing but rancor remains.

WARREN: I listened to what my country wanted. You were stubborn. You made a mistake and dedicated the rest of your life to defending it (*with small laugh*). Sometimes I think you took positions just because they were the opposite of mine.
HARRY: That's ridiculous.
WARREN: You were never my friend. Took me years to see it.[83]

And vitriol replaces argument.

HARRY: You were disorganized! Bill Rehnquist and I almost never agreed but at least he could run the Court! And you know what? We *respected* each other!
WARREN: People respected me—
HARRY: NOBODY did![84]

Until it ends in pathos.

WARREN: Now here we are, knee-deep in betrayal. And no way back. Humans have friendships for only one reason, Harry—because we're terrified not to. When we lose those friendships ... that really is the definition of eternity....
HARRY: I'm sorry. I'm sorry.
WARREN: Do I know you? (*WARREN exits.*)[85]

Blessing meets the challenge to make history relevant by making the political issues dividing Burger and Blackmun play second fiddle to the issue of friendship. Few of us get elevated to the Supreme Court but all of us do make and lose friends, an existential issue of being alive. He propels the stage action with two additional male and two female actors playing a host of background characters, from Nixon, to Blackmun's daughter Sally, who considered having an abortion herself, to President Clinton, to archivists literally tossing around the papers of Blackmun's historical hoard. He keeps things moving on stage while simultaneously engaging us in 30 years of history. Mission accomplished.

The Hourglass Project

Called by its author "a speculative comedy about the future," *The Hourglass Project*, like all good science fiction, explores human drama against a backdrop of breathtaking technological advances. In this case, six elderly indigent and terminally ill people awaken after a 23-week induced coma to find themselves 20 years old and healthy again due to "regenerative gene therapy."[86] Fortunately, the author has little interest in the complicated science behind this "miracle" and spends our time and his investigating the impact of this transformation upon the relationships and psyches of his nine characters across nine scenes.

Blessing prefaced the play with this epigram: "Old age is an island surrounded by death,"[87] which he told me he "ran across around the time I started the play."[88] The quote, from Ecuadorian author and essayist Juan Montalvo

(1832–1889) accurately describes the Brightfield island estate setting of the play and adds a fearsome foreboding to a play that quickly turns comedic, laughing at both old age and death.

Abby and Don, a less than happily married couple, Melissa, Carol, and Walter are the formerly elderly who delight at first in their new bodies:

> ABBY: My breasts look really good.
> DANA: Isn't that great?
> DON: You bet your ass it's great.[89]

Don's renewed sex drive and Abby's reticence deliver the best humor of the play:

> ABBY: You're staring at life through a fog of testosterone.
> DON: So?!
> ABBY: Right now we need to contemplate the nature of intimacy itself—
> DON: That's what I'm—
> ABBY: In our *minds*, and rediscover the deep, human connection that leads people to marriage in the first place. We have feelings to sort out. Sex comes at the end of that process, not the beginning.
> DON: How much ... sorting out are we looking at here?[90]

Each character reacts differently to this second chance at life. Melissa's hard times in her previous life give her no hope for the future. In fact, she signed up for this experiment, having read the contract detailing the odds of 10,000 to 1 against success, in high hopes it would fail and she would die:

> MELISSA: There's so much pain in life. I was married four times. None of my children lived. I don't want to go through it again!
> DANA: It doesn't have to be that way—
> MELISSA: Of course it does! It's life! My last husband had a heart attack when I was fifty. I was alone for so many years—My daughter died in the same wreck that crippled me! Life's a firing squad! They don't even give you a blindfold![91]

Does life bless or curse us? Certainly younger people usually begin their lives with big plans and high hopes. As we grow older those plans sometimes fail and those hopes often get crushed. Though inside younger skin, our characters remember the vicissitudes of lives already lived.

> CAROL: The minute we weaken, life's right there with its whip and its club. It doesn't just want to kill us; it wants to ... to punish us.
> STEVE: For what?
> CAROL: For thinking it cared about us. Ever. Even for a moment.[92]

The guys have high hopes, though: Walter wants to use his new youth to cash in on fame and fortune and cheers up Don with thoughts of a new, single life without Abby.

The action unfolds at the Brightfield estate on a private island within a

9. Plays of Death and Immortality 221

private lake patrolled by alligators and snapping turtles. The wealthy and aged Brightfields, Chuck and Martha, privately fund the experiment under the supervision of daughter Dana, a scientist, in hopes of discovering their own personal rejuvenation. When they arrive from similar successful and secret trials in Asia in new 20-year-old bodies, we learn that what differentiates the happily reborn (Chuck and Martha) from the newly young but terminally morose (Carol, Don, and Melissa) is the difference in all of our society's divisions: money, specifically the money of the 1 percent. Economic class, not science, dominates this story's moral.

While we know the course of new young life will not run smoothly we have fun along the way and the sex in newly nubile bodies supplies much of the humor:

>ABBY: Now when I wake up, I look out the window and see Don standing there in his pajama bottoms.
>MELISSA: Ew.
>STEVE: What's he doing?
>ABBY: Staring at my cabin.
>STEVE: In just his bottoms?
>ABBY: He's showing off his new body. He thinks it'll seduce me.
>MELISSA: Ew.
>STEVE: Are you sure that's what he's—?
>ABBY: Pretty sure. 'Cause at the same time he's also ... you know, saluting the dawn.
>STEVE: Saluting the—?
>ABBY: Displaying his manhood?
>STEVE: Oh.
>CAROL and MELISSA: Ew—!
>ABBY: Standing at attention?
>CAROL and MELISSA: Ew—!!
>ABBY: Tenting on the old campground?
>CAROL and MELISSA: EW-!!!
>STEVE: Thanks, we get the drift.[93]

Abby works to seduce Steve while resisting husband Don. Steve, we learn, is a ringer, and actually young, brought in to observe the newborns undercover, from within their ranks. He's also Dana's boyfriend, but that relationship may not survive Abby's successful advances. As Don cracks wise: "I'll never understand women. They're a mystery wrapped in a ... Fig Newton."[94]

When things get out of hand and the Brightfields plan to slip all the newly young, plus Steve, special amnesia sandwiches, Dana rebels and includes her parents in the forgetting. Last to fall asleep, Steve protests, but Dana does not relent:

>DANA: I can't go through life wondering if you're going to leave me and spill all our secrets—
>STEVE: I couldn't do that to you!

DANA: Of course you could! You were unfaithful with Abby!
STEVE: I was not! We were just dancing and ... kissing...
DANA: You're a man; you can't help being undependable.

Dana concludes, as Steve falls to the ground, asleep: "You'll be so much better a boyfriend."[95]

Originally commissioned through the Hendrix-Murphy Foundation Programs in Literature and Language, *The Hourglass Project* premiered at the Hendrix College Department of Theatre Arts and Dance in Conway, Arkansas, on February 24, 2014. Hendrix College, a highly rated small liberal-arts institution founded in 1876, and located 30 miles from Little Rock, has 1,400 students at a pricey $52,000 (2014) per year for tuition, room and board.

The Hourglass Project's mix of sex and philosophical ruminations (Is a second shot at life a good thing? Does money buy happiness?) and roles for nine 20-year-old actors make it a natural for college productions. In January 2015, Blessing attended the staged reading of the play at the University of Tulsa. While there, he talked to a reporter about the project and James D. Watts, Jr., filed this story:

> "I've received commissions from professional theaters in the past, but this was the first time a college had asked me to write a play," Blessing said. "It was an open-ended commission—I could write whatever I wanted—but they requested that the play have a large cast and that some of the characters be college age," he said. "I decided to give myself a bit of a challenge and have every character in the play be 20 years old. Then it became, how can I get nine 20-year-olds into the sort of world I wanted to write about?" Blessing cited Ray Kurzweil's book on artificial intelligence, "The Singularity is Near," as one inspiration for his story about people's lives being "reset." ... "It's not as far-fetched as it sounds," he said. "People have been studying how to expand human longevity, trying to determine what makes cells age and die, and ways to stop or reverse that process.... And that raises all sorts of ethical questions.... I think we're approaching a crossroads where some profound cultural and developmental ideas are going to be challenged, and I hope we humans are ready for it.... [Could there be an] 80-year-old mind in this 20-year-old body?"[96]

CHAPTER 10

Writing for Movies and Television

Throughout his playwriting career, Blessing also tried his hand at writing for television and the movies, with mixed success. To those outside Hollywood it may seem strange that one can make a living writing scripts that are bought outright or optioned for a specific time but never actually see the light of day at the multiplex. Of course, when a script does get translated to the big or small screen an author makes even more money. And playwrights must always concern themselves with income. As Blessing told one interviewer: "One really cannot assume that one can go through a writing career and make a living writing only plays."[1] As mentioned earlier, his play *A Walk in the Woods* appeared as a movie in 1988, directed by Kirk Browning with the original Broadway cast of Robert Prosky and Sam Waterston, and also shot in Spain in 1993 as a movie for television, *Un Passeig Pel Bosc*, in Catalan, starring Enric Arredondo and Abel Folk.

His career of writing original scripts for film seems to have begun with *Alive and Kicking*, in 1993, the story of three college students, credited to Phyllis Paullette, Jeanne Blake, and Lee Blessing. Undoubtedly it seemed natural for him to turn to his love for baseball for an early script and this resulted in the award-winning film *Cooperstown*, discussed in more depth in Chapter 3.

One of Blessing's more successful film projects, successful in that it finally saw theatrical release at least (in 1995), was his work on *Steal Big, Steal Little*, accomplished during a residency in Santa Barbara, California, from October 1993 through February 1994, though its strange development reveals a lot about how Hollywood works. The original screenplay dates to 1994 and credits as authors, Blessing, then-wife Jeanne Blake, and director Andrew Davis. A later script in the same year bears the names of Blessing and Blake alone. By May 1994 we have a rewrite credited as a "revised screenplay by Andrew Davis and Terry Kahn based on a screenplay by Andrew Davis, Lee Blessing, and Jeanne Blake." Keep in mind that scriptwriting fees get apportioned based on where in the credits your name appears. On May 2, 1995, it's a "screenplay by Andrew Davis, Lee Blessing & Jeanne Blake and Terry Kahn. Story by Andrew Davis, Theresa Tucker-Davies and Frank Perilli." The ampersand and the word "and" are not created equal either and more money goes to the name placed before the "and." When Savoy Pictures released the film, *DramLogue* reports: [Director Andrew] Davis also produces with Fred Caruso and wrote the screenplay with Terry Kahn based on a work he wrote with Lee Blessing & Jeanne Blake." Finally, various authors of the screenplay appealed to the Writers Guild of America to arbitrate the writing credits.[2]

The film, according to a Savoy Pictures interoffice memo, followed "twin brothers [as they] vie for control of a valuable ranch," and starred Andy Garcia in dual roles as identical brothers and featured Alan Arkin (who would later appear in Blessing's *Cooperstown*). The film drew poor reviews and failed at the box office.[3] Blessing and Blake wrote additional screenplays, "Two of Hearts" in 1993[4]; "Milo's Arms," "Billy the Kid," based on his play *The Authentic Life of Billy the Kid*, "Pranks," and "Aberdeen" in 1995; "Creative Writing" and "Magic Time" (set in Haiti) in 1996. In their prolific year of 1996, Blessing and Blake co-authored a "TV film treatment" of his play *Independence*, adding a bunch of male characters to the formerly all-female play: Sherry's boyfriend, now a psychiatrist, and a psychiatric patient, Marcus (based where Evelyn was once committed by Kess and now volunteers), who develops a romantic interest in her. In the now happier, though less believable, ending, Jo still leaves home but Marcus shows up to woo Evelyn, who may well not be alone for very long.[5]

In 1999, Blessing and Blake wrote "Minions," not to be confused with the 2015 animated movie. They collaborated as well in 1996 for a screenplay based on Blessing's play *Down the Road*, and, in 2000, on a screenplay based on his play *Going to St. Ives*. He wrote a screenplay entitled "Final Rounds" on his own in 2005. Of these, only the contested script for *Steal Big, Steal Little* and *Cooperstown* made it to the big screen.

Blessing found some frustration in writing for television. He revised a script by Vine Deloria, Jr., and Angela Rackley in 1986 for *The Trial of Standing Bear* for University of Nebraska Television, KUON-TV, which aired in 1988. The teleplay, based on historical events, followed a Native American Chief who sued the U.S. Army for release under *habeas corpus* in 1879. The trial judge ruled in his favor, declaring to the surprise of most white people at the time that "an Indian is a person." William Shatner narrated the PBS film. As Blessing told me: "I did indeed write a first draft of *The Trial of Standing Bear* for the PBS affiliate in Omaha, Nebraska. They later rewrote the piece and eventually produced it. But I was off the project by then, so little remained of my original draft."[6]

In 1995, Blessing collaborated with Jeanne Blake and David E. Kelly to write the *Picket Fences* TV series episodes "Jupiter Himself" and "Upbringings."[7] Blessing wrote the *Homicide: Life on the Streets* episode "Double Blind"[8] and, in 1997, Blessing, with Blake again, wrote the episode "Signs and Words" (Episode no. 5K12, story no. 4892) for the TV series *Nothing Sacred*.

As Blessing told me: "Writing for TV and the movies was better in the '90's and easier to make good money then. Nowadays movies fall into a handful of genres ... which need little English dialogue because they are all aimed at an international market. Serious art, by contrast, is about people (not explosions and car chases)."[9] Or, as he told another interviewer in 1996:

> In Los Angeles talent is a liability. Television is a business that has nothing to do with artistic aspiration.... I'm from Minnesota, where it gets down to 31 degrees below zero, but every day in Los Angeles you encounter temperatures far colder.[10]

Chapter 11

Curtain

I have applied no Freudian theory here. No Marxist theory. Semiotics? Post structuralism? Nah. No preconceived theories of any kind to impose, at least consciously, on another playwright. Just a need to read the plays and see and understand what's there. Why do we write plays? Why do we read plays or attend the theater? My context for understanding involves analyzing authorial intent and reader response. Does the playwright have something to say? Does the audience get the message? Has the playwright created art, and has the audience entered into the experience? Serious artists make us see our world more clearly by creating fictional worlds into which they usher us. They invite us to ask big questions and imagine new answers. They make us think and feel through the experience they create for us. Tennessee Williams was such an artist. He wrote in his memoirs:

> Plays are written and then, if you are lucky, they are performed, and, if their luck still holds, which is not too frequently the case, their performance is so successful that both audience and critics at the first night are aware that they are being offered a dramatic work which is both honest and entertaining and also somehow capable of engaging their aesthetic appreciation.[1]

I've always thought playwriting the second-most difficult genre of creative writing, behind poetry. Fiction allows a writer to share the internal musings of their character, to *tell* us how a character thinks or feels. A screenwriter can resort to voiceover narration to accomplish the same end, while a playwright must work within the limits of the stage, always looking for ways to externalize internal conflicts and to *show* us the inner workings of a character. Like poetry, playwriting depends upon concision and must work within tightly regulated forms of time and space. And in our own age of limited attention spans, competitive media choices, and rising theater admission costs, dramatic literature struggles for its share of public attention and finances. Blessing has faced these challenges and thrives.

11. Curtain 227

The second mark of a great artist is, I believe, someone who, having created art, keeps challenging themselves, keeps experimenting with form, exploring new themes, and risking failure. My favorite painter is Francisco Goya (1746–1828). His body of work over decades of painting demonstrates bold experimentation and constant change. Goya began as a skilled but restrained painter to the Spanish Royal family, incorporated the "Naked Maja," moved on to paintings of common folk, experimenting with prints in the *Caprichos*, and then to the powerful series "Disasters of War" when the French invaded his country, then to bull fights, and, finally, to the phantasmagorical nightmares of his "Black Paintings." His subjects, themes, and styles developed, morphed, and grew to enlarge our understanding of the world. Lee Blessing has honed his craft over four decades, evolving, growing, and consciously challenging his own talents.

Blessing, artist of the theater, has been writing plays for a long time without gaining the attention he deserves. Perhaps because he is not black, not gay, not female, not scandalous, not criminal, his body of work has largely escaped widespread notice outside the theater world. And yet his body of work is inseparable from U.S. theater of the last 40 years. You can find his plays on stage somewhere in the world at any given time.

Though it seems applicable to call him, in the words of critic, Mike Steele,

a relatively happy, relatively sane, relatively whole human being who has tried to add complexity to his life.[2]

I would add that through his writing this "normal" man, from America's rural Midwest, has chosen to travel through his imagination to some very abnormal places, seeking complexity. No one can predict Blessing's next project based on what he has written previously:

I've never known what plays I was about to write. It would be nice to have a defined project like August Wilson had, which could keep me busy for two decades, but my creative center seems to work a different way. I like surprising myself. As for hopes and aspirations, I have to say that's not really what makes me write. It's nice when things go well for the things one writes, but the impulse to write has to be internal, I think. The rewards for writing that the world supplies are far too unpredictable and random to be the whole point of it. Some writers are routinely over-rewarded while others are shamefully ignored. Nearly every writer, no matter how successful, goes through periods where the rewards just aren't out there. So I can't write plays because of anything the world may or may not offer. The fact is, I write because I'm a writer, because I can't *not* write. Writing is my identity.[3]

As I pressed him to identify some unifying feature to his body of work, he told me he writes of "extreme conditions that test our humanity," adding:

I suppose, for me, the most common thematic thread connecting my plays is loneliness. Most of my plays show people breaking apart, or staying apart, in one way or another. Happy families, even happy relationships, are a rarity in my work, generally achieved at high cost and often short lived.[4]

Failed marriages and broken relationships are features of plays like *Great Falls, Riches, Nice People Dancing to Good Country Music, Down the Road, Cobb, A Body of Water, Chesapeake,* and *The Scottish Play.* Burgeoning friendships abbreviated by circumstance are seen in *Going to St. Ives* and *A Walk in the Woods.* *Two Rooms* focuses on a man kidnapped and kept in solitary confinement in Beirut, separated from his wife for three years. *Independence* and *Eleemosynary* present families whose members cannot find a way to live together.

Other forms of "solitary confinement" are readily evidenced: Ty Cobb, isolated in limbo by his personal irascibility and racism; Carl, in *Black Sheep,* a black man adrift in a surreal world of white wealth and privilege which has adopted him but to which he can never belong; the office workers in *Good, Clean Fun* (the first half of *Flag Day*) separated by their racial differences, and the fearsome Dot in *Down and Dirty* (*Flag Days'* second half) also limited by race-based rage who cannot find it in her heart to save the life of a white accident victim. *Lake Street Extension* features prisons within prisons, taking place in the basement bedroom of a young man molested by his father and a refugee from military oppression in El Salvador.

His dramatic subjects range over a world of diversity and he does not repeat himself, making it impossible to categorize him:

> One of my great challenges as a playwright is my unwillingness to write the same play over and over. At times I feel interviewers scrutinizing me (as though searching for the spot marked "Attach Type-of-Playwright Label Here") and I don't know what to tell them. I've written broad farces, political commentaries, family dramas, sports plays, work plays, plays about crime, personal biographies, marriage plays—even a Western.... I always hope that a reader or audience member, at the point of experiencing a new work of mine, won't be able simply to "dial-in" a set of expectations before the lights go down: such and such a genre, tone, context, set of characters—all with relatively minor variations.... I want the world of each new play to open as many doors as possible, for the audience and for myself. I love exploring different kinds of human experience and different kinds of theatre. For me it keeps the process alive.[5]

Clearly, his subjects vary from play to play, but so do his techniques and play structures. *Nice People Dancing to Good Country Music, Riches, Unknown, Oldtimers Game, The Winning Streak,* and others all follow normal, "realistic" linear play structure. Some plays he sets in limbo or hell, like *Courting Harry; Cobb; Reagan in Hell; A User's Guide to Hell Featuring Bernard Madoff;* etc., and others follow a nonlinear structure as in *Thief River,* and *For the Loyal,* exploring the variables of time and human choice. Some are fantasies, like *Chesapeake* and *Whores.* Some are just for laughs, like *Nice People, Fantasy League,* and the *Scottish Play.* While others are *deadly* serious and scary, like *Flag Day, Lonesome Hollow,* and *Into You.* As he said more than twenty years ago:

11. Curtain

My ambition is to write plays that are different from each other so that the audience doesn't always know what it is going to get except, hopefully, a play [that is] compelling on some level.[6]

This work comes up against certain commercial exigencies. We rarely sit through a five-act, four-hour-long Shakespearean play today, nor Eugene O'Neill's three-act, three-and-a-half-hour *Desire Under the Elms*, nor even a two-act play from 20 years ago. By financial necessity and talent, Blessing has refined and mastered the 90-minute one-act (*Lake Street Extension*, *Riches*, *Patient A*, *Fortinbras*, etc.), the single and minimal set (basement, single hotel room, undifferentiated limbo), sparse props (a pair of wings in *Eleemosynary*), and a spare cast: just two characters in *Riches*, *The Winning Streak*, *Fantasy League*, *A Walk in the Woods*, *Going to St. Ives*, *Great Falls*; only three in *Eleemosynary*, *Down the Road*, *A Body of Water*, *The Roads that Lead Here*, etc. Shakespeare didn't stint, writing 34 characters into *Hamlet*, and a whopping 63 in *Richard III*, nor did a producer tell him he couldn't afford to pay that many actors.

On campus, I find my students much more interested in screenwriting, which I also teach, than playwriting, in part because by the time I get them they have seen many more films than plays and because they know well that writing for the screen pays much better than for the stage. I usually trip them up, however, when I describe film writing as a debased "art," where any time you don't know what to do you can simply throw in a car chase or blow up a building to keep the audience's attention. When I ask them to think of a movie with well-rounded characters and penetrating dialogue we usually find that that film is based on a play or crafted by a playwright.

Blessing has found the benefits in necessity:

> A single set signals the audience that its interest needs to center more on the issues of the play as expressed in the dialogue than on what fantastic visual effects might drop down on a rope or ooze through a trap door.... These plays are all about what the characters are saying, what choices they are making and what the costs of those choices are. Simple, even Spartan sets are appropriate and helpful here.[7]

He brings the same flair for dialogue, humor, and fully realized characters to plays that are personal as to those that are political. And if the personal plays examine people "breaking apart," his political plays display themes of individuals struggling with their governments, as in *A Walk in the Woods*, *Lonesome Hollow*, *Two Rooms*, etc., making a humanistic case for both individual freedom and a faith in cooperative action. Critic and author Mel Gussow observed: "[Blessing has the] ability to take a subject of public interest and turn it into provocative drama."[8] and the *New York Times* called Blessing "America's most imaginative playwright on public issues."[9]

Raising issues and questioning political norms can put audiences off, however. Not answering those questions and not wrapping up stories into "happily ever after" makes audience work harder than they might choose to. When accused of raising, but not answering, questions, Blessing responded:

> Life is more complex than that. I'm not here to tell people how to fix things, just to point out that often society thinks in schizophrenic terms. Sometimes, people, especially Americans, have a guarded reaction about seeing questions raised that aren't soluble—about plays that don't have a happy ending.[10]

Often Blessing's plays, such as those in which he is examining a political or social problem, ask us to dig a little deeper to reach an understanding, to even have a chance to approach a solution. When I asked him why, as in *For the Loyal* he revisits issues of the recent past (in this case, the pedophilia scandal at Penn State), he said:

> It's useful because when society moves forward on a particular problem to remind us of our old ways of thinking. We may feel "we took care of that one" but you go back and see when we didn't handle it so well. It makes us think there are other similar issues we are still not dealing well with.[11]

But, to a large degree, Blessing denies this separation between the personal and political in his plays:

> I think all theater is political. It's just that some plays are a little more conscious of it than others. It seems a curiously American point of view to think that there is a "private" life that is completely divorceable from a "public" one. Everything we eat is the product of a political system. The worth of our houses turns out to be a very volatile product of a political system. The clothes on our back, the gas in our cars—it's ubiquitous. Everything we do, think or say is done in the context of a political system. Political battles are fought in every sphere of our lives: cultural, business, aesthetic, religious, filial, romantic—you name it. Even choosing to ignore poli-

Lee Blessing, at a rehearsal for *Thief River*, Guthrie Theater, Minneapolis, Minnesota; 2002, photograph by and courtesy of Michal Daniel.

11. Curtain

Lee Blessing with his contemporary and fellow midwestern playwright August Wilson at the Eugene O'Neill Theatre Center in Waterford, Connecticut, where both men saw their careers launched with director Lloyd Richards; 1985, photograph by and courtesy of A. Vincent Scarano.

tics completely is, at base, an intensely political decision. Once a society has at least three members (perhaps only two) politics is born. This is the sadness and I suppose the majesty of politics. Who can imagine the Garden of Eden without a serpent?[12]

Sometimes he sounds pessimistic about critics and audiences:

> Straight plays—particularly non-British ones—are pretty much anathema to Broadway now. As we continue to disempower, underrate, impoverish, and vulgarize the potential audience there's little else that could logically result.[13]

And sometimes hopeful:

> Theatre has a relatively eternal feel, compared to the "quick-hit" quality of other media. This is, in part, because theatre is presented in these inescapable, 90-minute increments, but also because the province of serious theatre has come to be content. It can't do the spectacular, superficial things film can do or live for years at the center of the culture, like a hit TV series. But it can help us undertake those aspects of existence which are deadly serious and deeply unsettling and help us process our feelings about them. It does that better than any medium. For that reason, I think we'll always have theatre in some form.[14]

In a playwriting class five years ago, Blessing reminded us: "Plays are written to do something to an audience."[15] The stage is not about making money, entertainment, distraction, or recreation; at least none of those terms fully defines its role. Drama in ancient Greece grew out of religious observance, ritual, and sacrifice. The goal was transformation. Blessing stands in that historic perspective when he says:

> What I want to do more than anything is find a way to compel. I'm there to make the audience confront themselves and the way they think. That's the way, it seems to me, drama ought to be written.[16]

My late uncle Larry, may he rest in peace, told me, "I don't go to the theatre to learn anything." He confined his stage experiences to the big-ticket musicals and classic revivals. No doubt everyone has an Uncle Larry, and though we love them we cannot allow that mentality to describe contemporary theater. At one time Blessing received three commissions, one after the other (one became *Whores*), from three different theater groups, each of which were rejected as too controversial. For all three he had to seek new venues for their premieres. Blessing explains:

> When you commission a writer, that writer will write it the way he or she writes it. And you may not like it or it may not fit the image you want to project. It's very hard to get produced if you're writing controversial [plays] right now. A lot of regional theatres are scared of being controversial and turning off their subscription base. Times are tough and they read their subscription base as being more conservative and less tolerant of controversy.[17]

Blessing writes, in part, to fill the void in political theater today:

> You can write a play much quicker than you can make a film. Theatre is in a much better position to respond to the here and now. Theatre promises a very different perspective—it allows you to say more problematic things. It can talk about politics as no one else can and can challenge people to get involved. The impact of the arts has ebbs and flows. There are times when artists have a lot to say and people listen and other times when they don't listen as much.[18]

To keep going, Blessing takes a longer view:

> A playwright just writes plays, some of which strike a stronger chord than others in audiences, and go further in their initial productions, or last longer, or get rediscovered, or whatever.... My guess is that that play is the kind of play that people looking back on this period in history are going to be curious about, want to read, want to think about, and want to do.[19]

Or, as he told me:

> You can't worry about your legacy because there it is on stage and on the page. Shakespeare was mainly published posthumously. Sometimes I feel that I am writing for a generation beyond this one.[20]

Blessing has been at it for a long time, in spite of the obstacles:

> It's hard to write plays for this long a period of time. Usually the message in our society is you need to do this for a while until you can use it to leverage a career in writing for television or film, because those are the areas that pay a real living. If I lived only on what I

11. Curtain 233

make as a playwright I'd have to live in a hollow log in Maine. That's the reality of it. The fact that I've been able to do what I wanted, which was to create a body of work for the stage over a long period of time in a culture that's inimical to that, has been really satisfying.[21]

And he's not done yet. He premiered five new plays in 2013–14.

I am not contemplating retirement. I am always exploring a new world. I have no sense I've said everything I have to say or that I am repeating myself.[22]

With luck, ours and his, he'll go on writing much longer. I know no better way to close this book than with the playwright's own admonition to each of us:

All your life you will rub your heart against the world's disappointments, for which you must be grateful ... and yes—you'll feel joy anyway—which no one can explain.[23]

Appendix 1: The Awards

1971 Schubert Playwriting Grant
1978 Wulitzer Foundation Grant (residency in Taos, New Mexico)
1979 National Playwriting Award of the American College Theatre Festival (*The Authentic Life of Billy the Kid*)
1979 Amoco Bronze Medallion for Excellence (*The Authentic Life of Billy the Kid*)
1981 Jerome Foundation Playwriting Grant
1982 Jerome Foundation Playwriting Grant
1982 Great American Play Award (*Oldtimers Game*)
1983 McNight Foundation Playwriting Grant
1983 Participant, Eugene O'Neill National Playwright's Conference (*Independence*)
1984 Great American Play Award (*Independence*)
1984 Participant, Eugene O'Neill National Playwright's Conference (*Riches*)
1985 Great American Play Award (for *War of the Roses* [retitled *Riches*])
1985 Grant from the National Endowment for the Arts
1986 Participant, Eugene O'Neill National Playwright's Conference (*A Walk in the Woods*)
1987 Bush Foundation Playwriting Fellowship
1987 American Theatre Critics Association Award (*A Walk in the Woods*)
1987 Hollywood Drama-Logue Critics Award for Outstanding Achievement (*A Walk in the Woods*)
1988 Winner George and Elisabeth Marton Award (*A Walk in the Woods*)
1988 Grant from the National Endowment for the Arts
1988 Pulitzer Prize nomination in Drama (*A Walk in the Woods*)
1988 Tony Award nomination (*A Walk in the Woods*)
1988 Olivier Award nomination (*A Walk in the Woods*)
1988 Drama-logue Playwriting Award (*Two Rooms*)
1989 McNight Foundation Playwriting Grant
1988 Marton Award
1989 Guggenheim Fellowship
1991 Great American Play Award (*Down the Road*)
1992–93 Signature Theatre season in New York City devoted to plays of Lee Blessing (*Fortinbras, Lake Street Extension, Two Rooms,* and *Patient A*)

Appendix 1

1993 Winner Humanitas Award, Screenplay (*Cooperstown*)
1994 Delivered the Collins Lectures at Indiana University
1994 Drama-Logue Critics Award for Outstanding Achievement (*Riches*)
1994 Nomination (Best Movie) Cable Ace Award (*Cooperstown*)
1996 Participant, O'Neill Playwrights Conference, Waterford, Connecticut (*Going to St. Ives*)
1996 Herbert and Patricia Brodkin Award, Eugene O'Neill Center (*Going to St. Ives*)
1997 Prism Commendation (*Homicide: Life on the Street*, "Double Blind")
1997 L.A. Drama Critics Circle Award for Best Play (*Eleemosynary*)
1997 Michael Devereaux Award (*Eleemosynary*)
1997 Drama-Logue Award (*Fortinbras*)
1998 Awarded a Star on the Playwrights' Sidewalk in New York City (then comprised of 43 stars on a sidewalk in Greenwich Village for Off Broadway produced writers).
1999 Participant, O'Neill Playwrights Conference, Waterford, Connecticut (*The Winning Streak*)
2000 Participant, O'Neill Playwrights Conference, Waterford, Connecticut (*Thief River*)
2000 Ten Best Plays of 2000—*L.A. Times* (*Going to St. Ives*, La Jolla Playhouse)
2000 Visiting Writing Professor at The Michener Center for Writers, Austin, Texas
2001 Jonathan Reynolds Playwriting Residency, Denison University, Granville, Ohio
2001 Visiting lecturer, University of Tulsa and University of Nebraska at Kearney
2001 Participant, O'Neill Playwrights Conference, Waterford, Connecticut (*Black Sheep*)
2001 Drama Desk Award for Best Ensemble (*Cobb*)
2002 Great American Play Award (*Snapshot*)
2002 Drama Desk nomination for outstanding play (*Thief River*)
2003 Great American Play Award (*The Roads That Lead Here*)
2003 *Entertainment Today* newspapers Ticketholders Awards, Runner-up, best playwright (*Going to St. Ives*)
2003 University of Minnesota University Libraries Distinguished Writer (public reading and lecture), Minneapolis, Minnesota
2004 Best Playwright Nominee, Beverly Hills/Hollywood NAACP Theatre Award (*Going to St. Ives*)
2004 Keynote Speaker, New Play Festival, Madison Repertory Theater, Madison, Wisconsin
2005 Obie Award, Outstanding Ensemble (*Going to St. Ives*, Primary Stages, New York City)
2005 Outer Critics Circle Award, Best Off Broadway Play (*Going to St. Ives*)
2005 Lucille Lortel Award Nomination, Best Play (*Going to St. Ives*)
2005 Screenplay (*Cooperstown*) named one of the Ten Best All-Time Movies about Baseball by the National Baseball Hall of Fame in Cooperstown, New York
2005 Participant, O'Neill Playwrights Conference, Waterford, Connecticut (*Great Falls*)
2006 Steinberg New Play Award (*A Body of Water*)
2006 American Theatre Critics Award (*A Body of Water*)
2007 *A Body of Water* featured in The Best Plays Theater Yearbook

The Awards

2007 San Diego Theatre Critics Circle Awards, Outstanding Dramatic Production, Direction of a Play, Ensemble and Set Design (*A Body of Water*)
2008 Great American Play Award (*Great Falls*)
2009 Great American Play Award and American Theatre Critics Citation (*Great Falls*)
2011 Profile Theatre production of *Thief River* wins Drammy Awards for Best Ensemble and Best Direction
2010–11 Profile Theatre of Portland, Oregon, season dedicated to Blessing's works
2010 Barrymore Award nomination for the Independence Foundation Award for Outstanding New Play (*When We Go Upon the Sea*)
2010 *Into You* named one of four finalists for Attic Theatre Ensemble's 2010 One-Act Festival in Los Angeles (Produced by that theater in September 2010)

Appendix 2:
The Napkin Play

In May 2003, the Brooklyn Repertory Theatre Company began a festival of so-called "Napkin Plays" by seven playwrights: Arthur Kopit, Tina Howe, Lee Blessing, Dan O'Brien, Glen Berger, Ethan Youngerman, and Rachel Axler. Inspired by the legend of director Joe Papp asking playwright Samuel Beckett to write him a world premiere play entirely on a napkin at a bar, Brooklyn Rep presented a night of plays, many of which fit on a napkin, though some ran longer. With his permission I reprint Lee Blessing's "Napkin Play" here, in its entirety:

Napkin Play
by Lee Blessing

I waited for you.

This bar is wet with my tears &
Tequila ... and a little vodka.
Ok, and some gin—but mostly tears.
I waited Monday night, and Tuesday,
And Wednesday & Thursday. I ate
Nothing but bar nuts & one of those
Eggs—you know, in a jar?

The bartender held my hair
While I threw up.
On Friday he took me home.
No words, simply lifted me out
Of my stool and took me home.

He opened up a new world for me.
Showed me a life of beauty &
Honesty, of mutual caring

The Napkin Play

Looking past all the insignificant
Defects and petty grievances.
He pledged a lifetime of fidelity &
Taught me the True Meaning of Love.

He introduced me to his pets.
They were fluffy and small. I've never
Felt so warm & nurtured in my life.
All in all it was a pretty good weekend.
My words are running on this napkin.
They glisten in a pool of tears and booze & snot.

You've got one half hour.

Appendix 3:
The Plays

The Authentic Life of Billy the Kid, began life as "The Real Life of Billy the Kid," in 1975, at the Iowa Writers Workshop and premiered under its final title at the Kennedy Center in Washington, D.C, in April 1979, as winner of the American College Theatre Festival student playwriting competition. Published by Samuel French, 1980.

Nice People Dancing to Good Country Music, a two-act play, began life as two separate one-act plays: *Nice People Dancing to Good Country Music* (1982) and *Toys for Men* (1983) at the Actors Theatre of Louisville (Kentucky). World premiere by Actors Theatre of St. Paul, Minnesota, 1984. Published by Dramatists Play Service, 1983.

Pushups, written by Lee Blessing with Michael Robins and Alfred Harrison. The latter two acted in the production and drew material from their own lives for the script. Premiered at Illusion Theatre Minneapolis, Minnesota, in 1982.

Oldtimers Game, originally presented as *The Old Timers Game*, at the Sixth Annual Humana Festival of New American Plays at the Actors Theatre of Louisville (Kentucky), February 24 to April 4, 1982, under the direction of Paul Tovat. Cast: Anthony De Fonte as Jim Nealy; Ray Fry as Old John Law; Mel Johnson as Dave Pearl; Michael Kevin as Mr. Thompson; Ken Latimer as Crab Detlefsen; Frederic Major as Cal Timmer; William McNulty as Harly Nix; Kim Sullivan as Sut Davis; and Dierk Toporzysek as Jesus Luna. Subsequently produced as *Oldtimers Game* at the International City Theatre in Long Beach, California, on May 22, 1987. Directed by David Herman. Cast: Loren Farmer as Cal Timmer; David Taylor as Sut Davis; Andy Rivas as Jesus Luna; Mark Daneri as Harly Nix; Wayne Richards as Old John Law; Gary Bolen as Crab Detlefsen; David Watkins as Mr. Thompson; and Tommy Ford as Dave Pearl. Published by Dramatists Play Service, 1988.

Independence premiered professionally at the Actors Theatre of Louisville (Kentucky) during its Eighth Annual Humana Festival of New American Plays in February 1984, under the direction of Patrick Tovatt. Cast: Shelley Crandall as Jo; Deborah Hedwall as Kess; Gretchen West as Sherry; and Sylvia Gassell as Evelyn.

Marjorie. Blessing's first wife, Jeanne Blake, directed and was one of three actors playing Marjorie at various times in her life. The play was staged once, in Minneapolis. Wrote

The Plays 241

Blessing in an email to me (dated July 23, 2015): "*Marjorie* was a full-length play I wrote in the mid-eighties.... I later reworked the second of its three acts and turned that into *Riches*. Later, I borrowed the casting device from *Marjorie* for my play *Thief River*."

Riches, as *War of the Roses*, premiered at the Actors Theatre of Louisville (Kentucky) in the Humana Festival of New American Plays, February 19–March 30, 1985, under the direction of Bill Partlan. Produced in Paris at Theatre Rive Gauche. Published by Dramatists Play Service, 1986.

Eleemosynary premiered professionally at the Philadelphia Festival for New Plays from April 29 to May 10, 1986, under the direction of Gloria Muzio. Winner of four L.A. Drama Critics Circle Awards. Published by Dramatists Play Service, 1987.

Cold Water. First production May 27, 1986, at the Actors Theatre of Louisville (Kentucky), under the direction of Mark Sawyer-Dailey. Cast: Mark Nash as August; Edward Patrick Corbett as Russell; Helen Greenberg as June; and Jeffrey Crockett as Eric. Translated into Spanish and published in Art Teatral

A Walk in the Woods premiered at Yale Repertory Theatre, February 20, 1987, under the direction of Des McAnuff. Cast: Josef Sommer as Botvinnik; and Kenneth Welsh as Honeyman. It opened on Broadway at the Booth Theatre, February 28, 1988, directed by Des McAnuff, with Robert Prosky as Botvinnik and Sam Waterston as Honeyman. Opened in Moscow with the Broadway production, May 1989. The Broadway production was seen on PBS's *American Playhouse* in May 1989. Published by Dramatists Play Service, 1988, and Plume Books, 1988. Published by Oberon Publishing, 2011.

Cobb was produced at the Yale Repertory Theater, New Haven, Connecticut, on March 21, 1989, under the direction of Lloyd Richards. Cast: Josef Sommer as Mr. Cobb; James E. Reynolds as The Peach; Chris Cooper as Ty; and Delroy Lindo as Oscar Charleston. Published by Dramatists Play Service, 1991.

Two Rooms received its world premiere at the La Jolla Playhouse, La Jolla, California, on June 21, 1988, under the direction of Des McAnuff. Cast: Amanda Plummer as Lainie Wells; Brent Jennings as Walker Harris; Jo Henderson as Ellen Van Oss; and Jon De Vries as Michael Wells. Published by Dramatists Play Service, 1990.

Fortinbras received its world premiere at the La Jolla Playhouse, La Jolla, California, on June 18, 1991, directed by Des McAnuff, and received a Japanese production in 1999. Published by Dramatists Play Service, 1992.

Down the Road, commissioned by the La Jolla Playhouse, La Jolla, California, opened August 8, 1989, under the direction of Des McAnuff. Cast: Jonathan Hogan as Dan Henniman; Susan Berman as Iris Henniman; and James Morrison as William Reach. Published by Dramatists Play Service, 1991.

Lake Street Extension, commissioned by Ensemble Theatre of Cincinnati (Ohio), it opened May 13, 1992, under the direction of Jeanne Blake. Cast: Gordon Greene as Fuller, Keith Brush as Trace, and Enrique Munoz as Gregorio. Published by Dramatists Play Service, 1993.

Patient A premiered at Signature Theatre Company in New York City on April 25, 1993, under the direction of Jeanne Blake. Cast: Robin Morse as Kimberly; Jon DeVries as Lee; and Richard Bekins as Matthew. Published by Dramatists Play Service, 1993.

The Rights. Commissioned by the Ensemble Theatre Company of Cincinnati (Ohio), where it had its world premiere, in March 1994, and Theatre in the Square, Marietta, Georgia, where it opened in April 1994, under the direction of Jeanne Blakely. Rewritten as *Rewrites*, it was produced by Chicago's Dolphinback Theater in March 2001, directed by Ellen Larabee, and produced at Denison University in April 2001.

Going to St. Ives received its world premiere at A Contemporary Theatre in Seattle, Washington, in July 1997, under the direction of Leslie Swackhamer. Cast: Mari Nelson as Dr. Cora Gage; and Gloria Foster as May N'Kame. The play was also produced by the Studio Theatre, Johannesburg, South Africa, April 2006; that production was directed by Alan Swerdlow.

Chesapeake premiered at New York Stage and Film Company and the Powerhouse Theater at Vassar College, in Poughkeepsie, New York, in June 1999, under the direction of Max Mayer, and featuring Mark Linn-Baker as Kerr. Blessing himself has read, though not performed, *Chesapeake* at the Ransom Center in Austin, Texas, the Playwrights' Center in Minneapolis, the New Harmony Playwrights Conference, the Sewanee Writers Conference, Florida Stage, the Seattle (Washington) Repertory Theatre, Ensemble Theatre of Cincinnati (Ohio), and the Coronet Theatre in Los Angeles among others. Published by Broadway Play Publishing, 2001.

Thief River was originally given a staged reading at the O'Neill Playwrights Conference in July 22, 2000, and had its world premiere at Signature Theatre May 20, 2001, directed by Mark Lamos. Cast: Jeffrey Carlson as Gil 1/Jody; Erik Sorensen as Ray 1/Kit; Neil Maffin as Gil 2/Harlow; Gregg Edelman as Ray 2/Reese; Remak Ramsay as Gil 3/Perry; and Frank Converse as Ray 3/ Anson. Published by Dramatists Play Service, 2002.

Black Sheep had its world premiere at Florida Stage on December 14, 2001, directed by Michael Bigelow Dixon. Cast: Jonathan Bustle as Nelson Winship; Brandon Morris as Carl Winship; Caitlin Miller as Elle; Paul Tei as Max Winship; and Angie Radosh as Serene Winship. Published by Dramatists Play Service, 2003.

Tyler Poked Taylor premiered March 2002, at the Humana Festival of New American Plays at the Actors Theatre, in Louisville, Kentucky. Directed by Russell Vandenbroacke, with actor Jake Goodman as Loyal. It was published in *Snapshot: A Dramatic Anthology*, by Actors Theatre of Louisville in 2003.

The Roads That Lead Here had its premiere and only staging in 2002 at the Guthrie Theatre in Minneapolis, Minnesota, and was printed in *Ten-Minute Plays from the Guthrie Theatre: Volume 2*, by Playscripts, Inc., 2003.

34th and Dyer premiered September 11, 2002, directed by Nela Wagmen, acted by Cynthia Nixon and Keith Nobbs, at Town Hall in New York City on the one-year anniversary of 9/11. No copy of the script is known to exist.

The Napkin Play premiered at the Brooklyn Rep, where it was performed from May 23–31, 2003, one of seven scripts written to fit on a napkin. It is receiving its first printing in Appendix 2 of this present volume.

Fantasy League, produced by Mile Square Theatre's annual event, featuring baseball plays, in 2003. Based in Hoboken, New Jersey, the self-proclaimed birthplace of baseball, Miles Square is a regional northern New Jersey theatre which has featured an annual festival of baseball plays since 2003. They published *The Baseball Plays: 7th Inning Stretch* in 2008, which included *Fantasy League*.

Whores. A two-act version of *Whores* had its premiere in 2003 at the Contemporary American Theater Festival, West Virginia. A one-act version was a co-production of New Jersey Repertory Company and Playwrights Theater of New Jersey (where it was produced in February 2005). Directed by John Pietrowski, the cast included Lea Eckert, Carol Todd, Lily Mercer, Corinne Edgerly, and Jonathan Cantor. This play was originally commissioned by Florida Stage, in 2001, but that company found the work to be too controversial.

Flag Day premiered in 2003 at Contemporary American Theatre Festival, under the direction of Lucie Tiberghien. Cast: Lee Sellars as Rex; Roslyn Wintner as Dot; Albert Jones as Vandell; and Michael Flanigan as Adam. You can find a video of the 2009 Black Theatre Ensemble production of *Flag Day* on youtube at https://www.youtube.com/user/BlackTheaterEnsemble. Published by Dramatists Play Service, November 2007.

Perilous Night received a staged reading at Denver Center Theatre in 2008 and a full production by Nimbus Theatre in September 2013, in Minneapolis, Minnesota, directed by Liz Neerland, and featuring Kevin Carnahan, Ross Destiche, Dana Lee Thompson, and Shirley Venard.

Reagan in Hell was first produced by Naked Angels Theatre Company at the Culture Project in New York City as part of "Democracy" (September 14–October 2, 2004). Directed by Daniel Goldstein, the cast featured Robert Sella as Clark, and Frank Raiter as President Ronald Reagan. It was later published in the anthology *Naked Angels: The Issues Projects*, 2009.

The Winning Streak was originally produced at the George Street Playhouse, in New Brunswick, New Jersey, opening in January 2005. Directed by Lucie Tiberghien, the cast featured Brennan Brown as Ry Davis, and Dan Lauria as Omar Carlyle. Published by Dramatists Play Service, 2006.

A Body of Water had its world premiere at the Guthrie Theatre, in Minneapolis, Minnesota, opening June 15, 2005. Directed by Ethan McSweeny, the cast featured Michael Learned as Avis, Edward Hermann as Moss, and Michelle O'Neill as Wren.

The Scottish Play had its world premiere on September 20, 2005, at the La Jolla Playhouse, La Jolla, California, directed by Melia Bensussen, with music by Michael Roth.

Lonesome Hollow was originally produced at the Contemporary American Theater Festival at Shepherd University, in Shepherdstown, West Virginia, in July 2007, directed by Hal Brooks.

Great Falls was produced at the 2008 Humana Festival of New Plays at Actors Theatre of Louisville (Kentucky), directed by Lucie Tiberghien, with Tom Nelis as Monkey Man, and Halley Wegryn Gross as Bitch. *Great Falls* appeared in print in the anthology *Humana Festival 2008: The Complete Plays*, published by Playscripts, Inc., 2009.

Wood for the Fire appeared as part of "The Great Game: Afghanistan." The Tricycle Theatre, in London, mounted three continuous days of plays about the U.S./UK war in Afghanistan at their theatre in London, April 17-19, 2009.

Heaven's My Destination premiered 2009 at the Cleveland Playhouse, in Cleveland, Ohio, which had commissioned the play, under the direction of Playhouse artistic director Michael Bloom. The production ran April 29 through May 17. Cast: Katie Barrett as Actor E/ Ensemble; Kailey Bell as Actor D/Ensemble; Diane Dorsey as Actor F/Ensemble; Michael Halling as George Brush; Christian Kohn as Actor B/Ensemble; Courtney Anne Nelson as Little Roberts Girl/ Elizabeth/Rhoda May Gruber; Justin Tatum as Actor A/Ensemble; and John Woodson as Actor C/Ensemble.

When We Go Upon the Sea was first produced by InterAct Theatre Company in New York City on June 17, 2010, under the direction of Paul Meshejian. Cast: Conan McCarty as George; Peter Schmitz as Piet; and Kim Carson as Anna-Lisa. Published by Dramatists Play Service, 2012.

Into You won a playwriting contest of the Attic Theatre in Los Angeles, California, and was produced there in September 2010. It was also produced at the University of Maryland, Baltimore County, in 2009, and is currently scheduled for production at Tulsa University in 2016.

A User's Guide to Hell Featuring Bernard Madoff had its world premiere presented by the Project Y Theater Company, at the Atlantic Stage 2, September 7–28, 2013, under the direction of Michole Biancosino. Cast: Edward James Hyland as Bernard Madoff; David Deblinger as Verge; Erika Rose as Female Resident of Hell; Eric Sutton as Male Resident of Hell; and the chorus, featuring Noah Berman, Evan Coles, Jean Jisoo Hyu, Sarah Lusche, Molly O'Keefe, and Gadi Rush.

Unknown was performed by Michael Emerson in 2012, for the "'My America' Project of Baltimore's Center Stage." In 2013, Possible Films Company and director Hal Hartley made a feature film of these 50 monologues, available for streaming at Fandor Films.

Courting Harry had its world premiere in March 2013, at the History Theatre in St. Paul, Minneapolis, Minnesota, under the direction of Joel Sass. Cast: Clyde Lund as Blackmun; Nathaniel Fuller as Burger; with Jamila Anderson, Charlotte Calvert, Sam Pearson, and E. J. Subkoviak playing multiple other roles.

Seven Joys premiered at the Tricycle Theatre in London on February 9, 2012, under the direction of Nicholas Kent. Cast: Rick Warden as Cal; Michael Cochrane as Henry; Simon Rouse as Slava; David Yip as Wei; and Shereen Martin as Marianne.

A View of the Mountains premiered at the New Jersey Repertory Theatre, April-May 2014, under the direction of Evan Bergman. Cast: Katrina Ferguson as Isla Honeyman; Eva Kaminsky as Gwynn Branch; John Little as John Homeyman; John Zlabinger as Will Branch; and Jon Erik Nielsen as Andrei Honeyman.

For the Loyal had its world premiere at the Illusion Theater in Minneapolis, Minnesota, April-May 2015, under the direction of Michael Robins. The cast members included Michael Fell, Mark Rosenwinkel, Anna Sundberg, Sam Bardwell, and Garry Geiken.

The Plays

The Hourglass Project premiered at the Hendrix College Department of Theatre Arts and Dance at Conway, Arkansas, on February 24, 2014, under the direction of Hendrix theatre professor Ann Muse, in the Cabe Theatre. Published in *Dramatics Magazine*, November 2014.

Everything had a workshop/reading (under the title *Neutrinos*), May 27–29, 2014, at the Playwrights' Center, Minneapolis, Minnesota, and a workshop/reading (under the title *Neutrinos*), May 24, 2014, at New Harmony Playwrights Conference, New Harmony, Indiana. Blessing told me in an email (dated August 21, 2015): "Pay no attention to *Everything*. It's not done yet, & it's currently in the drawer."

Uncle had a reading, May 17, 2015, at Circle X Theatre, Los Angeles, California; a workshop/reading, May 27–29, 2015, at the Playwrights' Center, in Minneapolis, Minnesota; and workshop/readings at the Arkansas New Play Festival, June 15–28, 2015, Fayetteville and Little Rock, Arkansas.

Chapter Notes

Preface

1. Interview with Lee Blessing at Denison University, undated, Ransom Center, unnumbered box Gift 12088.
2. *Los Angeles Times, Calendar* section (December 13, 2012), S6.
3. Blessing email to author, August 1, 2013.

Introduction

1. Author interview with Blessing, December 6, 2014.
2. http://www.denverpost.com/theater/ci_14397304 (accessed July 10, 2015).
3. qtd. Text on back cover of Patient A and Other Plays.

Chapter 1

1. Author interview with Blessing, December 7, 2013.
2. Dana Bourke, "Lee Blessing: An Analysis of Three Plays" (master's thesis, Southwest Texas State University, May 1995), 3.
3. Ibid., 5.
4. http://minnetonka-k12.granicus.com/MediaPlayer.php?publish_id=106 (accessed July 20, 2015).
5. Jerry Tallmer, interview with Lee Blessing, *Villager Volume* 78 (November 5–11, 2008), http://thevillager.com/villager_288/keeptheirheads.html (accessed July 12, 2012).
6. Mike Steele, *Minneapolis Star Tribune*, September 24, 1989, 173:D-7.
7. Author interview with Blessing, December 6, 2014.
8. Rohan Preston, Blessing interview, Minneapolis *Star Tribune*, April 25, 2015, http://www.startribune.com/lee-blessing-s-for-the-loyal-premieres-at-illusion-theater/301224591/ (accessed July 28, 2015).
9. Ransom Gift 11843, Box 16, folders 1-2.
10. 2011 Minnetonka Distinguished Alumni Award, http://minnetonka-k12.granicus.com/MediaPlayer.php?publish_id=106 (accessed July 20, 2015).
11. Simon Saltzman, "Interview with Lee Blessing," TheaterScene.net http://www.theaterscene.net/ts%5Carticles.nsf/(AlphaI)/B28FD3331D783BBE85256F8200429DC3? (OpenDocument accessed March 22, 2014).
12. Preston, Blessing interview, *Minneapolis Star Tribune*.
13. Saltzman, "Interview with Lee Blessing."
14. Owen Hardy article, n.d., *Courier Journal* (Louisville, KY), Ransom Box 8, folder 8.
15. Author interview with Blessing, December 7, 2013.
16. *Reed Magazine* (Spring 2009), http://www.reed.edu/reed_magazine/spring2009/features/the_way_we_werent/2.html (accessed March 15, 2015).
17. Peter Vaughn, Blessing interview, the *Minneapolis Tribune*, January 22, 1982, 22.
18. Ibid.
19. Ibid.
20. Author interview with Blessing, December 6, 2014.
21. Ransom Gift 11843, Box 16, folders 1–2.
22. 2001 Commencement speech at Reed. http://cdm.reed.edu/cdm4/document.php?CISOROOT=/reedhisttxt&CISOPTR=18730&REC=3 (accessed May 12, 2015).
23. *Minneapolis Tribune*, October 10, 1971, 16-B.
24. Peter Altman review in the *Minneapolis Star Tribune*, n.d., Ransom Gift 11843, Box 16, folders 1–2.

25. Author interview with Blessing, December 7, 2013.
26. Jeanne Beach Eigner, Blessing interview, *La Jolla Light*, July 30, 1987, C9.
27. Jackie Demaline, Blessing interview, *Cincinnati Enquirer*, March 22, 1994, C-4.
28. Douglas Franl, Blessing interview, *Rutgers Focus*, April 5, 2002, 5.
29. *San Diego Union*, August 15, 1987, 1.
30. Ransom, Box 14, folder 4.
31. Ibid.
32. Philip Zwerling, "Playwriting (& texting quicker): Philip Zwerling Interviews Lee Blessing: Two Playwrights Talk Shop," *34th Parallel* 16 (October 2011), 26.
33. Author interview with Blessing, July 30, 2010.
34. Judith Rew, review of *Bad Dreams at the White House*, by Fred Hoffman, directed by Lee Blessing, University of Iowa, *Daily Iowan*, April 14, 1977, 6, http://dailyiowan.lib.uiowa.edu/DI/1977/di1977-04-14.pdf (accessed July 13, 2015).
35. Author interview with Blessing, December 7, 2013.
36. Blessing email to author, August 3, 2015.
37. Blessing email to author, April 3, 2015.
38. http://abcnews.go.com/US/historian-petitions-billy-kid-death-certificate/ story?id=29297799 (accessed March 1, 2015).
39. Carolyn Jack, Blessing interview, *Fort Lauderdale Sun-Sentinel*, December 9, 1990, F4.
40. Ibid.
41. Lee Blessing, *The Authentic Life of Billy the Kid* (New York: Samuel French, Inc. 1979, 1980): 7.
42. Ibid, 10.
43. Ibid., 16.
44. Ibid.
45. Ibid.
46. Ibid., 21.
47. Ibid., 22.
48. Ibid., 24.
49. Ibid., 27
50. Ibid., 31.
51. Ibid., 32.
52. Ibid., 40.
53. Ibid., 42.
54. Ibid.
55. Ibid., 45
56. Ibid., 49.
57. Julie Petrucci, review of *The Authentic Life of Billy the Kid*, by Lee Blessing, ADC's Corpus Playroom Theatre, University of Cambridge, http://www.bawds.org/authentic_life_of_billy_the_kid_review.htm (accessed June 13, 2015).
58. Ann Weltner, review of *The Authentic Life of Billy the Kid*, by Lee Blessing, The Spot, Arroyo Grande, California, *New Times*, January 6, 2015, http://www.newtimesslo.com/art/10614/kids-play-arroyo-grandes-the-spot-stages-lee-blessings-the-authentic-life-of-billy-the-kid/ (accessed 6/13/15).
59. Joan Crowder, review of *The Authentic Life of Billy the Kid*, by Lee Blessing, The Spot, Arroyo Grande, California, *Tribune*, February 12, 2014, http://www.sanluisobispo.com/2014/02/12/2922685/authentic-life-of-billy-the-kids.html (accessed June 13, 2015).
60. Mike Steele, Blessing interview, *Minneapolis Star Tribune*, September 24, 1989.
61. Christopher Burns, Blessing interview, *Minnetonka Sailor*, n.d., Ransom Box 17, folder 4.
62. reedhisttxt-rcmagaug2001art50001.jpg (accessed July 31, 2015).
63. Jerry Tallmer, Blessing interview, *Villager* Volume 78 (November 5–11, 2008), http://thevillager.com/villager_288/keeptheirheads.html (accessed June 15, 2015).

Chapter 2

1. Lee Blessing, *Four Plays* (Portsmouth, NH: Heinemann/Methuen, 1991), vii.
2. Ibid.
3. Ibid.
4. Ibid.
5. Priscilla Lister Schupp, Blessing interview, *San Diego Daily Transcript*, July 23, 1987, 4-A.
6. Author interview with Blessing, December 12, 2012.
7. Lisa Block, Blessing interview, *Arts & Entertainment*, March 2, 1984, 8, Ransom Center, Gift 11507, Box 5, folder 2.
8. Blessing, *Four Plays*, viii.
9. Author interview with Blessing, December 12, 2012.
10. Blessing, *Four Plays*, 8.
11. Ibid., 12.
12. Ibid., 13.
13. Ibid.
14. Ibid.
15. Ibid., 14.
16. Ibid., 19.
17. Ibid., 29.
18. Ibid., 30.
19. Ibid.
20. Ibid., 31.

21. Ibid., 32.
22. Ibid.
23. Ibid., 35.
24. Ibid., 36.
25. Ibid., 41.
26. Ibid., 46.
27. Ibid., 47.
28. Ibid., 50.
29. Ibid., 50–51.
30. Ibid., 52.
31. Ibid., 56.
32. Ibid., 57.
33. Ibid., 57–58.
34. Ibid., 58.
35. Philip Zwerling, "Playwriting (& texting quicker): Philip Zwerling Interviews Lee Blessing: Two Playwrights Talk Shop," *34th Parallel* 16 (October 2011), 27.
36. Nancy Scott, review of *Nice People Dancing to Good Country Music*, by Lee Blessing, *San Francisco Examiner*, March 12, 1985, E8.
37. Carla Walmer, review of *Nice People Dancing to Good Country Music*, by Lee Blessing, *Twin Cities Reader*, n.d., Ransom Center Gift 11507, Box 8, folder 4.
38. David Hawley, review of *Nice People Dancing to Good Country Music*, by Lee Blessing, *St. Paul Pioneer Press*, March 6, 1984, Ransom Center Gift 11507, Box 8, folder 4.
39. Author interview with Blessing, July 30, 2010.
40. *Summer in Clinton* script in Ransom Center Gift 11507, Box 10, folder 4.
41. Author interview with Blessing, December 7, 2013.
42. *San Francisco Examiner* and *Chronicle*, February 22, 1998, A-5.
43. Teresa Durbin, "Sibling relationships in selected twentieth-century American plays with three sisters" (dissertation, Bowling Green State University, 2000), 4.
44. Laura Tracy, *The Secret Between Us: Competition Among Women* (New York: Little, Brown and Co. 1991).
45. Blessing, *Four Plays*, 67.
46. Blessing letter, dated May 12, 1999, Ransom Center Gift 11507.
47. Blessing, *Four Plays*, 77.
48. Ibid., 78.
49. Ibid., 79.
50. Ibid., 80.
51. Ibid., 85.
52. Ibid., 87.
53. Ibid., 66.
54. Durbin, "Siblings" dissertation, 110.
55. Blessing, *Four Plays*, 78.
56. Ibid., 93.
57. Ibid., 95.
58. Ibid., 100.
59. Author interview with Blessing, December 12, 2012.
60. Blessing, *Four Plays*, 110.
61. Ibid., 118.
62. Ibid., 119.
63. Ibid.
64. Ibid., 123.
65. Ibid., 125.
66. Author interview with Blessing, December 12, 2012.
67. Review of *Independence*, by Lee Blessing, *Variety*, Volume 227, 40, 10.
68. Elias Stomac, review of *Independence*, by Lee Blessing, *Drama-Logue*, May 17–23, 1990 Volume xxi, no. 20.
69. Don Shirley, review of *Independence*, by Lee Blessing, *Los Angeles Times*, May 2, 1990, pg. F-1
70. Lawrence Enscoe, review of *Independence*, *Los Angeles Daily News*, April 30, 1990, page 22.
71. Blessing letter, dated May 12, 1999, Ransom Center Gift 11507.
72. Polly Warfield, review of *Independence*, by Lee Blessing, *Drama-Logue*, March 21–27, 1991.
73. Bruce Feld, review of *Independence*, by Lee Blessing, McFadden Place Theatre, Hollywood, California, n.d., Ransom Center 7.1.
74. Marion Ross, quoted by Elias Stomac, *Drama-Logue*, May 31, 1990, 4.
75. Ransom 7.3.
76. Blessing email to the author, July 23, 2015.
77. Jeanne Blake, quoted by Peter Vaughan, *Minneapolis Star* and *Tribune*, May 11, 1984, 2-C.
78. Unattributed review of *Marjorie*, by Lee Blessing, Ransom Center Gift 11507, Box 16, folder 3.
79. David Hawley, review of *Marjorie*, by Lee Blessing, St. Paul Pioneer Press (MN), May 13, 1984, 4-C, 86.
80. Carla Waldemar, review of *Marjorie*, by Lee Blessing, *Twin Cities Reader*, May 30, 1984, 33.
81. Kevin Kelly, review of *Riches*, *Boston Globe*, March 22, 1985.
82. Author interview with Blessing, July 30, 2010.
83. Blessing, *Four Plays*, 137.
84. Ibid., 138.
85. Ibid., 141.
86. Ibid., 149.
87. Ibid., 154.

88. Ibid., 151.
89. Ibid., 160.
90. F. Kathleen Foley, review of *Riches*, by Lee Blessing, *Los Angeles Times*, December 12, 1994, F7.
91. Lisa Grider and Marilyn Muljat, review of *Riches*, by Lee Blessing, *Easy Reader*, December 8, 1994, 39.
92. Ibid.
93. Hayley Barnes, "Playing Echo in 'Eleemosynary'" (thesis, University of Southern Mississippi Regional Campus, 2012), 7.
94. Author interview with Blessing, December 7, 2013.
95. Zwerling, "Playwriting (& texting quicker)," *34th Parallel*, 29.
96. Blessing, *Four Plays*, 167.
97. Ibid., 168
98. Author interview with Blessing, December 12, 2012.
99. Blessing, *Four Plays*, 183.
100. Ibid.
101. Ibid.
102. Ibid.
103. Ibid., 180.
104. Barnes, "Playing Echo," 21.
105. Blessing, *Four Plays*, 198.
106. Adam Langer, review of *Eleemosynary*, by Lee Blessing, *Chicago Reader*, http://www.chicagoreader.com/chicago/eleem(osynary/Content?oid=878831 (accessed August 16, 2015).
107. Frank Rich, review of *Eleemosynary*, by Lee Blessing, *New York Times*, March 10, 1989, Ransom Center Gift 11507, Box 5, folder 2.
108. Lawrence Bommer, review of *Eleemosynary*, by Lee Blessing, *Windy City Times*, February 12, 1987, 21.
109. http://ocw.usu.edu/theatre_arts/understanding_theatre/Literary_Arts_of_Theatre_3.html (accessed July 13, 2013).
110. Barnes, "Playing Echo," iv.

Chapter 3

1. Author interview with Blessing, December 7, 2013.
2. Frank Green, Blessing interview, *San Diego Union*, June 24, 1990, H-1.
3. Owen Hardy, Blessing interview, *Courier-Journal* (Louisville, KY), Ransom Center, Gift 11507, Box 8, folder 8.
4. Lee Blessing, *Oldtimers Game* (New York: Dramatists Play Service, 1988), 12.
5. Ibid., 24.
6. Ibid., 38.

7. Ibid., 40.
8. Ibid., 41.
9. Ibid., 50.
10. Ibid., 53.
11. Ibid., 61.
12. Ibid., 69.
13. Richard Stayton, review of *Oldtimers Game*, by Lee Blessing, *Los Angeles Herald Examiner*, May, 29, 1987, 29.
14. Dan Sullivan, review of *Oldtimers Game*, by Lee Blessing, *Los Angeles Times*, May 30, 1987, 2.
15. Alan Mootz, review of *Oldtimers Game*, by Lee Blessing, *Courier-Journal* (Louisville, KY), March 3, 1982, C-3.
16. Bruce Fred, untitled article, *Drama-Logue*, January 21–27, 1993, Ransom Center Gift 11507, Box 8, folder 8.
17. Unattributed review of *Cooperstown*, by Lee Blessing, *Entertainment Weekly*, January 22, 1993, Ransom Center Gift 11507, Box 8, folder 8.
18. John O'Connor, review of *Cooperstown*, by Lee Blessing, *New York Times*, January 26, 1993, Ransom Center Gift 11507, Box 8, folder 8.
19. Ray Loynd, review of *Cooperstown*, by Lee Blessing, *Los Angeles Times*, January 26, 1993, Ransom Center Gift 11843, Box 1, folder 6.
20. Eugene Manners, Blessing interview, *Rochester Democrat and Chronicle*, October 9, 1993.
21. Author interview with Blessing, December 7, 2013.
22. Dan Hulbert, interview with *Cooperstown* director Lloyd Richards, *Atlanta Constitution*, May 18, 1990, F-1.
23. Philip Zwerling, "Playwriting (& texting quicker): Philip Zwerling Interviews Lee Blessing: Two Playwrights Talk Shop," *34th Parallel* 16 (October 2011), 27.
24. Lee Blessing, *Cobb* (New York: Dramatists Play Service, 1991), 25.
25. Author interview with Blessing, December 7, 2013.
26. Susan Mendelsohn, article about *Cobb*, by Lee Blessing, *Preview*, 3.
27. Blessing, *Cobb*, 7.
28. Ibid., 14.
29. Ibid., 43.
30. Green, *San Diego Union*.
31. Blessing, *Cobb*, 31.
32. Ibid., 47.
33. Ibid., 50.
34. Green, *San Diego Union*.
35. Lawrence Clinton, Blessing interview, *Los Angeles Times*, June 24, 1990, B-44.

36. Unsigned article, March 31, 1989, Ransom Center, 11843, Box 1, folder 4.
37. Frank Rich, review of *Cobb*, by Lee Blessing, *New York Times*, March 27, 1989, B-9.
38. Malcolm Johnson, review of *Cobb*, by Lee Blessing, *Hartford Courant*, July 12–18, 1990, Ransom Center, 11843, Box 1, folder 4.
39. Unsigned review of *Cobb*, by Lee Blessing, *Coast Dispatch* (MD), July 5, 1990, Ransom Center, 11843, Box 1, folder 4.
40. Unsigned review of *Cobb*, by Lee Blessing, *Variety*, April 5–11, 1989, Ransom Center, 11843, Box 1, folder 4.
41. Unsigned follow-up review of *Cobb*, by Lee Blessing, *Variety*, July 2, 1990, 8.
42. Margaret Spillane, review of *Cobb*, by Lee Blessing, *New Haven Independent*, April 13, 1989, Ransom Center, 11843, Box 1, folder 4.
43. Bill Hager, review of *Cobb*, by Lee Blessing, *San Diego Tribune*, June 29, 1990, C-1.
44. Kevin Spacey, quoted in the *New York Times*, November 28, 2000, B-1.
45. Zwerling, "Playwriting (& texting quicker)," *34th Parallel*, 27.
46. *The Baseball Plays: Seventh Inning Stretch* (Hoboken, NJ: Mills Square Theatre, 2008), 6.
47. Lee Blessing, "For The Loyal," unpublished script, 2012, 4.
48. Ibid., 7.
49. Ibid., 8–9.
50. Ibid.
51. Ibid., 10.
52. Ibid.
53. Simon Saltzman, "Interview with Lee Blessing," TheaterScene.net http://www.theaterscene.net/ts%5Carticles.nsf/(AlphaI)/B28FD3331D783BBE85256F8200429DC3?OpenDocument (accessed March 22, 2014).
54. Lee Blessing, *The Winning Streak* (New York: Dramatists Play Service, 2006), 12.
55. Ibid., 13.
56. Ibid., 42.
57. Ibid., 24.
58. Ibid., 44.
59. Ibid., 80.
60. Ibid., 46.
61. Ibid., 47.
62. Bob Rendell, review of *The Winning Streak*, by Lee Blessing, "Talkin' Broadway," https://www.talkinbroadway.com/regional/nj/nj77.html (accessed March 22, 2014).
63. Mike Schulz, review of *The Winning Streak*, by Lee Blessing, Nighswander Theatre (Davenport, IA), *River Cities Reader*, http://www.rcreader.com/theatre/new-ground-ball-the-winning/ (accessed March 22, 2014).
64. Naomi Seigel, review of *The Winning Streak*, by Lee Blessing, *New York Times*, http://query.nytimes.com/gst/fullpage.html?res=9E06E2D71738F935A25752C0A9639C8B63 (accessed March 22, 2014).
65. Saltzman, "Interview with Lee Blessing," TheaterScene.net http://www.theaterscene.net/ts%5Carticles.nsf/(AlphaI)/B28FD3331D783BBE85256F8200429DC3?OpenDocument (accessed March 22, 2014).
66. For a full account of the scandal, see Tim Layden, *Sports Illustrated*, October 23, 2014, http://www.si.com/college-football/2014/10/22/penn-state-nittany-lions-football (accessed April 17, 2015).
67. Blessing, *For the Loyal*, 1.
68. Ibid., 8.
69. Ibid., 15.
70. Ibid., 9.
71. Ibid., 12–13.
72. Ibid., 18.
73. Ibid.
74. Ibid., 23.
75. Ibid., 28.
76. Ibid., 35.
77. Ibid., 42.
78. Ibid., 64.
79. Ibid., 73.
80. Ibid., 74.
81. Ibid., 101.
82. Ibid., 103.
83. Adam Szymkowicz, Blessing interview, May 31, 2010, http://aszym.blogspot.com/2010/05/i-interview-playwrights-part-184-lee.html (accessed March 22, 2015).
84. Dominic Papatola, review of *For the Loyal*, by Lee Blessing, Illusion Theatre (Minneapolis, MN), *Pioneer Press*, May 2, 2015, http://www.twincities.com/stage/ci_28028538/loyal-review-illusion-theater-play-is-intriguing-but (accessed August 18, 2015).
85. David and Chelsea Berglund, review of *For the Loyal*, by Lee Blessing, "How Was the Show?" online column, http://www.howwastheshow.com/2015/04/for-the-loyal-by-illusion-theater/ (accessed August 18, 2015).
86. Arthur Dorman, review of *For the Loyal*, by Lee Blessing, "Talkin' Broadway" website, http://www.talkinbroadway.com/regional/minn/minn329.html (accessed August 18, 2015).

Chapter 4

1. "Poetry on the Page, Poetry on the Stage," 3, Ransom G12153, Box 3, note at top Draft #1.

2. Author interview with Blessing, December 12, 2012.
3. Herbert Mitgang, Blessing interview, *New York Times*, January 21, 1988, Ransom Center Gift 11507, Box 12, folder 5.
4. Philip Zwerling, "Playwriting (& texting quicker): Philip Zwerling Interviews Lee Blessing: Two Playwrights Talk Shop," *34th Parallel* 16 (October 2011), 28.
5. Author interview with Blessing, December 12, 2012.
6. Sam Waterston, quoted in the *New York Times*, March 27, 1988, 19.
7. TimeLine Theatre study guide to *A Walk in the Woods*, http://www.timelinetheatre.com/walk_in_the_woods/TimeLine_WalkInThe Woods_StudyGuide.pdf, 13 (accessed March 1, 2015).
8. Author interview with Blessing, December 12, 2012.
9. Dana Bourke, "Lee Blessing: An Analysis of Three Plays" (master's thesis, Southwest Texas State University, May 1995), 18.
10. Lee Blessing, *A Walk in the Woods* (New York: New American Library, 1986), 7.
11. Ibid., 10–11.
12. Undated typescript in Ransom Center Gift 11507, Box 17, folder 3.
13. Blessing, *A Walk in the Woods*, 13–14.
14. According to American College of Rheumatology, Sjögren's syndrome is an inflammatory disease that can affect many different parts of the body, but most often affects the tear and saliva glands. Patients with this condition may notice irritation, a gritty feeling, or painful burning in the eyes. Dry mouth (or difficulty eating dry foods) and swelling of the glands around the face and neck are also common. Some patients experience dryness in the nasal passages, throat, vagina, and skin. Swallowing difficulty and symptoms of acid reflux are also common. http://www.rheumatology.org/Practice/Clinical/Patients/Diseases_And_Conditions/Sjögren_s_Syndrome/ (accessed March 3, 2014).
15. Blessing, *A Walk in the Woods*, 37.
16. Ibid., 50.
17. Ibid., 65.
18. Ibid., 69.
19. Ibid., 72.
20. Ibid., 87.
21. Ibid., 99.
22. Ibid., 101.
23. Ibid.
24. Ibid., 102.
25. Ibid., 104.
26. Ibid., 107.
27. Zwerling, "Playwriting (& texting quicker)," *34th Parallel*, 27.
28. Dr. Elaine Scarry, "Thermonuclear Monarchy: Choosing between Democracy and Doom," *Harvard Magazine* 116, No. 4 (March-April 2014), 48.
29. Ibid., 50.
30. Scarry, "Thermonuclear Monarchy," 51.
31. *San Diego Daily Transcript*, April 28, 1988, 9.
32. Priscilla Lister Schupp, untitled article, *San Diego Daily Transcript*, July 23, 1987, 4-A.
33. Ransom Center Gift 11507, Box 13, folder 1.
34. Carey Purcell, *Playbill*, September 30, 2014, http://www.playbill.com/news/article/a-walk-in-the-woods-with-kathleen-chalfant-opens-off-broadway-tonight-331793 (accessed August 19, 2015).
35. John Podhoretz, *National Interest* (Summer 1988), 168–169.
36. Barbara Cook, Blessing interview, *The Ottawa Citizen*, March 13, 1990.
37. Bourke, "Lee Blessing," 14.
38. Quoted in Podhoretz article, *National Interest* (Summer 1988), 169.
39. Robert Brustein, review of *A Walk in the Woods*, by Lee Blessing, *New Republic*, April 4, 1988, 25.
40. Letter dated March 22, 1988, Ransom Center Gift 11507, Box 12, folder 5.
41. Letter dated March 13, 1990, Ransom Center Gift 11843, Box 5, folder 2.
42. *Time*, January 4, 1988, 71.
43. Edith Oliver, review of *A Walk in the Woods*, by Lee Blessing, *The New Yorker*, March 3, 1988, 80.
44. Marshall Rine, review of *A Walk in the Woods*, by Lee Blessing, Gannett Westchester Papers, May 29, 1988, Ransom Center Gift 11507, Box 13, folder 3.
45. Dan Hulbert, review of *A Walk in the Woods*, by Lee Blessing, *Atlanta Journal*, quoted in Bourke, "Lee Blessing," 25.
46. Harry Bowman, review of *A Walk in the Woods*, by Lee Blessing, *Dallas Morning News*, quoted in Bourke, "Lee Blessing," 25–26.
47. Michael Billington, review of *A Walk in the Woods*, by Lee Blessing, *The Guardian*, April 4, 1988, Ransom Center Gift 11507, Box 13, folder 4.
48. Welton Jones, review of *A Walk in the Woods*, by Lee Blessing, *San Diego Union*, quoted in Bourke, "Lee Blessing," 11.
49. *New York Times*, February 29, 1988, 28.
50. Frank Rich, review of *A Walk in the*

Woods, by Lee Blessing, *New York Times*, February 29, 1988, http://www.nytimes.com/1988/02/29/theater/stage-a-walk-in-the-woods.html (accessed March 3, 2014).

51. John Podhoretz, *National Interest* (Summer 1988), 164.

52. Mel Gusso, review of *A Walk in the Woods*, by Lee Blessing, *New York Times*, March 8, 1988, Ransom Center Gift 11507, Box 14, folder 1.

53. Author interview with Blessing, December 7, 2013.

54. Tom Chesek, "Lee Blessing's Newest Is a Doom with a View," *Asbury Pulp*, May 3, 2014, http://asburypulp.com/2014/05/lee-blessings-newest-is-a-doom-with-a-view/ (accessed February 15, 2015).

55. Lee Blessing, *View of the Mountains*, April 2014 version, 109.

56. Ibid., 1.
57. Ibid., 13.
58. Ibid., 44.
59. Ibid., AUTHOR PROVIDE.
60. Ibid., 49.
61. Ibid., 18.
62. Ibid., 20.
63. Ibid., 24.

64. Marina Kennedy, interview with Blessing, April 18, 2014, Broadway world.com http://www.broadwayworld.com/new-jersey/article/BWW-Interviews-Lee-Blessing-Playwright-for-A-VIEW-FROM-THE-MOUNTAIN-at-NJ-Rep-20140418 (accessed March 22, 2015).

65. Ibid., 55.
66. Ibid., 56.
67. Ibid., 59.
68. Ibid., 89.
69. Ibid., 102.
70. Ibid., 105.
71. Ibid., 116.

72. Bob Rendell, review of *A View of the Mountains*, by Lee Blessing, "Talkin' Broadway," posted May 16, 2014, http://www.talkinbroadway.com/regional/nj/nj644.html (accessed February 15, 2015).

73. Ken Jaworowski, review of *A View of the Mountains*, by Lee Blessing, *New York Times*, May 9, 2014, http://www.nytimes.com/2014/05/11/nyregion/a-review-of-a-view-of-the-mountains-in-long-branch.html (accessed February 14, 2015).

74. Chesek, Blessing interview, "Asbury Pulp," http://asburypulp.com/2014/05/lee-blessings-newest-is-a-doom-with-a-view/ (accessed February 15, 2015).

75. Blessing, *A View of the Mountains*, 108.

Chapter 5

1. Elias Stimac, *Drama-Logue*, September 2–8, 1993, 4.

2. Terry Waite, quoted in *The Week*, July 24, 2015, 8.

3. Ibid.

4. Tim Weiner, *Legacy of Ashes: The History of the CIA* (New York: Doubleday, 2007), 408.

5. McAnuf, born 1952, directed at the La Jolla Playhouse, 1983-2007 and went on to serve as director of the Stratford Shakespeare Festival in Stratford, Ontario. While at La Jolla, he directed *A Walk in the Woods*, and later directed several motion pictures.

6. Lee Blessing, quoted in article by Robert Trussell, *Kansas City Star*, March 1, 1993, i–10.

7. Lee Blessing, quoted in article by Jackie Demalne, *Cincinnati Enquirer*, March 22, 1994, C-1.

8. Dana Bourke, "Lee Blessing: An Analysis of Three Plays" (master's thesis, Southwest Texas State University, May 1995), 38.

9. Lee Blessing, *Two Rooms* (New York: Dramatists Play Service, 1990), 8.

10. Ibid., 18.
11. Ibid., 12.
12. Ibid., 21.
13. Ibid., 28.

14. Alfred, Lord Tennyson in his poem "In Memoriam A. H. H.," Canto 56.

15. Ibid., 24.
16. Ibid., 25.
17. Ibid., 46.
18. Lee Blessing, quoted in Bourke, 37.
19. Ibid., 42.
20. Ibid., 48.

21. Brian D. Bethune, "Remaindered Subjects: A Lacanian Reading of Selected Plays by Lee Blessing," (PhD dissertation, Bowling Green State University, 1997), 88.

22. Blessing email to author, February 23, 2014.

23. *Time*, January 3, 1994.

24. Pamela Somners, review of *Two Rooms*, by Lee Blessing, *Washington Post*, March 15, 1993, 75.

25. Mel Gusso *New York Times* review, quoted in Bethune, 90.

26. Mel Gusso *New York Times* review, quoted in Bourke, 31.

27. Ibid., 45.

28. *Variety* review, quoted in Bethune, 88.

29. Dan Sullivan's *Los Angeles Times* review, quoted in Bethune, 87.

30. Walter Jones's *San Diego Union* review, quoted in Bourke, 45.
31. Lee Blessing, quoted by Russell Stomets in St. Petersburg (FL) *Times* clipping, n.d., Ransom Center Gift 11507, Box 11, folders 1–2.
32. Lee Blessing, quoted in Bourke 50.
33. http://en.wikipedia.org/wiki/Ted_Bundy+++ (accessed March 11, 2014).
34. Lee Blessing, quoted in Bourke, 53.
35. Ibid., 56.
36. Lee Blessing, *Down the Road* (New York: Dramatists Play Service, 1991), 21.
37. Ibid., 45.
38. Ibid., 18.
39. Lee Blessing, quoted in Bourke, 50–51.
40. Blessing, *Down the Road*, 22.
41. Lee Blessing, quoted in Bourke, 62.
42. Blessing, *Down the Road*, 26–27.
43. Lee Blessing, quoted in *Backstage*, article by Ira J. Bilowit, May 24, 1991, 11.
44. Blessing, *Down the Road*, 32.
45. Lee Blessing, quoted in the *Kentucky Standard*, article by Fred Allen, March 13, 1991, Ransom Center, Box 4, folder 5.
46. Lee Blessing, quoted in Bourke, 55.
47. Lee Blessing, quoted in article, "The Commercial Appeal," by Memphis writer Donald LaBadie, April 14, 1991, Ransom Center, Box 4, folder 5.
48. Lee Blessing, quoted in article by Kevin Nance, *Lexington Herald Leader*, March 12, 1991, D-2.
49. Blessing, *Down the Road*, 43.
50. *Drama-Logue*, September 2–8, 1993, 4, Ransom Center, Box 4, folder 5.
51. Unsigned review, source unknown, Ransom Center Box 4, folder 5.
52. Greg Evans's *Variety* review, quoted in Bethune, 17.
53. Sylvia Drake's *Los Angeles Times* review, quoted in Bethune, 138.
54. Clive Barnes's *New York Post* review, quoted in Bourke, 62.
55. Darryl H. Miller's *Los Angeles Daily News* review, quoted in Bourke, 63.
56. Lee Blessing, quoted in *Cincinnati Downtowner*, May 12, 1992, 28.
57. Mark Danner, "The Truth of El Mozote," http://globetrotter.berkeley.edu/people/Danner/1993/truthelmoz06.html (accessed March 17, 2014).
58. Lee Blessing, quoted in article by Jeanne Beach Eigner, *La Jolla Light*, July 30, 1987, C9.
59. Lee Blessing, quoted in the *Cincinnati Post*, May 8, 1992.

60. *Patient A and Other Plays: Five Plays by Lee Blessing* (Portsmouth, NH: Heinemann-Methuen, 1995), 185.
61. Ibid., 179.
62. Lee Blessing, quoted in Bethune, 19.
63. *Patient A and Other Plays*, 186.
64. Ibid., 182.
65. Ibid., 192.
66. Ibid., 197.
67. Ibid., 199.
68. Gabrielle S. Kaplan's *Chicago Reader* review of *Lake Street Extension*, by Lee Blessing, http://www.chicagoreader.com/chicago/lake-street-extension/Content?oid=889082 (accessed March 15, 2014).
69. Anne Kelly-Saxenmeyer's *Backstage* review of *Lake Street Extension*, by Lee Blessing, http://www.backstage.com/review/lake-street-extension_4/ (accessed March 15, 2014).
70. Julio Martinez's *Variety* review of *Lake Street Extension*, by Lee Blessing, http://variety.com/2002/legit/reviews/lake-street-extension-1200550213/ (accessed March 15, 2014).
71. Mel Gusso review of *Lake Street Extension*, by Lee Blessing, http://www.nytimes.com/mem/theater/treview.html?pagewanted=print&res=9E0CE0DB103BF931A35751C1A964958260&_r=0 (accessed March 15, 2014).
72. Kimberly Bergalis letter, *People Magazine*, December 23, 1991, 117.
73. Alisa Solomon, "Pursued By a Bear," *Village Voice*, May 11, 1993.
74. Lee Blessing, *Patient A* (New York: Dramatists Play Service, 1993), 39.
75. AIDS.gov/federal-resources/around-the-world/global-aids-overview/ (accessed March 3, 2014).
76. www.cdc.gov/hiv/statistics/basics/ataglance.html#ref3 (accessed March 3, 2014).
77. www.factlv.org/timeline.htm (accessed March 3, 2014).
78. Larry Kramer, quoted in Solomon, "Pursued by a Bear."
79. Author interview with Blessing, December 12, 2012.
80. George Bergalis, quoted in Solomon, "Pursued by a Bear."
81. Ibid.
82. Email to author from Florida Stage producer Lou Tyrrell, February 16, 2014.
83. *Patient A and Other Plays*, x.
84. Ibid.
85. George Gehman, article, *Morning Call*, January 13, 1995, D4.
86. Unsourced article, July 25, 1993, Ransom Center Gift 11507, Box 9, folder 2.

87. Patient A *and Other Plays*, xi.
88. Lee Blessing, quoted by Jennifer Armstrong, PerformInk 5 (June 1, 1995), 2.
89. Patient A *and Other Plays*, 255.
90. Blessing, *Patient A*, 7–8.
91. Ibid., 13.
92. Ibid., 37.
93. George Bergalis, quoted in Solomon, "Pursued by a Bear."
94. Bergalis, quoted by George Gehman in the *Morning Call* (Allentown, PA), January 13, 1995, D-4.
95. *Time*, May 17, 1993, 65.
96. Mel Gussow's *New York Times* review of *Patient A*, by Lee Blessing, http://www.nytimes.com/1993/04/29/theater/review-theater-trying-to-grasp-an-aids-tragedy.html (accessed February 19, 2014).
97. J. Wynn Rousuck's *Baltimore Sun* review of *Patient A*, by Lee Blessing, http://articles.baltimoresun.com/1996-03-13/features/1996073020_1_kim-loss-of-innocence-blessing (accessed February 20, 2014).
98. Alvin Kline's *New York Times* review of *Patient A*, by Lee Blessing, http://www.nytimes.com/mem/theater/treview.html?res=9F0CE5DE153FF932A15752C1A965958260&_r=0 (accessed February 16, 2014).
99. Lee Blessing, quoted by Katherine Burke in *Backstage*, February 23, 2001, Backstage.com text in Ransom Center Gift 11843.
100. Blessing email to author March 7, 2015.
101. Chris Jones, review of *The Rights*, by Lee Blessing, *Variety*, April 18-24, 1994, 73.
102. Michael Kape's review of *The Rights*, by Lee Blessing, WABE-FM (Marietta, GA), April 29, 1994, Ransom Center Gift 11507, Box 9, folder 5.
103. Lee Blessing, quoted by Richard Christiansen in the *Chicago Tribune*, February 25, 2001, http://articles.chicagotribune.com/2001-02-25/news/0102250542_1_iowa-graduate-writer-s-workshop-theater-play.
104. Lee Blessing quote, Ransom Center Gift 11507, Box 6, folder 3.
105. Lee Blessing, *Going to St. Ives* (New York: Dramatists Play Service, 2003), 13.
106. Ibid., 19.
107. Ibid., 20.
108. Ibid., 30.
109. ibid., 31
110. Ibid., 36.
111. Ibid., 45.
112. Ibid.
113. Ibid., 36–37.
114. Jeffrey Borak, review of *Going to St. Ives*,
by Lee Blessing, *Berkshire Eagle*, June 30, 2011, http://www.berkshireeagle.com/entertainment/ci_18381521 (accessed May 16, 2014).
115. Charles Isherwood, review of *Going to St. Ives*, by Lee Blessing, *New York Times*, March 30, 2005, http://www.nytimes.com/2005/03/30/theater/reviews/30ives.html (accessed May 15, 2014).
116. David Finkle, review of *Going to St. Ives*, by Lee Blessing, *Theatermania*, March 29, 2005, http://www.theatermania.com/new-york-city-theater/reviews/03-2005/going-to-st-ives_5834.html (accessed May 16, 2014).
117. Matthew Murray, review of *Going to St. Ives*, by Lee Blessing, "Talking Broadway" website, http://www.talkinbroadway.com/ob/03_29_05.html (accessed May 16, 2014).
118. Posted June 27, 20116/27/11, http://berkshireonstage.com/about-berkshire-onstage-and-larry-murray/ (accessed May 15, 2014).
119. Blessing, *Going to St. Ives*, 16.
120. Ibid, 16–17.
121. Lee Blessing, *Chesapeake* (New York: Dramatists Play Service, 2000), 10.
122. Ibid., 13.
123. Ibid.
124. Ibid., 24–25.
125. Ibid., 28.
126. Ibid., 30.
127. Chris Jones, review of *Chesapeake*, by Lee Blessing, *Chicago Tribune*, April 4, 2012, http://articles.chicagotribune.com/2012-04-03/entertainment/ct-ent-0404-chesapeake-review-20120403_1_kerr-chesapeake-bay-senator (accessed March 14, 2014).
128. Max Fischer, review of *Chesapeake*, by Lee Blessing, *Milwaukee Journal Sentinel*, http://www.jsonline.com/entertainment/arts/intandem-theatres-chesapeake-a-shaggy-dog-tale-of-culture-wars-b99210505z1-246793351.html (accessed March 14, 2014).
129. Tim Treanor, review of *Chesapeake*, by Lee Blessing, *DC Theatre Scene*, http://dctheatrescene.com/2011/04/18/chesapeake/ (accessed March 14, 2014).
130. J. Dakota Powell, quoted by Simi Horwitz in article for *Backstage*, August 12, 2002, http://www.backstage.com/news/theatreworld-remembers-sept-11/.
131. http://www.nytimes.com/2002/09/13/movies/critic-s-notebook-mountains-of-mourning-vistas-of-better-days.html (accessed July 25, 2015).
132. https://www.youtube.com/watch?v=6tTaeCcha5g (accessed July 25, 2015).
133. Robert Simonson, *Playbill*, http://

www.playbill.com/news/article/in-remembrance-of-9-11-starry-brave-new-world-offers-plays-songs-and-poems-107429/print (accessed July 25, 2015).
134. https://www.youtube.com/watch?v=6tTaeCcha5g (accessed July 25, 2015).
135. September 13, 2002, http://www.nydailynews.com/archives/nydn-features/lines-learned-heart-article-1.507323 (accessed July 25, 2015).
136. Robert Weber, review of "Brave New World," *New York Times*, September 13, 2002, http://www.nytimes.com/2002/09/11/theater/critic-s-notebook-theater-as-solace-in-a-time-of-anguish.html (accessed July 25, 2015).
137. Lee Blessing, *Whores* (unpublished script), January 1, 2004 draft, 23–24.
138. William Blum, *Killing Hope* (Monroe ME: Common Courage Press, 2004), 454–462.
139. Lee Blessing, quoted in Michael Killian's *Chicago Tribune* review of *Whores*, July 24, 2003, Ransom Center Gift 12343.
140. Blessing, *Whores*, 3.
141. Ibid., 5.
142. Ibid., 10.
143. Ibid., 13.
144. Ibid., 71.
145. Ibid. 26.
146. Ibid., 51.
147. Ibid., 41.
148. Ibid., 50–51.
149. Ibid., 70.
150. Ibid., 39.
151. Ibid., 87.
152. Ibid., 91.
153. Unsigned article, *Catlayst*, April 2005, http://www.catholicleague.org/another-catholic-bashing-play/ (accessed February 4, 2015).
154. Unsourced article, Ransom Center Gift 11507, Box 8, folder 4.
155. Robert Daniels, review of *Whores*, by Lee Blessing, *Variety*, October 12, 2004, http://variety.com/2004/legit/reviews/whores-1200530250/ (accessed February 4, 2015).
156. Blessing email to the author, April 3, 2015.
157. Julia Preston in the *New York Times*, April 11, 2014. http://www.nytimes.com/2014/04/12/us/salvadoran-general-accused-in-killings-should-be-deported-miami-judge-says.html (accessed February 8, 2015).
158. Julia Preston in the *New York Times*, March 12, 2015. http://www.nytimes.com/2015/03/13/us/general-in-el-salvador-torture-and-killings-can-be-deported-immigration-court-rules.html?ref=world (accessed March 17, 2015).
159. Ibid.
160. Blessing email to the author, March 21, 2015.
161. Julia Preston in the *New York Times*, April 8, 2015, http://www.nytimes.com/2015/04/09/us/us-deports-salvadoran-general-accused-in-80s-killings.html?ref=world&_r=0++++ (accessed April 9, 2015).
162. Blessing email to the author, April 9, 2015.
163. Bob Rendell, review of *Whores*, by Lee Blessing, "Talkin' Broadway" website, http://www.talkinbroadway.com/regional/nj/nj68.html (accessed February 4, 2015).
164. *The Economist*, February 19, 2011, 95.
165. Ibid.
166. Zwerling, "Playwriting (& texting quicker)," 29.
167. *The Great Game: Afghanistan* (London: Oberon Books, 2009), 113.
168. Ibid., 124.
169. Tony Kushner, *Homebody/Kabul* (New York: Theatre Communications Group, 2002), 67.
170. "A Defense of Poetry," in *Essays, Letters from Abroad, Translations and Fragments* (1840).
171. All reviews found at Stagegrade.com (accessed June 2, 2013).
172. Philip Zwerling, *After-School Theatre Programs for At-Risk Teenagers* (Jefferson, NC: McFarland, 2008), 5.
173. Zwerling, "Playwriting (& texting quicker)," 29.
174. *The Economist*, February 19, 2011, 95.
175. Author interview with Blessing, December 7, 2013.
176. *The Bomb: A Partial History* (London: Oberon Books, 2012), 6.
177. Ibid., 54.
178. Ibid., 55.
179. Ibid.
180. Ibid., 58.
181. Ibid., 62.
182. Ibid.
183. Ibid., 65.
184. Ibid., 66.
185. Ibid., 69.
186. Ibid., 74.
187. Ibid., 75.
188. Philip Fisher, review of *Seven Joys*, by Lee Blessing, "British Theatre Guide" website, http://www.britishtheatreguide.info/reviews/the-bomb-a-pa-tricycle-7238 (accessed June 18, 2015).

189. Sarah Hemming, review of *Seven Joys*, by Lee Blessing, *Financial Times*, February 22, 2012, http://www.ft.com/cms/s/2/cb6fbd26-5c92-11e1-911f-00144feabdc0.html#axzz1n8A4Gnxb (accessed June 19, 2015).
190. Charles Spencer, *Telegraph*, February 21, 2012, http://www.telegraph.co.uk/culture/theatre/theatre-reviews/9096699/The-Bomb-Tricycle-Theatre-review.html (accessed June 18, 2015).
191. *The Guardian*, February 21, 2012, http://www.theguardian.com/stage/2012/feb/21/the-bomb-review (accessed June 18, 2015).

Chapter 6

1. Blessing email to the author, February 20, 2011.
2. Author interview with Blessing, December 6, 2014.
3. Ibid.
4. Ibid.
5. Lee Blessing, *Black Sheep* (New York: Dramatists Play Service, 2003), 18.
6. Ibid., 8.
7. Ibid., 12.
8. Ibid., 25.
9. Ibid., 41.
10. Ibid., 42.
11. Ibid., 23.
12. Ibid., 15.
13. Ibid., 35.
14. Ibid., 14, 15, 16, 18, 20, 46, 48, 49.
15. Ibid., 18, 19, 23, 27, 28, 29, 30, 37, 39, 43, 44, 45, 46, 50.
16. Ibid., 14, 15, 24, 28, 31.
17. Ibid., 32.
18. Ibid., 17.
19. Ibid.
20. F. Scott Fitzgerald, "The Rich Boy," in *The Short Stories of F. Scott Fitzgerald*, ed. Matthew Bruccoli (New York: Charles Scribner's Sons, 1989), 318.
21. Blessing, *Black Sheep*, 40.
22. Ibid., 47.
23. Ibid., 11.
24. Ibid., 51.
25. Ibid.
26. Ibid., 52.
27. Ibid., 52–53.
28. Ibid.
29. Markland Taylor, review of *Black Sheep*, by Lee Blessing, *Variety*, July 25, 2002, http://variety.com/2002/legit/reviews/black-sheep-4-1200547170/ (accessed May 21, 2014).
30. Elyse Sommer, review of *Black Sheep*, by Lee Blessing, "CurtainUp," n.d., http://www.curtainup.com/blacksheep.html (accessed May 21, 2014).
31. Gail M. Burns, review of *Black Sheep*, by Lee Blessing, "Gail Sez," n.d., http://myvanwy.tripod.com/companies/barrington/blacksheep.html (accessed May 26, 2014).
32. http://gawker.com/unarmed-people-of-color-killed-by-police-1999-2014-1666672349 (accessed August 22, 2015).
33. Scott Heller, *Boston Globe* online, July 27, 2002, Ransom Center Gift 11843.
34. Lee Blessing, *Flag Day* (New York: Dramatists Play Service, 2007), 9.
35. Ibid., 11.
36. Ibid., 12.
37. Ibid., 15.
38. Ibid., 18.
39. Ibid., 19.
40. Ibid., 20.
41. Ibid.
42. Ibid.
43. Ibid., 22.
44. Ibid., 24.
45. http://www.holidayinsights.com/other/flagday.htm (accessed August 21, 2014).
46. Blessing, *Flag Day*, 29.
47. Ibid.
48. Ibid., 30
49. Ibid., 32.
50. Ibid., 39.
51. Ibid., 40.
52. Ibid., 43.
53. Ibid., 44.
54. SNCC Press Conference, July 27, 1967, http://www.thisdayinquotes.com/2013/07/as-american-as-apple-pie-cherry-pie-and.html (accessed September 22, 2014).
55. Ibid., 47
56. Unsigned review, *Flag Day*, by Lee Blessing, *Washington Times*, n.d., http://www.dramatists.com/cgi-bin/db/single.asp?key=3831 (accessed August 6, 2014).
57. Unsigned review, *Flag Day*, by Lee Blessing, *Potomac Stages*, July 15, 2004, http://www.haseltd.com/press/flagday04_ps.pdf (accessed August 6, 2014).
58. http://www.tcg.org/publications/at/dec09/blackandwhite.cfm (accessed September 23, 2014).
59. Stephen Dobyns, quoted in *The New Yorker*, October 6, 2014, 3.
60. Lee Blessing, *Perilous Night*, unpublished script, March 2008 version, 1.
61. Ibid.
62. Ibid.
63. Ibid., 5.

64. Ibid., 15.
65. Ibid., 23.
66. Ibid., 30.
67. From Gurlyand's *Reminiscences of A. P. Chekhov*, in *Teatr i iskusstvo* 1904, 28 (July 11, 1904), 521, http://berlin.wolf.ox.ac.uk/lists/quotations/quotations_by_ib.html (accessed August 23, 2015).
68. Blessing, *Perilous Night*, 32.
69. Ibid., 44.
70. Ibid., 45.
71. Ibid., 46–49.
72. Ibid., 49.
73. Ibid., 46.
74. Nick Huyck, review of *Perilous Night*, by Lee Blessing, City Pages (Minneapolis–St. Paul, MN), September 18, 2013, http://www.citypages.com/2013-09-18/arts/perilous-night-proves-to-be-a-challenge/full/ (accessed August 7, 2014).
75. Lisa Brock, review of *Perilous Night*, by Lee Blessing, *Minneapolis Star Tribune*, September 16, 2013, http://www.startribune.com/entertainment/stageandarts/223920991.html (accessed August 7, 2014.
76. Michael Opperman, review of *Perilous Night*, by Lee Blessing, "Aisle Say Twin Cities," website, http://aislesaytwincities.com/2013/09/27/perilous-night/ (accessed August 7, 2014).
77. Cain Burdeau article for the Associated Press, November 15, 2014.

Chapter 7

1. John Simon, review of *Marjorie*, by Lee Blessing, *New York Magazine*, June 4, 2001, 91.
2. Ibid.
3. Lee Blessing, *Thief River* (New York: Dramatists Play Service, 2002), 16.
4. Ibid., 19.
5. Ibid.
6. Ibid., 25.
7. Ibid., 28.
8. Ibid., 31.
9. Ibid., 39.
10. Ibid.
11. Ibid., 40.
12. Ibid., 48.
13. Bruce Webber, "Follow Your Secret Heart, Your Whole Life Through," review of *Thief River*, by Lee Blessing, *New York Times*, May 22, 2001, http://www.nytimes.com/2001/05/22/theater/theater-review-follow-your-secret-heart-your-whole-life-through.html (accessed November 16, 2014).
14. Lee Blessing, quoted in the *St. Paul Pioneer Press*, February 22, 2002, 12-E.
15. Blessing, *Thief River*, 57.
16. The Heterosexual-Homosexual Rating Scale, sometimes referred to as the "Kinsey Scale," was developed by Alfred Kinsey and his colleagues Wardell Pomeroy and Clyde Martin in 1948, in order to account for research findings that showed people did not fit into neat and exclusive heterosexual or homosexual categories. http://www.kinseyinstitute.org/research/ak-hhscale.html (accessed December 23, 2014).
17. *Newsletter of Signature Theatre Company* (Spring 2001), 1.
18. Kim Surkan, review of *Thief River*, by Lee Blessing, *St. Paul Pioneer Press*, February 22, 2002, 12-E.
19. *Ten-Minute Plays from the Guthrie Theatre: Volume 2* (New York: Playscripts, Inc., 2003), 65.
20. Ibid., 68.
21. Ibid., 69.
22. Ibid., 70.
23. Ibid.
24. Ibid., 71.
25. Ibid.
26. Ibid., 72.
27. Ibid.
28. Ibid., 73.
29. Ibid., 74.
30. Ibid., 71.
31. Blessing email to the author, August 23, 2012.
32. Lee Blessing, *A Body of Water* (New York: Dramatists Play Service, 2007), 7.
33. Ibid., 8.
34. Ibid., 9.
35. Ibid., 13.
36. Ibid., 14.
37. Ibid., 18.
38. Ibid., 18.
39. Ibid., 19.
40. Ibid., 20.
41. Ibid., 21.
42. Ibid.
43. Ibid., 22.
44. Ibid., 27.
45. Ibid., 31.
46. ibid., 32.
47. Ibid., 33.
48. Ibid., 37.
49. Ibid., 39.
50. Ibid., 40.
51. Ibid., 43.
52. Ibid., 44.
53. Ibid., 46.

54. Ibid., 47.
55. Ibid., 49.
56. Ibid., 50.
57. Ibid.
58. Charles Isherwood, review of *A Body of Water*, by Lee Blessing, *New York Times*, October 15, 2008, http://www.nytimes.com/2008/10/15/theater/reviews/15wate.html?_r=0 (accessed November 16, 2014).
59. Kerry Reid, review of *A Body of Water*, by Lee Blessing, *Chicago Tribune*, n.d., http://www.chicagotribune.com/entertainment/ct-ott-0322-on-the-fringe-20130320-story.html (accessed 11/16/14).
60. Bob Rendell, review of *A Body of Water*, by Lee Blessing, "Talkin' Broadway" website, http://www.talkinbroadway.com/regional/nj/nj431.html (accessed November 16, 2014).
61. http://www.straightdope.com/columns/read/2267/whats-the-story-on-the-curse-of-em-macbeth-em (accessed May 5, 2015).
62. Lee Blessing, *The Scottish Play*, unpublished script, 2002, 1.
63. Ibid., 16.
64. Ibid., 21.
65. Ibid., 42.
66. Ibid., 65.
67. Ibid., 67.
68. Ibid., 80.
69. Ibid., 90.
70. Ibid., 101.
71. Steve Oxman, review of *The Scottish Play*, by Lee Blessing, *Los Angeles Times*, September 27, 2005, http://articles.latimes.com/2005/sep/27/entertainment/et-scottish27 (accessed April 25, 2015).
72. Anne Marie Welsh, review of *The Scottish Play*, by Lee Blessing, *San Diego Tribune*, September 27, 2005, http://www.utsandiego.com/uniontrib/20050927/news_1c27scottish.html (accessed May 21, 2015).
73. Julio Martinez, review of *The Scottish Play*, by Lee Blessing, *Variety*, September 26, 2005, http://variety.com/2005/legit/markets-festivals/the-scottish-play-1200521514/ (accessed May 21, 2015).
74. Rob Stevens, review of *The Scottish Play*, by Lee Blessing, *Theatermania*, http://www.theatermania.com/new-york-city-theater/reviews/09-2005/the-scottish-play_6772.html (accessed April 25, 2015).
75. Lee Blessing, *Lonesome Hollow* (New York: Dramatists Play Service, 2011), 4.
76. *New York Times*, March 4, 2007, http://www.nytimes.com/2007/03/04/us/04civil.html?pagewanted=all&_r=0 (accessed January 15, 2015).
77. Blessing, *Lonesome Hollow*, 20.
78. Ibid., 9–11.
79. Ibid., 15.
80. Ibid., 29.
81. Ibid., 33.
82. Andrea Dworkin, quoted by Colleen McEneany, "Pornography and Feminism," FeministUtopia website, http://web.archive.org/web/20060720195949/http://www.amazoncastle.com/feminism/porn.shtml (accessed January 19, 2015).
83. Robin Morgan, quoted by Steve Chapman, unsourced article, November 5, 2007.
84. Blessing, *Lonesome Hollow*, 50.
85. Ibid., 19.
86. Ibid., 48.
87. Geoffrey Wansell, *Daily Mail* (UK), September 11, 2009, http://www.dailymail.co.uk/news/article-1212910/How-Britain-drove-greatest-genius-Alan-Turing-suicide—just-gay.html (accessed January 27, 2015).
88. Blessing, *Lonesome Hollow*, 21.
89. Ibid, 22.
90. http://dictionary.reference.com/browse/melodrama.
91. *Lonesome Hollow*, 39.
92. Ibid. 46.
93. Ibid. 48.
94. Ibid. 52.
95. Unsigned review of *Lonesome Hollow*, by Lee Blessing, *Washington Times*, Monday, July 9, 2007, http://www.washingtontimes.com/news/2007/jul/9/lonesome-a-hollow-misread-of-conservatis-51061785/#ixzz3JI2bfNXN (accessed November 16, 2014).
96. Katy Walsh, review of *Lonesome Hollow*, by Lee Blessing, "Chicago Theater Beat" website, http://chicagotheaterbeat.com/2013/02/16/review-lonesome-hollow-idle-muse-theatre/#review (accessed November 16, 2014).
97. Lee Blessing, *Great Falls* (New York: Dramatists Play Service, 2009), 12.
98. Ibid., 15.
99. Ibid.
100. Ibid., 16.
101. Ibid.
102. Ibid.
103. Ibid., 17.
104. Ibid.
105. Ibid., 19.
106. Ibid., 20.
107. Ibid., 24.
108. Ibid.
109. Ibid., 25.

110. Ibid., 31.
111. Ibid., 33.
112. Ibid., 36.
113. Ibid., 35.
114. Ibid., 39.
115. Ibid., 42.
116. Philip Zwerling, "Playwriting (& texting quicker): Philip Zwerling Interviews Lee Blessing: Two Playwrights Talk Shop," *34th Parallel* 16 (October 2011), 27.
117. Nina Metz, review of *Great Falls*, by Lee Blessing, *New City Stage*, January 1, 2009, http://newcitystage.com/2009/01/19/review-great-fallsprofiles-theatre/#sthash.fFxIUMLd.dpuf, http://newcitystage.com/2009/01/19/review-great-fallsprofiles-theatre/ (accessed November 16, 2014).
118. Judith Egerton, review of *Great Falls*, by Lee Blessing, *Louisville Courier-Journal*, February 29, 2009, http://archive.courier-journal.com/article/20080229/SCENE05/802290309/-Great-Falls-explores-stepdad-teen-s-bond (accessed November 16, 2014).
119. Unsigned review of *Great Falls*, by Lee Blessing, *Chicago Reader* online, http://events.chicagoreader.com/events/Event?oid=934664 (accessed November 16, 2014).
120. Lee Blessing, quoted by Linda Mack in the *Minneapolis Star Tribune*, February 17, 2002, F-5.
121. Blessing, *Great Falls*, 34–35.
122. Ibid., 30–33.
123. Michael McGregor, review of *Great Falls*, Oregonian, on October 3, 2010 at 2:05 p.m., updated October 4, 2010 at 8:39 a.m., http://www.oregonlive.com/performance/index.ssf/2010/10/theater_review_human_encounter.html (accessed December 16, 2014).
124. Lee Blessing, *Into You*, unpublished script, 2008, stage directions.
125. Time, http://time.com/3722834/the-hunting-ground-provocative-documentary-reignites-campus-rape-debate/ (accessed March 21, 2015).
126. Jake New article in *Inside Higher Education*, December 15, 2014, https://www.insidehighered.com/news/2014/12/15/critics-advocates-doubt-oft-cited-campus-sexual-assault-statistichttps://www.insidehighered.com/news/2014/12/15/critics-advocates-doubt-oft-cited-campus-sexual-assault-statistic (accessed March 21, 2015).
127. Ibid.
128. Blessing, *Into You*, 3.
129. Ibid., 4.
130. Ibid., 6.
131. Ibid., 10.
132. Ibid., 13.
133. Ibid., 15.
134. Ibid., 16.
135. Ibid., 17.
136. Lee Blessing, *Uncle*, unpublished script, 2015, 1–2.
137. Ibid., 1–3.
138. Ibid., 1–12.
139. Ibid., 2–24.
140. Ibid., 2–36.
141. Ibid., 3–48.
142. Ibid., 3–49.
143. Ibid., 4–67.
144. Ibid., 4–76.
145. Ibid., 5–94.
146. Ibid., 5–99.
147. Ibid., 5–101.
148. Ibid., 6–110.
149. Ibid., 6-111.
150. Ibid., 6-112.
151. Ibid., 6-113.
152. Ibid., 8–131.
153. Ibid., 9–138.

Chapter 8

1. Brian D. Bethune, "Remaindered Subjects: A Lacanian Reading of Selected Plays by Lee Blessing," (PhD dissertation, Bowling Green State University, 1997), 18.
2. Lee Blessing, *Fortinbras* (New York: Dramatists Play Service, 1992), 8.
3. Ibid., 8.
4. Ibid., 11.
5. Ibid., 14.
6. Ibid., 33–34.
7. Ibid., 45.
8. Ibid., 26.
9. Ibid., 36.
10. Ibid., 48.
11. Lee Blessing, quoted by T. H. McCulloh in the *Los Angeles Times*, June 21, 1991, F-15.
12. Blessing, *Fortinbras*, 56.
13. Time, June 6, 1992, 78.
14. Michael Phillips, review of *Fortinbras*, by Lee Blessing, *San Diego Union*, June 21, 1991, C-5.
15. Jeff Smith, review of *Fortinbras*, by Lee Blessing, *San Diego Weekly Reader*, July 7, 1991.
16. Quoted in Bethune, 186.
17. T. H. MicCollouh, review of *Fortinbras*, by Lee Blessing, *Los Angeles Times*, June 21, 1991, F-1.
18. Quoted in Bethune, 185.

19. Sylvia Drake, review of *Fortinbras*, by Lee Blessing, *Los Angeles Times*, June 25, 1991, F-8.
20. Quoted in Bethune, 184.
21. http://www.moma.org/collection/works/86028.
22. Lee Blessing, *Snapshot* (New York: Playscripts, Inc., 2002), 8.
23. Ibid., 23.
24. Ibid.
25. http://www.usnews.com/news/special-reports/the-worst-presidents/slideshows/the-10-worst-presidents/12 (accessed July 25, 2015).
26. Blessing, *Snapshot*, 24.
27. Ibid., 24.
28. Ibid.
29. Ibid.
30. Ibid.
31. Ibid.
32. Ibid.
33. *Naked Angels Issues Projects: Collected Plays* (New York: Samuel French, 2009), xiii.
34. Ibid., 3–4 (manuscript of play supplied to author by Blessing).
35. Ibid., 5.
36. Author email interviews with Blessing, September/October 2010.
37. http://www.theguardian.com/law/2011/feb/06/george-bush-trip-to-switzerland (accessed May 6, 2014).
38. Lee Blessing, *When We Go Upon the Sea* (New York: Dramatists Play Service, 2011), 8.
39. Ibid., 10.
40. Ibid., 15–16.
41. Ibid., 14.
42. Ibid.
43. Ibid., 19.
44. Ibid., 20.
45. Ibid., 21.
46. Ibid., 22.
47. Ibid., 24.
48. Ibid., 28–29.
49. Ibid., 31.
50. Ibid., 41.
51. Jason Zinoman, review of *When We Go Upon the Sea*, by Lee Blessing, *New York Times*, June 21, 2010, http://theatre.nytimes.com/2010/06/21/theater/reviews/21when.html?pagewanted- print accessed 3/9/2011.
52. Andy Propst, review of *When We Go Upon the Sea*, by Lee Blessing, Theatermania, htt://www.theatermania.com/off-broadway/reviews/06-2010/when-we-go-upon-the- sea_28096.html 6/18/2010, accessed 3/9/2011.
53. Joe Dziemianowicz, review of *When We Go Upon the Sea*, by Lee Blessing, *New York Daily News*, June 17, 2010, http://www.nydaily news.com/entertainment/music-arts/sea-review-lee-blessing-george-w-bush-bash-low-impact-controversy-article-1.183159#ixzz2y3e 3iUWE (accessed April 6, 2014).
54. J. Cooper Robb, review of *When We Go Upon the Sea*, by Lee Blessing, *Philadelphia Weekly*, April 4, 2010, http://www.philadelphiaweekly.com/arts-and-culture/stage/When-We-Go-Upon-the-Sea.html#ixzz2y3f8 odbg (accessed April 6, 2014).

Chapter 9

1. Jon Jory, ed., *25 Ten Minute Plays from the Actors Theatre of Louisville* (New York: Samuel French, 1989), 232.
2. Ibid., 236.
3. Ibid., 237.
4. Ibid., 234–236.
5. ibid., 233.
6. Ibid., 233–234.
7. Ibid., 234.
8. Ibid., 237.
9. Blessing email to the author, May 25, 2015.
10. Ibid.
11. Lee Blessing, *Heaven's My Destination* (adapted from Thornton Wilder's novel), playwright's script, July 2009, 2.
12. Ibid., 5.
13. Ibid., 15.
14. Ibid., 23.
15. Ibid., 61.
16. Ibid., 62.
17. Ibid., 63.
18. Ibid., 65–66.
19. Ibid., 68.
20. Ibid., 74.
21. Ibid., 96.
22. Ibid., 97.
23. Ibid., 108.
24. Ibid., 114.
25. Ibid., 117.
26. Ibid.
27. Bob Abelman, review of *Heaven's My Destination*, by Lee Blessing, *Ohio News Herald*, May 7, 2009, http://www.news-herald.com/general-news/20090507/review-heavens-my-destination-a-thought-provoking-wilder-ride (accessed May 23, 2015).
28. Christine Howey, review of *Heaven's My Destination*, by Lee Blessing, "Rave and Pan" blog, April 30, 2009 http://raveandpan.blogspot.com/2009/04/heavens-my-destination-cleveland-play.html (accessed May 23, 2015).
29. Lee Blessing, quoted at http://www.

Chapter Notes—9 261

projecttheatre.org/2013/08/users-guide-hell-featuring-bernard-madoff-2/ posted August 19, 2013 (accessed January 24, 2015).

30. Diana Henriques, *New York Times*, December 19, 2008. (Henriques offers a full appraisal of the Madoff crimes), http://www.nytimes.com/2008/12/20/business/20madoff.html?pagewanted=all&_r=0 (accessed January 25, 2015).

31. Diana Henriques, *New York Times*, December 12, 2013 (Henriques's update of the Madoff victims, five years after his arrest) http://www.nytimes.com/2013/12/08/business/madoff-victims-five-years-the-wiser.html?_r=0 (accessed April 16, 2015).

32. Lee Blessing, *A User's Guide to Hell Featuring Bernard Madoff*, playwright's script (dated June 2012), 19.

33. Ibid., 8.
34. Ibid., 20.
35. Ibid., 23.
36. http://www.holocaust-history.org/short-essays/josef-mengele.shtml (accessed January 31, 2015).
37. Blessing, *A Users Guide to Hell Featuring Bernard Madoff*, 32.
38. Ibid.
39. Ibid.
40. Ibid., 33.
41. Ibid., 35.
42. Ibid., 36.
43. Ibid., 45.
44. Ibid., 51.
45. Ibid., 52.
46. Ibid., 53.
47. Ibid., 57.
48. Ibid., 59.
49. Ibid., 61.
50. Ibid., 71.
51. Ibid., 72–73.
52. Ibid., 91.
53. Ibid., 95.
54. Ibid., 101.
55. Jason Zinoman, review of *A User's Guide to Hell Featuring Bernard Madoff*, by Lee Blessing, *New York Times*, September 9, 2013, http://www.nytimes.com/2013/09/10/theater/reviews/users-guide-to-hell-featuring-bernard-madoff-by-project-y.html?_r=0 (accessed January 24, 2015).
56. Carol Ditosti, Review of *A User's Guide to Hell Featuring Bernard Madoff*, by Lee Blessing, "Blog Critics," posted September 13, 2013, http://blogcritics.org/theater-review-nyc-a-users-guide-to-hell-featuring-bernard-madoff-by-lee-blessing/ (accessed January 24, 2015).

57. Diane Snyder, review of *A User's Guide to Hell Featuring Bernard Madoff*, by Lee Blessing, "Time Out New York," posted Monday, September 9, 2013, http://www.timeout.com/newyork/theater/a-users-guide-to-hell-featuring-bernard-madoff (accessed January 24, 2015).

58. Wendy Caster, review of *A User's Guide to Hell Featuring Bernard Madoff*, "Show Showdown," posted September 13, 2013, http://showshowdown.blogspot.com/2013/09/a-users-guide-to-hell-featuring-bernard.html (accessed January 24, 2015).

59. http://myamerica.centerstage.org/About-My-America+++).

60. Lee Blessing, *Unknown*, unpublished script, 1.

61. Lee Blessing, quoted by Mary Carole McCauley, *Baltimore Sun*, September 21, 2012, http://articles.baltimoresun.com/2012-09-21/entertainment/bs-ae-my-america-intro-2012 0921_1_monologues-neil-labute-anniversary-celebration/2 (accessed August 3, 2015).

62. Blessing, *Unknown*, 1.

63. Lee Blessing, *Courting Harry*, unpublished script, October 2012, 17.

64. Gradon Royce, review of *Courting Harry*, by Lee Blessing, *Minneapolis Star Tribune*, March 4, 2013, http://www.startribune.com/entertainment/stageandarts/195005391.html (accessed March 19, 2015).

65. Dominic P. Papatola, review of *Courting Harry*, by Lee Blessing, *Twin Cities Pioneer Press*, March 5, 2013, http://www.twincities.com/ci_22714839/theater-review-courting-harry-does-justice-st-pauls (accessed March 19, 2015).

66. Jill Schafer, review of *Courting Harry*, by Lee Blessing, "Cherry and Spoon," http://www.cherryandspoon.com/2013/03/courting-harry-at-history-theatre.html (accessed March 19, 2015).

67. Blessing, *Courting Harry*, set directions, n.p.

68. William Shakespeare, *The Tragedy of Hamlet, Prince of Denmark* (act 3, scene 1).

69. Ibid.

70. Blessing, *Courting Harry*, 3.

71. http://www.pbs.org/wnet/supremecourt/democracy/robes_warren.html (accessed March 20, 2015).

72. Blessing, *Courting Harry*, 11–12.
73. Ibid., 22.
74. Ibid., 26.
75. Ibid., 35.
76. Ibid., 41.
77. Ibid., 42.
78. Ibid., 52–53.
79. Ibid., 59-60.

80. Ibid., 62.
81. Ibid., 65–66.
82. Ibid., 78.
83. Ibid., 79.
84. Ibid., 82.
85. Ibid., 85.
86. Lee Blessing, *The Hourglass Project*, playwright's script, 2014, 5.
87. Ibid., preface, n.p.
88. Blessing email to author, March 16, 2015.
89. Blessing, *The Hourglass Project*, 8.
90. Ibid., 13.
91. Ibid., 16.
92. Ibid., 27.
93. Ibid., 57–58.
94. Ibid., 19.
95. Ibid., 108.
96. James D. Watts, Jr., Tulsa World article, January 19, 2015, http://www.tulsaworld.com/scene/artsandentertainment/geriatrics-get-their-youth-back-in-the-hourglass-project-play/article_4f201cba-39e1-5d6d-b4ff-9f87aa198773.html (accessed March 9, 2015).

Chapter 10

1. Lee Blessing, quoted by Kevin Wetmore, "Is Lee Blessing the Best Kept Secret in the American Theatre?" (undated interview at Denison University), Ransom unnumbered box, Gift 12088.
2. Ransom Center, Gift 11507, Box 9, folders 1-6.
3. Ibid., Box 10, folder 2.
4. Ibid., Box 10, folder 6.
5. Ibid., Box 7, folder 3.
6. Blessing email to the author, August 23, 2015.
7. Production no. 2K21, Story no. 4360.
8. Ransom Center, Gift 11507, Box 6, folder 4, script no. 518, draft dated December 2, 1996.
9. Author interview with Blessing, December 6, 2014.
10. Barry Johnson, "A Blessing to the Theatre" (interview with Blessing) February 1996, http://cdm.reed.edu/cdm4/document.php?CISOROOT=/reedhisttxt&CISOPTR=6779&REC=2 (accessed July 31, 2015).

Chapter 11

1. Tennessee Williams, *Memoirs* (New York: Bantam, 1976), 212.
2. Mike Steele quoted in Dana Bourke, "Lee Blessing: An Analysis of Three Plays" (master's thesis, Southwest Texas State University, May 1995), 2.
3. Philip Zwerling, "Playwriting (& texting quicker): Philip Zwerling interviews Lee Blessing: Two Playwrights Talk Shop," *34th Parallel* 16 (October 2011), 27.
4. Ibid.
5. Lee Blessing, Patient A *and Other Plays: Five Plays by Lee Blessing* (Portsmouth, NH: Heinemann/Methuen, 1995), xi–xii.
6. Lee Blessing, quoted by Jackie Demaline in the *Cincinnati Enquirer*, March 22, 1994, C-1.
7. Lee Blessing, quoted in Bourke, 67.
8. Mel Gusso, quoted in Bourke, 63.
9. *New York Times* quote reprinted on back cover of Patient A *and Other Plays*.
10. Lee Blessing, quoted in Brian D. Bethune, "Remaindered Subjects: A Lacanian Reading of Selected Plays by Lee Blessing," (PhD dissertation, Bowling Green State University, 1997), 216.
11. Author interview with Blessing, December 7, 2013.
12. "A Conversation with Lee Blessing" (Unattributed interview), http://www.diversecitytheater.org/?page_id=431 (accessed August 24, 2015).
13. Lee Blessing, quoted in Bourke, 7.
14. Zwerling, "Playwriting (& texting quicker)," 27.
15. From Lee Blessing lecture, San Francisco, July 30, 2010.
16. Lee Blessing, quoted in the *Minnesota Monthly* (January 1990), 35.
17. Lee Blessing, quoted by reporter Gary Wien, http://www.njrep.org/press_2002-2004.htm (accessed July 31, 2015).
18. Ibid.
19. Lee Blessing, quoted in Bethune, 21.
20. Author interview with Blessing, December 6, 2014.
21. Martin Rosenberg interview, Reed Digital Collections, http://cdm.reed.edu/cdm4/document.php?CISOROOT=/reedhisttxt&CISOPTR=13498&REC=14 (accessed March 16, 2015).
22. Author interview with Blessing, December 7, 2013.
23. Reed Digital collections, http://cdm.reed.edu/cdm4/document.php?CISOROOT=/reedhisttxt&CISOPTR=8778&REC=17 (accessed July 31, 2015).

Bibliography

Barnes, Hayley. "Playing Echo in Eleemosynary: A Creative Thesis Project." University of South Mississippi Regional Campus, 2012.
The Baseball Plays: Seventh Inning Stretch. Hoboken, NJ: Mills Square Theatre, 2008.
Bethune, Brian D. "Remaindered Subjects: A Lacanian Reading of Selected Plays by Lee Blessing." PhD dissertation. Bowling Green State University (OH), 1997.
Blessing, Lee. *The Authentic Life of Billy the Kid.* New York: Samuel French, Inc., 1979, 1980.
_____. *Black Sheep.* New York: Dramatists Play Service, Inc., 2003.
_____. *A Body of Water.* New York: Dramatists Play Service, Inc., 2007
_____. *Chesapeake.* New York: Dramatists Play Service, Inc., 2000.
_____. *Cobb.* New York: Dramatists Play Service, Inc., 1991.
_____. *Cold Water: 25 Ten-Minute Plays from the Actors Theatre of Louisville.* Edited by Jon Jory. New York: Samuel French, Inc., 1989.
_____. *Courting Harry.* Unpublished script, October 2012.
_____. *Down the Road.* New York: Dramatists Play Service, Inc., 1991.
_____. *Fantasy League.* Unpublished script, 2008.
_____. *Flag Day.* New York: Dramatists Play Service, Inc., 2007.
_____. *Fortinbras.* New York: Dramatists Play Service, Inc., 1992.
_____. *Four Plays.* Portsmouth, NH: Heinemann/Methuen, 1991.
_____. *Going to St. Ives.* New York: Dramatists Play Service, Inc., 2003.
_____. *Great Falls.* New York: Dramatists Play Service, Inc., 2009.
_____. *Heaven's My Destination* (adapted from Thornton Wilder's novel). Playwright's script, July 2009.
_____. *The Hourglass Project.* Author's script, 2014.
_____. *Into You.* Unpublished script, 2008.
_____. *Lonesome Hollow.* New York: Dramatists Play Service, Inc., 2011.
_____. *Oldtimers Game.* New York: Dramatists Play Service, 1988.
_____. *Patient A.* New York: Dramatists Play Service, Inc., 1993.
_____. *Patient A and Other Plays: Five Plays by Lee Blessing.* Portsmouth, NH: Heinemann/Methuen, 1995.
_____. *Reagan in Hell. Naked Angels Issues Projects: Collected Plays.* Edited by Mark Armstrong and Geoffrey Nauffts. New York: Playscripts, Inc., 2009.
_____. *The Scottish Play.* Unpublished script, 2002.
_____. *Thief River.* New York: Dramatists Play Service, Inc., 2002.
_____. *Two Rooms.* New York: Dramatists Play Service, Inc., 1990.
_____. *A View of the Mountains.* Unpublished script, April 2014.
_____. *A Walk in the Woods.* New York: New American Library, 1986.

_____. *When We Go Upon the Sea.* New York: Dramatists Play Service, Inc., 2011.
_____. *Whores.* Unpublished script, January 1, 2004.
_____. *A User's Guide to Hell Featuring Bernard Madoff.* New York: Dramatists Play Service, Inc., 2013. (The author also had access to the playwright's unpublished 2012 script.)
_____. *The Winning Streak.* New York: Dramatists Play Service, Inc., 2006.
_____. Email interviews. September 2010 and December 2010.
_____. Papers, 1995-2005. Harry Ransom Humanities Research Center, University of Texas, Austin.
_____. Personal interviews. July 30, 2010, December 12, 2012, December 7, 2013, December 6, 2014.
Blum, William. *Killing Hope.* Monroe, ME: Common Courage Press, 2004.
The Bomb: A Partial History. London: Oberon Books, 2012.
Bourke, Dana. "Lee Blessing: An Analysis of Three Plays." Master's Thesis. Southwest Texas State University, May 1995.
Durbin, Teresa. "Sibling Relationships in Selected 20th-Century American Plays with Three Sisters." Dissertation, Bowling Green State University, 2000.
The Great Game: Afghanistan. London: Oberon Books, 2009.
Hansel, Adrien-Alice, ed. *Humana Festival 2008: The Complete Plays.* New York: Playscripts, Inc., 2009.
Naked Angels Issues Projects: Collected Plays. New York: Samuel French, 2009.
Nauffits, Geoffrey, and Mark Armstrong, eds. *Naked Angels: The Issue Projects Collected Plays.* New York: Playscripts, Inc., 2009.
Snapshot. New York: Playscripts, Inc., 2002.
Ten-Minute Plays from the Guthrie Theatre: Volume 2. New York: Playscripts, Inc., 2003.
Weiner, Tim. *Legacy of Ashes: The History of the CIA.* New York: Doubleday, 2007.
Zwerling, Philip. "Playwriting (& texting quicker) Philip Zwerling interviews Lee Blessing: Two Playwrights Talk Shop." *34th Parallel* 16 (October 2011).
_____. *After-School Theatre Programs for At-Risk Teenagers.* Jefferson, NC: McFarland, 2008.

Index

Numbers in **_bold italics_** refer to pages with photographs.

Aberdeen 224
Actors Theatre of Louisville 21, 37, 38, 48, 97, **_158_**, 176
Alive and Kicking 223
Animals 12–13
At the Post Office 13
The Authentic Life of Billy the Kid 12–18

Billy the Kid 224
Black Sheep 134–138
Blake, Jeanne 18, 223, 225, 240
Blessing, Dean 8–9
A Body of Water 159–165
The Bomb: A Partial History 131–133

Chesapeake 116–119
Cobb 50–55
Cold Water 202–204
Contemporary American Theater Festival, 121, **_140_**, 172
Cooperstown (movie) 223
Cooperstown (play) 49–50
Courting Harry 214–219
Creative Writing 224

Down and Dirty 141–143
Down the Road 93–99

Eleemosynary 39–44
Eugene O'Neill Theater Center **_9_**, 13, **_76_**, **_231_**

Fantasy League 56–57
Final Rounds 224
Flag Day 139–144
For the Loyal 61–66
Fortinbras 188–193

Going to St. Ives 112–116
Good Clean Fun 139–144
Great Falls 174–179
The Great Game: Afghanistan 127–130
Goya, Francisco 227
The Guthrie Theater **_8_**, **_12_**, 150, **_152_**, **_154_**, 161, **_163_**, **_230_**

Heaven's My Destination 204–207
History Theatre 215, **_217_**, **_218_**
Homicide: Life on the Streets 225
The Hourglass Project 219–222

Illusion Theatre **_64_**
Independence (movie) 224
Independence (play) 27–33
Into You 179–181

Lake Street Extension 100–104
Lonesome Hollow 169–174
Lunatics 13

Magic Time 224
Marjorie 34
Marnich, Melanie 8, 18
Milo's Arms 223
Minions 224
Minnetonka, Minnesota 7, 8

The Napkin Play 238–239
A Nearly Perfect Weekend 34
Nice People Dancing to Good Country Music 20–27

Oldtimers Game 46–49
Overmyer, Eric 10

Un Passeig Pel Bosc 223
Patient A 104–111
Perilous Night 144–148
Pickett Fences 225
Pranks 224

Reagan in Hell 195–196
Reed College 9–10
Riches 33–39
The Rights 111–112
The Roads That Lead Here 156–159

The Scottish Play 165–169
Seven Joys 131–133
Signature Theater **90**, **103**, **105**, **191**
Sistena with Dirty Words 11
Steal Big, Steal Little 224

They Don't Name the Parts Though 9
Thief River 150–156
34th & Dyer 119–120
The Trial of Standing Bear 224–225

Tricycle Theatre 127
Two of Hearts 223
Two Rooms 85–93
Tyler Poked Taylor 193–195

Uncle 181–187
University of Iowa Writing Workshop 11, 12
Unknown 213–214
A User's Guide to Hell Featuring Bernard Madoff 208–212

A View of the Mountains 78–83

A Walk in the Woods 67–78, 223
When We Go Upon the Sea 196–201
Whores 120–126
Wilder, Thornton 204, 205
Williams, Tennessee 226
Wilson, August **231**
The Winning Streak 57–61
Wood for the Fire 127–130
The World Court 196–197

www.ingramcontent.com/pod-product-compliance
Lightning Source LLC
Chambersburg PA
CBHW051213300426
44116CB00006B/562